CORNELL '69

CORNELL '69

LIBERALISM AND THE CRISIS OF THE AMERICAN UNIVERSITY

DONALD ALEXANDER DOWNS

CORNELL UNIVERSITY PRESS
ITHACA AND LONDON

First published 1999 by Cornell University Press
First printing, Cornell Paperbacks, 2013

Library of Congress Cataloging-in-Publication Data

Downs, Donald Alexander.
Cornell '69 : liberalism and the crisis of the American university /
Donald Alexander Downs.
p. cm.
Includes bibliographical references and index.
ISBN 978-0-8014-3653-6 (cloth: alk. paper)
ISBN 978-0-8014-7838-3 (paper: alk. paper)

1. Cornell University—Strike, 1969. 2. Cornell University—Administration—
History. 3. Student movements—United States—History. 4. Black power—
United States—History. 5. Education, Humanistic—United States. I. Title.

LD1370.D68   1999
378.747'71–dc21   98-32348

Cornell University Press strives to use environmentally responsible suppliers and materials to the fullest extent possible in the publishing of its books. Such materials include vegetable-based, low-VOC inks and acid-free papers that are recycled, totally chlorine-free, or partly composed of nonwood fibers.

To the memory of my father, Donald A. Downs,
who believed in the liberating power of
education and sent me to Cornell.
And to my children, Jacqueline Downs
and Alexander Downs, who may
walk down the path
my father made.

We accept the falsity of the university's inward life.... The original sin stems from the pretension to be other than one's true self. It is our privilege to try to be whatever we wish; but it is vicious to pretend to be what we are not, and to delude ourselves by growing habituated to a radically false ideal of what we are. When the habitual behavior of a man or an institution is false, the next step is complete demoralization. And thence to degeneracy, for it is not possible for anyone to submit to the falsification of his nature without losing his self-respect.

—José Ortega y Gasset, *Mission of the University*

CONTENTS

PREFACE

I have written several controversial books, but none has generated as much heat as *Cornell '69*. Immediately upon publication in early 1999, Cornell University was forced to cancel a public forum on the book scheduled for February because of concerns about disruption and overflow attendance. A civil yet contentious forum was finally held on campus in April after emotions had settled down. Controversy continued as reviews with strong opinions were expressed by individuals arrayed across the political spectrum. After reading some early reviews, a friend of mine in the history department at the University of Wisconsin–Madison told me, "You appear to have upset both the left and the right—so you must have done something right!"

Whether or not *Cornell '69* did "something right" is for others to judge. The controversy it provoked, however, was hardly surprising given the personal, institutional, political, and moral matters that were at stake in 1969 and remained at issue thirty years later when the book appeared. On the level of normative policy issues, disputes raged in 1969 over many vital questions. For example, should the university's primary mission be to pursue truth and nourish intellectual excellence through respect for academic freedom? Or should it be to promote particular notions of social and racial justice, even if the way these goals are pursued engenders orthodoxy of thought? Should racial and social justice claims be addressed through liberal reforms emphasizing equal rights, diversity of viewpoints, and common citizenship, or through identity politics that stress difference, separation, and confrontation? Should universities strive to be "temples of reason" that downplay political engagement, or should they be open to powerful (even coercive) political pressures devoted to particular conceptions of justice? The responses to *Cornell '69* were updated replays of these very tensions that riveted Cornell and other campuses in the late 1960s.

At its core, the watershed crisis at Cornell—that veritable city on a hill—was about what kind of university it (and its brethren) should be. And though the politics of identity and academic freedom is less intense now than in 1969, it is still very much with us. Witness the conflict that has erupted in recent decades over such issues as free speech, speech codes, due process, affirmative action, intellectual diversity, and identity-based academic programs on campus—disputes still familiar to many Cornellians. The matter of affirmative action and a dispute over the aims of high education went all the way to the Supreme Court in 2003 when the Rehnquist court handed down its *Grutter v. Bollinger* (539 U.S. 306) opinion. And many writers have recounted the multitude of cases in recent years in which campus authorities have punished students and faculty for saying things deemed insensitive on grounds of race and other aspects of identity. The student who was charged with violating the University of Pennsylvania's speech code in 1993 for calling some noisy minority students "water buffaloes" (a nonracial term as it turned out) is but one famous example in a long list of such cases.

Beyond the seminal political and ethical questions at stake, *Cornell '69* also struck many personal nerves, for it exposed and probed existential matters of character that comprised the "human" side of the controversy. Not unlike Greek tragedy, Cornell's struggle with fundamental normative questions was propelled by powerful human passions and concerns exacerbated by the unprecedented circumstances. In this regard, it is useful to quote Milton Konvitz, a professor in Cornell's Industrial and Labor Relations School, who made the memorable observation that at the time Cornell was gripped by a "Hobbesian state of nature" as the central authority of the administration dissolved before our very eyes. I recall the very moment I, then a sophomore, experienced this feeling: right after President Perkins's failed convocation speech before 10,000 members of the Cornell community at Barton Hall on Monday afternoon of Crisis Week. I report on this feeling and its circumstances in the book; years later, the sense of disorder and confusion remains unforgettable. To paraphrase Yeats, the center no longer held.

Donald Kagan, who had resigned from Cornell's history department before the crisis for a job at Yale, observed in a remark quoted in *Cornell '69* that the situation reminded him of one of Thucydides' central teachings: crisis reveals true character. Indeed, elemental tensions of character were highlighted, dealing with such matters as courage and cowardice, independence and conformity, decisiveness and indecision, and whether one stood up to fear or succumbed to its pressure. The enormous public and media attention Crisis Week garnered no doubt heightened existential tension, for such exposure made it made it more difficult to ignore or retreat from what was happening. For many Cornellians, the crisis was as much existential as institutional, and not everyone met the existential test.

Though some readers have considered the character and existential aspect of the events a separate issue, I have always viewed this dimension as integrally related to the normative issues. This is so for a simple reason: institutions and principles are not pure ideas descended from heaven. They need to be defended and cultivated by individuals who are willing to put themselves on the line when the pressure comes. I paid due respect in *Cornell '69* to what motivated the students in the confrontation—an effort to understand that angered many reviewers on the right. But in the end I interpreted the faculty's and administration's reaction to the students' coercive threats as a capitulation that weakened higher education's fiduciary commitment to reason, civility, the freedom of inquiry, and diversity of thought—a posture the identity politics contingent on the left found unacceptable. Universities' distinctive moral charter is the pursuit of truth and knowledge; let the political chips fall where they may. Whether the threat comes from the right or the left, *Cornell '69* attempted to show why universities need to reaffirm their commitment to these principles if they are to be true to themselves and the society they serve.

Donald Downs
Madison, Wisconsin
April 2012

ACKNOWLEDGMENTS

Numerous individuals contributed to making this book possible, including the many who granted me personal interviews. I am grateful for their willingness to discuss this controversial event and set of issues after almost thirty years. In addition, I am in the special debt of certain members of the Cornell community who, for their own reasons, felt attached to the project and went the extra mile on my behalf by providing special assistance or data. These individuals, who represent a variety of views on the subject, include (in alphabetical order) Isadore Blumen, Joyce Cima, Dale Corson, George Hildebrand, Keith Johnson, Alfred Kahn, Robert Kilpatrick, Robert Miller, Richard Polenberg, Jeremy Rabkin, Paul Rahe, Allan Sindler, Art Spitzer, and Neal Stamp. Richard Polenberg and James Miller read the manuscript and made thoughtful and probing recommendations, as did an anonymous reader. Peter Agree, my editor at Cornell University Press, has been indispensable in the development of this project, and I thank him for his unflappable support and encouragement.

I would like to thank two others who worked on the manuscript: Catherine Rice of Cornell University Press, who worked hard and conscientiously on many aspects of the book, including procuring photographs, and Bruce Emmer, who did yeoman and excellent work as my copy editor. Finally, I would like to thank Elaine Engst, Librarian of the Kroch Archives at the Cornell University Library, and her excellent staff, for the professional assistance and friendliness they provided during my four trips to Ithaca.

I am indebted to those students at Madison who have either assisted me in research for this book or have inspired me by their active commitment to the principles of free speech and intellectual freedom on this campus, where the struggle, having begun in 1992, is now starting to bear fruit. Several such students merit mention: Juliet Berger, Katie Culver, Shira Diner, Bill Dixon, Christine Fredenberg, Evan Gerstman, Tim Graham, Anat Hakim, Lee Hawkins, Tim Hudson, Amy Kasper, Simon Olson, Mitch Pickerill, Christina Ruggiero, Ian Rosenberg, Kate Ross (who first had the idea for this book), Bob Schwoch, Jason Sheppard, Mark Sniderman, and Martin Sweet. Special recognition goes to Sheerly Avni and Kevin St. John—my intellectual consciences from different sides of the political spectrum. They did research on the Cornell crisis and the issues surrounding it and presented me with some of the most challenging and probing questions I have encountered from any research assistants. May we work together again, for, as Nietzsche said, *einmal ist keinmal.*

I owe a special debt to George Fisher and Stephen Wallenstein, whose unpublished manuscript *Open Breeches: Guns at Cornell,* written soon after the crisis ended, helped me to organize and clarify my thinking. I discuss this work and its authors at the end of Chapter One, where I explain my data and approach.

I am grateful to several colleagues and friends for their help and inspiration. Lester Hunt has taught me, in both word and deed, much about the principles at stake in this book. I also want to recognize Lee Hansen, who has demonstrated his commitment to academic freedom in word and deed, as have Mary Anderson and my colleagues on the Faculty Committee for Academic Freedom and Rights. So has my lifelong friend Dale McConnaughay. A newspaper editor with obstreperous hard-headedness and integrity, Dale has tirelessly forced me to face the problems of the university from an outsider's perspective, where we never look as good as we imagine. Robert Drechsel has enlightened me by his example in the trenches and with his scholarship. Stanley Kutler has given me characteristically enthusiastic and insightful encouragement from the start, as has John Wright, whose confidence and tireless effort on my behalf in the earlier stages of this project I will not soon forget. I hope that John's instincts will prove victorious.

Michael Gauger performed first-rate editing on an earlier version of this work and provided me with several articles and ideas concerning the project. A soldier on a winter's night, Michael has also enriched my thinking about the issues surrounding universities through his unique blend of knowledge, commitment to the life of the mind, and friendship. And last but not least, James Baughman has contributed to the manuscript in his own superb and inimitable ways, which include editing, providing relevant literature, ideas, and historical perspective, and offering friendship and advice that are fine beyond measurement.

Finally, I want to thank my wife, Susan Downs, for her understanding and partnership in the pursuit of the principles discussed in this book.

D.A.D.

CORNELL '69

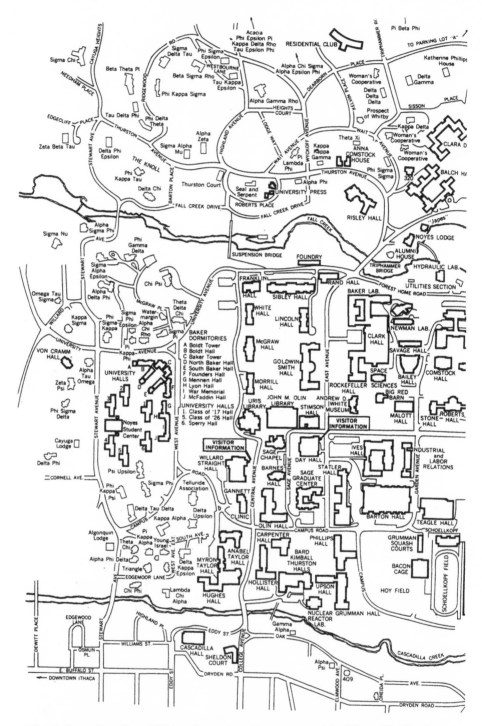

Detail of map from Cornell University student directory, copyright Office of Publications, Cornell University, 1968.

CHAPTER ONE

OVERVIEW OF THE CRISIS

Sunday, April 20, 1969, was perhaps the most infamous day in the history of Cornell University and a watershed day in American higher education. At 4:10 p.m. over eighty members of the Afro-American Society (AAS) marched in solidarity out of the student union, Willard Straight Hall, fists clenched in Black Power salutes. The march stood apart from all other upheavals of that era for one conspicuous reason: the protesters brandished rifles and other weapons. Never before had students introduced guns into a campus conflict.[1] The AAS did not take the guns into the Straight when they took it over; they smuggled them in for defensive purposes after some fraternity brothers broke in and the AAS feared further vigilante action. (AAS members and allies had purchased the guns earlier that year, encouraged to do so by the burgeoning Black Power movement.)[2]

As they walked across campus to their headquarters, the students held their weapons on high in salutes that imitated the famous Black Panther march into the state capitol of California in 1968. Thomas W. Jones, an AAS leader, boasted, "that was a moment in history—armed black people marching out of the student union at Cornell University in military formation. That was a moment that galvanized black people across this nation!"[3] The AAS minister of defense, one of the first students out of the door, wore a bandolier of bullets across his chest. The Associated Press photographer who captured the rifles, the bandoliers, and the exit in what came to be called "The Picture" won the Pulitzer Prize for the best photograph of 1969.

Two events precipitated the seizing of the Straight early the previous day: the burning of a cross in front of Wari House, the black women's cooperative, and the Cornell judicial board's issuance of sanctions against five AAS activists for disruptive demonstrations undertaken the previous December. The AAS's most immediate objectives were to get the sanctions—which it considered tools of oppression at the hands of the all-white board—nullified and to avenge the cross-burning. But larger issues lurked behind the takeover as well. For example, the AAS was protesting what it deemed the administration's inadequate progress toward an independent black studies program. Though the administration of President James A. Perkins and the Board of Trustees had recently authorized such a program, AAS activists considered it insufficiently premised on the tenets of Black Power and black consciousness. The students were also taking a broader stand against the legacy of racism at Cornell and in American and Western culture.

Negotiations turned panicky once the presence of guns became known. The Perkins administration soon agreed to all of the AAS's demands, offered amnesty for damage done during the takeover, promised to investigate the cross-burning, and pledged to present a motion for nullification of the sanctions to the faculty. Nullification became the central issue in the dispute, putting the faculty on the line. Would it be proper for the faculty to accept such an agreement, entered into under conditions of extraordinary duress?

By Sunday evening Cornell had become something of an armed camp. The AAS still had its weapons, and certain fraternities and other campus groups took up arms in reaction. Threats of violence and reports of vigilante activity poured into the Campus Safety headquarters and the "rumor clinic" that was set up down the street from the Straight. Bullets were fired into an engineering building, just over the heads of two students who were studying inside. Furthermore, the AAS, Students for a Democratic Society (SDS), and some radical faculty were threatening to seize other buildings—acts that could have brought several hundred armed deputies onto campus. The situation was careening out of control. As many observed, fear and paranoia raged throughout the campus that night.[4]

The next day the faculty refused to accept the agreement because they construed it as a capitulation to force. Making such a crucial decision under coercion would violate the fundamental principles of reason that should govern a university. For over a year Cornell had been subjected to disruptions by SDS and the AAS in the name of social justice, including classroom disturbances, a quasi-violent takeover of the Economics Department, the violent expulsion of bank recruiters from a building, and the manhandling of President Perkins at a major conference on South Africa. Three white students were beaten on campus; two identified their attackers as black, and the third, suffering brain damage, nearly died. In none of these cases was anyone sanctioned. Many faculty felt it was time to draw a line.

The faculty's recalcitrance escalated the stakes. Few students accepted the principles behind the faculty's stand. By Tuesday evening SDS had organized a massive assembly of students in cavernous Barton Hall who vowed to take over the administration building, at the very least, if the faculty did not reverse their vote at a new meeting called for noon the next day. That same evening Jones made an inflammatory radio address and then an equally incendiary speech at Barton threatening the university itself and specific faculty members opposed to lifting the sanctions, sending tremors throughout Cornell. Meanwhile, three hundred to four hundred armed sheriff's deputies remained on alert, at the campus's edge, in case the students made a move. Many of these deputies were intolerant young rural toughs, eager to unleash their brand of justice against the unruly students. Disaster seemed imminent if the faculty did not bend.

Under excruciating pressure, the faculty reversed their decision, for several reasons: fear, loss of control over the situation, a sense of necessity, and perhaps a genuine change of mind. The vote averted violence, but it amounted to a surrender to intimidation and to radical students' interpretation of the proper purposes of the university. The students in Barton Hall, the so-called Barton Hall Community, now controlled Cornell, a revolutionary situation leading to the founding of a student-faculty "constituent assembly" to restructure university decision-making power. (The assembly created a senate based on egalitarian principles of proportional representation, an arrangement that lasted until 1977.) And the AAS won not only nullification of the sanctions but also an African-American studies center based on tenets of Black Power and black consciousness; given its pedigree, it was one of the most politicized programs in the country.[5]

The Perkins administration tried to salvage its authority by proclaiming the virtues of the new order, but Perkins's days at Cornell were numbered: he resigned within weeks. By losing control of the situation, he had lost the support of key faculty members. Several prominent faculty also resigned in protest of what they considered capitulation and a surrender of the principles of liberal education. The extraordinary events profoundly affected scores of professors, staff members, and students—indeed, the very legacy of Cornell.

Cornell at a Racial Divide

The scene in front of the Straight astonished the Cornell community and the wider world, which had not been privy to the events that had riven the campus over the course of the previous year. Cornell had prided itself on being the most racially progressive of America's predominantly white universities. Had it not been a leader in providing the previously excluded with an opportunity to have an Ivy League education? Had not the administration striven to provide the AAS with a black studies program? And had not the previous generations of black students managed to adapt to Cornell and find some measure of acceptance? Though many activists empathized with the AAS's claims, most whites—students, faculty, and administrators—struggled to understand why such a confrontation had come to pass. On the other side of the coin, many AAS members expressed anger and disbelief at whites' inability or refusal to grasp what was at stake. Too few whites appreciated the racism many black students had had to endure at Cornell.

Under the Perkins administration (1963–1969), Cornell was the first major university to recruit minority students aggressively, particularly blacks from inner cities whose backgrounds differed from those of traditional Cornell students. This initiative was part of the Committee on Special Education Projects (COSEP) program that Perkins launched in 1963, which had increased the number of undergraduate minority students from 8 to 250 by 1968–69. The program embodied the best of the liberal intentions and policies of the civil rights era, which was cresting as COSEP was being formed.[6] Despite conflicts, COSEP's advocates remained optimistic about its prospects even as racial tensions in America intensified during the course of the 1960s. As late as October 1968, *New York Times* reporter John Leo wrote, under the headline "Cornell Is Seeking Nation's Best Negro Scholars," that the fledgling program was "the first to be set up by a major American university. With the rise of black consciousness, many colleges are under pressure to start programs in black history and culture, but no university has come so far so fast as Cornell."[7] Even on the eve of the Straight takeover, Ernest Dunbar wrote an article in the *New York Times Magazine* that chronicled the problems of the previous year before ending on a note of optimism.[8]

But a historical irony was waiting in the wings as COSEP took the stage: the consensus between black and white activists over civil rights was unraveling. As Tamar Jacoby noted, "By 1963, something new had crept into the equation. Even those [blacks] who 'wanted in' were growing impatient and volatile, possibly already beyond appeasement. More discerning white journalists understood this. 'Black nationalism,' one reporter wrote, 'is a mood to be found in every segment of the Negro population.'"[9] The integrationist, universalist, liberal, and legalistic tenets of the civil rights movement were giving way to the more militant and separatist doctrines of Black Power and black consciousness. Many young men and women had been influenced by the separatist, nationalistic teachings of Black Muslim leader Malcolm X, and the movement for rights had taken a more confrontational turn with the rise of the Student Nonviolent Coordinating Committee (SNCC) and similar groups. Riots exploded in the Watts neighborhood of Los Angeles in 1965. Two years later Stokely Carmichael and Charles Hamilton published their classic statement, *Black Power: The Politics of Liberation in America,* a book that abandoned all hope for meaningful integration and common standards of right between black and white. The authors proclaimed that Black Power "is a call for black people to begin to define their own goals, to lead their own organizations. . . . It is a call to reject the racist institutions and values of this society. The concept of Black Power rests on a fundamental premise: *Before a group can enter the open society, it must first close ranks.*"[10] Carmichael and Hamilton also coined the expression "institutional racism" (pervasive racism based on unconscious assumptions of racial inferiority), which soon would play a major role in the evolving crisis at Cornell. Cornell students were influenced by these trends. As Denise Raynor, a onetime member of the AAS, told me by the later sixties, "There was no one at Cornell who took Martin Luther King seriously philosophically. Everybody just wrote him off as, —'ah, who cares?'"[11]

Student activists had already staged disruptions at black colleges earlier that decade to force their schools to adopt black studies programs conducive to the new trends in thinking about race, the most prominent of which took place at Howard University. The movement then spread to major white universities, such as Northwestern, where a young man named James Turner led a building takeover to win a program. So the AAS had precedents from both black and white schools on which to draw.

All these tensions were captured by "The Picture." As the doors of the Straight opened for the AAS to depart, the SDS members who had stood guard to protect the AAS from danger dispersed to make room for the marchers. The AAS men formed a protective loop around the women in the procession, symbolic of the "empowered" black men who were now able and willing to defend their women (another key theme of the Black Power movement).[12] The marchers' impact on the crowd that anxiously awaited their exit was immediate.

"Oh, my God, look at those goddamned guns!" Associated Press photographer Steven Stark exclaimed.[13] Leading the procession was AAS president Edward Whitfield, a mathematics student in the new six-year Ph.D. program. Tall and intellectually serious, Whitfield had ranked near the top of his large high school class in Little Rock, Arkansas, where federal troops had intervened in 1958 to support integration. Not accustomed to using guns, the bearded, spectacled leader looked both scholarly and sheepish as he walked across the porch of the Straight, his rifle dangling from his right hand. Slightly behind him and to his left marched Eric Evans, AAS minister of defense. A transfer student from West Point, the stocky, bearded Evans wore thick-framed glasses and held his rifle proudly and confidently as he strode before the astonished onlookers. Across his chest was draped the bandolier that became perhaps the most famous symbol of the crisis. Tom Jones and another member marched near the back of the legion, toting rifles and holding their fists high in Black Power salutes. Jones's expression was more emotional than Evans's or Whitfield's, presaging the inflammatory rhetoric that he would soon unleash on Cornell.

Just behind and between Evans and Whitfield sauntered Homer ("Skip") Meade, Jones's staunch ally. The sarcastic and ironic expression on his face matched his attire: rifle, western poncho, field-hand hat, cigar hanging from his lips—a touch of Americana. He was Clint Eastwood, the "man without a name," the "high plains drifter." These marchers reflected the various aspects of the unfolding crisis: dead seriousness, consternation, fear, wry comedy, and individuation in the presence of solidarity. But a common theme could be read in each man's expression: victory over the university.

Visible behind Meade was a large black man wearing a white hat and sunglasses. Rudolph ("Barry") Loncke looked out of place, as indeed he was. A second-year law student and Vietnam War veteran, Loncke had paid little attention to student politics at Cornell, preferring to concentrate on his studies; but the administration had asked him to act as an intermediary between it and the AAS, and he accepted the challenge in the name of protecting the interracial community. Then there was Thomas J. Turner, the large black campus security officer who stood to the left of the front door from the marchers' perspective. Turner, one of only two black campus officers, had been called to the scene on his day off, and he felt the pressure. "It wasn't a comfortable position to be in," he recalled twenty years later.[14] But he accepted his responsibilities as a professional.

Vice Presidents Steven Muller and Keith Kennedy—the major negotiators with the AAS—took up the rear of the procession. It had been a most difficult two days for these worthy yet overmatched men, and they looked worn and beaten. A sinking feeling swarmed over them as they walked with the group across the campus to the AAS headquarters for the actual signing of the pact. The look on their faces told the tale of an administration on the verge of breakdown—indeed, perhaps already over the edge.

Despite the variety of positions portrayed in "The Picture," the dominant theme was racial division and confrontation. In the eyes of Gloria Joseph, a creative black woman who was the key administrator in COSEP and who walked with the women of the AAS in the procession, a racial divide greeted the marchers as they stepped out of the Straight. "Every time I retell that story, I get a chill just thinking, knowing the anger and the looks on their faces. It reminded me of those little black kids in Little Rock when they were trying to get to school. And those policemen standing there, and those crowds. . . . There was a mob. . . . This was [a] most prestigious institution with all its legacy and history. You don't have a raggle-taggle bunch of black boys, as they would say, [take] over an institution like that. And on Parents Weekend!" [15]

After leaving the Straight, the marchers proceeded across the campus to the AAS headquarters on Wait Avenue, just across the Triphammer Bridge, spanning one of Cornell's magnificent gorges. As he followed the cavalcade, Cornell Public Information Officer Thomas L. Tobin remembered "quite vividly" the astonished looks on the faces of people in automobiles who had chanced upon the scene. "It was just total and utter amazement and confusion." [16] Administrators and AAS leaders signed the deal at the building on Wait Avenue.

At the end of this most extraordinary day, weary administrators retreated to the shelter of home. Perkins sat down and turned on the news. What else would appear on the screen but the most important story of the day? As he watched the AAS departure from the Straight for the first time, Perkins suddenly realized that "we had one hell of a public relations problem on our hands." [17] Rather than solving anything, the agreement over the Straight had only led Cornell deeper into crisis.

Perkins and Liberal Education

Though the Cornell crisis swept many individuals into its vortex, no one personified what was at stake as much as James Perkins. Sporting a résumé studded with all-star national and international appointments, the tall, elegant Perkins was a quintessential progressive liberal of his era. He had done his best to further the cause of social and racial justice and had a hard time fathoming being a target rather than part of the solution. At bottom the Cornell crisis was about the meaning of the university in relation to claims of racial justice and threats of violence, and Perkins's educational philosophy and policies were cardinal issues in this debate.

Perkins's impressive history included a B.A. from Swarthmore (1934) and a

Ph.D. from Princeton (1937); extensive high-level service in Washington and Europe during World War II in the Office of Price Administration and the Foreign Economic Administration, where he mastered the art of cooperating and facilitating the policies of high-powered business and political leaders; vice president of Swarthmore (academic affairs, public relations, and fundraising); vice president of the Carnegie Corporation of New York and the Carnegie Foundation for the Advancement of Teaching; and board memberships or chairmanships of several educational and civil rights organizations, including the chairmanship of the board of trustees of the United Negro College Fund. He cut a very high profile. Noted Cornell historian Walter LaFeber recalled that even John Kennedy once asked, "'Who is this James Perkins? He is on everybody's list. Everybody mentions Perkins.'" "Perkins was very ambitious," LaFeber said.[18]

The Cornell presidency was a jewel in Perkins's crown. He appeared to relish the chance to influence social change through the opportunities his presidency afforded and the connections he had cultivated with influential individuals and organizations around the world. He traveled often, leading students and others to criticize him as an absentee president. ("Perkins was away a lot, and I think that was one of the problems," LaFeber acknowledged.)[19] But others appreciated Perkins's connections and travels. Board of Trustees secretary (assistant secretary of the corporation) Joyce Cima valued the "style" and "class" Perkins brought to Cornell.[20] He seemed to resemble Richard Cory in E. A. Robinson's famous poem: "He was a gentleman from sole to crown / Clean favored, and imperially slim. . . . / And admirably schooled in every grace: / In fine, we thought that he was everything / To make us wish that we were in his place."[21]

Perkins was an heir to the pragmatic and liberal progressivism that had dominated twentieth-century education theory. This tradition, indebted to such pivotal thinkers as John Dewey and William James, was premised on the tenet that education could and should be used as a tool of progressive social change, which included revitalized democratic citizenship, material prosperity, equality, and the development of ethical and intellectual virtue. A key principle in Dewey's thought was the belief that the individual's struggle with immediate pressing problems is the key to intellectual growth; consequently, education should stress developing thought processes that are applicable to various types of practical problems, not just the learning of great books and cultural legacies, the type of learning that had formed the core of the traditional theory of liberal education. (Rousseau had pioneered this new approach to education before Dewey.)[22] For Dewey it was a question of balance; traditional emphasis on great books and cultural legacy should be supplemented, not replaced. To many of his followers, however, the balance decidedly favored immediate experience and practical education.

Though the thinking of Dewey and James was subtle and complex, the pragmatic and progressive turn in education theory that was carried on in their names led to an emphasis on useful and instrumental knowledge in universities (the physical sciences, social sciences, and professional studies) over the traditional curriculum centered in the humanities (philosophy, theology, history, literature). According to

E. D. Hirsch, the 1918 National Education Association report titled *Cardinal Principles of Education* flagged the shift in emphasis from humanistic to pragmatic education. "The 1918 report implicitly accepted these [Rousseauian] ideas, to which they added Dewey's pragmatic emphasis on direct social utility as an educational goal. Thus, the most appropriate replacement for bookish, traditional culture would be material that is directly experienced and immediately useful to society." [23]

Indeed, Cornell had pioneered this way of thinking at the university level well before Dewey's time, espousing Ezra Cornell's ideal of social usefulness at its founding in 1865, decades before the dawn of the progressive and pragmatic eras. But Cornell University was a rather unique hybrid in this regard, as it had prided itself from the beginning on providing excellence in both practical and liberal fields of education. It was a unique blend of publicly funded schools (such as the College of Agriculture) and privately funded schools (Arts and Sciences, Engineering, Hotel Administration, and many others). Not coincidentally, the battles of 1969 were fought by students predominantly from the College of Arts and Sciences, where many students took a serious view of the normative issues of the decade and disdained the instrumentalism of the university. [24]

Perkins's educational philosophy blended the moral ideals and the instrumentality of the progressive and pragmatic ideal of education that was now dominant at the major universities. But Perkins brought a distinctive "social justice" twist to his progressivism that was consistent with the moral urges of liberalism in the early '60s. Perkins had been raised in the suburbs of Philadelphia, the son of a local banker father who supplied the family with solid middle-class respectability; but his moral compass was the product of two other sources: his mother and his lengthy experience at Germantown (Pennsylvania) Friends School, a school of the Quaker faith. Neither of Perkins's parents was Quaker, but his mother's social activism and conscience fit well with Quaker moral thinking. "My mother was a spiritually oriented woman with a very fine tuned social conscience," Perkins told interviewer Keith Johnson in 1994. In this interview he portrayed his first exposure to the social and economic divide between blacks and whites. When his mother took him and his sister to the home of the family's maid, "We were appalled at the circumstances under which she lived. It was absolutely another world. . . . I was sensitized to the fact that the blacks had been given a raw deal." [25] Perkins remained firm in this belief as he rose in the world of corporate foundations and higher education. In a 1968 speech titled "This Reckless Decade," delivered just days before an early eruption of racial strife on campus, he declared, "Does one really believe the university should curtail the admission of Negroes merely because there are complications involved? The integrated school and the integrated campus represent our best hopes for future understanding between black and white. No matter what the difficulties, we must never abandon this liberal dream." [26] In his interview with Johnson, he applied the mission of social justice to the mission of the university:

> The question of social justice as a national preoccupation and requirement began to impinge on the colleges and universities. . . . But the blacks were another case.

They were no further ahead [by the early '60s]. . . . Politically we began to break up the whole business of segregation in the United States. But the universities like the Ivy League and like Cornell really lived in a world that did not see the inevitable implication of this basic drift towards concern for the equality of opportunity. . . . They were living in a dream world. . . . They had to accommodate minority students; they to set up special programs.[27]

Though some observers questioned the depth of his commitment to COSEP, Perkins was rightly praised for his initiatives. James Turner, the first director of the black studies program at Cornell, called him "very much a visionary in terms of democratizing the university."[28] Perkins's belief in social justice was a genuine part of his educational philosophy.

The other part of Perkins's philosophy consisted of a more prosaic application of pragmatic education theory: the university's *raison d'être* is to be socially useful and relevant in an instrumental sense. Without this connection to the immediate perceived needs of the time, the university is bereft of meaning. Indeed, this mission was so imperative in Perkins's writings that the identity of the university became almost indistinguishable from the society it is meant to serve. Perkins presented his understanding of the university in his book, *The University in Transition* (1966), based on the Stafford Little Lectures he delivered at Princeton in 1965. In these lectures he traduced scholarship that is not part of the mission of usefulness; the pursuit of truth and understanding should never be ends in themselves but rather means subjected to the imperatives of social service (an ideal that is related to both pragmatic education theory and Quaker morality). Often deploying generative images, Perkins belittled the "intellectual chastity" of the nonpragmatic scholar (he spoke of the "barren discussions of medieval scholasticism") whose vocation renders the university "sterile and inert," "impotent," weak. What is needed is "experts" who respond to society's needs and demands for service:

> We should note again that this mixture of private pursuit and public purpose is hardly conceivable without the universities as partners, and this partnership would be impotent if the university had not come to embrace its complementary missions which have enabled it to digest new ideas, train new students, and participate in new applications. . . . A fundamental requirement posed for the educational system is the need for continuous change and innovation. . . . The world is faced with vast new ideas and for manpower trained in new areas of knowledge.[29]

As David Grossvogel said in an essay about the Cornell crisis, *The University in Transition* embodied "the words of one whose purpose is to identify and resolve the problems that the operative society posits as givens, and who has marked off, for a time, the university as the grounds for this operation. For him [Perkins], the university is consequently defined by its 'social involvement.'"[30]

In addition to establishing COSEP, Perkins brought other innovations to Cornell based on this understanding. For example, he oversaw the establishment of a program in which a college freshman could earn a doctorate at Cornell in six years. Critics alleged that this program was premised on assumptions of instrumental knowledge: get the student in and out of the university as quickly as possible. (Indeed, Perkins earned his Ph.D. only three years after receiving his B.A. It took him only a few months of intense work to write his dissertation.)[31] Cornell Government Professor Allan Bloom, a famous humanistic critic of Perkins's vision of the university who resigned in the wake of the '69 crisis, charged in his own controversial book about higher education, *The Closing of the American Mind,* that the six-year Ph.D. program, "richly supported by the Ford Foundation, . . . was intended to rush [students] through to the start of their careers. . . . The Cornell plan for dealing with the problem of liberal education was to suppress students' longing for liberal education by encouraging their professionalism, . . . providing money and all the prestige the university had available to make careerism the centerpiece of the university."[32]

In addition, Perkins reorganized and centralized the biological sciences, making them a primary area of concern. Critics maintained that he downplayed the humanistic liberal arts in favor of the applied and physical sciences. (For both substantive and political reasons, his major supporters during the '69 crisis came from the physical sciences, whereas his major critics hailed from the College of Arts and Sciences.)

It cannot be stressed too strongly that Perkins's instrumental philosophy of education was representative of his time. By the mid-twentieth century, major universities differed profoundly from their nineteenth-century counterparts, embodying what University of California President Clark Kerr, Perkins's friend and former Swarthmore classmate, called the "multiversity."[33] In a nutshell, the multiversity is a vast bureaucratic enterprise with a multitude of functions that differentiate it from the more tightly knit educational communities of lore. Kerr's and Perkins's images of the multiversity also resembled the ethic of "interest group liberalism" that Theodore Lowi dissected so devastatingly in his classic book, *The End of Liberalism,* published in 1969. In Lowi's portrayal, interest group liberalism's theory of leadership entails balancing and accommodating the myriad claims of visible interest groups in the name of maintaining equilibrium in the presence of constant change. Thus interest group liberalism is not guided by substantive authority or an authoritative vision of the public interest but rather by a process of accommodation.[34] As Perkins wrote in *The University in Transition,* "University integrity, then, is involved not with preserving things as they are, but rather, with maintaining the coherence of its various parts, and the harmony with which it is able to pursue its aims—whatever their specialized nature."[35] We will see that the crisis of authority associated with interest group liberalism haunted liberal authority at Cornell.

As Grossvogel and others noted, Perkins's understanding of the university was similar to that of activist students in the sense that both wanted the university to be more relevant to society and social justice. Yet Perkins's view differed from students' in two respects. First, many student activists of the late '60s had come to view American society as fundamentally corrupted by racism, militarism, and alienation; hence the university that serviced this society was also corrupt, virtually by definition. Perkins's emphasis on the university's obligation to be a part of that society played right into the hands of this critique. Second, Perkins's instrumentalism (if not his social justice side) ran counter to the quest for deeper understanding of self and society that motivated many students in the '60s. Thus when students grew powerful, Perkins and the administration had no pedagogical foundation on which to resist the forces of change. Without a soul of its own, Perkins's university dissolved under the force of pressures arising from within. In Freudian terms, the powers of the superego and the id overpowered the diminished ego. In other terms, power prevailed over persuasion.

A scene on February 27, 1968, presaged the fate of Perkins's authority at the hands of student leaders. Perkins and students held a "question and answer" session in the Temple of Zeus, the "artsy" coffeeshop in the basement of Goldwin Smith Hall that is adorned with ancient Greek and mythological sculptures. The *Cornell Daily Sun* reported, "Some 175 followers of the cult of president watching—with the skeptics outnumbering the faithful—made a less than pious pilgrimage to the Temple of Zeus yesterday to meet and greet James A. Perkins." [36] The front-page article featured a picture of Perkins bowing at the feet of Lawrence F. Kramer ('70) as Kramer placed a "ceremonious crown" on Perkins's head. On the surface it was all in good-natured fun—the president meeting and joking with student critics, Kramer smiling as he coronated the president. But the crown looked like a dunce's cap, and men and women of a serious bent considered the picture humiliating. A year later they considered the scene prophetic.

It is instructive to contrast Perkins's vision of the university with that of another university president, Robert Hutchins, of the University of Chicago (1929–1951). Though Hutchins was famous for his defense of the traditional liberal arts curriculum and the "great books" approach to liberal education, he did not disavow the claim that the university should contribute to society. Like Dewey, he believed that the university should serve the enterprise of democracy and that education in practical professions was a proper part of the university's offerings. It was a question of balance, and in Hutchins's world, the balance should decidedly favor humanistic education over vocationalism and the direct servicing of society. In this sense, Hutchins's thought and practice also differed from such humanists as Bloom, who were much more doubtful about the possibility of the university's providing leadership for the democratic experiment. Though Bloom repeatedly espoused the need for the university to lead the democratic polity out of the shadow of the cave and into the light of thoughtfulness, a deep pessimism ran through *The Closing of the American Mind* that is reminiscent of the despair of Plato, Bloom's historical mentor and the creator, in *The Republic*, of the metaphor of the cave. Bloom seemed content to make the university an elite island unto itself, protected from the corruption of the cave. Hutchins exuded more confidence in the university's partnership with democracy.

This said, Hutchins differed profoundly from Perkins in a cardinal respect: he believed the university should contribute to society *on its own distinctive terms,* which entailed educating students in what Hutchins called "the single-minded pursuit of the intellectual virtues." [37] The intellectual virtues included struggling with the works of the greatest minds who dealt with the enduring fundamental and universal questions. Hutchins would have agreed with Bloom's definition of liberal education: "recognition of important questions of common concern . . . the sense that learning must and can be both synoptic and precise . . . the specific intention to lead to the permanent questions."[38] Empiricism, instrumentalism, and vocationalism have their place in Hutchins's understanding of the university, but the fundamental purpose of the university is the development of the intellectual virtues nourished by the liberal arts. The key point, for our purposes, lies in Hutchins's belief that the university can serve society only if it *does not surrender its distinctive meaning and form* to external forces. It must not compromise its integrity, its wholeness, its honesty. Democracy and the professions will always see to their own practical needs: what the university has to offer them is an example of the exercise of the powers of the mind and (in a more utilitarian sense) the creative growth engendered by exposure to the intellectual creativity cultivated by a vital university that is proud of its intellectual heritage. Whereas Perkins viewed nonpragmatic scholarship as "sterile," Hutchins believed that unapologetic instrumentalism led to the greatest sterility of all:

> The only hope of securing a university in this country is to see to it that it becomes the home of independent intellectual work. The university cannot make its contribution to democracy on any other terms. . . . I suggest that vocationalism is not merely bad for the universities; it is bad also for the professions. I beg to lay down this fundamental proposition, that every profession requires for its continuous development the existence of centers of creative thought. To the extent to which universities and professional schools abandon creative thought and degenerate into trade schools the profession must degenerate into a trade. . . . [The university's justification] is to be found in the enduring value of having constantly before our eyes institutions that represent an abiding faith in the highest powers of mankind.[39]

That Perkins did not share Hutchins's burning faith in the distinct mission of the university may be related to Perkins's lack of interest in scholarship, a fact he acknowledged more than once in his interview with Johnson. In describing his decision to leave Princeton and join the Office of Price Administration, he presented a telling story:

> I knew in my bones that I was never going to be a research scholar. It wasn't my style or my quality. . . . And maybe that's why they began to think of me in administration right off the bat, coming to the same conclusion. I was writing a book at the time. I would go into my study, and I would look out the window and see all those other people having a nice time, and I was doing this drudgery work. So it became clear to them and to me and to everybody else the rest of my life that I know how the deal with scholars, but I was not going to be one.[40]

This attitude toward scholarship no doubt influenced how Perkins and many around him reacted to the conflict surrounding academic freedom.

Social Justice, Academic Freedom,
and the Meaning of the University

More than any other campus dispute of its time, the Cornell crisis featured a stand-off that cut to the heart of the conflict over the meaning of the university, a conflict that also made Cornell a harbinger of intellectual and political disputes that have rocked American universities in the 1990s: academic freedom versus the concern for racial justice. The threat of force (the guns) made this tension uniquely explosive at Cornell. As I will eventually argue, there need not be any real conflict between the worthy aspirations of social justice and academic freedom; yet the politics at Cornell brought them into fierce conflict in a manner that foreshadowed future campus wars.

Numerous writers and reporters have depicted how American universities have used speech codes, harassment policies, and other devices to limit or censure speech that is considered hostile to members of historically oppressed groups.[41] Although such policies are often well intentioned and can contribute to making the campus more hospitable and egalitarian (at least in theory—the evidence is hardly conclusive), they also stifle honest and critical thinking about such vital issues as race, gender, and equality and thus challenge the conception of the university as an institution dedicated to the pursuit of truth and critical understanding. This debate pits two academic cultures against one another, one committed to the principles of liberal education and academic freedom, the other committed to using the university to create an ideal of equality and social justice.[42] The conflict at Cornell epitomized this clash.

Cornell had on its faculty individuals who were keenly concerned about protecting academic freedom, especially in the History and Government Departments, where the leading conservative and liberal dissenters to the administration's policies resided. Many of the these individuals were master teachers for whom the life of the scholar-teacher was an all-consuming calling, not simply a profession. No one embodied this ethic as eccentrically as Bloom, who believed that education is ultimately about the discovery and training of the soul. At some point in his career Bloom established the annual ritual of taking his best students (usually graduate students) to his family's old house near New York City for the purpose of spending a weekend immersed in the legacy of Socrates, Plato, and the Academy. The scholars would drape themselves in Greek togas, drink wine, and impersonate the characters of Plato's dialogues, in particular *The Symposium,* Plato's dialogue on Eros and philosophy. At the end of the weekend, "Socrates" would be given the "hemlock," and the guests would return to campus. One can only imagine what someone of Perkins's temperament would think of such a practice! Other professors of the academic freedom camp were far less eccentric but no less dedicated to teaching. Walter Berns and Walter LaFeber, for example, were applauded after every lecture in their large courses, not merely after the last lecture of the semester, which was the normal student acknowledgment of a course well taught.

Like many other major universities, Cornell had been struggling for several years to protect the academic freedom of those who dissented from the antiwar movement on campus, as we will see in Chapter Two; but the tension between academic free-dom and racial claims erupted in spring 1968 when the AAS took over the Econom-ics Department in reaction to what it considered the racist teachings of a visiting professor from the Philippines, Father Michael McPhelin, in his class on economic development. AAS activists interpreted McPhelin's comments against the back-ground of the Black Power and black consciousness movements and their own often alienating experiences at Cornell. It was time to take a stand for racial justice. The McPhelin incident introduced the concept of institutional racism to Cornell and marked a turning point in the politics of race and academic freedom. It was the main catalyst in the movement toward a black studies program. The AAS also introduced an important point: What about the academic freedom of students who dissent from a professor's views?

Struggling for legitimacy in the face of the AAS's severe criticism of Cornell as the embodiment of institutional racism, Perkins redefined the meaning of academic freedom in a manner that made it congruent with the AAS's understanding of racial justice. Henceforth, professors and others who spoke against the new orthodoxy on matters of race were in jeopardy—a condition that increased over the next year and reached a peak during the Straight crisis.

It is also important to accentuate another set of casualties of academic freedom that was largely ignored administratively and publicly at Cornell: black students who did not agree with the AAS on substantive or tactical grounds. At no point did the AAS represent a majority of Cornell's black community. Cornell's black com-munity was as diverse as any other community on campus. Yet nonactivist black students were subjected, in ways we will examine in the book, to more coercion than anyone, thereby demonstrating the dangers of dividing the debate along color lines.

The AAS felt its own kind of jeopardy: exposure to institutional racism in the classroom, intolerable to personal and racial pride. The interests of the institution and the AAS, of course, were not necessarily incommensurate. The promotion of racial tolerance, human rights, and equality is properly part of the institutional fab-ric of a humanistic university.[43] And the thirst of many students for racial knowl-edge and justice was undeniable and noble. But the university entered more prob-lematic terrain by assuming that the AAS represented all blacks on campus and by framing the question of academic freedom in isolation from the institutional needs of liberal education. From the time of the McPhelin incident to the Straight crisis a year later, professors, students, and administrators were fearful of running afoul of the proper line on race.

This debate is still very much with us. A statement by professor Barbara Johnson of Harvard represents one side of the contemporary academic freedom versus social justice debate: "Professors should have less freedom of expression than writers and artists, because professors are supposed to be creating a better world."[44] The as-sumption is that freedom of speech and thought should give way to the ends of so-cial justice (whatever those might be) when the two seem to conflict.

On the other side of the issue are such thinkers as Yale's Jaroslav Pelikan, who wrote a book in 1992 reconsidering Cardinal Newman's classic work, *The Idea of a University.* Pelikan placed freedom of thought, intellectual honesty (expressing one's beliefs truthfully and accurately), and a commitment to reason at the center of liberal education: "It shall perhaps go without saying, but unfortunately the history of the university past and present makes it all too obvious that it does not, that the two fundamental intellectual virtues in the 'law of studies' are free inquiry and intellectual honesty.'"[45] Pelikan, however, was no intellectual anarchist. His understanding of academic freedom was based not on an abstract conception of freedom but rather on the purposes of the university as an institution. A subtle conclusion to be drawn is that academic freedom is both more and less extensive than general free speech under the First Amendment, depending on the context. For example, a professor should enjoy extensive freedom to publish but somewhat less freedom in the classroom, where institutional (and today perhaps legal) obligations—such as sticking to the subject matter, competence, and observing basic standards of decorum—prevail. Freedom requires responsibility, but a form of responsibility that does not thwart the freedom of the mind to pursue its truth. Certainly the teaching of all ideas germane to the subject matter should be protected in the classroom, however uncomfortable such ideas might be. Academic freedom also involves adherence to legal and constitutional norms and forms:

> The university will need to affirm old ways of being free and responsible, and to learn new ways of doing so, also because of the alarming increase in the tendency to politicize the university. For it remains true that "a liberal education is an education for freedom," but also that "the order necessary to keep that freedom from collapsing into merely competitive appetites or colliding gusts of anarchy is, in this country, a respect for law and processes of the law."[46]

In this statement Pelikan evokes two forms of responsibility for academic freedom. First, professors, especially when dealing with controversial issues, should be aware of the fact that they are treading on challenged terrain and should therefore be tolerant of dissenting viewpoints. This standard is a professional norm, not something that should be legislated in a punitive sense. It is consistent with the famous Statement of Principles on Academic Freedom and Tenure of the American Association of University Professors, the leading professional defender of academic freedom. Provisions relevant to the Cornell crisis state:

> Teachers are entitled to freedom in the classroom in discussing their subject, but they should be careful not to introduce into their teaching controversial matter which has no relation to their subject. . . . When [professors] speak as citizens, they should be free of institutional censorship or discipline, but their special position in the community imposes special obligations. As scholars and educational officers, they should remember that the public may judge their profession and their institution by their utterances. Hence they should at all times be accurate, should exercise appropriate restraint, should show respect for the opinions of others, and should make every effort to indicate that they are not speaking for the institution.[47]

Second, students, administrators, and others need to respect "the processes of the law." This standard has two aspects: (1) lawfulness needs to be respected because freedom and freedom of thought cannot exist in the presence of threats, coercion, or violence, and (2) respect for the processes of law is historically and logically linked to respect for the rights of others, which is in turn linked to the intellectual freedom of dissenters. Alexis de Tocqueville and others have understood how unreflective social moralism (what Tocqueville called the "tyranny of the majority") can trample dissent and minority rights when it is loosed from the restraints of the forms of law (the "forms of liberty").[48] This understanding is supported by such social contract theorists as Thomas Hobbes and John Locke, who construed the state of nature not simply as a domain of selfish individualism but also as a state where moral passion and fury are not tempered by the institution of law and common terms of justice. The state of nature is violent because there is no consensus over the meaning of justice—no rule of law. Moral anger—even that of groups with strong moral claims against history—can be dangerous. In the universalist thinking of Hobbes and Locke, no person or group is exempt from this possibility, however pure its moral lament.[49]

We will see that the Cornell crisis provided a laboratory for thinking about these interconnected principles. By the time the crisis reached its climax in 1969, the administration had more or less suspended the enforcement of the law for student militants and had forsaken the protection of academic freedom. The situation of lawlessness—which was grasped either consciously or subliminally by the Cornell citizenry—contributed to a breakdown of the sense of order and authority that more than one prominent participant portrayed as the outbreak of a Hobbesian state of nature. When the dust settled, the Cornell crisis was a crisis of liberalism, as professors and administrators entrusted with the protection of liberal principles of education and law proved unwilling or unable to uphold these principles in trying times.

The tensions over academic freedom have been exacerbated in recent years by the development of a type of pedagogy and politics that was also intensifying at the time of Cornell: identity politics, or the politics of recognition. In a nutshell, this has three essential features: (1) the desire to be recognized as a full, competent human subject; (2) identity defined on the basis of such ascriptive characteristics as race, ethnicity, gender, and sexual orientation; and (3) group solidarity along these lines.[50] Identity pedagogy and politics can be constructive, as they can deepen one's sense of cultural heritage and provide a home in a hostile world. They can also serve as points of origin from which to enter the civic culture of shared citizenship on a more propitious basis than that of abstract individualism.[51] Yet such politics and pedagogy can also be problematic if they lead to negative forms of solidarity and sectarianism that limit or stifle the intellectual creativity of the university community and individual minds. *University* means "many within one"; knowledge is manifold but ultimately one. Taken to an extreme, identity politics is inconsistent with intellectual freedom because the solidarity and group pride (group forms of "self-esteem") that it exalts are naturally inhospitable to the tolerance of pointed criticism that is the hallmark of liberal education. If inculcating group pride is essential to education, criticism that affronts this pride is naturally considered inconsistent with educational goals. Under the banner of identity politics and pedagogy, groups affirm their right to freedom of speech at the same time that they assert their ostensible right to freedom *from* speech considered hostile to group pride.

At a deeper level, the politics of identity and recognition contain the potential for serious confrontation, as the struggle for recognition is ultimately a matter courage in the face of the oppressor. The writings of such thinkers as Hegel and Malcolm X portray this conflict as ultimately a life and death struggle.[52] This point will be developed more fully in a later chapter; suffice it to say that this aspect of the politics of recognition played a surprisingly meaningful role in the Cornell crisis. At the peak of the crisis, the courage (on both sides) to defend principles with which one identified emerged as a cardinal virtue; the crisis confronted individuals with fundamental existential and philosophical questions involving personal and institutional integrity.

Perkins's posture toward academic freedom at Cornell was consistent with his uneasiness about scholarship. He and others in the administration (there were exceptions) did not truly grasp the concerns of those who felt themselves threatened by the emerging order, either because they disagreed with its objectives or, more commonly, because they opposed its methods. This failure was partly a function of Perkins's lack of experience as a scholar and teacher who had to put his reputation on the line whenever he entered the arena of intellectual controversy. It was also a function of his philosophy: if the role of the university and the scholar is to serve ends outside of the pursuit of truth and understanding, there can be no solid normative justification for thoughts and scholarship that allegedly thwart what a majority or an intense minority feels is right.

Perkins's posture differed from such progressive defenders of academic freedom and free speech as Dewey, who was a pioneer in the defense of academic freedom from a progressive and pragmatic perspective. Indeed, the most prominent defenses of free speech in the twentieth century have come from the progressive and pragmatic schools of thought; social progress and democracy require the fullest possible testing and criticizing of views.[53] But progressive and pragmatic defenses of free speech are always less secure than defenses that are grounded in less empirically contingent principles, especially when the person mounting them is less beholden to the life of the mind than Dewey.

Statements by various Cornell citizens involved in the '69 crisis capture the debate over academic freedom at Cornell. On one side were activists such as two former AAS members now involved in higher education who maintained that academic freedom should yield to the primary principle of "human rights." Andre McLaughlin, a tall, energetic African-American woman who now teaches minority issues at Medgar Evers College, declared, "We always say at Medgar that there are no academic rights, there are human rights, that first everybody must be considered a human being."[54] Much as Perkins did in the aftermath of the McPhelin affair, Irving McPhail, now president of a community college in inner-city St. Louis, emphasized the need to balance academic freedom with "responsibility" to the norms of identity politics. The legacy of historical oppression weighed heavily on McPhail's thought:

> I think academic freedom must carry with it responsibilities. Those responsibilities must include respect for people and some principles and values that respect the goals of a pluralistic campus community. . . . I think that in contemporary American higher education, we must hold ourselves to a higher standard. And I think that the goal of a pluralistic, multicultural community represents that standard, and I don't think that "anything goes." Insulting members of another race or cultural group, whether they be black, white, brown, red, et cetera, is not to be tolerated. Therefore, academic freedom must be viewed in a more realistic context.[55]

The camp represented by McLaughlin and McPhail was joined by many (mostly younger) progressive professors who believed that eradicating racial and other injustices was a primary goal of the university. During the crisis, these individuals associated themselves with a group calling itself the Concerned Faculty, which was sympathetic to the Afro-American Society's claims against Cornell and the AAS's view of what the university should be.

Other professors lined up on the other side of the issue. Walter LaFeber, leading left-oriented antiwar professor and nationally acclaimed "revisionist" historian of American foreign policy, was a forceful critic of the compromise of academic freedom. When asked if his views had changed nearly three decades later, the hard-headed, forthright LaFeber replied in the language of a progressive still animated by the principle of intellectual freedom:

> Of course not. Because . . . what a university is all about is rational discourse. What these people were doing was essentially raping the major principle of the university. Once you introduce any kind of element of force into the university, you compromise the institution. To me, that is totally unforgivable. . . . We have to make a distinction between procedure and politics. What I am talking about is procedure. I'm a relativist in terms of object and conclusion. I don't think I am necessarily right. What I am absolutist about is the procedure you use to get there. Which means the university always has to be open and it cannot be compromised.[56]

LaFeber was joined by several other liberal-progressive types, including History Department colleagues Frederick Marcham, Joel Silbey, and Richard Polenberg (Polenberg later modified his position somewhat) and the chair of the Government Department, Allan Sindler, who became perhaps the most important faculty member in the entire yearlong affair. These were a few of the small number of liberals who were willing to fight for academic freedom. The abandonment of liberal principles of freedom by the majority of liberals (for whatever reasons) was a powerful subplot of the Cornell story.

Sindler, verbally threatened by AAS leader Tom Jones after the siege at the Straight, was proud to be the first professor to resign from Cornell. The next two were conservative colleagues in the Government Department, Bloom and Berns (Berns had also been threatened). Berns, Bloom, and three other colleagues in the Government Department had studied under the renowned political theorist Leo Strauss at the University of Chicago. Strauss believed that the best liberal education required immersion in the texts of the great thinkers, especially such ancients as Socrates, Plato, and Aristotle, who taught that there are standards of virtue and truth that can be learned through the proper intellectual discipline. Unlike LaFeber and the liberal tradition he represented, the Straussians believed there is a moral truth; indeed, Berns had even made his reputation by writing a book in which he criticized the relativistic liberal tenets of the Supreme Court's emerging free speech jurisprudence and argued for censorship in the name of virtue.[57] But when it came to academic freedom, Berns favored the protection of all ideas, for such freedom is necessary to the dialectical pursuit of truth, and the university is a special place where this process should be most revered. In the matter of academic freedom, the Straussians and the few liberals who were willing to commit themselves were comrades in arms who have maintained respect for one another to this day. The Straussians brought their own distinctive stamp to Cornell and were as responsible as anyone for making the conflict between academic freedom and racial justice the centerpiece of the crisis. In *The Closing of the American Mind*, Bloom defended academic freedom in words with which LaFeber would not quarrel: "Freedom of mind requires not only, or not even especially, the absence of legal constraints but the presence of alternative thoughts. The most successful tyranny is not the one that uses force to assure uniformity, but the one that removes the awareness of other possibilities."[58]

The Legacy of Cornell '69

The issues posed by the Cornell crisis are especially relevant to the university today. The Cornell crisis was a watershed in terms of the tension between the pursuit of social justice and academic freedom, which in turn reflects the larger debate over the meaning of the university. The issue is not only over the ends of social justice, though that issue is important, especially because there are many competing views about the meaning of social justice. (Hence if the university, as an institution, commits itself to one brand, that in effect marginalizes competing notions within the institution. This is a recurring problem in universities today.) The debate is also over the means whereby social justice is to be pursued. In sum, what should be the principal meaning of the university, and what is the relationship between this role and the pursuit of justice?

I will argue that the Cornell experience shows the dangers of not preserving the distinct intellectual integrity of the university as we pursue our thirst for justice. Justice cannot prevail in the absence of respect for truth derived through a process of critical intellectual freedom, respect for the rights of dissenters, and commitment to equal protection of the law. These principles form the heart of constitutional citizenship. History has shown time and time again that the alternative is coercion and brutalization of nonconforming individuals in the name of a higher power or authority. The only sound basis for the pursuit of racial justice is freedom and respect for the rights of all, as Martin Luther King Jr. understood so well. King rode the back of truth, freedom, and common constitutional citizenship, believing that only the realization of these virtues could unlock the gate to the promised land.[59] Until the waning of the civil rights movement, it was always assumed that social justice and freedom of speech went hand in hand.[60] As Vaclav Havel, the Czech philosopher-president, declared, the intellectual's distinctive obligation is to speak one's personal truth to power, to "live in truth."[61] Abandoning this obligation is tantamount to accepting the notion that there is no distinction between truth and power—a conclusion that frees power from restraint. Hutchins was right: the university serves democracy and justice best when it is true to its distinctive integrity.

The Cornell story also suggests the limits of the otherwise promising politics and pedagogy of identity or recognition, as these forces thwart the honest and critical pursuit of truth if they are not ultimately held accountable to the more universal norms of critical inquiry. Similarly, the Cornell story shows the dangers of pursuing separatism too far from the moorings of integration and assumptions about the common powers of the mind that transcend race or ascriptive difference. The pursuit of difference must ultimately lead back or take place within an a priori commitment to the principles of intellectual unity and common citizenship. This is what it means to have a *university*, a one made of many. Developing the intellectual power of individual minds is the university's preeminent contribution to constitutional democracy.

Yale University Law Professor Stephen Carter expressed this ethic in a 1991 book in which he wrestled with the tensions between racial pride and intellectual obligation. Decrying the ways in which the prevailing "shibboleths" of identity politics have compromised intellectual integrity, Carter endorsed a dialectical relationship between racial pride and intellectual individualism. Carter's resolution of the tension within him stands as a fitting statement of the university's integrity:

> The entire point of the argument is that the majority view is irrelevant to the intellectual, whose authority must be the authority of reason. The views I express must be the ones I have reasoned out, not the ones that will make me popular. . . . The task of the intellectual, finally, is to answer not the cautions of friends but the call of the mind. . . .
>
> For those of us holding dissenting views, to content ourselves with silence would represent a tragic rejection of our history as a people. The battle for the right to read, the right to learn, the right to question and to think and to understand and to challenge, has been fought at far too great a cost for us now to pretend that the struggle was really about having a black orthodoxy rather than a white one imposed upon us. . . . We of all people—we who are black—ought to understand the costs of silencing independent voices.[62]

The Cornell story is about the failure of liberalism to protect intellectual freedom in the face of imperative social justice claims, thereby providing a blueprint for the severing of these principles that compromises higher education to this day. It is my hope that this first full telling of the Cornell story will spark the desire to reunite these worthy aspirations in the university, thereby renewing the university as a model for constitutional democracy.

The Scheme of This Book

This book is based on research at the Kroch Archives at Cornell, which contains presidential papers, large quantities of material on the crisis and its aftermath, and Oral History interviews with major participants conducted during and right after the crisis. The Oral History interviews were conducted by several students and other individuals under the aegis of Gould Coleman, an archivist at Cornell. The interviews and data collection were intended to assist research and establish a historical record. In addition, I personally interviewed dozens of participants over the course of the past several years. Though some individuals' views changed during the intervening three decades, most have the same feelings and beliefs today.

I also draw on a rather remarkable manuscript, *Open Breeches: Guns at Cornell*, written by two young men who were involved with Cornell in 1969, George Fisher and Stephen Wallenstein. The manuscript has attained cult status among the few Cornellians who know of it. Fisher was a journalist who worked in the Cornell Public Information Office. He had access to press accounts and individuals who were present at key meetings, and he conducted taped interviews with major figures in the aftermath. Wallenstein, a senior at Cornell, was one of the main interviewers for the Oral History interview project and maintained contacts around the campus. Today he is executive director of the Global Capital Markets Center at Duke University, where he is a professor of law and business.

The manuscript was never published. An incomplete version was available in History Professor Joel Silbey's papers in the archives, but I obtained the complete version from a friend of someone close to Fisher. Though my work and research are original, I draw on Fisher and Wallenstein's observations in many instances and am grateful to and respectful of their work.[63] Their manuscript is accurate and consistent with other data I have found on the crisis.

I was unable to obtain interviews with many participants; several refused to be interviewed (or did not respond), including Perkins, Jones, and other AAS leaders. I interviewed several members of the AAS, and though I raise questions about the implications of their stance, I am grateful for their insights and have striven to tell their story fairly and honestly. Perkins has refused to discuss the crisis with reporters or researchers for decades (he even avoided the subject in his lengthy interview with Keith Johnson), yet his position was portrayed in other materials I cite.

This book follows a mostly chronological pattern. The chapters in Part I deal with key background issues that led to the Straight takeover. Chapter Two covers the rise of student activism at Cornell, emphasizing the nonracial student movements that began in 1958 and the links between movements at Cornell and those on other campuses across the country. It provides background material that I draw on throughout the book. In Chapter Three I discuss the rise of the Afro-American Society and racial conflict at Cornell. In Chapter Four I analyze the pivotal McPhelin case and its implications. Chapters Five and Six address the politics of the black studies program, and Chapter Seven deals with the struggle over the judicial board.

In Part II I focus on the Straight crisis and its aftermath, devoting a chapter to each of the five days from the takeover to the second decisive faculty vote. In Part III I trace the circumstances leading up to Perkins's resignation in the wake of these events and offer some reflections on the implications of the crisis for Cornell and the country.

THE ROAD TO
THE STRAIGHT

CHAPTER TWO

STUDENT MILITANCY

To gain perspective on racial politics and the events of 1969, we need to look at pertinent aspects of student militancy in the 1950s and '60s. I will focus on two areas: student political movements, and student conduct and adjudicatory policies.

From one viewpoint, the clash between social justice and academic freedom in 1969 reflected a tension built into Cornell's institutional fabric. The New York State Legislature established the Cornell Agriculture School as a land grant public institution under the Morrill Act of 1862, but Cornell set up its College of Arts and Sciences as a private college. Ezra Cornell founded the university in 1865 as "an institution in which any person may find instruction in any study," a motto that appears on Cornell's shield. The school's first president, Andrew Dickson White, a pioneer of nineteenth-century higher education, strove to make Cornell a combination of the traditional liberal arts university and the modern research institution dedicated to social progress, based on the German model of the research university. A blend of private and public and of liberal arts and practical studies has been Cornell's distinctive staple since its inception.[1] The 1960s would heighten these tensions to the breaking point. Most of the student and faculty activism would come out of the Arts College. In this Cornell reflected a nationwide pattern: liberal arts was the natural spawning ground of student activists, and liberal arts colleges in universities were domains of resistance to the larger institutions within which they were embedded. Such students opposed what Michael W. Miles called the "industrialization of the university."[2]

During Cornell's first century, authority over student conduct had shifted between faculty and administration, often creating confusion. In his definitive history of the university, Morris Bishop wrote that "University discipline, originally administered by the faculty as a whole and later by the separate colleges, gradually got out of hand as our numbers increased. A University Committee on Student Conduct was formed in 1902."[3] This arrangement lasted until 1955, when the Board of Trustees returned some power to the faculty through the Faculty Committee on Student Conduct. Still, the president was able to maintain substantial control.

The first important student activism began during the presidency of Dean Malott (1951–1963). John Marcham, a man who held a variety of positions at Cornell that gave him a unique knowledge of the university (student, administrator, local journalist, editor of the *Cornell Alumni News*—a role he would make pivotal in 1969—and son of History Professor Frederick Marcham, who would play a key role in the events of 1969), observed that "in the past, students accepted discipline on campus. . . . Students began to challenge both the rules and the process in the later '50s."[4] The biggest battle of the late '50s concerned the policy known as *in loco parentis,* especially Cornell's rules requiring chaperones for women students and prohibiting apartment parties, which reflected Malott's and the Committee on Student Affairs' concerns about the growth of off-campus living (Cornell's was the only coed Ivy League campus at the time). In spring 1958 Kirkpatrick Sale, former editor of the *Cornell Daily Sun* student newspaper, and his roommate, Richard Farina, led a mass student demonstration against the rules. Over a thousand students shouted obscenities, threw rocks at Malott's home while Malott was meeting inside with the Board of Trustees chairman, and chanted such slogans as "We have parents now, who needs more?"[5] This and other demonstrations over parietal rights were minor compared with what lurked on the horizon, but they were important because they represented the dawn of student skepticism of authority, new calls for freedom, and the decline of moral consensus.

Also, in the wake of the Sale-Farina-led disturbance, the stunned Malott yielded control over student conduct to the faculty and named John Summerskill, a psychologist in the Student Clinic, as vice president for student affairs. Under Summerskill's aegis, Cornell instituted a new form of student government with greater authority over student affairs; the new Student Executive Board remained in operation until fall 1968, when it was abolished due to student indifference. At the same time, three adjudicatory bodies were created: the Faculty Committee on Student Affairs (FCSA), which reviewed and considered policy concerning student behavior; the Undergraduate Judicial Board (UJB), consisting of students who would hear cases of students charged with violating the university code; and the Faculty Committee on Student Conduct (FCSC), which would review cases the UJB decided. In this scheme the faculty held ultimate power because it could overturn UJB decisions or increase penalties. Nonetheless, students (especially women) gained greater freedom under this new arrangement over the next several years as the FCSA and related university bodies increased the amount of freedom students enjoyed (permitting coed visits to dorms, off-campus living, drinking in dorms, later curfews, and so on). Some observers worried that the new system failed to delineate the relationship between the president's and the faculty's authority over student conduct.[6]

Two further issues during Malott's tenure merit attention. First, in 1952 and 1953 the House Un-American Activities Committee (HUAC) accused two Cornell professors of being communists: physicist Philip Morrison, who had worked on the atomic bomb in World War II, and biologist Mark Singer. Though Malott secretly had a special trustee committee investigate Morrison (it concluded he was not guilty), the president vigorously supported Morrison in public, and eventually Morrison was vindicated. Singer presented a tougher case because a federal district court had found him guilty of contempt for refusing to testify before the HUAC. As soon as Singer was indicted, Malott removed him from his teaching but not his research. Eventually an appeals court reversed Singer's contempt conviction, whereupon Malott reinstated Singer as a teacher. Overall, Malott took a stronger stand in favor of academic freedom than most university presidents at the time. "The general posture of the campus toward [Morrison's and Singer's] refusal was careful defense of their academic freedom," two Cornell professors wrote. "Given the character of the first McCarthy period, the defense was very courageous indeed."[7]

Second, Cornell responded to the historic Supreme Court decision against segregation in education, *Brown* v. *Board of Education of Topeka* (347 U.S. 483, 1954; 349 U.S. 294, 1955), by forming a commission to investigate discrimination in housing and in Cornell's extensive fraternity system (the university had the third largest number of fraternities of any college in the country). Some progress was made for Cornell's small number of black students; for instance, in 1961 a black man, Edmund Furtick, was elected freshman class president, and six fraternities rushed him.[8] Issues concerning social discrimination at Cornell would persist throughout the next two decades. Parietal issues faded in importance.

The Rise of the Multiversity

At the same time that campus protest was increasing, universities such as Cornell were busy transforming themselves into the "multiversity" discussed in Chapter One. In *The Uses of the University*, published a year before the Berkeley student movement that launched student revolts in the '60s, Clark Kerr said the term *multiversity* had replaced *university*, which "carried with it the older versions of a unified 'community of masters and students' with a single 'soul' or purpose." The new "Alma Mater was less an integrated and eternal spirit, and more a split and variable personality." Reflecting the growth of specialization and expertise in the new mass society, the multiversity was a research-oriented institution with multiple functions, interests, and connections to society.[9]

The multiversity contributed to student militancy because students viewed it as an integral part of the alienating, bureaucratic, industrial machine. Indeed, Kerr called the new university a "knowledge factory." It is precisely this perception of the university (bureaucratic education without a human face) that led to the student revolt at Berkeley, where Mario Savio cried that resisting the cogs of the machine through liberating speech was necessary to save one's humanity. The knowledge factory suffocates freedom and true individuality. "Never, at any point, is provision made for [students] taking their places as free men!. . . . Maybe somehow we could take our place as free men also!" [10] Such progressive liberals as James Perkins believed that the multiversity served social justice by serving society, yet students had two counters to this claim: the liberal society was corrupted by racism, an illegitimate and murderous war, and alienation of the human spirit; and the university is implicated in this corruption on many fronts. According to Miles, "Mass lectures, the low priority of teaching, the dominance of the values of research, and the university as a 'service station' to the industrial economy were all elements of the student left's critique of the multi-faction university." [11] Along these lines, Tom Hayden, a founder of Students for a Democratic Society, announced it was time that the university dedicated itself to addressing the larger moral and intellectual potential of the self and to developing a "public" space in which broader moral, social, and political issues could be addressed—in short, the university should be more of a polis. "The old promise that knowledge and increased rationality would liberate society seems a lie. . . . The real question is whether or not society contains any prophets who can speak in a language and concept that is authentic for us, that can illuminate the inner self that burns for understanding. . . . The University must work relentlessly at being a face-to-face, rather than a mass, society," Hayden said. [12] As noted in Chapter One, the ultimate target of student discontent was liberalism and the society and politics it had wrought.

In the multiversity, professors are inclined to be entrepreneurs, with their own funding and research agendas, and the attention they give to their careers detracts from their attention to the polis. Students of the 1960s were seeking freedom, social justice, and a meaningful community. And although they wanted professors to be engaged in society, they also wanted professors to attend to students' thirst for understanding and justice. Interestingly, as we will see, it was not only professors of the left who met these needs (though Cornell had many) but also some on the right, especially at Cornell. These professors were master teachers who were dedicated to a polis at Cornell. Professor Allan Bloom, describing the crisis in higher education in words that challenged Kerr, declared, "The character of the experience of Socrates is important because it is the soul of the university." [13] Walter Berns, Bloom's colleague in the Government Department, found Kerr's notion of the university "absolutely disgusting." Kerr had "absolutely no sense of the noble role of the university," which Berns considered a "calling." [14] Bloom, Berns, and colleagues at Cornell who were dedicated to the Socratic ideal and the university polis became mentors to many students, including, ironically, some of those who would turn on them in the late '60s. These educators agreed with the radicals' critique of the multiversity's corruption of liberal education and the spirit of enlightened inquiry, but they were far less radical and less disturbed by the university's involvement with power in society and more prepared to defend the university for preserving a haven, however diminished, for Socratic inquiry into more fundamental questions. Though many radicals admired this dedication to deeper truth and reflection, many also considered the defense of the university naive and even complicit in the corruption.

As students looked to faculty for moral and pedagogical leadership, many professors were too busy with their research and what the students considered questionable social service to focus on the key issues affecting society: the Vietnam War, civil rights and racial justice, student power, and national and personal liberation. In the '60s, for example, Cornell contributed to the Vietnam War effort by allowing the U.S. Army's Reserve Officer Training Corps (ROTC) to operate on campus and by its association with the Cornell Aeronautics Laboratory in Buffalo, which conducted research on air warfare and reconnaissance. The university had a myriad of other connections and investments that involved it with the military-industrial complex and with the racist regime in South Africa, another target of student outrage. Liberalism had betrayed the hopes with which it was associated earlier in the decade. As Paul Berman expressed it, the '60s gave birth to a myriad of conflicting utopian hopes. "A worldwide shift in power from elites to the masses. A society of individual liberty (as per the revolution in middle-class customs). A society of spiritual grandeur (as per the revolution in the zone of the spirit). Something soulful. A moral advance. And in the glow of that very grand and utopian idea, a thousand disparate events from around the world, . . . seemed to merge into a single tide. And the tide swept forward, unstoppable, all-powerful. It was the new society coming into being. That was the source of our exhilaration." [15] The exhilaration would be short-lived.

Student Groups

In the early 1960s the Cornell Liberal Union became "the first large left-of-center group to appear on campus in a decade," in the words of Irving Louis Horowitz and William H. Friedland.[16] The group concentrated on civil rights, signaling the growth of student concern for the rights of black Americans. By the end of 1963 Cornellians had become active in voting rights struggles in Fayette County, Tennessee, a springboard for student political education at Cornell and elsewhere. (Student involvement in the direct action movements in the South, along with the arrival of the Congress for Racial Equality in the San Francisco Bay Area in 1963 to engage in direct action for jobs and equality, set the stage for the free speech movement at Berkeley.)[17] Another organization, Students for Education (SFE), adopted a different focus, protesting the inadequate selection of books at the Cornell bookstore, the grading system, large classes, lack of faculty contact with students, President Perkins's frequent absences from campus, and the proctor's and dean of student's alleged lack of respect for student concerns, especially restrictions on marijuana. Formed in 1965, SFE styled itself after the Berkeley reform movement but was less confrontational, refraining from making threats or attempting to take over university property. It had the support of student government, the *Cornell Daily Sun,* and the administration. As Nathan Tarcov pointed out, "Cornell's administration, more than Berkeley's, tried to be responsive, undoubtedly from fear of large-scale disruption and consequent adverse publicity as well as from genuine sensitivity to student feelings and concern with improvement." [18]

When one hundred SFE members demonstrated over the quality of undergraduate education in March 1965, the day before Cornell's centennial celebration at Lincoln Center in New York City, Perkins strode into Provost Dale Corson's office, a *Daily Sun* story about SFE in hand, and said, "I'm going to New York. This is yours." [19] Corson was a nuclear physicist from Kansas and a man of common sense, scientific expertise, and substantial administrative experience. Before coming to Cornell he had worked at nuclear laboratories at the Massachusetts Institute of Technology and at Los Alamos and as a technical adviser to the War Department during World War II (1943–1945). In 1948 he had received the Presidential Certificate of Merit from President Truman, a fellow midwesterner whom he resembled in looks, temperament, and style. Since coming to Cornell's Department of Physics in 1946, Corson had worked his way through the professorial and administerial ranks, including full professor, chair of Physics, dean of the College of Engineering, and provost, a position he attained in 1963 when Perkins became president. Steeped in the credentials of science and administration, Corson fit the profile of the preeminent multiversity man. Yet he transcended this profile in two powerful respects: he was dedicated to Cornell as an institution and a polis (he had not taken a sabbatical leave since anyone could remember), and he was devoted to social justice, especially for blacks. The consummate polis man, he assumed responsibility for dealing with SFE, as he would deal with later student disruptions. Impressed with the caliber of the SFE leaders and the reasonableness of their demands, he worked closely with them on an agreement: the students got a new bookstore, and over the next few years some major faculty commissions would issue reports on undergraduate education that would lead to reforms. (Unfortunately, by the time the reports came out, they had lost relevance in the face of revolution at Cornell.) [20] Corson's discussions with SFE set a precedent for taking students' claims seriously and trying to meet them halfway, an approach that was vindicated in this case yet would fare differently as student demands grew more strident. Leaders in the group had earlier asked Walter Berns to be their faculty adviser. He declined because he planned to be on sabbatical in 1964–65. "When I came back after a year," he recalled, "they were all in SDS." [21]

The Radical Left

As the '60s developed, students came to believe that the battle for justice was rooted in a battle for power. Activists contended that the only way to achieve a just and nonalienated society was to shatter the prevailing liberal order, the ideals of which were merely rationalizations for maintaining privilege and the status quo. As W. J.

Rorabaugh noted, "The social turmoil of the sixties was really a battle over power. College students, young blacks, members of the New Left, and hippies believed that power should flow from the bottom up rather than from the top down."[22] This logic played a major role at Cornell, especially in the conflict between claims of racial justice and academic freedom, as militants and their faculty sympathizers viewed the faculty's claims of academic freedom as justifications for perpetuating the privileges supported by racism.

In 1962 Tom Hayden and Todd Gitlin joined other activists to found Students for a Democratic Society (SDS), the leading student protest organization of the decade; it came to the Cornell campus in 1964.[23] For a while SDS at Cornell was largely an intellectually oriented group dedicated to theoretical inquiry rather than confrontation. During the summer of 1966, however, burgeoning discontent with the war helped to swell its membership and make SDS the main group devoted to progressive politics at Cornell. The Ad Hoc Committee to End the War, which had been involved in national antiwar mobilizations in Washington, D.C., had been the major antiwar organization on campus, but it dissolved in the summer of 1966, leaving the field to SDS. An energetic press operation provided an anchor for this new form of activism. In the summer of 1965 Joe and Pat Griffith set up Glad Day Press, a small mimeograph operation that was to grow into a major publisher. Veterans of the Fayette County project, the Griffiths turned the press into the center of radical activity on campus; it "quickly became a national center for reprinting and distributing antiwar and related articles, the mailing address for every left-of-center group on campus, a meeting place for student activities, and a general social center."[24]

Cornell's SDS ranks continued to grow as anger over racism and the war intensified. Students with leadership skills and a devotion to confrontational politics began to play more significant roles, David Burak, Chip Marshall, and Joe Kelly most prominent among them; a key founder of the group, Bruce Dancis, was also coming to believe in confrontational action. By 1969 Cornell's chapter was the third largest in the country, with as many as three hundred members.

In the fall of 1966 Dancis became president of the SDS chapter. Many observers considered him the moral leader of the organization and student activism because of his deep personal commitment to resist the war: he was the first SDS member in the nation to destroy his draft card, on December 14, 1966, for which he served twenty months in federal prison (just after the Straight crisis).[25] Earlier that spring, he and others organized the Mobilization, Cornell's part of an antiwar effort around the country that culminated in a national demonstration in November. The five hundred– to six hundred–member Mobilization had a predecessor, Students for a Constructive Foreign Policy (SCFP), which Burak, Marshall, and Bruce Cohen formed in the spring of 1965. SCFP strove to educate students about the war, its members spending hours leafleting and holding discussions in dorms about Vietnam.[26]

Flush with this success, Dancis and a handful of other students decided in spring 1967 to start an organization called the Resistance, dedicated to receiving the pledges of five hundred students to refuse to be drafted or inducted into the military. That spring they were an important ingredient in the "Sheep Meadow" draft card burnings in Central Park, which were widely publicized. Antiwar professors, administrators, and members of Cornell United Religious Work (CURW) assisted the Resistance, and after its dissolution a man associated with CURW, the famous Catholic priest, brother Daniel Berrigan, carried on in its wake.[27]

In addition to sparking a confrontation with the university that I will discuss shortly, the Resistance movement split SDS between a faction that endorsed a more intellectual and educational approach based on study groups and a faction dedicated to more confrontational action. Dancis's drive for the Resistance, recalled SDS member Peter Agree, "produced the first . . . split within the organization that fall [1967]"; the group "fell apart . . . in November or December or so, and it wasn't reformed until February . . . at Burak's insistence."[28] Dancis wanted to dissolve SDS in favor of an umbrella group known as the Movement; Burak prevailed, although SDS remained split into several factions. Commitment to the organization nevertheless revived just before the key 1968–69 academic year, thanks in part to SDS's "success" in disrupting Columbia University in the spring of 1968.

SDS Factions

Though the factional lines at Cornell would remain inchoate until the SDS national meeting in Chicago in June 1969, by 1968 some outlines were emerging. The three major groups were the Labor Committee, the Anti-Imperialists, and the Action Faction. Tony Fels established the Labor Committee at Cornell after the national SDS founded a similar committee in New York and Philadelphia in the summer of 1968. Most concerned with economic issues, capitalism, and the problems of the working class, this group pressed the university to assist in alleviating the housing problems of the poor in Ithaca in 1968–69. The Anti-Imperialist faction emphasized the war, America's role abroad, and Third World revolutionary movements, focusing on such issues as ROTC and the university's involvement in military research and oppression around the world. The Action Faction, which gained in influence between 1967 and 1969, identified with these and other issues but accentuated confrontation. Its ideology was an amalgam of the policies of the other groups, enhanced by a belief in the ideological and political efficacy of confrontation. The Action Faction at Columbia, led by Mark Rudd, established a model for confrontation in spring 1968, bringing the administration to heel over such issues as urban expansion into the ghetto, racism, and war research.[29]

The Action Faction made the decisive jump from the Resistance to SDS. After Marshall spent the summer of 1965 working with Stokely Carmichael and H. Rap Brown in the Student Nonviolent Coordinating Committee (SNCC, pronounced "snick") in the South, he, Burak, and Cohen decided to influence student government and SDS by radicalizing them. According to Marshall:

> Burak kept saying, "Listen, I know the Resistance is fine, but we've got to build an organization because what good is it if it's not nationwide?" . . . So he finally broke

us down and convinced us that we should join SDS. I think it was sort of like, OK, a bunch of us will come in and we'll just take over and that kind of deal. And then we managed to. Burak was very good at this, although he was more traditional left than, say, Joe [Kelly] and I were. And Bruce Dancis was convinced to come into SDS. Bruce was the kind of moral force of the whole thing.[30]

In addition to taking over SDS, the Action Faction entered candidates in the elections for the Student Executive Board. Winning a place on the board, Marshall then played a role in dissolving the board, leaving Cornell without organized student government during the fateful 1968–69 year—a vacuum that SDS filled in ways we will examine.

The members of the Action Faction exemplified the rise of a new breed of radical leadership: committed, dynamic, "cool." Marshall and Burak were involved in sports (including boxing), journalism, music, and fraternities as members of Sigma Nu. Burak even walked around Cornell with a large live snake wrapped around his neck, and Marshall always seemed ready for action of some sort.

Burak hailed from upstate New York, the son of a military father (a colonel). Devoted to the polis of Cornell as he understood it should be, he was a ubiquitous presence on campus in the mid- to late 1960s: SDS leader; teaching assistant to Professors Sindler and Hacker in their course on race and politics; journalist; organizer of numerous teach-ins, demonstrations, and educational functions; member of the Sindler Commission; and President Perkins's assistant and confidant on a variety of matters, such as research on higher education, including work with the United Negro College Fund (Perkins would fly him down to meetings).[31] Burak acknowledged his sense of bravado: "One of my strengths—and weaknesses—at the time was that I wasn't afraid of authority. I didn't have that [reaction] of step back in awe or apprehension. Part of the reason is that I was brought up in a military family, and I was around uniforms all the time. So it was like no big deal. I made friends with some of the campus cops."[32]

Marshall came from a different background. His parents were well-educated liberal activists ("definitely left-wing" but more classically liberal). His father took him to see Martin Luther King's March on Washington when the youth was a senior in high school, and the young man identified with the concerns of the black community. Like Burak, Marshall worked as a political reporter for the *Ithaca Journal*. Marshall got politicized when he joined the new government program VISTA (Volunteers in Service to America) after seeing a promotional display in the Straight in 1965, and he subsequently spent a year in Atlanta working with SNCC.

Some people admired the swagger of the Action Faction; others frowned on their macho ways. One of the latter was Sheila Tobias, an administrative assistant who would play an important role in the aftermath of the Straight crisis. She was involved with politics yet stayed away from SDS because of "my annoyance—and that's the best word—with the radical student left male leadership. *Macho* is the word, confrontational . . . [Their attitude was that] women were there to get laid: 'Don't say "no" to men who "won't go." '"[33]

Others appreciated the Action Faction's willingness to put itself on the line, especially after the calamitous events at Columbia in the spring of 1968. But such leadership, coupled with the factionalism that existed, also meant that SDS would not have a coherent political philosophy or strategy, consigning it to episodic action. During 1968–69, the main political activity on campus revolved around the AAS, leaving SDS as a kind of sideshow. When the Straight crisis erupted, the Action Faction would spring at the opportunity to play a leading role.

SDS also worked closely with such activist professors as Douglas Dowd of Economics and Douglas Archibald of English. The tall, imposing Dowd, whose son, Jeff, was a major player in SDS, despite being only a student at Ithaca High School, was the most influential radical professor on campus, and he worked on several committees that dealt with students. He was also a leading antiwar activist and radical critic at the national level. Dowd was deeply committed to radical change in America and believed that the university should be an agent bringing about social change or should at least provide an institutional base for groups dedicated to politics and change. Delivering a lecture on activism and social justice in 1967, he told a packed house in Anabel Taylor Hall's Founders Room, "There is no social justice without the attempt of men to gain social justice, and that is my definition of activism." Social justice means "a world in which men can live decently and freely, and in some sort of equality." Dowd acknowledged that no such society had ever existed, yet he singled out America for special blame. America was the ultimate hypocrite about justice and lacked the historical excuses that exonerated such countries as India. America was "the very worst society that history has ever known," he told the gathering.[34] Though he viewed the university and America as deeply flawed, Dowd did respect the intellectual functions of the university, and colleagues told me that he did not impose his ideology on students in the classroom.[35] According to Dancis, professors such as Dowd and Archibald helped to make SDS more level-headed and intellectually serious than some action types were inclined to be.[36]

SDS also had ties to the administration, despite an antiestablishment stance that disposed some of its members to destroy the university in the 1969 crisis. As noted, Burak worked with Perkins on a variety of fronts. The administration kept several student activists close as sources of information, following the advice of Mario Puzo's Godfather: keep your friends close but your enemies closer. Though this policy made practical sense, it also reflected the deeper problems discussed in Chapter One. It reflected the permeability of Perkins's concept of the university to political forces within, and it was consistent with Perkins's policy of governing via the tenets of the leading public philosophy of the time, interest group liberalism (or pluralism), in which factions were placated to maintain balance and order. Interest group liberalism is the sine qua non of the multiversity as Kerr described it. Like many presidents of multiversities, Perkins often spoke in a Newtonian discourse that emphasized "forces," balances," and "accommodations" rather than substance.[37] The problem with interest group liberalism, as the most perceptive thinkers on the left and right observed in the '60s, is that it had no underlying substantive philosophy to guide it. As Theodore Lowi pointed out in his classic critique, *The End of Liberalism* (1969), "Interest group liberalism seeks pluralistic government, in which there is no formal specification of means or of ends. In pluralistic government there is, therefore, no substance. Neither is there procedure. There is only process."[38] As John Schaar, a leading professor supporter of the student revolt at Berkeley, said, the biggest problem in the multiversity and mass society of the '60s was the lack of meaningful authority worthy of respect.[39] Other than nihilists (such as the Weatherman faction of SDS), many student militants respected authority that was backed by moral force, reserving their wrath for what many considered an empty liberalism. The liberalism of administrative elites (what Miles called the "official liberalism" of the "managerial core") was well intentioned but lacked a philosophical compass.[40]

It is interesting to note in this regard that political science's foremost advocate of interest group liberalism, David Truman, was provost at Columbia when it exploded in 1968. Among Truman's arguments was the claim that there is no such thing as an overriding public interest: public interest is merely the quantitative cumulation of private preferences.[41] Such leading practitioners of interest group liberalism as Truman, Kerr, and Perkins were drowned by forces of change that their philosophies could not fathom. Given the forces of change and disruption that erupted in the '60s, few university leaders could have been expected to have the wherewithal to avert chaos.[42]

Nonetheless, Burak's networking would prove indispensable at the single most dangerous moment of the crisis in 1969. He was a graduate student in the School of Industrial and Labor Relations, a teaching assistant in the first class on race and politics taught in the Government Department by Allan Sindler and Andrew Hacker in 1967, and a campus reporter for the *Ithaca Journal,* the major town newspaper. He worked with individuals from a variety of organizations, including CURW, campus security, and the local police. Construing his part in SDS as a learning experience for the campus and the country, he favored nonviolent confrontation, thinking it had educational value, and was critical of individuals who crossed the line into violence (though, as we will see, he had his own moments of weakness in this regard). Along with Government Professor Eldron Kenworthy, Burak defused the threat of massive violence in April 1969. The extensive ties he had nourished over the years proved especially valuable in this regard.

Changes at the *Sun* and the Fall of Student Government

Two other background factors should be mentioned about student activism. The first concerned the *Sun,* the center of student opinion and politics and, in student Art Kaminsky's words, "potentially the single most powerful element on the Cornell campus." Traditionally the *Sun* editors balanced criticism of the university with basic defense of the status quo, but by the mid-'60s the newspaper was being affected by what was happening around it and grew opposed to the administration, fraternities, and student government. "The *Sun* became increasingly critical of [student government] failures [and] weaknesses and less enamored with its successes," Kaminsky wrote.[43] The paper thus helped to undermine student government. It should be noted, however, that when events turned more radical and potentially violent in 1968–69, the *Sun* took a more balanced approach and even recoiled at much of what transpired. One reason was that the *Sun* always maintained some diversity of opinion on its staff. Another reason was that a *Sun* reporter had been beaten up covering an event (we will return to this in a later chapter); more than one observer told me that this act turned the *Sun* against the AAS and part of SDS.

The second factor was the demise of student government. With the rise of student radicalism, the more traditionalist Student Executive Board lost respect and student allegiance; voting in elections for student officers declined rapidly in the face of widespread student indifference to the board. When Marshall became a member, he contributed to a referendum movement that led to the board's abolition at the end of 1967–68. This was precisely the same time that the new judicial system was being instituted and the AAS was growing militant. Some observers, including Government Professor Clinton Rossiter, believed that the demise of student government opened a vacuum into which more militant groups and chaos flowed—a theory that comports with political science teachings about the role of conventional democratic politics in providing stability and compromise that forestall radicalization and instability.[44] Others were less certain, for student government had already become so marginalized that its formal dissolution merely confirmed what had already happened in reality. Still, the demise of student government left a vacuum that made it more difficult to counter militancy. This point gains poignancy with recognition of the fact that student activists at Cornell, as elsewhere, were a distinct minority even after the explosion of student movements across the country from 1967 to 1969. (Over one hundred colleges and universities had protests in the 1967–68 academic year, and over five hundred in 1968–69.)[45] As Miles and others have shown, student rebellions in the '60s achieved success when the majority of "sympathetic" but nonactivist students joined the activists in confrontation with campus authorities.[46] A dearth of established institutional mechanisms for majority rule would naturally play into radicals' hands. Student representation at Cornell remained on a small scale, on the Faculty Committee on Student Affairs, yet that, too, was discredited over conflicts in the judicial system.

The Harriman and ROTC Incidents

Student activists were involved in a number of campus confrontations, seeds that would germinate in the Straight crisis. Shortly after the SFE demonstration, an incident that many Cornellians considered the era's first major threat to academic freedom occurred in May 1965 when Averell Harriman, U.S. ambassador to South Vietnam, came to speak on campus. A few weeks earlier, members of the Ad Hoc Committee to End the War walked out of New York Governor Nelson Rockefeller's speech at the Charter Day Convocation, with decorum and without incident. But as Horowitz and Friedland observed, "This was the first and last 'respectable' demonstration; future protests were obstructive as student activists dropped their concerns about appearing respectable."[47] After Rockefeller's speech, up to three thousand Cornellians had attended Cornell's first teach-in on the war, so when Harriman arrived, critics were ready. They deprived him of the microphone and insulted him as an "agent of imperialism," seriously disrupting his speech. "That, I think, was the first time when there were developments on the campus that nobody had the slightest idea how to deal with," Corson said. "I had discussions with [the students], and they hadn't the slightest interest in academic freedom."[48]

A few days after Harriman's misfortune, the Ad Hoc Committee disrupted the annual review of the ROTC at cavernous Barton Hall. Though the proctor had warned committee members they would be punished for any disruption, such threats no longer intimidated students. When the review started, seventy-six students sat down to interrupt it, triggering a potentially violent counterdemonstration by many of the twenty-five hundred observers in the balcony. Only astute moves by Perkins (who carried out the review) averted violence. Three days later the Undergraduate Judicial Board reprimanded the students; five days after that the Faculty Committee on Student Conduct reviewed the matter in a lengthy session and increased the penalties to probation for the rest of the term for sixty-nine students. The penalty, however, was less severe than it appeared, for the term had just a few days left.

As more cases involving war protests came before the judicial boards, the panels began to lose legitimacy. Protesters' gains "were indicated not only by the numbers of new supporters they won in each trial, but also in the decreasing severity of their punishments and the growing disaffection of student members of the UJB and CSC review procedures," Horowitz and Friedland wrote.[49] Late 1967 brought ROTC demonstrations to a head. On November 17 nearly two hundred protesters and thirty counterdemonstrators engaged in pushing, shoving, shouting, and obstruction during an anti-Marine protest at Barton Hall. One-hundred thirty students were cited for blocking the Marine recruiters; on December 4 the UJB voted 4–3 not to act on the demonstrators' demand to reconsider university policy concerning both the accommodation of recruitment and the dangers to which penalties might expose the students. On December 14, however, the FCSC overturned the UJB's decision and issued "reprimands" to 129 students. This action provoked the immediate resignation of Sociology Professor Robert McGinnis and in late January the resignations of three members of the UJB (its chairman, Neil P. Chodorow, '69; Alan D. Brush, '68; and Tom Jones, '69). The crisis of the judicial boards was at hand.[50]

The *Trojan Horse* Incident

In January 1967 another incident took place that was humorous on the surface but would also have an impact on the way the administration handled the Straight takeover. While Perkins and the administrative hierarchy were in New York City for a Board of Trustees meeting, the head of the Safety Division, Jim Herson, confiscated copies of the student literary magazine, the *Trojan Horse*, on the grounds that it was obscene (among other things, the publication included the sexual ruminations of a local teenage girl). After Perkins returned, the university dropped the matter, yet District Attorney Richard Thaler, a Cornell alumnus, obtained a court injunction against *Trojan Horse* sales and had sheriff's deputies come to the Straight to seize the magazine, which was being sold in defiance of the order (the *Sun* announced the time when the sales were to begin). Two thousand students and several professors and administrators were on hand when Thaler and deputies showed up to arrest students selling the magazine, the first time in Cornell's hundred-year history that civil officials had come on campus to arrest students (*in loco parentis* had made the university responsible for students' law violations). Students surrounded Thaler's car in a threatening manner and tried to trip a deputy. According to John Marcham, one of the top-ranking administrators on campus at the time, the incident "was another challenge to the whole structure. The morale question was significant, a fear of students running rampant over other university employees. We were starting to get into the street theater that came with the New Left."[51]

Soon after the affair the Scheduling, Coordination, and Activities Review Board (SCARB) voted unanimously to allow the publication to be sold, the Interfraternity Council offered to bail out arrestees, over fifteen hundred students and faculty signed a form admitting they bought the magazine, and Marcham said he would not interfere with sales. Chastised, Thaler abandoned his crusade. A state court soon overturned the injunction, ruling that the magazine was not obscene.[52]

Other than again exposing the folly of the human condition, the *Trojan Horse* affair had two important consequences. First, some faculty joined hands with students even though the students had engaged in intimidating actions. Second, the case alerted the administration to the dangers of letting local law enforcement authorities get involved with student conduct on campus. "The entire incident was embarrassing to the university, which had generally managed to avoid external intervention."[53]

Draft Card Destruction

In 1967 students in the Spring Mobilization to End the War organized a national movement to obtain pledges to destroy draft cards. SDS sought permission to set up a pledge table at the Straight on March 7, but SCARB balked, claiming the solicitation was illegal. (First Amendment law was less protective of advocacy of illegal activity than it would become by the end of the decade.)[54] The issue marked the reemergence of *in loco parentis* in a new, politicized form, for the university maintained it had a responsibility to prevent students from engaging in political crimes, in this case criminal solicitation, on campus. On March 16 SDS ignored SCARB and began to solicit pledges, bringing in the proctor, who stopped the solicitations and suspended several demonstrators. Next came a large sit-in at the proctor's office and a teach-in that filled the large lobby of the Straight.

Speakers at the teach-in provided views that epitomized rising tensions between two understandings of moral obligation in the context of university citizenship: social justice versus rule of law. (An identical debate surfaced in the 1969 crisis, although by then the stakes were much higher.) Dancis, who had dropped out of school a few months earlier to devote his full attention to opposing the war, downplayed legalities and emphasized the killing in an illegal war. "We cannot be hung up here while people are dying in Vietnam. . . . We say we cannot go along with this, and we must appeal to you to feel the same way: to say no to this government, and to destroy your draft card when we're going to do it on April 15." Burak added to his case, saying, "If we can't have the freedom of advocacy in the universities of America, then where can we have it? I'll answer that. No place! We're going to have something else. We're going to have what may be fascism. . . . This is what we see now." [55]

SCARB chairman Art Kaminsky represented what could be called the morality of rules that led to institutional responsibilities.

Cornell, no matter what you may think of it, is a society, a bit of society unto itself. It lives by rules and it dies by rules being broken. . . . As you have a responsibility to yourselves, to your consciences, to fight with all you have against this evil war, as an individual, I tend to think that I've done my part to fight this war. But . . . the members of SCARB have a moral responsibility to their position . . . and this meant to follow the rules as prescribed. . . . If you live in a society, and you do, you do not break the rules and then change them; you change them first.

Burak and Dancis embodied a view that was becoming prominent in movement thinking across the country: the moral enormity of the war was more important than the morality of the law to which Kaminsky felt obligated; in other words, the ends are more important than the means. In the university context, this logic pointed ineluctably to another conclusion: the principles of the university, such as academic freedom and rules of conduct, should not stand in the way of the imperatives of moral action. [56]

Over the next week, confrontations occurred at noon daily between activists and campus authorities at the Straight, capturing the attention of the university community. The proctor started dropping cases at the doorstep of the judicial boards, and tensions heightened. The suspensions continued, impelling several students and faculty to resign from the judicial boards. The politicization of the campus had permeated the judicial process, pitting coalitions and faculty against each other and helping to prod the overhaul of the judicial system.

The Hershey Directive: Intellectual Freedom and the Open University Defended

On October 26, 1967, prowar forces in the Johnson administration decided to retaliate against the antiwar movement and the people responsible for the successful march on Washington that had just taken place. In the most notorious action, General Lewis B. Hershey, director of the Selective Service System, announced that local draft boards could cancel the draft deferments of students who were alleged to have interfered with the draft or military recruitment. Hershey had already earned a reputation for vindictive actions against college students. In 1966 he had concocted a policy under which local draft boards could induct students who ranked in the lower levels of their classes, as determined by grades or a special exam the Selective Service planned to conduct in May. As Tom Wells observed in *The War Within: America's Battle over Vietnam,* "Suddenly students were being told that they could be carted off to die in the jungles of Vietnam. The shock on campuses was palpable." [57] In reaction the national SDS created a "counterexam," which it offered at nine hundred sites; Dancis organized the exam at Cornell. [58] Eventually the government dropped the Hershey plan in the face of widespread opposition.

Hershey's 1967 directive contained some vague guidelines to use in quashing deferments; simply demonstrating against the war could suffice, so students could lose their coveted deferments merely for exercising a basic constitutional right. Because SDS and the Resistance had organized a number of antiwar rallies and confrontations with military recruiters at Cornell, the directive could affect many students. Also, the order conflicted with the principles of campus authority as articulated in the Sindler Commission report on the campus judiciary, which the faculty was now considering. Ultimately courts repudiated this dirty business, but only after the policy had caught thousands of students in its web.

Cornell had an answer to the directive, which key faculty and the Perkins administration considered an attack on the principles of the open university. On November 16 Perkins publicly condemned the directive and called for a reconsideration of the policy "in view of the overwhelming necessity to maintain the integrity of the university campus." [59] A few weeks later, on December 5, the fifteen-member Faculty Council issued a statement strongly supporting Perkins. The statement was the product of several meetings in which the council struggled to strike the right balance between order and the rights of principals on all sides of issues:

> The Faculty Council believes that on-campus exercise of fundamental rights, such as those of freedom of speech and assembly, should not be infringed, directly or indirectly, whether by official University actions, by activities of adherents of opposing viewpoints, or by agencies outside the University. Maintenance of these rights is fundamental to society and, especially on the campus, to the educational function of the University.

In this spirit the Faculty Council reaffirms its support of the principle of the "open campus" at Cornell University. This means that this campus must remain open for the free expression of ideas, without interference from either outside or inside the university community. [60]

For some observers the stance against Hershey represented liberalism's finest hour at Cornell. Others feared that it constituted an illegitimate politicization of university leadership; it is inappropriate for the university as an entity to take sides in such a debate.[61] And would Cornell take a stand in favor of the principles of an open university when the threat came from within, not without? As Berns said about the lack of a similar response in 1969, "If the threat had come from the McCarthyite outside, they would have rallied to a man!"[62]

Despite the institutional response to Hershey, two Cornell students were shocked to find themselves reclassified from 2S (student deferment) to 1A (highest level of draft eligibility) because of the actions of the assistant registrar, C. Edward Maynard. The Poughkeepsie, New York, draft board reclassified Daniel J. Greene ('67) 1A in September 1967 after Maynard notified them that Greene had made insufficient progress toward his degree. And in February 1968 Maynard asked a draft board to reclassify Michael N. Singer ('68) after Singer burned his draft card. News of Maynard's actions took Cornell by storm, and Maynard was rebuked by the administration, which announced a freeze on university correspondence with the Selective Service until the registrar's policy was rectified. (The registrar's office continued to serve as a link between students and draft boards at students' requests but ceased to act in Maynard's fashion.)[63] Undeterred, draft boards, however, did start reclassifying Cornellians who destroyed their draft cards in a public manner. On November 20, 1967, the *Sun* reported that English Professor James H. Matlack and Nathaniel W. Pierce ('66) had been reclassified for this reason.[64]

The Sindler Commission

The rise of student power and protest at Cornell caused a crisis for campus adjudication of student misconduct, the *Trojan Horse* incident showed the danger of allowing external officials to deal with protests, and antiwar and anti-ROTC cases had prompted splits and resignations on the judicial boards. Consequently, on May 10, 1967, the Faculty Council and the Faculty Committee on Student Affairs created a commission to review university policy on student misconduct in the wake of campus disruptions. The panel was known as the Sindler Commission, after its chairman, Government Professor Allan Sindler, the epitome of the polis citizen.

The recipient of a Ph.D. in political science from Yale, Sindler had come to Cornell a few years earlier from Duke, where he had been an active participant in the civil rights movement (and the target of criticism from colleagues for his stance). A serious, deliberate man, Sindler was widely respected for his judiciousness, conscientiousness, and integrity. Though small in physical stature, his intellectual presence cut an imposing figure. He had several important responsibilities at Cornell during the time of our story, including the chairmanship of the Government Department and membership on the Educational Policy Committee and the revamped Faculty Committee on Student Affairs. During the racial crisis of December 1968 (to be described shortly) he was one of Perkins's most incisive advisers. Like Perkins, he was a New Deal progressive liberal who believed in social justice. But he differed from Perkins and many other liberals at Cornell in several respects: he was committed to the proposition that social justice must be anchored in such liberal norms as individual freedom, responsibility, and accountability; he believed strongly in the principles of liberal education and the university as an autonomous institution with its own distinct *raison d'être;* and he was willing (some would say driven) to fight for these principles regardless of the strength of the opposition. Sindler and many of his colleagues in the Government Department believed strongly in equality and equally strongly in the principle of color-blindness, that race should bestow no special privileges on anyone.[65] Sindler was especially proud of the pioneering changes his commission crafted for the judicial system. "Allan Sindler had devoted his heart, mind, and soul to the Sindler Commission," said his department colleague Andrew Hacker. "He put a lot of time into it as a scientist, as a person. [It showed] his loyalty to Cornell, which had grown very quickly and very firm." John Marcham described Sindler as "a tremendous community person" with "a huge heart."[66]

Sindler's commission, consisting of thirteen distinguished faculty, administrators, and students (including Burak), met twenty-five times and took testimony from faculty, law enforcement officials, students, administrators, and local lawyers. Befitting its chairman, it produced a meticulous report of eighteen thousand words released to the Cornell community on September 27, 1967. It said the university's primary objective should not be law enforcement, which was the proper concern of public authority. Rather, the university should "protect the opportunity of all members of the Cornell community to pursue their educational goals effectively."[67]

Further, the report ushered in the end of *in loco parentis* by redefining the balance and meaning of freedom and responsibility. If students wanted more freedom, they had to accept more responsibility, and the "working relationship" Cornell had developed with the Ithaca police no longer made sense. Under this approach, the proctor would intervene when a student had violated the law and direct the prosecution of the case. Modeled on the typical legal procedures for adjudicating juvenile criminal cases, this arrangement entailed handling the case with special procedures and wiping out any permanent police record to protect the student's reputation. "Although well-intentioned and humane in purpose, this practice retards the development of responsibility and maturity among students," the report said. Trying to insulate the offender from the "ordinary consequences" of a willful act undermines the concept of student freedom and promotes disrespect for the law, however unwittingly. "Students must recognize that they are members of the larger Ithaca community and that they are obliged to behave in accord with the law without special immunity because of their status as temporary residents."[68] Thus the report made a distinction between violations of university regulations and violations of local, state, and federal criminal law: the university would handle university code violations, and public authorities would handle law violations. As for cases involving violations of both jurisdictions, the commission concluded that public authorities should handle only serious offenses and Cornell should deal with less serious offenses, such as those involving marijuana use. But it insisted that an exception be made for misconduct that demonstrated flagrant disrespect for the rights of others or that constituted a serious threat to others in the university community, an exception that would prove important when the road to the crisis opened late in 1968.

The commission also addressed shortcomings with the adjudicatory system, in which the FCSC had complete review power over all UJB decisions. Though it typically upheld the UJB, the FCSC sometimes overturned rulings in cases involving controversial rules such as parietal rules and sexual behavior (and as we have seen, conflicts had broken out over the treatment of antiwar protests). Given the rise of student power considerations, the report averred: "Students evidence a declining confidence in the representativeness and the fairness of the system. Specifically, they feel that the student role in the University justice has been reduced to offering advice or recommendations, only especially with respect to those matters provoking divergent generational views on the part of students and faculty. In a phrase, they feel that the system gives students the form but not the substance of authority, and hence mocks the goals of responsible student freedom and respected University justice." [69] Moreover, the present system had been too disorganized, building little or no institutional memory for case law and providing almost no guidance for advance thinking on how to deal with sticky problems. Hence the system "reflects badly on the capacity for the rationality claimed for an educational community. And it is a damaging strategy as well, since it accentuates the willingness of students to escalate conflicts and confrontations to crisis proportions in the sure knowledge that crisis, at least, demands and gets fast attention." [70]

The commission urged that a student conduct board decide all complaints of student code violations and that an appeals board made up entirely of faculty be given power to review only cases in which a defendant appealed or in which a penalty of suspension or expulsion had been ordered. The appeals board could not increase penalties, as similar bodies had done earlier. Under "extraordinary circumstances" the Faculty Council or the entire faculty could review decisions of either board. Finally, the commission favored establishment of a "university student conference" of faculty, students, and administrative staff members that would serve as a policy forum on conduct codes and issues.

To illustrate its points, the report dealt with three highly relevant issues: political advocacy, dissent, and civil disobedience, especially in the form of draft card destruction, marijuana use, and freedom of artistic expression. Normally public authorities would handle the first set of cases if laws were broken; the university should not adjudicate typical cases, for such demonstrations do not disrupt educational objectives. Nevertheless, the commission recommended rules against excesses of dissent that violated the rights and freedoms of other members of the Cornell community. On marijuana use the report cited medical authority in concluding that it was detrimental to social and educational processes and said most marijuana and drug offenses should be treated as offenses against the university, not public law. (This position was already anachronistic, as marijuana and other drug use was widespread on campus.) Regarding artistic freedom the commission essentially endorsed a committee report in the aftermath of the *Trojan Horse* incident, which called for an end to SCARB's powers to censor what the panel deemed obscene, although it did not suppress the magazine. Yet it also urged greater student responsibility in exercising this freedom, saying somewhat naively that "more could and should be done to upgrade the quality and taste of student publications." [71]

On the whole, responses to the report were full of praise. It became instant news in the world of higher education; several universities contacted Sindler or the university for copies and advice on their own reforms. A writer in the *Cornell Alumni News* said it was to the commission's credit that it was impossible to label its conclusions either liberal or conservative, as they rejected the polar opposite views of *in loco parentis* and the perspective of the university as a "service facility" that dispenses knowledge without regard to students' maturity.[72] Douglas Dowd, who would later ridicule the new judicial system as unfair to students in political and racial cases, told the Faculty Senate in November 1967 that "students with whom he had talked appeared generally to favor the report, save for the provisions relating to marijuana."[73] David Burak, who also later rallied the campus against the judicial system, told me, "I was on the Sindler Commission, and I knew that the effort to make an unbiased and fair judicial system was substantive. . . . I thought it was a good system."[74]

But others expressed concern about the report, foreshadowing problems that would haunt Cornell during the Straight crisis. Cornell counsel Neal Stamp was exasperated because of what he termed the lack of concrete guidelines. "This is one of the things that really disgusted me about the Sindler Commission," he said. "There were all these philosophic statements, but it didn't come down to something specific that would give us a road map."[75] John Marcham wrote in the *Alumni News* that although the report offered an improvement over the status quo, it left unresolved the question of who's in charge.[76] Isadore Blumen, professor of Industrial and Labor Relations, claimed that the commission somewhat naively ignored the threats to campus integrity that could arise from sources (such as students) *within* the university—something Sindler would learn to his dismay the next year.[77]

The report sparked intense debate for several months across the campus and at meetings of the faculty and the Faculty Council. Eventually, however, the council recommended passage on February 6, 1968, the full faculty adopted the proposals with amendments eight days later, and the faculty approved a modified adjudication system on May 1.[78] The final legislation ordered student representatives to draw up a code in accordance with the February 14 faculty action, with the university Faculty Committee on Student Affairs overseeing the project to ensure compliance. It made the dean of students the code administrative office through which complaints would pass, a screening device that supplanted the proctor. The Student-Faculty Board of Student Conduct (four faculty and five students) was created to hear cases referred by the code administrator; the Student-Faculty Appellate Board (five faculty and four students) was charged with reviewing all decisions of expulsion, though it could not increase a penalty.

The legislation departed from the commission recommendations in eliminating the review power of the Faculty Council in "extraordinary" cases and in combining faculty and student representation on each board. Critics such as the *Sun* had expressed concern that the Faculty Council could lead to a backdoor negation of student influence over adjudication, and others worried about undue faculty-student conflict over appeals.[79] But the enabling legislation provided an important escape clause: "The faculty retains the right to intervene to overrule actions of the Adjudicatory Board on its own motion." This provision gave the faculty as a whole—not the Faculty Council, which sometimes was as much a tool of the administration as of the faculty—the power to intervene in extraordinary cases. It would subject the faculty to enormous pressures in the crisis of '69.

Ironically, the commission's work would redound against the panel when the new system confronted what had to be unexpected pressure as soon as it began. It was like a young bird being asked to go to war against a battalion of eagles. The trustee who conducted extensive hearings after the 1969 crisis, William Robertson, told me that a general uncertainty about lines of authority characterized the year leading to the crisis.[80] This state of affairs, combined with the explosive political environment and the inability or unwillingness of the administration to apply the rules, led to a breakdown of governance.

In the end the Sindler Commission's report represented the essence of liberal justice: individual freedom conjoined with personal responsibility. As we will see, Sindler was very involved in other educational issues at Cornell, so the report and its primary author embodied the links between liberal principles of justice and liberal education. When these principles came under attack, Sindler and the members of the judicial boards (faculty and students) defended these principles with heart, but they were left out on a limb by students, the faculty, and the administration.

A few months after the faculty adopted its version of the Sindler Commission report, an event shook Cornell: the AAS took over the Economics Department to protest allegedly racist comments by a visiting professor, Father Michael McPhelin. Nothing like this had ever happened at the university; earlier demonstrations had challenged laws, university rules, and free speech in the public forum without threatening academic freedom in the classroom. The takeover occurred the very day that Martin Luther King was assassinated. In the wake of these two stunning developments, Cornell turned down the path to the Straight.

CHAPTER THREE

THE RISE OF

RACIAL POLITICS

T he rise of racial politics at Cornell paved the road to the Straight. The key elements were the COSEP program and the Afro-American Society (AAS). But
the origins go back to a scene that took place at Cornell in spring 1962, more
than a year before James Perkins became president. Malcolm X, the outspoken Black
Muslim and black nationalist, and James Farmer, the head of the Congress for Racial Equality (CORE), engaged in a debate titled "Separation versus Integration."
Farmer, an African American, made the classic case for integration based on the
tenets of the burgeoning civil rights movement, which entailed an appeal to white
consciences. "We are Americans," he said. "This is our country as much as it is
white America." Then Malcolm spoke, "steely and intense," in the words of Tamar
Jacoby. He denounced integration in favor of "complete separation" and accused
men like Farmer of being "Uncle Toms" and "not black enough." According to Jacoby, the largely white audience left the debate very troubled by the message "that
blacks didn't like or trust whites, that the ghetto wasn't interested in their help, that
there was nothing they could do to make up for the past—no way, as King was suggesting, 'to redeem the soul of America.'"[1] Though Malcolm's message was strange
for the Cornell of that time, it was about to grow in influence as new students arrived on campus.

COSEP

In 1963 Perkins appointed the Committee on Disadvantaged Students, under the
chairmanship of Vice President for Student Affairs John Summerskill. Perkins
charged the committee to "recommend and initiate programs through which Cornell could make a larger contribution to the education of qualified students who have

been disadvantaged by their cultural, economic and educational environments."[2] The committee eventually changed its name to the Committee on Special Education Projects (COSEP) because the students objected to being characterized as "disadvantaged," an issue that always haunted the program. The burgeoning black consciousness and Black Power movements had begun to take issue with integrationists' practice, in their efforts to win support for civil rights and social programs, of depicting blacks as having been "damaged" by racism. According to Daryl Michael Scott in a book that traces the links between social policy and claims about the "damaged black psyche," the rejection of "damage imagery" was now imperative. "By the late 1960s, reshaping the image of African Americans became an important movement within many of the social sciences, attracting leading talents. . . . From the perspective of the present, the dismantlement of damage imagery seems a preordained event, a logical outgrowth of the Black Power and New Left movements. . . . Just as grassroots activists challenged liberal politicians, radical intellectuals challenged liberals in intellectual and policy-making communities."[3]

The committee reflected the progressive view of the university that Perkins brought to Cornell. In a 1994 interview, he stated:

There was only a handful [of Afro-Americans] in each class, and I was told that that's the way in which the Administration and even the Board, perhaps, wanted it.

I felt that that was a situation in which a modern university could not stay. . . .

So in talking to my colleagues and others, and fortunately some of them were enthusiastic members of the campus, we set up an organization called COSEP. . . . It would try and recruit black students, where the principals and teachers in their schools would write a letter saying, "We believe that if John or Jane So-and-So is admitted to Cornell, they have enough academic promise that they will be up to the average of those who enter and graduate."[4]

The first committee, which consisted of Summerskill and such key progressive professors as Douglas Dowd, Chandler Morse, Benjamin Nichols, and Walter Slatoff (each of whom would play significant roles in the events that led to the crisis), had to decide what the committee's mandate meant. According to Gloria Joseph, COSEP's most important administrator, "There was a group of faculty we called 'The Tired Seven' because every time there was a problem or a situation involving a black student, these seven faculty members were right there on our side doing their thing, trying to place the so-called problem situation in perspective."[5]

At the beginning no one considered black studies to be part of the committee's mandate. COSEP was originally a recruitment and fund-directing program, not an academic program, but it was a visionary effort for its time. Anyone considered "disadvantaged" could apply (including whites; a racially restrictive program could have violated federal and constitutional law), yet in practice blacks were the primary beneficiaries. Still, at this point the committee had little guidance from the administration, and Perkins rarely attended its meetings. Committee members, many of whom were active in the civil rights movement, wanted something more radical that would have a more immediate impact than established programs to assist disadvantaged students. So, according to Slatoff, "rather than develop any programs or junior high school activities or summer programs, we decided to see what we could do about recruiting a certain number of students to come to Cornell from ghetto high schools where there hadn't been much feeling that students could go to college. We thought we wanted to confine it to a relatively few schools at first so that there would be the feeling that good students could get into a place like this and could be financed."[6]

Three issues arose right from the start. First, funding was always a struggle. The administration was reluctant to commit too much money, especially because the program was never formally approved. "We didn't feel . . . at the beginning that we got whole-hearted support for this program" from President Perkins and the administration, Slatoff admitted.[7] Critics alleged that Perkins used the program primarily to enhance his liberal credentials—some called it "window dressing"—and to serve as a stepping stone to a national position.[8] Yet Perkins was also criticized for pushing too fast in this area; and like all university presidents, he had limited resources with which to work.

Second, the committee's relationship to the faculty and normal university procedures was tenuous. Given that the program would soon reach out to students whose credentials were often considerably lower than the Cornell norm, and given the unusual nature of the admissions process under consideration, the program was bound to raise questions. Slatoff's portrayal of the committee's decision to avoid clearance by the faculty opened the blinds on this matter:

> I suppose another thing which cast a lot of light on our attitudes later on [was] the question we always had—should we bring this before the faculty? Could we get total faculty approval for the program—say at a University faculty meeting or at an Arts College faculty meeting? And our best guess always was that the faculty would find ways of dragging its feet, raising enough questions that essentially the program would not grow under these conditions; that all kinds of questions about standards, about fairness would be raised—why should black students with lower scores receive scholarship aid when white students with equivalent scores weren't receiving scholarship aid, and so forth. The general questioning would be such that essentially we would get no program at all.[9]

William Robertson, a leading member of the Board of Trustees who headed the special committee that investigated the causes of the Straight crisis in 1969, stressed how lack of faculty input created problems for COSEP down the line:

> COSEP was just getting started when I went on the board, and I'd heard some grumblings from some alumni, and . . . remarks from some faculty members that I knew, that they didn't like what was going on. Jim Perkins was a great guy, but he was a Quaker, and he was a pacifist, and he would do anything to avoid confrontation. And he was a little scared to announce all this to his faculty. So he just sort of went around them. We mentioned [this problem] in our report. Mentioned in

there, [Perkins] sort of brought it in the back door. He didn't talk a great deal about this [COSEP] with the board. . . . I think [the COSEP program] was mostly done by the administration, and those few people in the administration he had working with him to put [the program] over.[10]

Thus the committee and the administration made the fateful decision to proceed without the usual faculty clearance. This pattern would be repeated when the administration and the AAS struggled to put together a black studies program from 1967 to 1969. The relatively marginal and disconnected status of these programs exacerbated the tensions and fears on all sides as Cornell moved toward the crisis of 1969, for lack of common ground and familiarity made it easier for fears to prevail over common sense and objectivity.

Faculty members on the other side of the fence sensed that they were being bypassed. Economist George Hildebrand observed that the COSEP program shot itself in the foot by not reaching out. "There were on this campus experts in intergroup relations, and I refer to Professor Robin Williams as one example, who could have helped the faculty to devise means of anticipating problems, discovering opportunities, uncovering ways and means for making this program work. This was simply not done. . . . The emphasis or bias if you wish of the COSEP recruitment program was in favor of activists, militants. . . . Middle-class Negro students were not welcome at Cornell."[11]

Third, the committee was torn over two conflicting goals. On the one hand, the panel wanted the program to reach out to minority (mainly black) students whose credentials had prepared them for Cornell. On the other hand, the committee wanted to go further by bringing in students who were less qualified in the traditional sense. Along these lines, the committee recommended that Cornell establish a scholarship fund for "students whose credentials will appear marginal or worse by the usual Cornell admissions standards but who otherwise give evidence of being able to compete at Cornell."[12] This fund did not receive money until the Rockefeller Foundation provided a grant in 1965, after which the COSEP program began to flourish.

COSEP did not have the authority to handle admissions itself, but it played a major role in the advocacy and recruitment of minority students. Some sources claimed that students themselves came to play influential roles in this process as part of the politicization of admissions; others downplayed this connection.

Before 1964 each freshman class of twenty-three hundred students had only four black students. Under COSEP, eight black students entered in 1964, thirty-seven in 1965, forty-nine in 1966, sixty-seven in 1967, and ninety-four in 1968; as many as 170 were expected in fall 1969, yet the number was lower because several such students were scared away by the events that spring. Most of this increase came from the ghettos of northern cities or from the South. When promising students had low standard credentials, the committee gave such attributes as motivation and leadership skills more weight than the SAT scores, grades, and extracurricular activities that counted for whites. The committee then submitted its list to the relevant colleges, whose admissions committees would make the final decision. Until 1969 the admissions committees judged COSEP students in a pool against one another, not the general pool of student applicants. Under this approach virtually all blacks with good SAT scores within each category were admitted. But this approach also meant that students competed only with other students in their own group; accordingly, many students from group 1 or group 2 with superior credentials were not admitted while those with inferior credentials in group 3 were admitted.[13]

In 1969 the procedure changed, with applicants divided into three categories. The idea was to make the top-notch black applicants compete as a separate group with the whites, but internal pressures from concerned faculty resulted in the new process following the same path as its predecessor.

In addition to being underfunded until outside grants came to the rescue, the committee was also understaffed and unprepared to deal with the academic and social problems that many of the new admittees would encounter. As Charles McCord, an original member of the committee, observed, "Looking back, we were definitely ill-prepared."[14] It was more or less assumed that the COSEP admittees would use the academic counseling and tutoring services provided for the other students. Like many white students, the new black students did not take advantage of these services. Furthermore, many black students considered the white staffers patronizing, so they stayed away until a black woman of exceptional ability was brought on board.

Gloria Joseph, a black graduate student in educational psychology and an activist and writer, began working for COSEP in 1964, providing academic counseling as an assistant dean of students. For many black students, Joseph *was* the COSEP program. One AAS leader told me she was instrumental in his success at Cornell. "Gloria Joseph was our savior . . . the glue that held us together. Gloria was the person we turned to for support, a shoulder to cry on. Gloria was our adviser, our counselor, our mentor, our everything. She was our home away from home, our support system."[15] Andre McLaughlin remarked that "she was just a resourceful person, she was the person who gave us the moral support to continue, to do well in school and to attend to the first business, which was school. She was a no-nonsense person and always available to help people. And I think her support of the students meant more to us than [the efforts of] anybody else on that campus."[16]

Before long Joseph and others came to realize that social adjustment and politics went hand in hand under the circumstances. Joseph portrayed her role in an interview decades later:

> For one thing, every single student who came on that campus I had into my office, sat down, and gave them a good old-fashioned talking to. I would be there to help them and help them with their program. . . . [It was important for them to know] that there was someone or two or three persons who were sincerely interested in their welfare, someone who knows the adjustments they have to make.
>
> Another problem was following through with their academics because racism abounds. They'd be in the classroom and they would state a fact that would be just well known to and accepted by blacks, and white faculty would say, "Is that fact or fiction?" [It was a] clash of cultures.[17]

Joseph took on a Herculean task, and as word of her efforts spread around the national community of higher education, she found herself in demand as a consultant and conference participant. At Cornell she worked closely with COSEP and the various colleges in admissions, recruitment, and academic counseling. Most of the COSEP students in the earlier years were admitted to the Arts College, so Joseph developed a working relationship with Arts Dean F. Dana Payne and his assistant, Barbara Hirshfeld. Together they crafted a program for every COSEP student. Payne gave Joseph the power to sign course cards in the college's name, so that students did not have to shuffle back and forth between offices, and to offer academic counseling. By becoming exceptionally knowledgeable about such things as black students' backgrounds, objectives, and needs, Joseph strove to fit their programs with the requirements of the university.

These efforts improved the quality of COSEP's work, but the Admissions Committee of the College of Arts and Sciences still cited problems in late 1967. Its "Report on Arts College Admissions, 1967" foreshadowed the concerns that the Robertson report identified, pointing out that "most members of the admissions committees endorse and support the COSEP Program at Cornell but have certain reservations about the existing operation of it, notably the lack of definition about its function within the larger context of the Arts College admissions. Obviously, the program is costly and the expense necessitates some quotas, however flexible. . . . We are too often shooting in the dark and operating on a risky chance basis when making our decisions."[18]

Eventually Joseph managed to put together a small staff (Faye Edwards and Charisse Cannady, who had been in the first COSEP class). Problems still arose despite their earnest efforts. And as the campus moved toward the crisis year of 1968– 69, Joseph would find herself torn, like many other professors and staff, between obligations to the university; responsibilities to all minority students, not just the militants; and obligations to AAS objectives. After the Straight crisis, Joseph's relationship with Payne and Hirshfeld deteriorated dramatically.

Joseph's counseling also involved instilling black pride. She joined the Black Power and black consciousness movements, which were starting to roll. (In April 1968 she would beseech the Williams Committee looking into the McPhelin affair to declare an economics professor guilty of institutional racism.) A fact sheet on COSEP published in 1969 (no author is cited, but Joseph must have been involved) described the counseling program:

The Negro student at Cornell today, like his fellow black students at other predominantly white universities throughout the country, is part of a minority group on campus that is not only growing larger but increasingly concerned with establishing a sense of identity and racial pride. Furthermore, in the changing national climate any group of Negro students is inevitably bound to the black movement.

Under these circumstances, one can hardly expect a black student to deny his blackness or to slip into the role of what the blacks refer to as an "Uncle Tom" in his relations with the rest of the university community. The subtleties of racism, so long smoothed over by the tacit etiquette of academia, are now out in the open, and the burden of keeping them there is one of the insistent pressures felt by nearly every Negro on a white campus.[19]

This report also presented data on COSEP's selection process. In 1965 – 66 the thirty-seven COSEP students had median SAT scores of 570 verbal and 600 math (the range was 430 – 670 and 380 – 730, respectively), compared to median scores of 622 and 671 for all Cornell freshmen and 660 and 685 for freshmen in Arts and Sciences. In 1966 – 67 COSEP median scores for verbal and math were 540 and 570 (ranging 340 – 740 and 410 – 760), compared to 631 and 682 for all Cornell freshmen and 683 and 700 in Arts and Sciences. (Note that the COSEP scores were going down while those for others were going up.) This trend continued in 1967 – 68 and reversed the following year. In 1967 – 68 COSEP medians were 530 and 540 (ranging 400 – 710 and 420 – 700), compared to 634 and 683 for all Cornell freshmen and 703 and 716 for Arts and Sciences freshmen. In 1968 – 69 COSEP medians were 548 and 559 (ranging 383 – 740 and 347 – 790), compared to 637 and 684 for all Cornell freshmen and 690 and 705 for Arts and Sciences freshmen. The report downplayed the upward COSEP trend of 1968 – 69, claiming that it does not represent a change in philosophy and that SAT scores are poor indicators of future performance.

Finally, the report discussed the academic achievement of COSEP students. It pointed out that very few COSEP students had dropped out and that overall performance was "very satisfactory." Only three of thirty-seven who entered in 1965, two out of forty-nine who began in 1966, and one out of sixty-seven who arrived in 1967 flunked out, and not many more had withdrawn for other reasons. As of 1969, thirty-three remained who entered in 1965, forty-three from 1966, and sixty-five from 1967. The report concluded that the intellectual hurdle was less of a problem than the "social sacrifice" that students must make.

The Robertson report was less positive: "we have been told by some [professors] that the optimistic academic reports given on the program so far are suspect for two reasons," it stated. Some professors, "for whatever reasons, have tended to mark black students easier than whites; and some blacks were allowed to stay in school longer than whites with similar records would be."[20]

On the other side of this debate, some black students claimed that they were graded more harshly than whites, particularly in classes involving urban issues, in which their experiences differed from the presumptions of the professor or the texts. Several students told me they disagreed on empirical or normative grounds with courses that accentuated their backgrounds as "disadvantaged." AAS Treasurer Stephen Goodwin recalled performing badly on a midterm exam in a course on urban poverty. When the professor expressed surprise, Goodwin replied, "You're not going to understand this, but I didn't know until I met you that I had all these problems!"[21]

James Turner, whom the administration recruited avidly in 1969 to chair the new black studies program, stressed the importance of challenging damage imagery:

We were concerned [that] all the social sciences had a "problem-focused, deficit-focused" perspective on blacks. So we are all talking about exclusion and how it is affecting the paradigm of education in America, [that] there was exclusion in the curriculum, that what [students] were getting in these economics classes and political science classes was not an accurate representation of the life of black people, that most sociology courses were based on the notion of black people being unable to defer gratification. We said, "What is that? That's not true!" We live in families where our parents stretch two cans of pork and beans. . . . My father is an ununionized, working-class guy trying to send me money at school, and we didn't have any automobile. . . . The sociologists saw our religion as emotive, with no culture or theology. We said, "What?"[22]

Since more blacks were gaining racial consciousness and enrolling in courses dealing with urban and racial issues, these concerns spawned a desire for classes taught from their own perspective. The stage was being set for developing a black studies program.

Despite these problems, many COSEP students excelled at Cornell and went on to have meaningful careers. Edward Whitfield, the president of the AAS during the April crisis period, had graduated fifth in his large class at the famous Little Rock Central High School in Arkansas and was enrolled in Cornell's special six-year Ph.D. program. Like many AAS leaders, Whitfield felt a deep sense of responsibility in being at Cornell. He told the *Cornell Chronicle* in its 1989 commemoration of the Straight seizure that black students were at Cornell because their great-grandparents had been slaves, so "being at Cornell was not only a great privilege, but also a great responsibility. Could we use the opportunities, experiences and knowledge that could be gained to serve the needs of our communities and correct some of the existing social injustices that were the result of that slavery?"[23] Whitfield is now a community organizer in North Carolina.

Several other AAS members have gone on to achieve success in their endeavors, some of which deal with racial issues. Tom Jones is now a major figure on Wall Street and a member of the Cornell Board of Trustees. Irving McPhail is the president of a community college in St. Louis that serves the black community. Andre McLaughlin is a professor at Medgar Evers College in a predominantly black neighborhood of Brooklyn. Irene Smalls is a nationally known writer of children's stories featuring African Americans. AAS Secretary Zachary Carter (who, like Jones, declined to be interviewed for this book) is the U.S. attorney for the eastern district of New York.[24] Stephen Goodwin has made a career on Wall Street and runs a small investment firm. Robert Jackson, a former AAS president and executive committee member, is an administrator and a professor of food and nutritional science at the University of Maryland. Paul DuBois, an early AAS member, is a nationally connected community organizer who runs a media company with his wife, Frances Moore Lappé, the author of *Diet for a Small Planet*. John Garner, the most influential AAS leader in its militant phase, had close to a 4.0 grade average in engineering and was a brilliant synthesizer of theory and practice for the AAS. Garner, who came to envision the Cornell movement as a step in a revolutionary process, left Cornell just before the Straight takeover and went to work in the black community back home in Dayton. He ended up in medical school but died of a kidney disease during his internship. Denise Raynor became a medical doctor, and Reuben Munday is a leading attorney in Detroit.

Many AAS activists appreciated the educational opportunities that Cornell offered, sometimes at the same time that they felt compelled to destroy the institution as a prominent representative of the racist order. One AAS officer who helped the group purchase guns in the months leading up to the Straight incident told me that Cornell was like a candy store that offered opportunity and creativity everywhere you looked. Another AAS leader said that he and many other members of the group spent much of their time inside the Straight during the takeover studying for upcoming exams. The AAS also invited speakers of a variety of views to its meetings, at least before the overt militarization in 1968. For example, Tom Jones invited Walter Berns to speak. Berns recalled talking about opportunities for minorities in the military and the war—"not saying what they wanted me to say."[25] The AAS provided an education within the education at Cornell, as it were. As always, the picture beneath the surface is complex.

Racial Tensions

But the successes of the COSEP program were matched by problems to which I have alluded, involving overt racism, institutional racism, and cultural confrontations. Many of the problems were due simply to a lack of mutual understanding. Furthermore, a generational clash within the black student community appears to have affected how students responded to these problems. Those oriented more toward integration hid their wounds or felt less alienated in the first place. Yet it is also true that in some respects integrationists had more reason to be disappointed. After 1965 or 1966, COSEP students were much more inclined toward separatism, so they were less tolerant of the racism that permeated the institution.

Though many of the COSEP students came to Cornell with a sense of self and accomplishment, it was hard for them to avoid cultural clashes. Blacks experienced taunts and hate speech, and some who attained a reputation for militancy received threatening phone calls and letters. Many black students felt alienated by the rural, overwhelmingly white setting of the campus. With a mixture of humor and seriousness, Irene Smalls remarked: "Well, it was rural, and they had cows. It was like a culture shock. It was different—the smells were different, it was just totally different than Harlem. I was homesick and desperate to come home, but my mother wouldn't let me come home. Cottage cheese—I had never seen people who ate cottage cheese before in my life! They were eating this weird stuff! They looked different, they acted differently, they talked differently. It wasn't so much a matter of race. I didn't think of it in terms of race because . . . I [too] was bright."[26]

Smalls's first roommate at Cornell was a white student from a rural town. "I put up a poster of Malcolm X, which she tore down off the wall. . . . She was this girl from the Midwest, farmer and stuff like that. And she had this attitude that black people weren't that important or very impressive and that she could do what she wanted." Andre McLaughlin encountered similar problems in the dorms: "I think that they wanted us to have a multicultural experience, but I don't think that they thought it out in terms of personalities and people's backgrounds. . . . It was normal conflicts, but it was also exacerbated by people's ignorance about other cultures. . . . And so people felt inclined to ask and say things that were so ignorant." [27]

Stephen Goodwin related a story that paints a revealing picture of Cornell:

In 1967 or '68, we were sitting at a table in Willard Straight Hall . . . called the Gaza Strip. . . . because the WASPs sat on [one side of the lunchroom] . . . and the Jews sat on [the other side]. The jukebox at the time only had three soul records on it. . . . There was not even a *good* soul record.

So the guy came in to change the jukebox records, and these five black guys accosted him. He said, "Look, look, look, just give me a list of what you want and I swear to you that I'll bring it back!" He obviously thought we were going to beat him up or something. You've got to remember, at this era in time, when four or five black guys stood around a white person, the white person panicked. This guy, he broke down, tears were coming down, he was crying. So we sat him down at the Gaza Strip table and we proceeded to produce a list. Next week that guy came back with every soul record we asked for.

So the significance of the story is twofold. Cornell was the kind of place that if you could articulate clearly what you wanted and the benefits were not only to you but to everybody else, they were able to give it to you. And Cornell had the kind of student body, whites as well as blacks, who had that kind of capability. Hey, the administration, the faculty—they conceded the wisdom of what you were saying. And it didn't take much to convince them. [28]

Some blacks detected a lack of respect from white students for their intelligence or achievements. When he got a good grade, Goodwin said, "People said to me that I was lucky. Well, how come I can't be smart? How come I can't know? So when I couldn't get recognition as a scholar, I decided to become a capitalist. And even as a capitalist, I couldn't get into campus 'Who's Who' because they decided I was an opportunist, not a capitalist." [29]

McLaughlin described the racism she encountered at Cornell and downtown:

[In] '66, there were people who were definitely very resistant to change. Matter of fact, there were people who made no bones that we weren't welcome, on the campus. I didn't run into too much of that at the College of Agriculture, interestingly enough, because I was going to school with a lot of farm boys. And people from the country, I think, have less sophisticated attitudes that I found to be quite the contrary when I think about the experiences of my classmates in the College of Arts and Sciences. We didn't have professors that we were running around screaming about. [30]

Then there was the fraternity and sorority system. Before the late '60s, the Greek system was the centerpiece of Cornell's social life. It was mistakenly assumed that the fraternities would be receptive to black members. Some fraternities could not recruit black members because of racist national charters, and others were reluctant. As more black students came to Cornell, especially from the inner city and the Deep South, the problem intensified. Fraternities and sororities are in the business of recruiting members who fit their image of themselves; they are not meant to be showcases of cultural pluralism. As Sociology Professor Charles ("Charlie") Ackerman often told Cornell fraternity men, one sociological function of fraternities is to provide a closed community within which students of a large, impersonal campus can withdraw. Therefore, it is not surprising that COSEP students met chilly receptions when they rushed.

It should be noted, however, that several prominent AAS members had fraternity ties. Tom Jones was a member of Zeta Beta Tau, a Jewish fraternity (he was also president of his freshman class), and Earl Armstrong, president of AAS before the radicalization of the organization in fall 1968, was the president of his fraternity. During the Straight crisis, the president of a fraternity that suffered a major fire, Chi Psi, was a black student, Otis Sprow. Goodwin also belonged to a fraternity with substantial ties to Wall Street.[31] But these black men were adept at dealing with the white world, and many AAS members came to question these individuals' racial authenticity as the AAS grew more separatist. (Some sources construed Jones's extreme militancy in 1968–69 as a reaction to this perception. Jones came from the professional middle class; his father was a physicist. More than one commentator has cited black students' guilt about being at Cornell as a factor in the politicization of the AAS.) "There was almost a guilt trip for some of the wealthier kids; they had to be more back to the roots," former SDS member Harris Raynor said.[32] Similarly, black students, including AAS leaders, had developed close ties with white professors, including the professors who were most opposed to what took place in 1969. Walter Berns was Tom Jones's adviser and intellectual confidant. And Whitfield, the president of AAS during the Straight takeover, was a student of Allan Bloom's whom Bloom was cultivating as the first "black Plato."

Yet many blacks encountered discrimination, a problem that was not limited to rushing. For example, in October 1966, when the university was seriously considering the role of the Greek system on campus and in race relations, Phi Delta Theta charged black students money to get into a dance that featured a local band. Whites were not charged. The fraternity claimed that it charged a fee to keep townspeople out of the crowded party and that only friends of fraternity brothers were admitted free of charge, but Reuben Munday, a black member of Sigma Phi, told the *Sun* that only blacks were charged and that the doorman attempted to charge him while letting his white fraternity brothers in free.

Gloria Joseph told the *Sun* that she was "deeply concerned" about the Phi Delta Theta incident and that "many Negro students have complained to her." The incident "exemplifies the contrast between overt discrimination which is condemned in the United States and what she considers a more subtle form which usually goes unpunished."[33] An investigation by the Cornell judicial board concluded that the policy, though not originally intended to be discriminatory, was used for discriminatory purposes. The board placed Phi Delta Theta on social probation for a year. Meanwhile, the AAS unsuccessfully attempted to foment a boycott of fraternity rushing. More important, the affair intensified the move toward Black Power. AAS member Cleveland Donald observed:

> After the Phi Delta Theta incident, black students continued to adopt the black power ideology. During the remainder of the academic year, blacks attended all SNCC-sponsored conferences devoted to black power, particularly those concerned with the manifestation and expression of black power at the college level. Through a joint effort of both the IFC [Interfraternity Council] and the Afro-American Society, a Soul Week was held during which many national advocates of black power appeared, including Stokely Carmichael. At this time, black men were permitted to establish a separate all-black dorm for themselves . . . Elmwood House.[34]

Interestingly, just a day before the Phi Delta Theta incident, the *Sun* published a special supplement on Black Power and black identity. In the lead article Gloria Joseph wrote about the ideas of Malcolm X and Stokely Carmichael. She opened with a rhetorical question that would frame the emerging racial debate at Cornell and other universities for years to come: "Is it possible for a white man to understand the black man in America, or is it always a case of alienated knowledge?"[35] Also, during the 1966–67 academic year numerous prominent speakers came to Cornell to advocate Black Power and related doctrines.

The growth of the AAS and the establishment of Elmwood House as a black men's dorm furnished alternatives to the Greek system. In 1964 and 1965 the faculty and student government established the Human Rights Commission to work on eliminating discrimination in the Greek system. The commission, headed by Walter Slatoff, promoted legislation requiring fraternities and sororities to attain local autonomy to circumvent national constitutions that mandated religious or racial discrimination. The faculty eventually adopted the legislation, but just as the Greek system put it into effect, "the movement toward a greater degree of separatism and an unwillingness to be the 'token black' in a fraternity or to try to keep on having to fight this battle with whites and so on began to develop [among black students]."[36]

Dorm confrontations, especially among women, were a constant problem that sparked the creation of Wari House. Black women in the dorms confronted hostility when they gave themselves Afro hairdos, as some whites objected to the Black Power image or even the smell of the procedure (in one case a black woman's white roommate called campus authorities because she suspected the smell was marijuana smoke!). The Human Rights Commission got involved after fights broke out between white and black female roommates.

The most notorious case involved Alicia Scott, who received a medical suspension from a white psychiatrist after several confrontations with white women in her corridor during 1967–68. The white women charged that she played her soul music too loud and that she grew hostile when they asked her to turn it down. According to Smalls, who rallied to her support, Scott was aggressive and did get into fights with her roommate and hallmates. But as was often the case, cultural differences lay at the heart of the problem:

> She got into a fight. . . . I knew that her mother would kill her if she came back home. I also felt that they weren't being fair. All that they did was listen to the white girl's point of view, and no one was talking to Alicia. Alicia was kind of brash and loud—she wasn't easy to talk to, I'm telling you—but I felt that there was a matter of equity here.
>
> I set up a series of meetings with this man [either Mark Barlow or the dean of students] and said that there was no way I was going to allow him to kick her out of school without due process. In [Scott's] cultural environment, what she is doing is perfectly normal. So what you are saying is that she is not conforming here, but I don't think that is a completely valid argument. Because when you recruited people, you knew where they came from. You can't tell me that if I am from France and speak French, "You can come here, but you can't speak French." That's who I am; that's all I know. You are asking me to be a fish out of water.[37]

In response to the medical leave, a handful of Scott's friends, led by Smalls (who was chairwoman of the AAS's Black Cooperative Committee) held a demonstration and made a demand for a black psychologist who understood problems peculiar to blacks. This demand would not be met until over a year later, when AAS pressure forced the administration's hand. But in reaction to the Scott conflict, the AAS asked the dean of students in February 1968 to consent to the formation of a black women's dorm on campus. At the time, only senior women were permitted to live off campus, so the group could not solve the problem logistically. Smalls also discussed the matter with Patricia Stewart, a member of the Board of Trustees who had been involved with her recruitment to Cornell. In a public statement released in the *Sun* on February 15, 1968, the AAS declared a new coop was necessary because the environment at Cornell "implies that the cultural background of these black co-eds is inferior."[38]

A subcommittee made up of COSEP staff, members of the Human Rights Commission, and the Faculty Committee on Student Affairs announced support for the residence in April 1968. Taking its name from the Swahili word for "home," Wari House accommodated thirteen of Cornell's hundred black women. Though it was officially open to all COSEP students (COSEP was by definition not exclusively for blacks), only blacks used it. The New York Civil Liberties Union threatened a lawsuit on grounds of racial discrimination but did not pursue the case. Assistant Dean of Students Ruth Darling defended the segregationist policy by citing the need for affirmative action. "There has been a great deal of discrimination against blacks in the past, and you have to do more than just say blacks and whites should have an equal chance. You have to move to positive discrimination."[39] The establishment of Wari was a response to racism in the eyes of the AAS. In the eyes of some others, however, it was another step toward separatism and conflict and another example of dishonesty about intentions: though technically open to all races, no one involved really intended a policy of racial inclusion to prevail.

The passage of time between the establishment of Elmwood House and the founding of Wari featured a major paradigm shift in race relations at Cornell. Elmwood relieved racial tensions, and authorities viewed it as a positive alternative to the fraternity system. The forces behind the establishment of Elmwood were able to draw on arguments of universal moral appeal that did not divide the university community. The moral arguments behind Wari, though, were less clear-cut. The right to play loud music in a dorm and the right to physical confrontation have less obvious moral standing than the right not to be a victim of discrimination. With Wari's founding, something troubling was in the air. "The demand for a COSEP female cooperative shattered the university's sense of gradually improving racial relations. Unlike Elmwood, Wari's establishment exacerbated racial tensions," Donald said.[40]

Scott's moral standing was ambiguous. But Cornell had its share of less ambiguous encounters that support the allegations of racism, overt or institutional. Two incidents among many are indicative. The first involves the freshman basketball team of 1967–68 (at the time freshmen could not play varsity basketball or football). Of the twenty-five or so men who tried out for the twelve-member team, three were black, two of whom had a fighting chance of making the squad. They did not make the final cut. This was not prima facie evidence of racism, for there were reasonable differences of opinion about the players' ability. The problem arose in the shower after the coach announced the cuts: a couple of white players made comments with racial undertones about the results while the black players huddled at the other side of the shower.[41]

The other incident concerned a discussion section in a class in the fall of 1968. The material for that week covered segregation and race relations, and the class was discussing an article by a columnist in which he dwelled on the fact that African tribes or villages had not developed the technological skills of the West. The columnist wondered why so many villagers lived by the sea yet had never conceived of the sail. The teaching assistant in the course marveled at this remark and repeated it in a sarcastic tone, claiming that it showed how difficult it would be for the races to live together. The lone black student in the class sat near the door, looking humiliated. He said not a word and turned his eyes to the floor; the teaching assistant had acted as though this student were not there.

It is not clear that this instructor's comments were racist or, if they were, that they should be proscribable. (Such matters are discussed in Chapter Four.) But these cases revealed something about the environment for blacks at Cornell. The fact that black students frequently encountered such insensitivity fueled their desire to establish their own studies program. Joseph recalled an incident that showed subtle racist thinking on the part of Cornell whites:

I remember once teaching a class I'll never forget. I was a student assistant, and it was the first day of class, and a student stepped into the room, and he looked at me and stood dead in his tracks. He had on this blue blazer, looked like a preppie. And he took out his course card and looked at it, and looked at the title of the course on the board, and he couldn't believe it. He was from the Deep South and he had never walked into a classroom and seen a black professor standing there. He thought he was in the wrong room. That's how drastic the situation was.[42]

AAS Coercion of Nonconforming Blacks

Another of the problems black students confronted at Cornell will be discussed more fully later but deserves mention here. As Cornell advanced toward April 1969, certain AAS members grew progressively intolerant of black students who did not conform to the "party line" and put intense pressure on reluctant blacks to show solidarity. Blacks who roomed with whites were special targets in 1968 and 1969. In one case that was not atypical, an AAS contingent came to the room of a black who roomed with a white student and browbeat him mercilessly, reducing him to tears. This student did not break under what his roommate described as crushing pressure, but he paid a dear price.[43]

A student who left the AAS informed President Perkins in early 1969 that some members of the AAS were threatening nonconforming blacks with violence and that the administration was ignoring the interests of these students in favor of the more vocal minority. On May 14, 1969, Dean of Students Elmer Meyer Jr. wrote a letter to associate deans and directors of programs "on behalf of those students, particularly many of our black students, who are feeling the strains, pressures, and anxieties of their present situation at Cornell to such an extent that to continue studying, attending class and preparing for examinations is an impossible task."[44] In the days before the Straight takeover, unidentified blacks beat two whites for no reason. These incidents triggered great debate over the AAS's responsibility. Finally, at an AAS meeting in spring 1969, an unidentified man threatened the life of Alan Keyes, a Ph.D. student in government, studying under Bloom, according to a Security Division document. The document referred to "Paul Irwin . . . he was upset that Dr. Perkins had not been able to talk to him yesterday afternoon. He said it was not only Alan Keyes who had been threatened, but others. Any black who dates a white has been told 'they will get it' . . . He added that students, black and white, are living in fear." The division took the threat seriously, and Keyes felt so threatened that he left Cornell for good.[45]

Fall 1968 was a pivotal period for the AAS, as Tom Jones and John Garner fought for the leadership. The dispute was partly over personality and partly over philosophy; Garner was more radical and serious than Jones. Around this time the two factions had what amounted to a brawl, replete with chains and knives. DuBois observed: "I spoke with several dozen black students who were similarly alienated from the Society's actions and from the autocracy that seemed to be functioning. . . . Moderate black students have in fact been beaten, have been threatened. I talked with a black student two days ago who did not want to be identified as a moderate black student, although that student next year will be [attending school elsewhere] . . . because he's afraid that more militant students will [come after him]. . . if he in any sense interrupts their plans for the fall." DuBois also pointed out that Joseph had told him that many black students were planning to leave Cornell because of the stress and that more moderate AAS members (such as graduate student Bob Jackson) had told her that undergraduates complained to him all the time about not being able to withstand the pressure.[46] The pressure intensified after the McPhelin incident and Martin Luther King's murder in April 1968. "Before that, everything was very liberal and everybody could think what they wanted to think. After that, nobody could do anything but the party line," Denise Raynor said. After this point, Raynor was ostracized because of her SDS ties and her white boyfriend.[47]

DuBois told me that several AAS members maintained secret ties with him after he left the organization. Sometimes they would sneak over to his apartment to confide their "true feelings" about racial politics at Cornell. "I also personally felt bitter some of the time about some of the attacks and so on; it was too easy to retreat. . . . I was trusted by some who would come to my place, my apartment quietly, secretly, you know, 'I don't want to be seen talking with you, but Paul, here's what I'm really thinking.' There was an awful lot of that."[48]

Pearl Lucas, an assistant dean of Arts and Sciences, opposed what she considered the corrupting influence of militant leaders, and she disagreed with Joseph's claims that most COSEP students came to Cornell already politicized. She met with many students who felt intimidated and wanted to leave Cornell. "It's often very subtle, and the bullies pick on the weakest and most immature students. And it's usually not as direct as it was in the case of Alan Keyes, where he was physically threatened."[49]

Dana Payne and Barbara Hirshfeld talked about pressure exerted on students to take "relevant" courses rather than such courses as science or world history. Payne also discussed the case of a white student (a "Jewish liberal") who had been kidnaped by a group of black students over Halloween in 1968 in front of Anabel Taylor Hall and taken out to the countryside, verbally abused about being white, and threatened with a knife. At first this student did not want to press charges, but he changed his mind. And "then he was discouraged" to do so by campus authorities. Payne could not elaborate because the student "was out all last term."[50]

Payne averred that the black student community at Cornell had as much potential for diversity as the white student community. "I'm sure that if there were a free climate here, we'd have as many different groups within the black community as we have with the white. But with the threats of all sorts of violence and . . . to a smaller degree, threats of isolation, if they're talking to the wrong white people or something, I have little optimism that . . . the black students will sort of become individuals. I'm afraid they're going to be just one solid group, and this makes me very concerned."[51]

The Afro-American Society

Black students founded the AAS in early 1966, the second full year of the COSEP program's operation. It had a rather fluid leadership style, with an executive committee and a steering committee. The group held weekly meetings (except during crises, when meetings were held as often as every night); attendance varied, depending on the issue at hand. The usual strategy of leadership was governing by consensus, so most AAS actions were based on the consent of the majority. Sometimes, however, radical splits prevailed, as in the fall of 1968, when the Jones and Garner factions were engaged in their struggle. Dale Corson told me the administration was most afraid of violence during this period because no one really controlled the AAS, and the factions strove to outdo each other in terms of revolutionary consciousness and the tactics of confrontation.

The AAS's purpose was "to initiate and support programs which were to aid in the dissemination of factual material concerning the history of black people, and to initiate and support programs which are devoted to the eradication of the social, economic, and psychological conditions which blight black people." [52] Originally the AAS included both whites and students of color, but younger members moved in a separatist direction in fall 1966, when the influx of new students with Black Power and black consciousness beliefs changed the tone of the organization. Soon whites were barred, except by special permission. Though graduate students and instructors were members, the organization was primarily an undergraduate group. According to a *New York Times* reporter, "The creation of the Afro-American Society sent shock waves through the Cornell faculty." He quoted one liberal professor: "There are many people here, white liberals and even radicals, who felt they had been fighting for integration so long, and they just couldn't turn themselves around that fast. They had been fighting fraternities for refusing to admit black students and Orientals, and now they saw themselves faced with what looked like a very familiar pattern—this time by the blacks." [53]

Cleveland Donald, a graduate student in history and an AAS member, points out that factions and generational splits marked the politics of the AAS. The key variable in this development was the rise of Black Power ideology, which gripped Cornell's blacks after the summer of 1966, when SNCC mounted the move to admit James Meredith to the University of Mississippi. Black activists were growing impatient with Martin Luther King's emphasis on integration and nonviolence. Many of them identified with Black Power and black consciousness ideologies, and running into old friends back in the inner city also made many feel guilty or uneasy about being at an elite white university. In writing about the situation at Cornell and other elite schools, Miles wrote, "The militancy of black students at these institutions was also a function of an awareness of their privelege [sic] in relation to the black masses, and a resulting collective guilt." [54] How could they stay at Cornell and yet contribute to the cause?

When the students returned to the Cornell campus, two key developments awaited them: the Phi Delta Theta incident, which crystallized their feelings about the fraternity system, and the second wave, or "generation," of COSEP students. "The second generation, which came in the fall, had not been a party to the social contract that existed between whites and the black first generation. . . . This generation stridently attacked the whites and the black first generation for the racial situation on the campus. In the process they legitimated themselves as the oracles of black power on the predominantly white college campus," Donald observed. [55]

Irving McPhail, a leader of the new wave in the AAS, depicted the conflict between generations in more confrontational terms:

Let me suggest that the African-American students who were there when we got there were of a different ilk than those who came in '66. I'm thinking of a couple of students in particular who clearly came from the black middle and upper class, whatever that is. . . . These were guys who were really not a part of the inner-city ghetto, if you will, experience that most of us who came in in '66 were a part of. So these folks had basically framed a very integrated society, the AAS. Frankly, I was shocked when I went to the first meeting to see all these white people basically making decisions and engaging in discussion about what clearly in my view, and in the views of some of my colleagues, was a black experience. So . . . we formed a totally new organization, which we dubbed the Black Liberation Front. [The vanguard was from twelve to fifteen members.] This was an African-centered organization for African-American students only, with an agenda. The previous group had no agenda. . . .

We basically transformed that organization. I would say chief among this group would be the late, great John Garner. He was the intellectual as well as the spiritual leader of our movement. Here's a guy who went to all-black schools in Dayton, Ohio. Here's a guy who came to Cornell to major in electrical engineering. Here's a guy who couldn't afford to buy a slide rule (these are precomputer days). John literally did all of the calculations in his head. John had a straight 4.0 average in electrical engineering. Not only was he blowing everybody away in the school of engineering, but John was very deeply immersed in learning his culture and in motivating those of us who were around him who were his friends (I consider myself his best friend) to delve deeply into the legacy of African-American excellence. John was a part of that consciousness-raising movement in that society. I was a part of that; people like Andre McLaughlin were a part of that. There were key people who were a part of transforming that organization and making it a prototype of the black student movement for white campuses.[56]

Over the next two years, the AAS grew and developed. It entered the fray over the fraternities, and it was behind the Scott affair and the establishment of Elmwood House and Wari House. It served both social and political purposes. McLaughlin provided a picture of the multifaceted role of the AAS over the next couple of years:

We really had stimulating conversations; sometimes we had speakers to talk on different topics. It was a combination of several things. A part of it was socializing, seeing everybody, from the different schools. Another part of it was political: we were developing in what the world was, what was our position in the universe, and we helped each other make sense. . . . We had elected offices, we had an agenda . . . and the beginning of the Black Power movement, so people were really doing, becoming aware, just becoming aware of who we were, what our history was, and for many of us, this was the first time we were being exposed to this information. . . . We organized programs, cultural and political programs, to have speakers, to have musicians. . . . We were cooperating, to create a climate that was friendly for us.[57]

James Turner, who would eventually become the director of the Afro-American studies center that emerged out of the Cornell struggle, depicted how the discovery of a distinct black identity galvanized the new generation of students and how this movement led to pressure to create a black studies program. A key issue, epitomized by the publication of Harold Cruse's *The Crisis of the Negro Intellectual* (1966), concerned the ends to which the black intellectual should devote his or her work and mind: intellectual development or political cause.

> For the black students on the college campus . . . the issues of how to resist the issue of racial exclusion in the curriculum of American higher education began to become very critical to us. Where was the linkage, the historical link to African Americans? What was our historical point of origin? What was our historical being? The Negro had no historical being in American thought—we were a southern invention. There's this intellectual tradition that is segregated from the white intellectual tradition. White scholars knew nothing of these people—Charles Wesley, Benjamin Quarles—they didn't know these people, . . . [not] even John Hope Franklin, who is now very respected. . . .
>
> Then *The Crisis of the Negro Intellectual* was published, and I don't think there is any other book that had the kind of single impact on my generation as that book did. . . . Professor Harold Cruse's book created a raging debate within our circles . . . [about] the role and the responsibility of the black educated class, of the black intellectual. And then by extension, that debate was taken up in the black arts movement. What is the role of the black writer? What is the role of the black artist? Is it art for art's sake? And these were very pregnant discussions.[58]

The question of racial consciousness in relation to white culture and learning had deep roots in the history of the black community. In 1903 for example, W.E.B. Du Bois announced his famous theory about the "double consciousness" of the black man in *Souls of Black Folk*, speaking of "his two-ness, an American, a Negro; two souls, two thoughts, two unreconciled strivings, two warring ideals in one dark body."[59] In the 1920s, DuBois and others in the "New Negro" movement called on blacks to assert themselves politically and to take pride in their "negritude." The movement took hold on many black college campuses (Hampton Institute, Shaw University, Florida A&I, Fisk University, and Howard University), where students challenged parietal policies and curricula that reflected the norms of white bourgeois culture. The movement was dedicated to carving out a realm of authentically black culture within the dominant white society, including an education system that built on the realities of black virtues and social oppression.[60]

In 1938, James Weldon Johnson, executive secretary of the National Association of Colored People in the 1920s, professed that students should learn a blend of African and black American culture to "give our youth a new and higher sense of radical self-respect, and will disprove entirely the theory of innate racial inferiority." Johnson also believed such a program should be guided by high intellectual and academic standards, including principles of academic freedom. "I do not in the least advocate that our colleges become any part of political machinery or touched by partisan politics, but I firmly believe that special political education of Negro youth is a proper and necessary function for them. The political history of the race should be reviewed; independent political thinking should be inculcated." Though faithful to liberal education, Johnson opposed assimilation to white culture, for assimilation "depresses and crushes at the same time the spark of genius in the Negro by making him feel that his race does not amount to much and never will measure up to the standards of other people." [61]

Beholden to white authority, the leaders of black colleges and universities resisted the New Negro movement, and the movement waned with the advent of World War II. Yet it returned on the heels of the war with the emergence of several black issues: blacks' expectations of equality sparked by the participation in the defeat of Hitler; continued black migration to urban areas, especially in the North; the rise of the civil rights and Third World Nationalism movements; the eventual rise of the Black Power movement. By the mid-60s, these and related forces had renewed the debate over the autonomy of African-American education, this time with a more radical edge.

The first major student revolt on a black campus arose at Howard University in spring 1967 with students protesting the Hershey directive and the white orientation of the curriculum; ultimately they demanded an autonomous black college and amnesty for a building takeover. Howard remained the scene of activism through the sixties, and eventually the students won more freedom and a black studies program. From Howard, the movement worked its way to other campuses, including Cornell. At its core, the movement rejected "the system of the black bourgeois," according to Miles.[62] In 1968–69, at least eighty-five predominantly white colleges witnessed black protest, including Cornell.[63] The most significant and sustained action took place at San Francisco State, where blacks, Chicanos, and Asian students formed the Third World Liberation Front and forced the university to shut down as they pressed for a variety of radical changes. (University president S. I. Hayakawa did not honor the agreements in the end.)[64]

Virtually all of these movements led to various forms of black studies programs rather than autonomous colleges based on the "black college" model introduced at Howard. Yet some programs were more separatist than others; at Yale, for example, concerted efforts were made to link the new program to established departments and programs, whereas at Cornell the new studies center was among the most militant in the country.[65]

Thus, the black student movement at Cornell was indebted to predecessors. In 1967 Robert Jackson led the second generation to power when he became AAS president. He helped to radicalize the AAS with a tenuous combination of Black Power ideology and Marxist theory, which he balanced with teachings based on his ties with the Government and History Departments (he was a student of Berns and Sindler). According to Donald, he accepted the conclusions of observers such as Assistant Labor Secretary Daniel Patrick Moynihan and Stanley Elkins, author of *Slavery*, who maintained that black women's control of families had a deleterious effect; consequently, Jackson and the AAS emphasized male leadership, relegating women to secondary roles, a point that remained an issue within the AAS throughout the period covered in this book.[66]

Jackson had a hard time keeping the growing factions together. But this period was a time of intellectual and political ferment within the AAS, and the groundwork was being laid for positions and actions. From the fall of 1968 through the Straight crisis, the AAS would be riven by power struggles between and within the two political factions, which crystallized into identifiable forms as 1968 wore on. The social faction drew heavily from the first generation. The politically moderate faction consisted of members old and new who were gaining black consciousness but also were wary of overly militant postures; these individuals also saw more virtue in the traditional university, though they wanted very strong reforms. And now a third faction emerged: the radicals, who wanted militant revolutionary confrontation and, at different points, wanted to destroy the university as a bastion of white oppression or to establish an independent black entity within it modeled on the theories of Black Power and black nationalism.

Donald portrayed the factions somewhat differently in his article "Cornell: Confrontation in Black and White." He identified the factions the Yippies, the Converts, and the Radicals. The Yippies (so called by the Radicals) were less politically oriented and more artistic and "cool." "They resisted the constant preoccupation of the other factions with the white devils by asking black students to forget the honkey and to concentrate on love and respect within the black community. The implication of their philosophy meant withdrawal from the politics of dealing with white society and the development of strong interpersonal relationships among black students."[67] The leader of this faction was a prep school graduate who established *Watu*, a black literary magazine. This individual and others, among them DuBois, ran into considerable difficulties with the more militant factions. The Converts were typically middle-class and of the first generation, but their experiences with the fraternity system politicized them and gave them black consciousness. The Radicals were the ones who wanted meaningful revolution.

Finally, Donald discussed the importance of black men protecting black women. Perhaps this concern was a reaction to the "damage imagery" that accused black men of lacking masculine authority; it was also a function of the masculinist tenets of Black Power. In addition, the issue of interracial dating and sex was important at Cornell and elsewhere during this period. Tolerating interracial relations was one of the benefits of the civil rights movement, and blacks at Cornell took advantage of it. Goodwin stressed that he and many of his friends dated white women, for example. But interracial relationships became suspect—at least officially—as the new generation exerted its power. Malcolm X and others taught that black men should stick to black women as a matter of black pride and support. Accordingly, a debate over the appropriateness of dating white women broke out within the AAS. Donald stated, "Before the advent of black power, the black woman's life on campus was degrading and frustrating. . . . Black power, or more precisely black nationalism, sought to redefine and expand the traditional concept of manhood in such a manner that it took into account the realistic condition of a black community. . . . Manhood as expressed in the black nationalism that came to Cornell said, 'We must protect our women; we must love our women.' Love and protection of women became synonymous with the acceptance of oneself and of the black community."[68] In April 1969 it would be a putative white attack on the women's residence, Wari House, that precipitated the takeover of the Straight. And as the AAS walked out of the Straight after the agreement was struck, the men protected the women in actual and symbolic fashion by placing them in the middle of the procession, surrounded by men in arms.

CHAPTER FOUR

RACIAL JUSTICE VERSUS
ACADEMIC FREEDOM

Like an omen, Martin Luther King's murder occurred just hours after the Afro-American Society carried out the central act of the McPhelin affair, a quasi-violent takeover of the Economics Department offices. These two events galvanized the militant AAS faction; the McPhelin incident also pitted claims of academic freedom against claims of racial justice in the starkest manner possible. This was the first time that the conflict had erupted onto the public stage at Cornell, and the administration's response set a precedent of avoidance that would come to haunt the university. In short, the McPhelin affair was a trial run for April 1969.

Economics 103

Father Michael McPhelin, a visiting lecturer from the Philippines, began his second semester teaching the large lecture class of 338 students on January 30. The material in "Economic Development" (Economics 103) was potentially racially charged, covering such subjects as poverty, the economy of the ghetto, cultural and biological factors related to economic success and development, and Western values compared to those of other cultures. No students had lodged complaints the previous semester, but race relations had taken a downward turn since then. Equally important, three committed members of the AAS were enrolled in the course that spring: John Garner, Robert Rone, and Bert Cooper. (Four or five other black students were in the class as well.) If the rise of black consciousness was the sine qua non of the AAS, Garner was its heart and soul. AAS members spoke of Garner in reverent terms. Cleveland Donald's description was typical:

In the beginning there was blackness; blackness was Zimbawa [Donald's fictitious name for Garner], and Zimbawa was radical. A brilliant engineering student and a good chess player, Zimbawa's mind plowed through fertile fields of unconventional thought. Nearly every militant or revolutionary concept known to black Cornellians had issued first from Zimbawa's mouth. . . . The Yippies often said that if Zimbawa ever slept with only one white woman he would change his ideological perspective. To which the Radicals replied, probably so, but if Zimbawa ever slept with a white woman Zimbawa would not be Zimbawa. In a group of black students where the disease of blacker-than-thou had not been eradicated completely, Zimbawa was truly black.[1]

Garner and his allies charged that McPhelin's teachings constituted racism—if not overt racism, then institutional racism. Their reaction to the course proved pivotal in Cornell's history. The following portrayal of McPhelin's course is drawn from the testimony of several witnesses before the commission that investigated the incident, the Williams Commission.

McPhelin began the course with a general discussion of economic development, a process that he characterized as preeminently a product of Western civilization.[2] Garner's group construed this emphasis as a form of institutional racism because it excluded the experiences of blacks in America and in Africa. In a written statement to the commission, the group said:

From the beginning of this course, the lecturer has consistently and subtly constructed a philosophy of racism; to clarify, we do not mean individual or overt racism, but institutionalized, or covert racism, that type by which attitudes of white superiority are perpetuated.

This philosophy was first introduced as soon as the course began, upon discussion of the topic of economic logic, in which the lecturer assumed and emphatically repeated the "fact" that the rational decision involved in economics, and the study of economics as such is solely the product of the Western man.[3]

In his testimony before the commission, Garner defined institutional racism as "any type of statement where the person will point out a difference and in so pointing out this difference implies that the way in which he acts or the way in which the group he supposedly represents acts is superior or is better than the way in which the group which he is talking about or which he is defining actually acts."[4] Garner's definition was beholden to the concept of institutional racism that had recently been coined by Stokely Carmichael and Charles Hamilton in *Black Power*. Institutional racism differs from "individual racism" in the sense that it "is less overt, far more subtle, less identifiable in terms of *specific* individuals committing the acts. But it is no less destructive of human life. . . . [It] originates in the operation of established and respected forms in the society, and thus receives far less public condemnation than the first type. . . . Institutional racism relies on the active and pervasive operation of anti-black attitudes and practices. A sense of superior group position prevails."[5]

Garner reported that the only times McPhelin explicitly mentioned blacks was when he excluded them from economic development and when he later referred to the Moynihan Report, a famous study in which Assistant Labor Secretary Daniel Patrick Moynihan discussed the ways in which the deterioration of the family in the ghetto contributed to social pathology and the widening of the socioeconomic gap between blacks and whites.[6] A very sensitized person could find racism lurking in such remarks, but that conclusion is not self-evident. Several commission members pressed Rone and Garner on this point. It was one thing to exclude blacks from the analysis for reasons of prejudice and quite another thing to report that they had been excluded in a factual sense. In its report, the commission stated, "Even when reports were in exact agreement as to what was actually said—and the specific words and sentences spoken—there were radically different reports of perceived meanings, intentions and implications."[7]

Regardless of the cause, factual differences exist between the races concerning such matters as wealth, health, opportunity, accomplishments, and cultural practices. But under what circumstances does the recording or analysis of these differences move from objective reporting to prejudice? The distinction can be especially treacherous when the practices with which one is dealing are normatively loaded, such as economic productivity or the greater crime and illegitimacy rates among black Americans compared with whites. Garner's definition provides a basis for finding racism in the reporting of such facts unless one presents them with the utmost caution. Yet such sensitivity can have a chilling effect on the good-faith pursuit of truth, leading to self-censorship and intellectual dishonesty. The least agile instructors are in the greatest danger. A teaching assistant alleged that McPhelin did not encourage discussion or challenge during the lecture and that students had to wait for discussion sessions to air their disagreements. A more able teacher might have been able to walk the delicate line.

The traditional concept of racism—that certain groups are inferior to others because of biological or genetic factors—is less open to interpretation than the definition Garner proffered. The concept of institutional racism, by focusing on attitudes and subconscious assumptions, invites a more complex and more subtle understanding that is truer to the intricacies of history and power in society. Still, it opens the door to subjectivity and allegations of "unconscious" racism that are virtually impossible to refute. In other words, the concept has the potential to be enlightening and McCarthy-like at the same time.

Rone told the commission that his class notes showed that McPhelin's comments about economics in the first lecture did indeed exclude blacks from the definition of *Western*. "He said that Western man was meaning the European nations and America, but he also qualified that by saying except for Negroes."[8] What did "except" mean? So much depended on one's assumptions and emphases and on who had the burden of proof. But Garner thought such distinctions obscured the truth. When commission chairman Robin Williams asked him, "Was it a specific statement that Negroes were left out because of the lack of . . . ," Garner interjected, "Well, I don't think it matters." They then engaged in an exchange that captured the difference between the traditional notion of racism and the new notion of institutional racism:

> Williams: My question was whether he specifically excepted Negroes on the ground that they had not been part of the historical Western development or whether he did it on the basis that they were somehow not capable of the economic rationale.
>
> Garner: I think they both would be racist.

Garner and his colleagues wanted to challenge McPhelin during the first lecture but demurred because of their "shock" and because of the difficulty of finding the right words under the circumstances. "You would have to go into his entire way of thinking, you'd have to delve into his entire logical approach. This could not be met."[9] Garner and McPhelin "chatted regularly after class" as the semester progressed, so dialogue was maintained. Yet the lectures grew more controversial, especially after the initial suspicions had emerged. On February 6 Rone and McPhelin debated the virtues of communism over capitalism. On February 13 McPhelin spoke about the relationship among such factors as human resources, biology, inheritance, and climate. Garner pointed out that his sources were out of date and questioned McPhelin's interpretation of Marx. McPhelin added fuel to the fire on March 14 by a discussion of poverty besetting the urban poor, which set the stage for the explosive lecture on "poverty, American-style," on March 19. That lecture dealt with the nature and causes of poverty. (Here McPhelin delved into the Moynihan Report.)

McPhelin ventured into the supercharged area of theories about poverty and character. He pointed out that hunger and privation can build character "within the proper environment" (Garner's reporting), as can "transient" (temporary) poverty. Garner told the commission, "Then he pointed out that there have existed frugal, ambitious people who rose by their own efforts, people with aspirations who made their way out of poverty with the help of the growing economy." McPhelin next compared the nature of poverty and schooling for seven-to-seventeen-year-olds in 1969 and 1870. Garner raised his hand to object to the comparison, pointing to McPhelin's earlier claim about the historical specificity of poverty. "Upon which he completely ignored me, and continued with his lecture."[10] Sometime in this discussion (the record is not clear when), McPhelin made the remarks that incited the AAS to confrontation. The "Initial Statement of Economics 103 Students" submitted by Garner, Rone, and Cooper to the commission covered this matter more fully than the testimony:

> The ultimate insult to the blacks, as well as white psyche, occurred during the lecture on Tuesday, March 19, 1968, in which the lecturer directed his comments toward the urban poor. "Children are without fair opportunity . . . their games are sickly and perverted, stress cunning for survival as in the jungle. . . . Slums pro-

duce young people inclined toward crime and violence, four-fifths of youths in San Francisco have been arrested by the age of seventeen. . . . The atmosphere is stagnating, there are no pleasures except those satisfying the lower tastes." . . . Furthermore, throughout the lecture the lecturer implied that certain segments of the poor were poor because they lacked ambition to rise through their own efforts.[11]

Recall that many black students—like their peers and scholars across the country—had qualms about the use of "damage imagery" to portray black culture and psychology.[12] McPhelin was treading into an area of delicate expectations and sensitivities, and he was doing so in front of the leading advocates of Black Power on campus. Worse, McPhelin entered this fray with fewer strategic skills than other professors who managed to get away with similar remarks in class. According to Nathan Tarcov, who lived in the same house as the visiting priest, McPhelin was a friendly, decent man who had the misfortune of being obtuse. "He really just could not fully comprehend what was happening to him," Tarcov said. "He just didn't get it."[13]

The commission questioned whether the remarks about race and poverty were racist per se, for, as Williams observed, "he's talking about poor people, he's not talking about race"—and most poor people are white. Also, Williams said, "there is specific reference [in the Moynihan Report] to broken families, which again is fact." Garner responded, "Well, aren't you, in effect, trying our case before we finish presenting it?" The rest of the commission's discussion of this point revolved around the report's conclusions and the difference between the presentation of facts and theories or values that might be derived from those facts.

Not surprisingly, McPhelin had a different interpretation of everything. He began his testimony by critiquing the concept of institutional or covert racism that Garner and his colleagues articulated. "This was a statement made at a university, used as a charge against a university professor, and I wonder, you know, in this kind of presumably scientific atmosphere, whether that would be acceptable, exact, and precise." For example, it was "certainly true" that some parts of the world have experienced more economic advancement than others, and "there's nothing especially it seems to me racist about a statement like that."[14] He also defended his more controversial comments about "cultural inheritance," pointing out that cultural values (how people "value labor," for example) and ideas affect economic development, as do things such as climate. What about the controversial concept of "biological inheritance"? McPhelin claimed his comments about biological inheritance were not racist because they involved differences within, not between, racial or ethnic groups. "What I said was that if you take only the Irish, you know among the Irish you find some who are weak, some who are strong, some who are smart, some who are stupid . . . but that itself is not, as I see it, a racist statement."

Then McPhelin addressed the "ultimate insult" to blacks: his comments about sick and perverted games. He said he directed his comments only to the urban poor in general, not the black urban poor per se. He intended to discuss the black urban poor on April 4, but Garner and his colleagues disrupted the class before he could do so (more details will be given later). When he spoke of children playing "games sickly and perverted," stressing survival in a jungle, he maintained that he was drawing on literature he had read (for example, Herman Miller's *Studies of Poverty in the United States*) as well as statistics about crime and violence in the urban environment. But he admitted, "I could bite my tongue for having used 'sick and perverse.'"

Garner confronted McPhelin after the March 19 class and challenged his assessments and remarks. In response, McPhelin apologized to Garner and his colleagues in front of the class on March 21. After this class, Garner pursued the matter. McPhelin then "tried to advise him in a friendly way that . . . his sensitivity could be a block to his learning." Along these lines it is interesting to note a conversation that Gloria Joseph reported having with Rone. Joseph pointed out that Rone had come to see her early in the semester to complain about the racist undertones of the course. At the same time, Rone told her and some other AAS members "that in a way he found it challenging because he [McPhelin] encouraged him to go out and come back with facts to present to Professor McPhelin." [15] With McPhelin's March lectures, however, being insulted overwhelmed being challenged.

As a result of the reaction to his teaching, McPhelin began to check his thought processes. "I began myself to have the sense that I couldn't go into class and say 'tropics' without [his hearing] 'black tropics' . . . I couldn't say 'poverty,' or talk about its consequences, or talk about slums, it seems, without his hearing that I was talking about black poverty." Nevertheless, McPhelin received some support for his defense that his teaching was not racist. First, the Economics Department had received no complaints from students who took the same course the previous semester. Second, the Williams Commission received a petition signed by a large number of students who attended his April 11 lecture that called the charges "unjustified and invalid. We offer our full support of Professor McPhelin and urge the administration to do the same." [16] Finally, students wrote to the *Cornell Daily Sun* in support of McPhelin. This support buttressed McPhelin's claims, although it could not settle the matter. One would expect blacks and whites to view the matter differently, especially if institutional racism existed. After McPhelin's more extreme comments, some students laughed. Perhaps this reaction by whites intensified the black students' feelings of alienation.

Andre McLaughlin recalled the impact of the McPhelin incident on her and her colleagues. She pointed to McPhelin's pedagogical style as well as the content of his remarks: "Well, that professor, I wasn't in that class, but it was very disconcerting. He was blatant in his attitude: 'If you don't like what I'm saying, get out.' I think what he was saying was so racist. And the attitude was typical in the academy of the teacher. We got daily reports on what was happening in the class. We always heard what was going on in different classes, what teachers were saying. But this guy, he was kind of like outrageous. . . . He was the lightning rod." [17]

Another AAS member had a similar view. Irving McPhail said, "Here you had a professor who, as I recall, made explicit and overt racist statements about black women on welfare. That kind of behavior was just not to be tolerated. Our response was appropriate to the insult and to the absence of the search for truth that learning and higher education institutions are supposed to be about."[18]

The Department Takeover

McPhelin's apology on March 21 did not satisfy Garner and his colleagues, who demanded that the educator be fired or removed from the class, to be replaced by an instructor more congenial to their position. But the students were not aware of the normal channels through which to file a complaint against a professor, and Cornell administrators made things worse because of their own ignorance of the procedures. No students had ever accused a professor of racism, and none had demanded removal of a professor or the hiring of another with an alternative point of view. In addition, Cornell's administrative labyrinth was enough to perplex the most seasoned bureaucrat, let alone students with little knowledge of the institution. The AAS interpreted the hurdles as signs of institutional racism.

The day after the March 19 class, Garner's group went to register an official complaint with Mark Barlow, the vice president of student affairs. Barlow was not available, so a secretary sent them to Dean Stanley Levy in the dean of students' office. Levy then sent them to Stuart Brown, dean of the Arts College. Levy perceived the students as very serious. "I've rarely, frankly, seen three angrier yet more composed individuals, who were really irate about the attitude they felt that this professor had been expressing. . . . It wasn't so much any direct references as it was innuendos or interpretations of the urban problem."[19]

Brown met with them briefly and had his secretary set up a meeting between Garner and Tom Davis, the chairman of the Economics Department. The students told Brown they wanted an apology, McPhelin's dismissal, and a black professor to teach from their perspective. Brown told the group that it had a legitimate complaint but that procedures had to be followed. The threesome construed this as a runaround (accurately—Brown later admitted that he wanted to stall them in the hope that they would cool off and drop their complaint.) Then when they went to see Davis, he was unavailable because of an exam. His secretary made an appointment for 1:30 the next day—or so she thought—but when Davis showed up for this meeting, the three did not appear, having misunderstood the secretary's scheduling. Eventually, Garner made an appointment to see Davis on April 2, right after spring break.

Eric Evans, the AAS's future minister of defense, joined Garner, Cooper, and Rone when they met Davis on April 2. The meeting was a disaster. "My response to the students centered on two things," Davis remarked. "One, the general issue of academic freedom, which it seemed to me they had no comprehension of at all, we were just speaking completely different languages. . . . And I believe it was Mr. Garner, at this point, [who] said, 'What are you going to do?' And I guess a direct question deserves a direct answer, but I have a tendency to use passive voice where active voice would be far more effective and instead of saying what I was going to do,

I said nothing would be done."[20] According to Rone, "We felt that he was trying to pull something over on us, you know, give us the runaround."[21] Davis wanted to tell the students that he would pursue the matter with the dean, but they stormed out the door.

The group was now at wits' end. "We thought that . . . the time had come to try to get our grievances aired in any way possible."[22] So it took the case to the AAS, which had a meeting scheduled for the next evening. At this meeting the group precipitously decided the Garner group should go to McPhelin's class on April 4 and read the statement to the class (the same statement with demands that was taken to Davis).[23] Joseph, in her role as the AAS academic adviser, contributed to this decision. "My advice was to go to the person with whom they had their grievance rather than running all over the campus again."[24]

On April 4 Garner and company entered the classroom right after McPhelin had begun lecturing. Garner went up to McPhelin and asked to read the statement the group had prepared. Startled, McPhelin asked to read the statement first, but Garner started to read it to the class as McPhelin read it to himself. McPhelin then told Garner to stop, declaring, "I run the show." But Garner continued to read the statement out loud. McPhelin asked the students whether they wanted to hear it and got a mixed response. Garner kept reading, at which point McPhelin invited the class to start singing "The Star-Spangled Banner." Garner continued amid growing chaos until McPhelin canceled the class.

Garner and his colleagues then went out and gathered allies from the class and at the Straight. During the confusion a band of students led by Tom Jones started looking for McPhelin, bent on confrontation (the students did not find him). After some heated discussion in the Straight, the AAS group decided to take over the Economics Department. The protesters left the Straight and marched to Goldwin Smith Hall, a couple of hundred yards away on the Arts Quad. At around 10:30 or 10:40, fifty to sixty students, white and black, entered the two main offices of the department in Goldwin Smith. They closed the door, posted a note on it saying the offices were closed until further notice, took over the phones, and unplugged the typewriter. Davis was inside with three secretaries. The first twenty to thirty minutes were pretty chaotic. The protesters handed Davis a letter with the three demands and told him they would not leave until he arranged a meeting with someone in authority who could do something about their demands. Davis refused to do anything until his office was cleared out and things settled down.

After about twenty minutes, Lowell George, supervisor of public safety, arrived with two plainclothes campus police officers. The students did not allow them to enter, so George said, "If you do not open the door, you will be subject to discipline and possible suspension. We will have to break the door down." The threat was ignored. (This scene would be replayed almost to the letter a year later at the Straight.) The crowd outside the office grew to about sixty, and several students brought in food. Gloria Joseph and her aide Julian Mayfield, a writer who was also teaching a class, continued to go in and out of the office, carrying communications between Provost Dale Corson and the AAS.

An exchange between Garner and Law Professor Norman Penny at the committee hearings captures the flavor of the standoff that now ensued:

> Garner: So at that time we really became more or less very set that he was not going anywhere until we got a meeting. . . . He was free to leave as soon as we got a meeting. But only so soon as we got a meeting.
>
> Penny: To use the modern term, positions hardened. Is that right?
>
> Garner: Well perhaps in view of the fact that he was obviously lying to us, yes.

The confrontation settled down to a standoff. During this time AAS members used the phones to make unauthorized long-distance calls, including one to inform the *New York Times* of the controversy. Sometime after noon George came back and began signaling Davis through a window, asking whether he wanted campus police to free him. Davis signaled back "no" several times, fearing that such an attempt would lead to violence. At 2:00 p.m. two representatives emerged from the offices and read a statement about the reasons for the takeover and the three demands. Then Paul DuBois left the office to talk with Provost Corson—the first serious step toward a resolution.[25] Joseph had been running back and forth among Davis, the AAS, and the Corson group, hoping to mediate. There was little coordination amidst a fury of phone calls, messages, and runners.[26]

At this point Davis observed something that foreshadowed April '69: "Rumors went through that room at a wild and furious rate. Every half-hour or so I overheard in the conversation or was told that this person was coming or that person was coming or that this action had been taken or that action had been taken—all of these things, to the best of my knowledge, subsequently were shown to be without foundation. . . . The next thing I knew was that the statement was made that the provost was coming to meet in the Economics Department office."[27] The rumor explosion drew energy from the fears and racial paranoia that seemed to grip both sides. The blacks suspected the worst from the whites, and many of the whites involved were intimidated by the sight of angry, militant blacks. For the next year racial paranoia would reign at Cornell, peaking with the guns at the Straight.

Finally, at 3:15, the first meeting with university officials, AAS leaders, and Davis took place. It included Corson, Faculty Dean Robert Miller, and Economics Professors Douglas Dowd, Chandler Morse, and Frank H. Golay. After almost two hours of negotiations, Corson promised to meet with the students to deal with their demands, to pay for an outside lecturer "of the Society's choosing," and to investigate the entire matter. Corson described the scene when he entered the fray at 3:15:

> One of the things that characterizes discussions like this is that everybody is terribly angry; rationality has almost nothing to do with it. What you try to do is get the level of rhetoric down to the point where you can be rational. And that was often impossible during that period. The black students were so angry that they were irrational. There were two groups of black students, and just three or four in the inner office or four or five, with Tom Davis, and in the outer office, twenty or more. Perkins was in Williamsburg and I was to call him at five. I told these students that

I had until five, and I will come back when I finish this call. I went to leave and someone said, "Nobody is going to leave this room." And I said, "I told you I am leaving this room, and I *am* leaving this room." And one of the black students went with me, Steve Goodwin, who is now working on Wall Street. He said, "I am going to walk over with you to protect you." He didn't ever develop that kind of angry confrontation.[28]

Some threatening incidents occurred during the takeover. First, around 1:00 p.m. George decided to stop black students from coming into the room (by now whites were not allowed in) and assigned two plainclothesmen to block the door. When five students appeared, the officers told them they could not enter. The five then pushed their way past the guards, causing a major scuffle. According to one source, one of these officers placed his hand on his service revolver but did not use it.[29] Officers were taught not to bring guns to such encounters, but this rule was neglected in this case. Corson said it was a perilous moment.[30] George said, "A number of students . . . came out and attacked the two officers and hit them about the face with their fists, knocked them to the floor, and everybody ran in and they slammed the doors."[31] The two officers had to go to the infirmary. Tom Jones, who was involved in this incident, told the commission that he had stepped outside to get a soda and that the two officers would not let him back into the room. His version of the clash differed from the officers'. "They offered no identification whatsoever, so for all I knew, they were just bystanders who had taken it upon themselves to decide how the course of events would go. So I told them that I was going back in the room and they said, 'no, you're not.' So I said that they were going to have to kill me to keep me out, and then I went to put my hand on the doorknob, and the next thing I knew I was lying in the hall, about five feet away from the door; my glasses had been knocked off."[32] Jones said a gun had dropped out of the pocket of one of the officers after the scuffle.

As a result of this clash, George replaced the two officers with three uniformed officers, one of whom was black. When three more students, two of them women, started pushing and screaming at these three officers to get in, George dropped the policy of no entry. This scene set an eerie precedent: a year later at the Straight, George and the administration once again adopted a policy of letting AAS members in while sealing off whites. It was under this policy that the AAS smuggled in the guns.

Another incident concerned a secretary's access to pills. The activists would not allow Davis or the secretaries to use the phones or have access to their desks. When one secretary moved to get her pills from her purse, a woman student angrily confronted her and denied her access. Eventually a male student intervened and let her get her pills, although the conflict made the secretary "quite nervous." But observers testified that individuals and groups within the seizing party differed in terms of hostility and anger. Another secretary remarked that she grew less frightened as the conflict progressed. "I realized that the incident between this female student and Mrs. Otis wasn't really representative of all the students who were there."[33]

Eventually Corson managed to work out an agreement with Garner and his entourage, promising to look into the AAS's complaints about McPhelin and the university. Several questions were left dangling, however: How would the university investigate the AAS's complaint? How would it handle the individuals who took over the Economics Department and physically assaulted the officers? With passions high on all sides, these were treacherous questions.

King's Assassination

A few hours after the takeover ended, Martin Luther King Jr. was murdered in Memphis. Though many AAS students had moved away from King's teachings and assumptions, his death was nevertheless devastating.[34] On the heels of the McPhelin affair, it was a defining moment at Cornell. Public officials and other prominent individuals at Cornell and across the country eulogized King. Allan Sindler, the architect of the new judicial system and a participant in the civil rights movement in the South while at Duke, lamented: "There is universal shame for the nation that allowed King to be killed when he had so many more years to give in service to his people and his country. There is not much more that can be said at a time like this."[35]

But the lines between black and white were hardening. Violence and alienation flared across the nation and in Ithaca. What could have been an opportunity for the races to come together in mourning and purpose turned into a wedge between them. Though the Cornell white community seemed genuinely saddened by King's death, racist incidents against blacks and the inability of many whites to fathom fully the enormity of King's death added fuel to blacks' sense of alienation. Whites who did understand and did care too often failed to convey their sympathy simply out of shyness or the sense of unease they felt in the presence of the anger and sorrow that gripped their black acquaintances. Perhaps the move toward separatism was a fait accompli. Many blacks and whites no doubt wanted reconciliation, although like a struggling married couple they failed to do, or were unable to do, the little things that could bring them together. Denise Raynor's recollections were illuminating:

> Martin Luther King was a major turning point for the community, because before that everything was liberal and everybody could think what they wanted to think. After that, nobody could do anything but the party line. I can remember Stephanie Bell turning to me that night and saying, "We can't afford to have white friends anymore!" There was a clear dividing line, that was it. And after that, people [blacks] would cross the street and not talk to me [because my boyfriend was white].[36]

More blatant, many Cornell blacks received threats from anonymous sources. In one incident, rowdy white undergraduates shouted racial epithets as they shot off toy cap guns in the dorms. Word of such insufferable actions spread like wildfire through Cornell's black community. Several black students reported shootings in scuffles with whites.[37] In the women's dorms, blacks felt isolated "in otherwise white corridors," so they joined black friends in other dorms. In an AAS meeting after a campus memorial service for King, AAS president Robert Jackson urged Cornell's black students "to stay home and off the streets." In an interview with the *Sun*, he laid out the new rationale for self-defense. "The white people should be made to understand that the police department is not doing its job in protecting black people. White people—students—should know that threats will not continue without black response. Students, regardless of where they are from—Cleveland, Watts, Georgia—have been shown by the events of the past five days that you can be a so-called 'good Negro' and still be murdered. Racism is so pervasive that no black person is safe."[38]

Meanwhile, three Ithaca businesses were targets of firebombs, and several arson fires were attempted. Someone threw a rock through a window at the *Ithaca Journal*, wrapped with a message that read, "You are as much to blame as anyone." When Ithaca police arrested Paul DuBois that night for possession of a dangerous weapon (a sword cane) and for shooting a weapon inside city limits, he told them he had armed himself because he had received racist death threats and because a white man had shot at him. The day after the takeover and King's death, a group of forty blacks, demanding equal time to respond to an editorial "or else," barged into the student radio station, WVBR ("Voice of Big Red"). A spokesman declared over the air that "no longer can black people dream, no longer can black people have faith in this white racist society."[39] Though this takeover violated federal law, authorities initiated no legal action against the students. Over the next several days fires broke out all over Cornell and downtown, fires that came to be known as the "alphabet fires." First, a traditional bar in Collegetown (an area of shops on the eastern edge of campus), Alt Heidelberg, burned to the ground, followed by major fires at the Triangle Book Store and Lyon Tower. Though officials determined that accidental causes were involved in the latter two cases, "an ominous theory circulated: arsonists were attempting to spell 'ATLANTA.' This theory was bolstered the following Monday when a $50,000 fire gutted the chapel of Anabel Taylor Hall. ATLA had been spelled out."[40] (King's congregation was in Atlanta, and on the eve of his death he had made a famous speech there about the courage to face death.) With community awareness aroused, however, no more fires broke out.[41]

A memorial service for King was held at noon on April 5 at Bailey Hall, convened by Cornell United Religious Work. "It was the only segregated event that anyone could remember," Fisher and Wallenstein wrote.[42] Twenty-two hundred people crowded into Bailey, and five hundred more listened to the service at the Straight and another building. A whole section of seats in Bailey Hall had been roped off "for blacks only." After most of the audience had arrived, the blacks entered in solidarity and took their seats en masse. Provost Corson spoke, along with two AAS members (John Garner and Larry Dickson) and three CURW clergymen (Daniel Berrigan, Paul E. Gibbons, and Gordon Brewster). Corson called King's murder "a cruel loss to the community of reason." Brewster recalled working with King at a church in Atlanta, and Berrigan spoke about King and the Vietnam War. Then a tape was played of King's great "I Have a Dream" speech from the 1963 March on Washington. An entire era seemed to separate that speech from the words that immediately followed: "There is something that I must say to my people . . . ," King's voice intoned. "In the process of gaining our rightful place, we must not be guilty of wrongful deeds. Let us not seek to satisfy our search for freedom by drinking from the cup of bitterness and hatred. We must forever conduct our struggle on the high plane of dignity and discipline. We must not allow our creative protest to degenerate into physical violence. Again and again we must rise to the majestic heights of meeting physical force with soul force."

Gibbons followed King's call for nonviolent resistance with words that drew the first applause from the section of blacks. "The practice of nonviolence by whites has been dead for over three hundred years," he shouted. Then Garner spoke. "Dr. Martin Luther King was a black man who loved humanity, and perhaps that was his mistake. Dr. King's dream was for freedom, and this dream will live on." Then it was Dickson's turn. According to Fisher and Wallenstein, he "worked himself into a frenzy. Before he finished, he was screaming":

> Maybe it's *time* we started defending our homes and our families from this vicious honkey. . . . When this honkey drives through your neighborhood like they are going to do tonight, and they start shooting at your houses, brothers and sisters: YOU SHOOT BACK AND YOU SHOOT TO KILL! . . . I don't believe that white man has any good in him. . . . When Martin Luther King died, nonviolence died, baby! . . . All I want you brothers and sisters to do is remember: your life is in danger. Right here in Ithaca, your life is in danger. . . . They're talking about they're going to kill us. I'll be goddamned if they going to kill me! (applause from blacks) . . . Now if you honkies think you bad enough to fuck with us, just try it!

Dickson jumped off the stage to shouts of "Black Power, Black Power" from the audience. Those in attendance who did not subscribe to violence sat in stunned silence. SDS leader David Burak then addressed the assembly "in a half whispered, conspiratorial tone," saying: "The call for nonviolence in the face of what is impending is amoral. I speak to the white people." Authorities in New York State had stockpiled "super weapons" to use against blacks, he contended, and many cities had designs to "commit genocide" against blacks during the upcoming summer. "These weapons must be destroyed by any means possible." Burak's claim reflected an ominous rumor that was spreading through the black militant community in America: the government and hate groups were collecting weapons to use against blacks. That many people accepted this irresponsible claim, for which there was no evidence, reveals the eerie state of fear that was coming to grip race relations in certain institutions. Within a few months AAS members began to purchase guns. The AAS then left Bailey in solidarity to march downtown.

The following Monday the *Sun* was chock-full of stories about McPhelin and King. The newspaper editorialized about the "White Problem," and two graduate students wrote op-ed pieces about the memorial service. Paul Anisfield bemoaned the move toward violence and the blaming of all whites as a desecration of King's memory. Cleophus Charles, a black history graduate student, titled his article "A Time for Action." Ambivalent over the continuing validity of King's vision, the article advocated militant but nonviolent action. It struck an ominous tone of moral power and tension: "Make no mistake, ugly America, though I am a moderate, I hate you (as you presently stand) with a burning hatred which can never be quenched by a mere assassin's bullet. So long as there remains a black man alive or a white civil rights advocate, Martin Luther King cannot, and I pray will not, have lived and died in vain. The die is cast: the time for meaningless talk and tokenism is long gone. Act now, America, before it is too late."[43]

King's funeral was held April 9; Cornell canceled classes and held a teach-in on racism. Two thousand students met in Barton Hall to listen to nine professors and President Perkins. Many discussed the concept of institutional racism. Government Professor Andrew Hacker asserted that it was time for blacks to choose their own leaders and that whites were inherently racist. Hacker reveled in his reputation as a maverick and an iconoclast. "There is nothing we can do about it," he said. "We whites can't look at a black person as a man." Only Sindler took issue with this view. "The assertion that unless a white man, seeing a black man, sees not a black man but a fellow human being, then he remains fundamentally a racist, is misapplied. . . . I do not think an abdication or suspension of judgments comports with any person, white or black."[44]

That all the other speakers took the Hacker line shows that Garner and his forces had begun to win the war of public opinion at Cornell. Regardless of what the Williams Commission and the university judicial boards might rule, the most public voices had accepted the logic of institutional racism. The university was now awash in racial shame.

A final reaction to King's murder should be noted. In a book on the 1960s published in 1987, Edward Whitfield, president of the AAS in 1969, said that within a few days of King's death, "there were reports that some white students in a fraternity drinking club called the Mummies were out buying guns and ammunition and talking about they were going to kill some niggers."[45] Though the rumor proved untrue, its presence was important for two reasons: it signified the hysteria that was gripping Cornell, and it contributed to the AAS's decision to procure arms.

The McPhelin Incident and Black Studies

In reaction to the McPhelin incident, the university intensified its efforts to develop a black studies program. Graduate student and AAS member Cleveland Donald wrote:

> The demand for black studies was analogous to the situation of black Mississippians demanding a part in the jury system. As a small segment of the university community, blacks could not change the educational process without resorting to force or the help of a third party. The McPhelin incident demonstrated the futil-

ity of expecting people with a stake in the system to change that system. Consequently, the black students sought to create a structure within the university community where the notion of professorial privilege would serve the black community. They wanted a program where black professors could teach black ideology, just as, in their view, white professors reflected the dominant ideology of their society.[46]

Even before the McPhelin incident, pressures had been mounting for black studies. Professors such as David Brion Davis, a history professor who had recently won a Pulitzer Prize for his book *The Problem of Slavery in Western Culture*,[47] had been devising a black studies program of high quality, and other departments had recently created courses dealing with racial issues. One of the first was a government course on race and politics, taught by Sindler and Hacker in spring 1967, and their teaching assistant was none other than the redoubtable Burak. In addition, in March 1968, just before the McPhelin incident, the embryonic Afro-American Studies Program was initiated under the aegis of Ben Nichols, an engineering professor who was an activist on campus (later he would become mayor of Ithaca) and other prominent professors on the left, such as economist Douglas Dowd. This program was the first version of what would become the new Africana Studies Center after the "revolution" of spring 1969.

Davis envisioned a "fully developed program" and set about to form a lecture series that brought in distinguished scholars, black and white, to speak on racial topics. Like James Weldon Johnson in the 1930s, Davis wanted to ensure that the program would avoid ideological and political dogmatism, trends he feared would compromise the intellectual integrity of the program. The program should be consistent with the principles of free inquiry and academic standards.

Nichols, for his part, envisioned something closer to what the student activists wanted (based on identity politics) and something that would serve as an agent of social change. In late 1968 he said, "From the beginning what we were talking about here was a program primarily for black students. . . . The change in the need for the independence and self-identification and power of the black community was something that I didn't start with, certainly. But I came to appreciate the need for it over the last couple of years."[48]

The McPhelin affair added urgency to this process and ultimately gave momentum to Nichols's approach over Davis's. On March 9 Nichols met with several interested faculty and a few students to discuss a program (disappointingly, only four students showed up). At this meeting, Economics Professor Thomas Sowell took a hard line on black studies, claiming that black students had to learn the basics of economics and other disciplines before they ventured into black versions.[49]

On April 15 Nichols headed a group, including AAS students Dalton Jones and Tom Jones, that presented the case for a program to the Committee on Undergraduate Education (CUE), which included such top administrators as Perkins, Corson, and Robert Sproull, the vice president of academic affairs. The group wanted CUE to authorize two black studies courses for fall '68, to be taught by two activist white professors: a "black economy" course by Dowd and a course on black literature by English Professor Dan McCall, who had been involved with COSEP.

Two issues confronted the proponents of a black studies program: How "scholarly" should it be, as opposed to being "political"? And how "separate" should it be in terms of structure, teachers, and students? People such as Sindler and Davis wanted the most scholarly program possible, a program that was integrated with the rest of the educational establishment at Cornell and the country. But the AAS and its supporters sought a more autonomous program run by and for blacks and devoted to the tenets of Black Power and black nationalism. As Irving McPhail observed, "What Perkins was doing was basically kind of designing a black studies program designed by whites for blacks, which obviously was never going to work. The whole issue was that as African-American students, we felt very strongly that we should design the program. It was more than we had to be consulted; we should be the principal architects of the program." [50]

A debate over the inclusion of white students in Dowd's and McCall's new courses provided a preview of the confrontation coming in the fall. Though it temporarily conceded to established white professors teaching the courses in the embryonic program, the AAS drew the line when it came to the students who would take the courses. CUE, however, had no choice but to disagree with the proposal, for federal, state, and university rules prohibited discrimination on the basis of race.[51] But Perkins and CUE had an idea: explicit exclusion based on race could be achieved by limiting enrollment through a traditional device, requiring students to obtain the "consent of the instructor" to enroll. The instructors, who were sympathetic to the AAS's desires, could then use their discretion to keep whites out.

Nichols took this "compromise" back to the AAS for discussion. At this point, "my feeling was that my role was to push through whatever the students insisted I should be pushing through." [52] After much debate, the AAS agreed to the compromise because "this would in fact accomplish what was wanted anyhow." In the meantime, a steering committee for the Afro-American Studies Program was established with student and faculty membership, under the auspices of the Center for Research and Education headed by Nichols.

In late April the steering committee met with the Educational Policy Committee (EPC). History Professor Donald Kagan, one of the members of the EPC, presented the most forceful opposition, largely on the grounds that the courses were exclusively for blacks, albeit in disguise. In the end, the EPC voted 5–1 (Kagan against) for the courses and the consent-of-the-instructor rationale. But when Stuart Brown wrote a letter to the faculty explaining the EPC vote on May 13, all hell broke loose. Symptomatic of this response was a letter Nichols received from a "liberal" faculty member. The faculty member enclosed a copy of Brown's letter with the sentence that proposed a program of courses "for black students only" underlined in red and scolded Nichols in words that captured the shift in pedagogical philosophy and thinking about race that Nichols epitomized: "That this could be suggested at Cornell is at the limit of credibility. Ben, when did you make the transition from teacher to politician?" [53]

So pressure was brought on Dowd and McCall to keep the courses open. In the end, Dowd admitted four whites among the nineteen students he accepted in the course (seventy applied), an act that caused Tom Jones and some other black students to walk out of the class in protest.

Finally, Nichols and others worked hard to raise money for the fledgling program. Steve Goodwin raised some money from connections at IBM, and the administration pledged some funds. Discussions with faculty and administrators commenced about how to proceed. From these discussions one name arose as someone who would be a good candidate to chair the new program temporarily: Chandler Morse. He was a scholar of African economics and a member of the Faculty Council. Over the summer Morse and others in the administration worked on developing the program, and DuBois came up with a definitive plan. We will return to this development in the next chapter.

The Williams Commission

Meanwhile, back from spring break, the Garner group met April 8 with the administration to present its basic demands concerning the McPhelin matter. Perkins established a commission to investigate a broad range of issues, including McPhelin's class, the Economics Department takeover, and racial problems at Cornell. In addition, Tom Davis agreed to pay for an outside lecturer to present a different point of view. There was also the issue of university security and conduct boards' investigations of three possible charges against the individuals involved in the takeover: for disrupting McPhelin's class, for holding Davis and the secretaries hostage, and for assaulting the security officers.

The very inception of the commission under the chairmanship of Robin Williams, an expert on group relationships, raised procedural and compositional questions. Two procedural issues stood out. First, the normal procedure to be followed when charges could lead to a dismissal of a professor (the case with McPhelin) required a preliminary investigation by the dean of the college (in this case, Stuart Brown), to be followed by a hearing and investigation by a panel of one's peers if the dean deems the evidence sufficient to pursue the case. In addition, the process would have included confronting one's accusers.

By giving the commission immediate authority to conduct the investigation, though, the administration circumvented these procedures. In effect, this meant it had accepted Garner's charges as substantial enough to go straight to the second stage of investigation, though in this case the commission was not exactly one of McPhelin's "peers," as it consisted of administrators and students in addition to professors.

The other procedural issue involved the relationship between the commission's task and the erstwhile independent investigation of the students' conduct. According to Lowell George, Corson asked security to postpone the investigation until the commission had finished its investigation. George acknowledged that this "freeze" could hamper finding the truth because the best time to investigate is when the evidence is fresh and because security is better equipped by training and resources than the commission to conduct an investigation. The decision to forestall the normal investigation was made at a special three-hour meeting that Corson called in early April, attended by numerous administrators and faculty chairs of committees. This group decided that the extraordinary nature of the issue called for extraordinary procedures.

Regardless, the relationship among the three investigations remained unclear and confused. George concluded his testimony: "We were instructed to discontinue it temporarily. It doesn't mean we won't start again, but we won't start until we're instructed."[54] Security never was so instructed. What was certain was that the administration signaled that the established standards of legal accountability and due process were not applicable to the situation. This logic matched that of the AAS, which proclaimed, "The gravity of our grievances makes any possible disciplinary action resulting from our bold venture unjustified."[55]

The composition of the Williams Commission was also unusual. Its nine members consisted of professors and administrators and two students. Given the stakes, it would have been naive to expect a "neutral" commission, but some members had strong personal stakes in the outcome, and two were parties to the dispute. On the one side, Gloria Joseph was the most important administrative contact for the AAS, and she had even advised the AAS to take the case directly to the Economics Department. Joseph also testified before the commission as a witness. When Williams called her to testify, he told her to "pretend you are in from the outside." Student member Earl Armstrong was about to become the next AAS president (though compared to Garner he was basically a figurehead). Joseph and Armstrong would ultimately dissent from the commission's moderate position on institutional racism. On the other side, Professors Norman Penny of the Law School and George Hildebrand of Economics were strong defenders of academic freedom; Penny was the chair of the Committee on Academic Freedom and Tenure. And student member Art Kaminsky had taken a strong law-and-order stand against the draft card solicitors in 1967 as SCARB chairman, as we saw in Chapter Two.

The biggest debate on the commission was over institutional racism. Joseph pushed that line in her testimony and her questioning of witnesses. She and Penny engaged in numerous debates over racism and Joseph's role in the takeover (Penny seemed to try to pin her down as an instigator, and she had many conflicts with Penny and Hildebrand over academic freedom and racism). At one point in her testimony Joseph maintained that the real culprit was Cornell. "The critical issue in the minds of the students and expressed by the students was the perception of racism in education, and this is their major complaint. This is what they've been talking about and this is the point that to me the Commission keeps overlooking and hanging onto technicalities and procedures." When one member stressed the importance of academic freedom, Joseph replied, "I think they were much more concerned with righting one of America's worst wrongs, and that's racism . . . for racism is killing us."[56]

After six days of listening to nineteen witnesses, the commission came to its conclusions and issued its report on April 26. Despite the range of its charges and the perceptions that it was established to avoid judgment, it made some forceful statements and thoughtful suggestions. It worked hard to get the facts straight and to take the claims on both sides seriously, making probing points about academic freedom and the racial problems at Cornell. The panel also formulated some carefully considered ideas about how to proceed with COSEP in a manner that better prepared students and faculty for the problems that had arisen. Some critics maintained that the commission did not settle the academic freedom versus racial justice conflict, but it is not clear that anyone possessed the wherewithal at this point to accomplish that task.

The majority adopted the traditional, narrower definition of overt racism, though it did pursue the larger context of racial problems at Cornell. It exonerated McPhelin of racism on this count, a conclusion with which even the dissenters (Joseph, Armstrong, and Diane Weinberg) concurred. "It is our conclusion that Professor McPhelin was not aware of the full cognitive and evaluative interpretations to which his remarks were subject when heard by black American students in 1968, and more specifically, that he saw no grounds for anticipating the depth and intensity of the responses actually encountered." [57] Thus McPhelin was not guilty of *conscious* racism, but what about *unconscious* racism, the essence of institutional racism? The minority differed from the majority on this question, discerning a link between McPhelin's insensitivity and institutional racism at Cornell.

The commission also condemned the students' conduct and referred the case to the student conduct boards, which were undergoing reform (the McPhelin affair contributed to the final faculty decision that spring to have both student and faculty representation on the trial-level and appellate judicial boards). But it recommended not punishing the students: "In light of the information available to the Commission as to the whole background and sequence of events, however, we recommend that the relevant University agencies refrain from severe punitive actions against individual students. . . . If individual 'blame' is to be assigned, many must bear its burdens, including faculty and the administration as well as students." [58]

With the ball back in its court, the administration (Perkins, Miller, and Barlow) had to decide whether the students should be charged. During the incidents, administrators had been receiving correspondence from faculty. For example, Perkins received a letter from History Professor Frederick Marcham, who had earned a reputation as one of Cornell's most conscientious and able academic citizens. Marcham said that he considered "the actions which caused Professor Davis to be imprisoned in his office for some hours" to be "criminal acts" and encouraged Perkins to defend "the tradition of free personal utterance on the part of members of the faculty" and the right of students "to challenge the utterance of a professor." [59]

Despite such pleas, the administration decided that the students involved in the disruption should not be charged. Miller explained why he moved to this position. He said of the entire affair that "there was a highly developed sense of paranoia running through all of this, and that at least one of the students [John Garner] was extremely ingenious in demonstrating that something that most people regard is perfectly innocuous was in fact a racial phenomenon."[60] Miller also said Davis had decided that he did not consider himself a "hostage" in any coercive sense, so pursuing the charges "was not going to be very profitable."

More important, in a crucial meeting with Miller, Brown, and the Garner group after the takeover, Corson had indicated to Garner that he (and therefore the administration) essentially sided with them. Interviewees described Corson as among the most level-headed administrators at Cornell. During the serious events of April 1969 he seemed to be the most in control. When Perkins resigned in June 1969, everyone looked to Corson to lead Cornell out of the wilderness. Corson believed in academic freedom and the mission of the university to pursue the truth. He also believed strongly in social and racial justice. More than one interviewee described him as "an abolitionist born one hundred years too late." At this meeting the abolitionist side shone through. Miller observed:

> We once again fell into a discussion of institutional racism which by now was a word that everybody was talking about, and speculating as to exactly what it meant. . . . And the Provost made a statement which I cannot quote, but my interpretation of his intent in making this statement was that it was high time that this community woke up to this issue. . . . Well, what he said was words that in effect said to the black students—this is what they heard—"We appreciate what you have done to make this community aware of this problem." Well, the impact of that statement was just obvious and the expressions of these three kids. . . . They were sitting there expecting the worst from institutional racism. They were expecting to get expelled, I'm sure. Now what they heard was a pardon with praise from The Man. And you could just see it in their faces.[61]

Miller therefore recommended to Perkins to intervene and prevent the issuance of sanctions. Given that the judicial system was undergoing reconstruction, Perkins had more discretion to intervene than he would have the following term, so the charges were essentially dropped.

This left one issue: whether to pursue charges against McPhelin. The Williams Commission had "exonerated" him, yet the dean of the College of Arts and Sciences, Stuart Brown, still had to make a determination. Brown pondered the matter, received correspondence from interested faculty, including Walter Slatoff, who urged that McPhelin not be charged but that the university dedicate itself to eradicating institutional racism, and consulted with key administrators. He decided not to charge McPhelin. In the three-page report he sent to Perkins and the faculty explaining his decision, however, he accused the university of institutional racism. This report made official what Corson had told Garner and his cohorts earlier, that *the real culprit was the university.*[62] McPhelin was not guilty because everybody was guilty.

Brown did not mention academic freedom once in his report. He redefined the mission of the university as the pursuit of racial justice, beseeching Cornell "as an institution" to "commit ourselves fully and at once to the solution of the great educational and social problems revealed by this incident." The letter sent waves of approval or alarm around the campus, depending on one's position:

> In some sense of "racist," McPhelin and I and most whites are racists in some degree. We are all in some degree ignorant of and insensitive to the plight of black people . . . [amounting] in practice to unconscious and well-meaning arrogance and patronage. . . . That the ignorance and indifference displayed . . . characterizes the entire white community proves it has nothing specifically to do with the teaching of Economics 103. . . .
>
> I think they [black students] have the right to demand of us . . . that we make an immediate and resolute effort to teach ourselves about black problems, and that we dedicate ourselves as an institution to finding solutions to these problems.[63]

Faculty members such as Slatoff agreed with the conclusion of Brown's letter. Others, such as Hildebrand, saw it differently. "This astonishing, extreme position indicates to me that the administration found the Williams Commission report completely unwelcome. . . . To my knowledge not one of those recommendations was ever adopted by the Perkins administration."[64]

The Aftermath

Brown's letter—which was sent too late in the term for the faculty to debate it in a meeting—indicated that the administration had moved away from the balanced approach of the Williams Commission. In fact, the evidence suggested that the administration had tried to keep the commission report from being made public until after the semester ended and summer vacation had begun. (The administration claimed that the mimeograph machine had broken down.) The *Sun* received only a copy of the commission's dissent, which meant that the public was aware of only that side of the conflict. The administration never made the report available to the faculty during the semester, so there was no public airing of its conclusions or findings.

On April 24 Isadore Blumen, a conservative member of the School of Industrial and Labor Relations, wrote a letter to Miller, imploring him to arrange the release of the commission's findings so that there could be a full accounting of the issues. "There is a special responsibility . . . that justice be done by regular lawful means," he wrote. Blumen also called on Miller and the administration to make a strong statement in favor of protecting freedom in the classroom. "There should be a full and prompt airing of the issues implicit in the Williams Commission report and in the items above. This means that this topic should be the first matter of business for the next faculty meeting, special or regular."[65]

Miller replied that the tactics of delay were advisable, saying a stronger stance could lead to the type of mass disruption that had taken place at Berkeley, Columbia, and Wisconsin. His logic of preventing more trouble differed from Blumen's logic of standing for something worth causing trouble. The reply provided a good look into the mind-set of the administration:

I believe in deliberate speed, controlled reflexes, and moderation. These make for no exhilarating triumphs, but neither do they make for shattering defeats. Let me remind you that Professor McPhelin is still teaching Economics 103, the student protestors are still in his class, no other classes have been disrupted, our Trustees were not locked in by SDS . . . , the Afro-Americans have not become active allies of the SDS, we have not expelled any students nor fired any faculty members, and, so far, the Dean of the Faculty has not resigned. We have not escaped Scott-free: we've had arson, mostly unsuccessful; we've had disorderly conduct; we've had threats exchanged by students, but we've had no bloodshed, no mass arrests, no lawsuits, and no all-night faculty meetings. What the future holds, I do not know: Maybe a big bang made bigger by our low-key approach. I hope not, and I'm gambling that Berkeley, Wisconsin, or Columbia never happen at Cornell.[66]

By moving away from the Williams Commission's balanced approach as it did (the commission had taken concerns about *both* academic freedom and racial justice seriously), the administration ended up siding with the Garner faction. According to Donald Kagan, however, the administration's actions alienated both sides. On the one hand, the AAS viewed the commission as a whitewash, so the administration's backpedaling was always suspect; on the other hand, faculty concerned about academic freedom felt betrayed over the administration's burying of the commission's report and by the signals that Brown's letter sent. Kagan maintained that normal procedures should have been followed; this would have meant taking the students' claims seriously at the same time that the students would be held accountable for their seriously disruptive behavior. According to Fisher and Wallenstein, who spoke with Kagan, "The McPhelin incident taught many people that Perkins didn't care about academic freedom or the complaints of students, but was more concerned with not having any 'trouble.'"[67]

On April 22 the executive committee of the Cornell chapter of the American Association of University Professors (AAUP), chaired by Ben Nichols, sent a letter to Perkins expressing its concerns about McPhelin's constitutional rights. The AAUP, the major defender of constitutional rights and academic freedom at universities, had promulgated the most authoritative set of standards by which colleges and universities should abide.[68] The Cornell chapter alleged that the timing and charges of the Williams Commission "have resulted in an arbitrary and substantial infringement of a legal right of a member of the Cornell faculty." As noted earlier, the university procedure called for a preliminary investigation by the dean and then an investigation by a panel of the professor's peers in cases involving complaints against the faculty. "In our judgment, the arbitrary departure from the prescribed legal process, in and of itself, has resulted in a substantive denial of justice to a member of the Cornell faculty and has established a precedent which can seriously compromise a principle which the Cornell community heretofore has cherished."[69] In his reply Perkins stressed that Nichols had attended the meeting in which the commission was established and that representatives of the faculty had approved of the procedure. Also, because "the atmosphere" of the campus "was tense, the necessity for a university-wide approach seemed vital."[70]

Nichols's role as the chapter president placed him in an interesting position. As seen, he was also a leading faculty proponent of the emerging black studies program, and his vision for this program derived largely from what the students wanted. Nichols was a pivotal figure at Cornell, caught between his commitment to traditional civil liberties and his commitment to the pedagogy of identity. Later Nichols would downplay the threats to academic freedom at Cornell in 1968 and 1969. "I just don't see where academic freedom was jeopardized. What some people call their academic freedom is their right not to have to justify themselves, not to be able to face arguments from students; they are not willing to engage in real debate, as far as I can see, or question their own assumptions, which I think is part of being a faculty person."[71]

On May 17 Perkins and the Garner group were the featured guests at the annual meeting of the chapter. The theme of the meeting was, naturally enough, academic freedom and racial justice. Nichols introduced Garner, Rone, and Cooper, who declared there was no conflict between academic freedom and the goals of the AAS. Then Nichols introduced Perkins, who gave a speech on academic freedom. Perkins offered balm to both sides of the debate—a lot of "academic freedom . . . but" comments and metaphors of "fluidity" rather than "drawing the line." In so doing he redefined the university as an agent of social justice and social change, consistent with the general theory of the university he enunciated in his Princeton lectures. The redefinition justified limiting academic freedom or melding it imperceptibly with the other goals of the university. Academic freedom should be approached pragmatically, not as a principle worth spilling blood over, for how much intellectual freedom can the university tolerate if "repressive" speech thwarts the fundamental mission of the institution?

Perkins began by talking about the historical origin of academic freedom: as a product of the secularization of the university.[72] But today the university has a "dual role." The AAUP secretary's notes recorded the basics of Perkins's statements:

On the one hand, the university as the creature of society served as an agent of society and, on the other hand, the university became the chief critic of society. [Today the] balance between these roles is fluid and presently shifting towards emphasis on the agency role with recognition that provision of higher education to those members of society capable of taking advantage of such an education is a responsibility of the state. . . . The agency role has been enhanced by the emergence of "activist" elements who share the belief that the university community should become "involved" in seeking solutions to social problems. . . .

Under the present volatile and tense circumstances, the scholar must recognize an obligation to exercise academic freedom with responsibility. In the area of race relations, which President Perkins singled out as the single "most necessary adjustment facing Cornell over the next five years," the University community is challenged to convince the blacks that their consensuses are our concern. Only if we successfully meet this challenge can we expect black Americans to suppress the feeling they now share widely that they must produce direct action.[73]

In a nutshell, the university must adjust its objectives to prevent conflict with minorities.

Conclusions

The McPhelin affair was important for several interrelated reasons. It revealed the growing racial awareness of many students in the AAS and their determination to no longer tolerate what they considered racial insults. By galvanizing the AAS and sympathetic faculty and by moving the administration, the affair set the stage for the coming year. Miller and the top administrative brass had hoped that their policy of avoidance would prevent Cornell from becoming Berkeley, Wisconsin, or Columbia; events would prove them wrong. In Sindler's view, one reason was the pattern of appeasement that the administration now embraced. "The McPhelin controversy made highly visible for the first time elements of what came to be understood as a patterned set of defective responses by the administration. . . . From an institutional viewpoint it would be hard to devise a posture more damaging than that voluntarily and presumptuously assumed by the dean of Arts and Sciences with the tacit approval of the president."[74]

There is no doubt truth in Sindler's appraisal, but the picture he and many of his persuasion painted was one of a guilt-ridden administration and faculty who did not have the courage of their convictions to defend the principles of a liberal university. This portrayal was true for many. Yet another, deeper force was at play, a force to which Perkins gave rather clumsy voice in his speech at the Cornell AAUP: a new conception of the university as an instrument of social progress and social justice, not simply as an instrument for the Socratic pursuit of truth. In normal times the two conceptions coexist in various states of constructive or potentially destructive tension.[75] These were not normal times, however, and Cornell would undergo the throes of conflict. The McPhelin case offered the first glimpse of the central battle that would come to higher education in the ensuing years.

The administration's reasons for establishing the Williams Commission and circumventing established procedures signaled this deeper change. The established procedures the Cornell AAUP endorsed had been crafted during the McCarthy era. Unlike the cases of the 1950s, the McPhelin case put the entire institution on trial for unconscious racism. In such a then unprecedented case, the established procedures—which dealt with questions of individual culpability, not general or societal guilt—were inadequate as well as substantively out of tune with what was happening. (A similar conflict between individual versus group rights and individual versus societal responsibility also came to the constitutional law and politics of equal protection at this time—a conflict that has still not been resolved.)[76]

The response to McPhelin also represented a move away from liberal notions of justice, which are premised on individual responsibility and accountability. Such individualism also comports with the liberal notion of the mission of the university, which Richard Hofstadter defined as "intellectual individualism" in his famous speech at Columbia's graduation in 1968 amid the turmoil there.[77] Moreover, the reaction to the McPhelin affair contributed to engendering a distrust of the new judicial system that was coming into being under the aegis of Cornell's paradigmatic liberal, Sindler. As seen in Chapter Two, Sindler premised the new judicial system on principles of freedom and individual responsibility. But the administrative response to McPhelin circumvented the system, and the emerging doctrines of Black Power and racial sensitivity, which emphasized group recognition and allegiance, challenged the presumptions of individualism and individual responsibility on which the system rested. As we will see, many Cornellians were unsurprised when students flouted the new judicial boards in 1969.

In rejecting established procedures for adjudicating responsibility, the university was rejecting liberal notions of individualism in favor of a communal obligation to prevent racial offense. Henceforth individuals and their ideas would be accountable to the collective egalitarian goals of the evolving institution. The AAS, which was gaining a political sophistication that dwarfed that of any other group on campus, including SDS and the administration, understood this. It knew that it had the political and moral high ground and that the administration feared it. The AAS had not yet achieved what it wanted, an autonomous black studies program premised on the political and pedagogical tenets of Black Power. Only the politically naive could honestly hope that such a group would fold its fledgling wings. Though the AAS and its supporters' lack of appreciation for academic freedom in the McPhelin affair was troubling, some supporters of traditional notions of academic freedom were remiss in failing to grasp what was at stake for black students and for forgetting that students should also have a meaningful measure of academic freedom; McPhelin's inability to respond adequately to criticism was a factor in this regard. Furthermore, racism—which denies the very reality of individual responsibility and thought—undermines the principles of liberal education just as much as race-conscious restrictions on what should be taught, said, or even thought.[78]

Among other things, the Cornell upheaval of the late 1960s was also a product of the more general rise of student power in relation to traditional authority, including that of professors. Sheila Tobias, then an administrative assistant at Cornell, remarked that the Cornell crisis represented the birth pains of a more egalitarian ethic of higher education. In relation to the McPhelin case, she remarked, "There were big issues here—academic freedom, the responsibility of the faculty. This was a transition from yesterday's universities to tomorrow's, you and I would say today. . . . [Today] I'm responsible for the ideological base of my curriculum. I have to justify it, and I have to present equal time."[79]

The AAS's claims against McPhelin merited concerted attention, but they were troubling in their own right. McPhelin's views were not overtly racist; and once we move from the moorings of the traditional notion of racism to embrace the logic of institutional racism, any remark that could insult the self-esteem of an affected group can be labeled racist, including ideas presented in intellectual honesty rather than for the purpose of derogating or debasing anyone. In other words, though the concept of institutional racism can be useful in illuminating the effect of racism in society and institutions, it can cripple intellectual freedom when it is operationalized or used as the basis for academic policy. And what is a university for if not to provoke thinking and learning through the presentation of *all* relevant ideas? At the conclusion of the crisis of 1969, a leading Cornell liberal and critic of the government's Vietnam policy accused students and the university of supporting a new kind of McCarthyism in following the logic of institutional racism.[80] That logic, which emerged in the wake of the McPhelin case, essentially made any meaningful criticism of minority students' views off limits at the university. It constituted a license to be free from criticism and critical thought—the ethic of self-esteem (a component of the pedagogy of recognition) as opposed to the ethic of liberal constitutional citizenship that presupposes intellectual toughness. Sindler maintained that this state of affairs operated over the next year. In addressing Brown's letter on the McPhelin case, he argued:

A concern for academic freedom was conspicuously absent from the Dean's gloss. This absence implied that academic freedom was irrelevant to the McPhelin controversy . . . or that it was secondary to eradicating "institutional racism." . . . The impression gained by some faculty was that the president was aware of the obligation, but that he would not permit academic freedom to be used as a "cloak" for offending the sensitivities of blacks and other students. During the academic year, he was quoted as characterizing his position on the possible conflict between academic freedom and campus pursuit of social justice as that of a "mugwump." At times it appeared that he considered academic freedom to be mostly an attribute of faculty authority and privilege, a vested interest of one side of a power dispute.[81]

How could Cornell ensure the education opportunities of minority students in the classroom without violating academic freedom? No one knew. And by burying the Williams Commission report and adopting measures that in effect avoided dealing with this difficult question publicly and forthrightly, the administration short-circuited the difficult deliberations, building of alliances, and mutual understanding under pressure that were necessary (if not sufficient) to moving toward a solution.

The absence of democratic politics was a cardinal mistake because there was little common ground among the contending parties (this was also a function of the multiversity). Government Professor Peter Sharfman, who had just arrived at Cornell, observed that the lack of mutual understanding was striking during the year that led to the Straight crisis. Sharfman considered himself a progressive who sympathized with student activists. His observation showed how shocking the revolutionary turn was to many Cornell faculty and how divided the university was by factions wearing ideological blinders:

> I had not only no sympathy but also *no comprehension* of those who wanted to change Cornell itself. And there was no counterview provided by those in the Government Department, so I was totally unable to see the other side. Even Hacker did not [provide a counterview]. Even those who disagreed with Sindler accepted his premises. It was not until things went "kablooie" that I was even *exposed* to the other point of view. This was typical of those I talked to. For most faculty, you were on the left or the right, and that's who you hung around with. There was almost no communication between the two. I always stuck to my position about the responsibilities of the university. The university must offer an arena for alternative views about how the country is to be run, to avoid the slippery slope toward communism or fascism.[82]

The AAS's tactics were further troubling because they politicized the teaching and study of racial issues to an extent that made honest discussion and analysis of such issues extremely difficult. Professors told of student "monitors" appearing in class, keeping their ears open to what was said about race. After McPhelin, who would dare to say something in favor of, say, the Moynihan Report, even if it were honest and relevant? In this respect Cornell was yet again a microcosm of broader national trends: the Moynihan Report was rejected across the country. As Andrew Kull remarked in 1992, "The political furor that engulfed the Moynihan Report entirely overshadowed its implicit policy recommendations, and it placed further inquiry into black cultural disadvantage virtually off-limits for the generation of sociologists that followed. Twenty-five years later, the reverberations of that old controversy still obscure the extraordinary interest of the document as a political and historical landmark."[83] Moynihan's intention was to build a national consensus behind affirmative policies to alleviate poverty. Shelving his report was therefore symptomatic of the retreat from common solutions based on an integrationist ideal.

This is not to say that the Moynihan Report was not fair game for criticism—far from it. Most important, as Garner and others claimed, the report unfairly lumped the black community together as a whole in its analysis of family pathology. And racists could, and did, pounce on its conclusions concerning dysfunction to justify racist positions. Furthermore, it should be acknowledged that the report did spark an avalanche of criticism, especially studies on the strengths of black families and cultures (studies countering the damage imagery embodied in the report) and the viability of alternatives to the white, middle-class approach to family arrangements. These studies represented an orthodoxy in their own right.[84]

But it is one thing to criticize and another thing to silence. The report could have served a constructive purpose because of the grains of truth it contained and because wrestling with its conclusions and critiquing it in an intellectually honest fashion would have contributed to advancing knowledge in this crucial domain. As free speech theorist Jonathan Rauch has said, "We all benefit enormously from living in a society which is rich with prejudices, because strong opinions, however biased or wrongheaded, energize debate. . . . The notion that error is never a crime—[and] may indeed be an inspiration—frees us to think imaginatively."[85] Yet the left's reaction to the report engendered a moratorium on discussing such issues in public until conservatives broke the silence in the 1980s, thereby stealing the debate over the family from liberals. By the 1990s liberals had finally joined the bandwagon, publishing works on the need for strong families that echoed the report.[86]

Applying these points to McPhelin's class, we can draw a number of conclusions. There is no way around the conviction that McPhelin's ideas should have been protected, for any other stance derails the pursuit of truth in favor of one set of ideas. Garner's comments before the commission show the desire to prevent ideas deemed unfavorable or insulting to the politics of recognition. But there is a difference between causing offense as a consequence of the honest presentation of ideas and causing harm for the sake of hurting per se. There was no evidence that McPhelin said what he did for the purpose of discriminating on grounds of race. That said, students have academic freedom, too—a principle with special meaning when controversial ideas are professed. McPhelin's true error lay in his reluctance (even refusal) to allow meaningful student response. In other words, the answer to the dilemma posed by the McPhelin incident lies in promoting the academic freedom of all parties and keeping the market of debate open. McPhelin also simply failed to be a good teacher who is aware of the meaning and consequences of his statements. Even Walter Berns, for whom the McPhelin case was a defining moment at Cornell, admitted in our interview that McPhelin should have been more "careful" and that poor teaching was a part of the problem. But this is a pedagogical issue that should be dealt with informally (and carefully, as such considerations can be disguised forms of censorship); it is not something that can be legislated. And Berns was unequivocal about defending McPhelin's academic freedom once the line was drawn. Like many others who take this position, it was out of respect for the students, expecting them to respond to what they considered erroneous ideas with intellectual arguments, not obstruction.

Finally, the reaction to McPhelin and the Moynihan Report reflected the national disintegration of the liberal consensus about race and justice. Kull depicts the historical process at work:

> Events conjoined in the summer of 1965 to mark a watershed in the struggle for racial equality. . . . When the Moynihan controversy was at its height, the background of recent events included not only the enactment of the Voting Rights Act and the Howard University address [in which President Johnson called for the War on Poverty and universal equality in America], but also the Vietnam buildup, the commitment of American ground troops to combat, and the riot in Watts. The vehemence with which the Moynihan Report was condemned, particularly on the political left, suggests the suddenness with which the familiar liberal assumptions about the preconditions of racial equality were perceived as erroneous.[87]

The assassinations of Martin Luther King Jr. and Robert Kennedy in 1968 represented a fatal blow to the liberal integrationist consensus. Kennedy and King were the last prominent national politicians to possess credibility across the racial and economic divides. With them gone, no leaders stepped forth to uphold the liberal and integrationist principles. The Republican Party, led by Richard Nixon, had already begun its policy of racial division based on its famous "southern strategy," and the Democratic Party was only a few years from adopting principles of identity politics for party delegates and decision making.[88] The crisis of liberalism was now at hand at Cornell and in the nation; liberal notions of education, justice, and citizenship were openly challenged. Whether Cornell could find a way to reconcile liberal principles with racial justice was the most important question for the future of the university.

CHAPTER FIVE

SEPARATION OR
INTEGRATION?

The McPhelin incident made the development of a black studies program all the more imperative in the eyes of all concerned. It also legitimated more student input than most participants had been inclined to accept.

But two tracks were emerging: a program more consistent with the established principles of liberal education versus one based on Black Power, student power, and the politics of recognition. As seen in Chapter Three, institutions of higher learning were starting to wrestle with this tension by 1968. A similar debate had also been raging in the famous battle over "community control" in the Ocean Hills–Brownsville school districts in Brooklyn, where local activists were seeking to institute a curriculum based on Black Power and self-help in the name of fostering pride and inspiring youngsters to learn. Tamar Jacoby, Diane Ravitch, and others have shown how this struggle engendered intense controversy, and the anti-Semitism that had been festering in the thinking of some blacks erupted.[1]

The Ocean Hills–Brownsville dispute served as a precedent for Cornell, especially as many AAS members hailed from New York City and Brooklyn. Jacoby said, "Liberal integrationists [the Ford Foundation and similar organizations], trying to do good, had backed and bankrolled a band of angry separatists, then watched, not understanding, as the militants killed all hopes of racial harmony."[2] The main difference was that whereas the liberal teachers' unions led by Albert Shanker managed to thwart—at great pain—the ascendency of the movement in Ocean Hills, no such institutionally entrenched resistance existed or arose at Cornell.

During the fall semester a struggle broke out over which faction would have its ideology expressed in the black studies program. The Black Power faction won over the moderate faction and told the university, in effect, that it would destroy Cornell if the program was not adopted. This faction's excesses and failures led to the ascension of a less radical faction early in the next semester.

The black consciousness movement spoke to deeply felt needs of self-identity and collective identity and the desire to atone for America's greatest historical injustice. As James Turner said, black students wanted a program and a curriculum that addressed their desires to discover their historical, group, and individual identities. Irving McPhail portrayed the drive for a black studies program in terms of political awareness: "That agenda basically derived from both an acceptance of our needs as African-American students at Cornell and an awareness of what is happening on other campuses as well as a growing political awareness from reading and studying culture. We were the foundation for black studies, in a very significant sense. My pride of my involvement and our involvement in that period is the fact that we were really the vanguard group."[3]

The politics and psychology of respect stood at the center of the movement at Cornell and in America. Malcolm X, whose teachings changed the lives of many AAS leaders, taught that separation, independence, self-defense, and solidarity would help to secure the important goals of respect and recognition. Malcolm endorsed black nationalism for reasons that echoed in the stand of the AAS. He observed that decolonized Africans "have gained . . . recognition and respect as human beings much faster than you and I. . . . Our people are within our rights to protect themselves by whatever means necessary. . . . Education is an important element in the struggle for human rights. It is the means to help our children and our people rediscover their identity and thereby increase their self-respect."[4] The black studies program that many envisioned at Cornell would build on this understanding. As Tom Jones said in the aftermath of the Straight crisis, "Our struggle for self-determination has been operating on three levels: the political, the psychological, and the economic. . . . About March 1968, black students began a program of trying to develop a black studies program. . . . The purpose of our black studies program was, number one, to give us that psychological freedom of self-definition, to define what we are now, what we have been as a people and as a nation in the future."[5]

The politics of recognition also sprang from Hegel, who spoke of the relentless "struggle for recognition" as the fundamental human drive in society. The fight for freedom and the drive for recognition are sides of the same human coin. The struggle, epitomized by the master-slave encounter, can lead to violence and domination or a precarious state of equality based on mutual respect—the basis for equal citizenship.[6]

Hegel's bottom line is that the struggle for recognition and respect is an important part of our being, but it is fraught with conflict and tension, for even though the quest for recognition is the drive that establishes community, it also embodies conflict and violence that can destroy the sense of community. That is why the eruption of the politics of recognition at the university promised a just community at the same time that it threatened conflict.

At Cornell the crisis over black studies jumped back and forth between these two impulses. In history, whites "won" by dominating blacks, particularly in the form of slavery.[7] It was now time for black assertion in the face of this domination. Turner said that the works of Frantz Fanon were crucial to the development of black consciousness in the 1960s. In *The Wretched of the Earth,* Fanon advocated revolt as a means to regain the "full stature of man": "A people's victorious fight not only consecrates the triumph of its rights; it also gives to that people consistence, coherence, and homogeneity. Armed conflict alone can really drive out these false-hoods created in man which force into inferiority the most lively mind among us and which, literally, mutilate us."[8]

From this perspective, the politics of recognition that began in the '60s is not a new phenomenon but a culturally specific embodiment of a universal struggle.[9] It was time to confront the oppressor. The question would be whether this confrontation would embody a new freedom or a new form of oppression in its own right.

In this view, freedom means confronting the historical oppressor and risking one's life, if need be. Malcolm X knew that whites' willingness to defend freedom with their lives was the secret to their power and their freedom and that black men and women could learn from this inner truth. In addressing the ultimate showdown between "master and slave," Hegel maintained that overcoming the fear of death is a crucial step in attaining recognition and freedom. "It is solely by risking life that freedom is obtained. . . . The individual who has not staked his life may, no doubt, be recognized as a Person; but he has not obtained the truth of this recognition as an independent self-consciousness."[10]

Racial minorities were not the only ones to grasp this logic in the 1960s. Indeed, SDS cofounder Tom Hayden also captured the heroic ethic of life-risking commitment in an interview with James Miller in the 1980s. "On a theoretical level, you can say that we believed in wanting to make history and achieve civil rights. But there was something else: the middle-class emptiness of alienation that people talk about, and then suddenly confronting commitment. The whole emotion of defining not only yourself, but also your life by risking your life, and testing whether you're willing to die for your beliefs, was *the* powerful motive, I believe."[11]

As the clamor for a black studies program grew louder at Cornell, the activists sought to "heighten the contradictions" between black and white and developed an almost romantic willingness to put their lives on the line in the name of freedom. AAS members with more perspective felt that such sentiments constituted excess.

The emerging ideology and politics were captivating and uplifting. But they also posed problems for the university. First, they corresponded to the values of the activists and militants who did not represent all blacks on campus. Activists accused nonconforming students of "false consciousness," thereby justifying their acting as a kind of vanguard party, as Lenin had once justified in *What Is to Be Done?* Other black students, however, were less hostile to the university and whites and more integrationist in their thinking. Paul DuBois said, "The only action that we can uncover does have an integrationist bent to it, in part, because not only do we have to go where the resources are, we also have to get a lot of people throughout this society involved who are simply not of our color. That means, of course, we've got to have those skills, that philosophy, that ethic that involves all the people across this society who are willing to do something about racism."[12]

DuBois's posture seemed more consistent with the traditional notion of the university, which embraces the idea of universality within the diversity of peoples and minds. Experiences, interests, and viewpoints vary among individuals, groups, and cultures, but reason is universal. It is therefore possible to have one community of the mind that overrides—even transcends—the conflict of the many. It is also therefore possible to have a principled rule of law that provides justice for all.[13] To the extent that the radical version of black studies (as opposed to the more liberal, moderate versions that competed with it) contested the very possibility of universality, common reason, and transcendence of difference, it challenged the very foundation of liberal education and law.[14]

The AAS also challenged the university for other reasons, each of which reflects the deeper conflict just mentioned. Cornell, like many universities, had rather strong policies of faculty control of educational policy, including the selection of courses and curricula, the granting of course credits and academic degrees, and the hiring criteria for instructors. The basic idea was that the faculty are the best source to ensure academic standards in the educational programs and in staff. Of course, the very notion of such standards presupposes that intellectual criteria transcend politics and self-interest, at least to some sufficient extent. But the activist wing of the AAS was beginning to contest this assumption, as were other student activists, including members of SDS. In their eyes, academic standards were smoke screens for white power and control and the protection of the status quo.

Academic standards also included such key ingredients as academic freedom and free inquiry, faculty control, and academic credentials. But the McPhelin case convinced activists that academic freedom protected racism; and at that time the number of black instructors with sufficient academic credentials was very limited. As David Brion Davis and others sought to bring distinguished black talent to Cornell to teach, they found themselves in competition with universities all over the country. Credentials were hurdles.

The civil rights movement and SNCC had shown how important it was to put one's life on the line, an action that was as good a credential as the Ph.D. Activists wanted to be able to recruit instructors who were making history, not just studying it. A key example was Cleveland Sellers, a SNCC leader who came to Cornell to teach a course on black ideology in the spring of 1969 (he was part of the second phase of the fledgling black studies program). Having faced great danger and the murder of colleagues in SNCC's drive to bring civil rights and the vote to blacks in the Deep South, Sellers epitomized the activist willing to face death for the cause. He portrayed his struggle in moving fashion in *The River of No Return: The Autobiography of a Black Militant and the Life and Death of SNCC*, published in 1973.[15] But Sellers's appointment also caused dismay among many faculty, including Allan Sindler, who viewed Sellers—at least as a professor—as an ideologue rather than a scholar.[16]

Still, AAS activists such as John Garner were also very concerned with intellectual power as well as political and social relevance. Indeed, it appears that black students often had more respect for higher education than many white activists, perhaps because many blacks took their opportunities less for granted. Cornell AAS members often had critical things to say about their white allies in this regard, portraying some, perhaps unfairly, as spoiled children.

By broadening the notion of credentials, new ideas would pour into the curriculum that had excluded black ideas. But the strong emphasis on change and social relevance also challenged the notion of the university as a place fundamentally based on ideas. The advocates of social change, black and white, were opening the door to the politicization of the university in a manner that represented a qualitative change. Such things as politics, social justice, and social relevance would be not unavoidable by-products of higher education but essential ingredients of education's purposes. Of course, as seen in Chapter Two, the multiversity's many contracts with industry and the government had already compromised the ideal of the ivory tower; Cornell's Aeronautical Lab in Buffalo had been found to be producing chemicals for the Vietnam War.[17] So many felt that the university had already forsaken any claim to intellectual autonomy.

Cornell's First Response: The DuBois Plan

Responding to the McPhelin affair and the invigorated drive for a black studies program, Cornell officials held several meetings on May 20, including one of the Committee on Undergraduate Education. At this meeting Stuart Brown's comments were telling. According to the notes of that meeting, "A subtle shift had taken place, Mr. Brown explained, in the Afro-American students' demands for courses for black students only. . . . The students argue, and many agree with them, that the experience of living in the ghetto as a black person provides insights into modern Negro literature, in particular, which white students cannot have until they have studied the experience substantially. . . . The crucial issue in the next few years is racism in the University, the special needs of blacks, the question of contact with students on academic affairs is a first priority."[18]

At a CUE meeting on May 14, David Brion Davis had articulated a more balanced, less politicized vision of a program. He had just visited Yale and presented a report of his impression of its new program of black studies, which was being established as an interdisciplinary program. (Indeed, Davis was a key figure in forming the Yale program.) Davis proposed an extracurricular Program on the Black Experience for 1968–69 that would feature distinguished speakers on a variety of subjects, including art, culture, music, economics, history, politics, segregation, migration, the civil rights movement, and black nationalism and Black Power. Davis would get his program for the following year, but by then it was more or less a sideshow. "At Cornell [and] nationally, the separatist militant anti-white aspect of the Black revolution moved so far ahead that a lecture program of this sort was almost obsolete before it was conceived," Davis concluded in late 1968.[19]

Officials met several other times before the school year ended to discuss these and related issues. Then summer came and AAS leaders returned home. The plan developed by Ben Nichols and the AAS (see Chapter Four) had established the two courses by Dowd and McCall to be taught the next fall, as well as a course on black literature to be taught by John Matlock, but the conflict over the inclusion of white students had alienated the activists.

Into this vacuum stepped Paul DuBois, who had helped to broker the settlement over the McPhelin incident. DuBois was an original member of the AAS, but his integrationist views had begun to alienate him from the emerging leadership of the organization. He had developed close ties with President Perkins and, like Burak, was a consultant to the president. Perkins considered DuBois a spokesman for the AAS. DuBois had already assumed the position of heading the summer intern work-study program for black students, which placed black students in companies in upstate New York.

In late spring DuBois told Perkins that he and his associates would formulate a blueprint for a black studies program. DuBois seemed like the perfect choice: he was skilled at cultivating sources of potential financial support, and he was sharp, enterprising, and affable. Yet one crucial ingredient was missing in the arrangement: neither Perkins nor DuBois had cleared his assignment with the AAS.

DuBois had several goals. He wanted to increase the number of black students at Cornell, especially in the graduate programs (at that time there were only eighteen); ensure the educational quality of the program, a program that included black studies as well as practical economic and professional skills (it had to include such courses, DuBois remarked, "if it is to be anything more than a black literature, black history, black theory kind of haven for black ideologues or whatever"[20]); increase scholarship money for COSEP students; and establish a good home for the program. The structure of the program struck a balance between student power and traditional academic standards.

In private DuBois mocked the program that Nichols and the Joneses, Tom and Dalton, were struggling to put together. When word of this derision spread in the fall, it did nothing to mend relations between Tom Jones and DuBois. In the spring Perkins told DuBois to proceed with his plan during the summer. He also set up a big meeting for all concerned in September to consider DuBois's blueprint.

DuBois began meeting with interested graduate student friends, including Bob Jackson, Janet Williams, Bob Brown, and Steven Norris, who was white. The meetings dealt with such important questions as the nature of the courses, the role of whites, and whether the program should be set up as a center, a department, or a separate college. The group decided to push for a department whose faculty shared appointments in established departments (joint appointments, they felt, was the best method of ensuring quality, integration, and acceptance on campus). Unlike the AAS activists, the DuBois group appreciated the reasons why the process of faculty appointments was so arduous.

During the summer the group acquired money ($3,000 in an initial grant from Professor Chandler Morse, who was involved with the Center for Education), offices, and equipment such as typewriters. It also accumulated "an incredible amount of information . . . that swayed a lot of people's minds in preparation for this September meeting in which we got final approval for what we wanted" DuBois said.[21]

At the September 5 meeting DuBois presented his plan to Perkins, who had just spent several weeks in Europe. Fifteen people attended this meeting, including five students. According to Nichols, "It was kind of an amazing meeting in some ways. . . . Perkins would always check with Bob Jackson and Paul. . . . He was being very careful to make sure that anything that was going to go ahead had Bob Jackson's and Paul's OK."[22] Perkins assumed that Jackson and DuBois spoke for the AAS; Jackson had just completed his term as AAS president.

Sources recall that DuBois's proposal had good ideas in it, but they were not presented very well. Consequently, Perkins did not adopt the proposal but agreed to use it as a springboard. He did make the important decision to set up an advisory committee of students and faculty, as well as a committee to screen names for membership on the committee (Jackson, Morse, and Stuart Brown). The group decided to give the AAS steering committee the power to pick the student members. Eventually the membership included DuBois, Dalton Jones, Tom Jones, Janet Williams, Fenton Sands, Gayla Cook, Sandra Hearn, and Bert Cooper; Professors Morse, Nichols, McCall, Ulric Neisser (Psychology), and William F. Whyte (Industrial and Labor Relations); and administrators Stuart Brown, W. Donald Cooke (dean of the Graduate School), Faye Edwards (the aide to Gloria Joseph who was in charge of programs at the Straight), and David C. Knapp (dean of the College of Home Economics). Perkins then asked Morse to be the acting director, pending the appointment of a permanent director to be chosen by the committee and the AAS steering committee. Morse, an economics professor who specialized in rural poverty in Africa and elsewhere, was reluctant to assume the position, for he had doubts about his administrative abilities in this context, but he went along because he knew the position was temporary. The committee's mandate was to establish a program on the model of "area studies," which meant an interdisciplinary major in black studies that drew on existing programs and staked out its own territory. Perkins started it with $15,000 out of his contingency budget, with the stipulation that an official budget would be forthcoming.

DuBois and Jackson were emphatic about one thing: the entire project was contingent on approval from the AAS, which had scheduled a meeting in two weeks to discuss the issue when its members arrived back at school.

AAS Resistance to DuBois

When AAS members returned for the fall, the more militant ones greeted the new proposal with scorn. They felt that Perkins had adopted a moderate program behind their backs. At the end of the September 5 meeting, Morse had sensed a problem: "The students' approval was not the approval of the Afro-American Society as a whole."[23] When he came back, Tom Jones wondered, according to Nichols's recollection, "why Perkins would entrust DuBois with the responsibility of writing that proposal. . . . Why was there so much faith, apparently, that the black students would want to accept this, especially from people who hadn't been deeply involved in efforts [in the spring]?"[24]

DuBois realized he had a problem, so he met with the AAS's two leading militants, Tom Jones and John Garner, and the AAS steering committee in a three-hour session in mid-September. A week later he met with them again. At these meetings,

Jackson, Faye Edwards, and Don Lee, a resident lecturer on black poetry who was also part of the influx of activist lecturers, praised what the DuBois group had done.

Though it made the effort to appoint student members to the Advisory Committee, the steering committee (which consisted of Jones, Garner, Earl Armstrong, and others) never took the full issue to the AAS as a whole. Consequently, the Advisory Committee never achieved the legitimacy within the AAS that it had anticipated, leaving the door open to the more militant approach that Jones and Garner were now pushing. Nor did the black members of the Advisory Committee pass on the information about the committee's proceedings to the AAS. DuBois felt he was being stabbed in the back.

The reasons for the failure of the committee's promise were at least threefold: the committee's own incompetence, subversion by individuals who wanted a more radical and autonomous program, and the administration's reluctance or failure to ensure coordination. According to Davis, "There was, I think, a rather deplorable breakdown in [intrauniversity] communications in this respect since I had no idea what the administration was planning or what Professor Morse was doing, and this proved to be a liability when we in the History Department were urged and were very eager to go ahead in making an appointment in Afro-American History."[25]

Another problem was that the Advisory Committee, in Nichols's words, "never did produce . . . philosophy and aims." Nichols chaired its "substantive" subcommittee, whose task it was to develop a philosophy. But he demurred in this role because "I did not propose as the white faculty member to write a statement of philosophy and aims for Afro-American Studies."[26] Thus was the committee entrusted with developing what Dean Brown had proclaimed the single most important task of the university condemned to entropy.

Bert Cooper, one of the students who had complained about McPhelin, did not even attend the first two meetings of the committee. When he came to the third meeting, Morse presented a list of black scholars who could be brought in to teach in the spring and who could also join the Advisory Committee. Cooper construed Morse's presentation as an attempt by the committee and the administration to co-opt the AAS. During the fall semester black members and visitors to Advisory Committee meetings often had disagreements about the qualifications of instructors in the new program: Why did they have to have "homes" in departments? Why did they need Ph.D.'s? As the semester wore on, DuBois grew progressively alienated from the proceedings. The committee worked on little except "a desperate search for a director." Cleveland Donald maintained that the appointment of Morse contributed to the problem. Like Nichols, Morse was so beholden to student power that he was reluctant to lead. Morse's inability (or refusal) to lead, coupled with the lack of communication among the relevant parties, compelled the activists to take matters into their own hands.

The failure of the Advisory Committee was another turning point, for it discredited the administration's efforts and shifted power to the militants in the AAS. According to Donald, the committee's actions and inactions "pulled the Radicals, who had given up on black students, back into the Afro-American Society, for now they had the opportunity to use a program to politicize and radicalize black students and to institutionalize their ideological perspective." And Armstrong's succession to the presidency of the organization had contributed to the vacuum because Armstrong was a first-generation student who "was a relatively uninspiring person," "an independent who lacked enthusiasm and the desire for leadership."[27] He had won the AAS election in late spring because black women voted for him against Jackson, who had relegated women to backseat roles in the AAS.

By early October two major conflicts broke out within the AAS: a fight between the militant radical factions of Garner and Jones and a struggle between these individuals' followings and DuBois. DuBois's not-so-subtle criticism of Jones's black studies program infuriated Jones, and DuBois's successful effort in recruiting people such as Nichols and Dalton Jones to his group added salt to the wound. DuBois described his rivalry with Jones and Jones's wife, Stephanie, as long-standing and bitter. "We exchanged very bitter words the . . . night Martin Luther King was shot, and generally I've despised both of them since around that time," DuBois remarked in 1969. The ascendency of Jones and Garner by late November forced DuBois to abandon the Advisory Committee. But DuBois called Garner "my single biggest political enemy."[28]

The battle between Jones and Garner for the leadership of the AAS was vicious. The only two inside sources I have been able to find on this battle were Corson and DuBois's report, but their observations are consistent with what others have said about related matters. "At one point he [Jones] and Garner were having a feud and threatened to kill each other and at one point I actually thought that . . . John Garner and his friends would in fact kill Tom Jones," DuBois said. "And so at an Afro-American Studies Program Advisory meeting I loaned Tom Jones a gun, I gave it to him in a little box. He accepted it with gratitude in order to help him protect his wife. I figured that from then on maybe Tom Jones and I would be friends." Later, however, Jones accused DuBois of planting the gun on him to get him into trouble.

DuBois described scenes of Jones and Garner threatening to kill each other and of them prowling around the Straight with chains, looking for one another. At one AAS meeting Garner's forces showed up with guns and knives. Jones and his ally Skip Meade drove up. As they left the car, Garner's group surrounded them, and they barely made it back to safety. And when they started to drive away, the assailants broke Jones's car window and threatened his pregnant wife. It was after this incident that DuBois loaned Jones his gun. In March 1969 Corson asked Jones about the battle with Garner. "I'd heard about a fierce fight, a physical, violent fight with chains, going after each other before the December 6 business. He said that between them, they controlled ninety percent of the black students, and they would resolve their differences in order to present a unified front."[29]

By the end of November Jones and Garner had decided to end their war and join forces, albeit precariously. Their ascendency dramatically changed the orientation of the AAS, as Donald described:

The initial contest for control of the Afro-American Society erupted, after a meeting in early October of 1968, into a fight between the major factions. Saddened and shocked by what happened, black students during the week ahead sought an explanation for their behavior. . . . They fixed responsibility for their behavior on the racist nature of the Cornell community, on the actions of Chandler Morse, on the university administration, and on themselves. Believing that the immediate problem of establishing internal unity could best be solved with and after the expulsion of whites from all activities impinging upon black people, the major factions decided to remove all whites from the Afro-American Studies Committee.[30]

The battles of October paved the way for the more unified actions of November.

The Howard Conference and the November Actions

On November 6 and 7 a professor of economics from Fairleigh Dickinson University spoke in Dowd's black economics class. Robert Browne talked about black studies and the need for an independent "black university." The talk was based on a paper, "Financing the Black University," that he was going to deliver the following week at a major conference at Howard University called "Toward the Black University."[31] The paper addressed the need for a black college that is relevant to blacks' needs and for financial resources from reliable sources. Black students at white universities, Browne contended, "are being taught from a perspective, from invalid premises, and in terms of an inimical value system." Acknowledging that established institutions must be committed to integrated courses and staff, Browne championed an independent college based on separatist logic and laid out a program and format for expenses. His talk intrigued students and gave Garner the idea that what blacks at Cornell really needed was "a building and a million dollars." Cornell administrators circulated copies of the paper among themselves for perusal.

A few days later the Advisory Committee supplied AAS students with funds to attend the conference at Howard. Jones and Garner had a heated argument over who should be selected.[32] Jones, DuBois, Garner, McPhail, Irene Smalls, Gayla Cook, and two dozen others attended, driving to Washington from Ithaca. The conference featured speakers on a variety of topics; the highlights were talks by Stokely Carmichael and Harold Cruse. Cruse's recent book *The Crisis of the Negro Intellectual* was already a classic in the black consciousness movement that had set the stage for the advent of Black Power.[33] Cruse and others brought serious intellectual weight to the conference, matched by Carmichael's political credentials, earned by putting his life on the line at SNCC. According to McPhail, the conference was intellectually and emotionally a "transformative experience."[34]

The conference was important for another reason: James Turner was in attendance. Jones and Garner concluded that the Advisory Committee had to go and that the program needed a director of their own choosing. They had already drawn up a list of possible directors, including Browne and Charles Hamilton, coauthor with Carmichael of the recently published classic *Black Power*. Turner, who had gained national recognition for leading the takeover of a building at Northwestern University in a drive for black studies not long before the conference, appeared on a panel that addressed the responsibility of the black university to the black community. Turner made a good impression on many people. The Cornell students approached him after the session and arranged a breakfast meeting with him the next morning. Turner recalled, "At this meeting they were explaining that we have this committee, a black studies committee, and we are looking at people who might be able to come to campus and give it shape or substance. All they knew was that there was exclusion in the curriculum, that what they were getting in these economics classes and political science classes was not an accurate representation of the life of black people. That most sociological courses were based on the notion of black people being unable to defer gratification."[35] The students decided then and there to push for Turner when they returned to campus.

The students returned to campus ready to act. At the conference they had learned the art of making nonnegotiable demands. The drive for a black university within Cornell also provided a way for activists to attain respect and further the cause without leaving college.

The militants made their first move at the Advisory Committee meeting of November 19. Larry Dickson, Gary Patton, and two other students in Garner's faction showed up and read a statement that declared that there was no point in negotiating with the enemy and that what they wanted was "a million dollars and a building."

In late November Morse had a discussion with President Perkins, Provost Corson, Steven Muller (vice president for public affairs), and others about the budget for the program. The administration had committed $76,000, but Morse and the AAS wanted considerably more. Muller then confided to Morse that "it was going to be difficult to raise money."[36] He also told Morse the administration could work on finding money, but not if the program segregated whites. A few days later Morse met with Jones at Jones's apartment and informed him of Muller's comments. Jones got angry and told Morse it would be foolhardy for the AAS to meet with Muller. A few days later the December uprising commenced. According to observers, Jones underwent a "great shift" after meeting with Morse and started cooperating with the Garner faction. According to Donald, once the Garner faction gained temporary control, "the coalition had fed them [AAS] a steady diet of drums, honkeyisms, and black unity."[37]

The December Actions

After Dickson's announcement at the November 19 Advisory Committee meeting, the students asked the committee to postpone meetings until the AAS planned its next move. But the panel did schedule Turner to come to campus on December 6 to meet with the committee.

On Tuesday evening, December 3, Dalton Jones chaired a meeting of forty to fifty AAS members to review the status of the Afro-American Studies Program (AASP). (The lack of attendance at AAS meetings was discussed, indicating that the brewing confrontation was not a mass action.) According to the AAS's report of the meeting, Tom Jones asserted that the "whole structure of the Advisory Committee had to be changed because we [black students] never had anything to say about the structure in the first place, but were more or less co-opted into the 'package deal' developed over the summer by Paul [DuBois] and accepted by President Perkins." Garner then said that the AAS should "take over the committee completely." Jones replied that such a move would require the input of all 259 black students at Cornell, but Garner said the present group should decide to move now. After a lengthy report on the Advisory Committee's action that term, Garner reiterated his belief that blacks should be the masters of their own program, "controlling it completely." Garner moved that they "break all ties with the whites on the committee and assume total control of finances and decision-making processes." [38] They therefore created a twenty-two-member "all black advisory board" consisting of members of Tom Jones's and John Garner's factions and some members of the previous committee (Hearn, Edwards, and Williams, but not Jackson or Dalton Jones). The group then decided to wait until after Turner's visit before taking further action.

The next day the new committee met briefly and developed an embryonic plan for an "institute." The director, they concluded, should be someone "oriented toward a black nation and the whole concept of nationalism, who had contacts with other black potential staff members." The purpose of the institute was "to create the tools necessary for the formation of a black nation." The building at 320 Wait Avenue would serve as the AASP's home next semester (the university had already set the premises aside for this purpose beginning in fall 1969; at the moment it housed the Department of Science Education). The committee also stressed that more blacks should be recruited to Cornell and that all black students recruited to Cornell be required to "take certain courses offered in the Institute, in replacement of requirements such as Freshman Humanities, etc." The next evening the members decided to take over all the money under Morse's jurisdiction at Turner's meeting with the old Advisory Committee the next day.

On December 6 Morse showed up to meet with Turner in the Planning Office in the basement of Day Hall, the administration building. The AAS had scheduled Turner's visit on the spur of the moment. Morse said, "The reason for the timing and the short notice and so on was quite obvious; it was part of the tactic." [39] Fifty students, many uninvited, confronted Morse and a handful of his colleagues. Bringing in large numbers of students, unannounced, represented a new tactic that the militants had adopted after the Howard conference. It would be used again.

Turner sat down at a table across from Morse. Garner then read a statement disbanding the Advisory Committee and asked Morse to turn over an accounting of the committee's finances by Monday (in three days). He then issued the ultimatum: the fifty students present constituted the new Advisory Committee. The new committee ceremoniously voted 50–0 to exclude whites. All this time Turner sat implacably across the table.

The action continued on Friday. At noon six black students evicted a professor and two employees from 320 Wait Avenue, the university-owned building that the administration had previously approved (that same morning) as the home of the

Afro-American Studies Program beginning in fall 1969. The six left after posting a note on the door that proclaimed that as of noon Saturday the building would come under the exclusive control of the "Afro-American Institute."

The administration took what can best be described as a qualified hard stand on the takeover. "We don't accept the coup d'état of Friday," Muller told the press. "Everybody is hopeful this can be solved on this campus without violence." Still, after what the *Sun* called "an extraordinary series of weekend meetings by top University officials, including President James Perkins," and "desperately seeking information from Afro-American Society spokesmen, who were not easily found," the administration issued a statement that upheld the right of the program members to continue using the building, at the same time warning that denial of use of the building to others would be a cause for disciplinary action.[40] But the administration advised the current occupant, the Department of Science Education, to stay away, and when classes resumed for the spring term in February, the administration made the entire building available to the AAS, giving it effective control.

On December 7 Dickson spotted *Sun* reporter (and future managing editor) C. Barton Reppert across the street from 320 Wait. Without warning, he struck Reppert in the face, knocked him down, and seized his film. (Reppert filed harassment charges in city court rather than relying on the student conduct boards because he had no confidence in the university system of justice. In April 1969, Dickson pled guilty to harassment in Ithaca city court, receiving a suspended sentence of fifteen days.) Dickson also attacked the photographer who accompanied Reppert. According to sources, this act turned the *Sun* against the movement for the remainder of the academic year.[41]

Friday, December 6, the traumatized administrative staff met from about 7:30 p.m. until 1:30 a.m. The next morning Corson received a call from Garner, asking the provost to supply him with information about the decision-making channels of the university. Corson complied. At 4:00 p.m. Saturday, members of the Faculty Council, the Faculty Committee on Student Affairs, and department chairs met and decided that Perkins should write a response to the AAS.

At noon on Monday, December 9, Corson and Morse went to 320 Wait Avenue to receive the AAS's formal demands. They had decided that Perkins should not come and that they would not sign anything on the spot. Perkins had contracted a disabling case of the flu, so he was indisposed in any case. Unfortunately, the illness served to exacerbate the tensions between Jones and Perkins. At 11 o'clock the previous night Jones had called Perkins at his home, inquiring as to whether the president was going to attend the meeting at 320 Wait on Monday. Perkins was sleeping off his illness, so his wife, Jean, answered the phone; she would not let Jones talk to the ailing president. Bad words passed between Jones and Mrs. Perkins. Chafing under the growing pressure, she said things that were not advisable.

When Morse and Corson arrived at 320 Wait, they spotted Jones, Garner, Faye Edwards, and the secretary of the AAS sitting in four chairs in the middle of the room across from three empty chairs. Fifty to sixty AAS members lined the walls of the spacious room. The first person to speak was Jones, who was agitated; he pointed out the "significance" of the empty chair that was meant for Perkins. He then launched into an attack on the Perkinses, asserting that Jean Perkins's words had exposed the truth that her husband hoped to rid Cornell of black students. The couple expected the AAS "would try to burn down the University and she hoped they would and that they would burn themselves up with it." [42] Corson and Morse found the setting and tactics of the meeting so distressing that the president's staff decided that a top-level university official would not meet again with the AAS on its own turf, only on the administration's or at a neutral site.

Garner then asked Morse for a statement of the committee's expenditures and presented the demands. The centerpiece of the demands was the establishment of an autonomous program, funded by the university but controlled and administered by black students. The AAS presented a constitution, "Charter: College of Afro-American Studies," and demanded Perkins's authorizing signature by the next day, December 10. The constitution called for a governing board of directors that included a black director, black staff, and black students, with the students controlling half the board's votes; power for the college to define its own degree and degree requirements; 320 Wait as the home of the college; and a minimum budget of $250,000 per year, with $50,000 in an "emergency fund" to be available "at all times."

An AAS member—code-named "Warema" by Cleveland Donald—created a model constitution "that attempted to camouflage the organization's radical concepts behind the foliage of traditional academic rhetoric" and liberal concepts of antidiscrimination and equality before the law.[43] Warema assumed that this model would then be applied by students for revolutionary ends. But the militant faction, which had less trust in the university and the future director, substituted its own model, which provided details and set up a structure of control that sanctioned separatism. A source who requested anonymity, who had a contact involved in the internal AAS debate over the constitution of the proposed college, reported that on the surface (disregarding Donald's claim that it was a smoke screen) the original model looked a lot like the new program at Yale. The initial constitution was the product of a painstaking effort to be consistent with the bylaws and educational norms of the university. But AAS leaders rejected it because they wanted a more radicalized program that would also challenge the foundations of the university.

> The week before the crucial week [December 6–13] there had been a good bit of conflict within the Society. Indeed, for several weeks there had been a fairly rapid fluctuation in [the] leadership pattern with rather bewildering shifts in allegiance and in the particular people who went together in given factions. Because of the nature of the situation, those who could condemn others for their seeming Uncle Tomism or their subservience to white standards were thrust into more powerful positions, and consequently leadership turned less on the reasonableness of one's appeals than on the antiwhite content of one's rhetoric, and this tended to bring a younger and more militant group to the front.[44]

Donald noted that the constitutional shift provided an answer to a dilemma that confronted black activists: how to participate in revolutionary change while remaining at an elite white campus (SNCC members had left school to risk their lives). Staying made sense only if the confrontation with the university was taken to a new level. Employing the dialectical logic of revolutionary Marxism, Donald observed that if black students remained, "they should constantly *heighten the contradictions, that is, they ought to raise and prove, through word and deed, that integration had not worked. . . .* Tactically this could be done through the process known as *confrontation. . . .* The radicals desired to *raise the level of awareness* by heightening the contradiction through the process of confrontation. . . . Simultaneously, Radical ideology combined the objective of raising the level of awareness among blacks with another objective, the destruction of the university—if not its complete destruction, at least its disruption."[45] Reconceptualizing the university as the antithesis (and hence the enemy) of black class and self-interest was now an integral part of the movement toward true freedom and self-respect.

With the demand for the autonomous college, Garner presented a document of "other needs" at the December 9 meeting. These included $59,560 to finance the 1969 spring term, exclusive use of the Elmhirst Dining Room in the Straight for blacks, a black psychiatrist by February, payment of black students' tuition fees directly to the new college, power for the college to pick students to work in the admissions and financial affairs office "with full control over the admission of black students to Cornell University and the allocation of financial aid," delivery to the college of library books deemed relevant to the college, and complete files of all examinations given over the last five years (the AAS correctly pointed out that fraternities already had such compilations and that this gave fraternity brothers a big competitive advantage). After this remarkable meeting, forty-five top administrators and faculty members conferred for over two hours.

Between December 6 and 22 an avalanche of meetings took place. Perkins conferred with deans, staff, and professors whose judgment he trusted, among them Miller, Davis, Sindler, LaFeber, Dowd, and Morse. Sindler reported that he attended fourteen meetings during this period and that the average meeting lasted four hours. He characterized the meetings as "performing a kind of group therapy . . . in terms of hard advice and so on, it was a very, very time consuming and chaotic and formless way to try to solicit advice."[46] Others, however, found them exceptionally focused and astute. During this period the administration considered itself under siege. According to Corson, the period from the December actions through the end of February was more unnerving than the week of the Straight takeover. "The militants had only recently gained control of the Afro-American Society, and they were completely unpredictable. . . . In taking possession of 320 Wait Avenue they were forgoing any discussion of issues—something that Jones and Garner had consistently done. It was a new, and different, game."[47]

Perkins knew that he could not accede to the new demands. To buttress his case, he instructed Cornell legal counsel Neal Stamp to research the legal status of the proposal. The answer was clear: state law prohibited discrimination and also prohibited the establishment of a college without state approval. Perkins would henceforth use the legal obstacles as his primary justification for not endorsing an independent college. Some critics, such as LaFeber, contended that this strategy was doomed to failure. Perkins should have been more forthright with the AAS, telling them point blank that establishing an autonomous, racially exclusive college is not only illegal but also inconsistent with the fundamental principles of the university. Did the president have the stuff to take this stand? What did he believe, and why? And how willing was he to fight for what he believed? Was he as willing to risk a great deal as the morally serious students he confronted?

On December 10 Perkins wrote a memo to Gloria Joseph that revealed his growing sense of desperation at the turn of events and of the AAS's refusal to sit down and talk about the matter. The flu must not have enhanced his emotional state:

> I am most anxious to talk to and with members of the Afro-American Society who want to change the present structure of the Afro-American Studies Program. I am frustrated! First, they don't want to talk—just present demands which I am to sign at a specified time and place. Second, it suggests that a new structure is to be completely autonomous with no obligations or liabilities of any kind to Cornell. . . .
>
> You must try to explain to them the Office of the President cannot, repeat cannot, ever respond to an ultimatum. . . . If I were to respond to a demand under the threat of an ultimatum, every group would correctly decide that the way to get their share of the pie would be to coerce by ultimata. The Cornell community would be replaced by the Cornell jungle.[48]

Perkins's desperation was born of perplexity. In a rational world, reasonable men and women could work out their differences, no matter how far apart their views. And had he not been the great man who had opened the door to the promised land for the historically oppressed? By many accounts, he failed to grasp the depth of the militants' historical lament and the degree to which they held the liberal establishment accountable. He failed to comprehend that he and Cornell were now not the benefactors but the enemy, at least in the eyes of the militants. In this failing he was not alone. In his 1994 interview with Keith Johnson, however, Perkins maintained that he did indeed grasp the nature of his demonization. "It was only when the situation got very mean later on that they would become glaringly hostile, and they just wanted to make sure that I understood that I was the enemy. And I understood that. I mean, I got that message. And one of them said to me, 'Mr. President, don't think that we think the better of you because you're Chairman of the United Negro College Fund, because we know that all nigger lovers think well of the black colleges, because that's where they want us all to be.'"[49]

Among those who truly understood the revolutionary implications of the AAS's new stance were professors who would stand against the AAS in April, such as Berns and Sindler. Ironically, these individuals paid the AAS the most respect by taking the organization's goals seriously. According to Paul Rahe, a *Sun* columnist, in the AAS's eyes, "Perkins personified the weakness at the heart of late-sixties liberalism. . . . But there was respect for Berns, because Berns stood for something. They were afraid of Berns. But there was always respect." [50] In a twist of fate from which liberalism is still reeling, the great liberal benefactor was not only to be distrusted but was now also the enemy.

An example of the intensity that drove the militant faction is found in a report by Robert Rone, the AAS chairman of publications and public relations and a leading member of Garner's faction. The report, "The Need for Thought and Direction in the Black Revolution," was a memo to the AAS on the strategy and mentality that should govern the AAS's movement toward an autonomous program or college. Chiding his less militant colleagues and advocating an autonomous college, Rone mixed moral exhortation with the demonization of whites:

> We don't seem to realize that what we are really asking for is "power." We don't seem to realize that the beast we are dealing with will use all means at his disposal to maintain control of power. The beast is fighting throughout the world to maintain and increase his power. . . .
>
> In the context of Cornell, what "tools" do we have? Our Black bodies can be a tool, not necessarily the most effective one. Our minds are tools. The average honkie can be a tool if we know how to use him. . . .
>
> I am not saying don't hate white people. Hate can be a very effective tool to drive people, to organize them, and give them direction, but a tool is all that hate should be for a true black leader. A leader of black people cannot allow himself the luxury of hate. . . .
>
> If the Afro-American Studies Program can be achieved by threatening the honkie and not letting him on the committees, that's good. I'll be happy to see this tool added to our arsenal. [51]

On Monday, December 9, the AAS issued its ultimatum for a black college at 320 Wait, but Perkins did not sign on the dotted line. On Thursday, December 12, a story appeared in the *Sun* under the headline "Deadline Passes." The AAS held a meeting to determine how to respond. At this meeting the Garner faction made "rather fervent appeals for violence," according to sources. The faction simply could not gain enough support to carry the day, yet the moderates could not prevail either. "They could not speak out without fear of being castigated for the racist reasons I've mentioned," a source said. "There were no real ways they could communicate among themselves without great danger" at this point. Caught in a stalemate, the AAS had to decide to let the deadline pass and wait and see. [52]

Perkins's official response on December 11 combined firmness with concessions. He could not sign for a completely autonomous college or program, he wrote, because state laws did not permit discrimination and the law gave the power to create colleges to the state Board of Regents. Furthermore, if the program intended to operate within the framework of the existing colleges at Cornell, the faculty and the Educational Policy Committee would have to approve courses, credit, and faculty appointments. Perkins continued by stressing that the university was committed to a program of Afro–American studies "to be operative at the opening of the academic year 1969/70. There should be no doubt about this commitment." He also pledged that he would seek funds to start the program "on an interim basis" by the start of the semester that was a few weeks away.

Perkins also agreed to making 320 Wait Avenue the headquarters of the program (exclusively for its use) as soon as possible, to hiring a black psychiatrist "as soon as an appropriate candidate can be discovered," to securing a "Black Director" at the earliest possible opportunity, and to designating "appropriate space for a dining room" for the AAS. Moreover, he offered a fig leaf concerning the "possibilities of conferring greater autonomy on a program." Although there "are several reasonable possibilities" for creating a program with greater autonomy than other programs, such possibilities "cannot be developed by ultimatum. They have to be discussed." By not basing his reply on fundamental principles of liberal education, Perkins prevented himself from taking the initiative in the negotiating. The only way to gain the upper hand was to act from conviction. Belief and strategic power went hand in hand, as the AAS leaders knew so well.[53]

On Wednesday evening, December 11, black students met for the fourth consecutive night. The room was emotionally charged. "The largest number of black students to attend a meeting all year packed a room where candles glowed, incense burned, and brothers beat a warm rhythm on drums that Perkins had purchased for the Society," Donald wrote.[54] Perkins's response had gone only part of the way and had heightened the contradictions.

Garner began by telling the story of the students' struggle that year. Then, out of the shadows, came Tom Jones's voice. "Last year on the night Martin Luther King died while lying in a ditch, the pigs' bullets whirling over my head, I decided that Ithaca is too small a town to die in," he declared. Jones's remark took Garner aback; he considered it flippant and antirevolutionary. Jones explained, "All he wanted to do was prove to the brothers and sisters that the honkey was no good, and now that this had been proved everyone could go home better prepared to understand the nature of the racists' society." A physical confrontation almost broke out before order was restored. Though they agreed to take further action, the students left the meeting feeling adrift and shattered. "Since its takeover the coalition had fed them a steady diet of drums, honkeyisms, and black unity. Now their world had turned downside up as everyone stood isolated and alone. It is impossible to describe what happens when a black dream has been shattered," Donald reported.[55] The meeting revealed the precariousness of the coalition's grasp on power. Only forty to fifty students had been regularly attending meetings, and Garner's faction had only about fifteen members, of whom only seven or eight were truly dedicated to Garner's militancy and revolutionary call.

In the midst of the confrontation between the administration and the AAS, Stan Chess, the *Sun*'s editor, wrote an analytical piece designed to puncture the "white myth" that all Cornell's blacks thought alike. Chess pointed out that a majority of Cornell's blacks opposed the proposed AAS constitution and that AAS meetings usually amounted to little more than tactical sessions for the various planning groups.[56] Later in the spring many leaders admitted that the call for a completely autonomous college was misguided, "but at the time, people were threatened, you know, if they didn't go along with it."[57]

On Thursday afternoon, December 12, seven members of the militant faction took matters into their own hands by going on a toy gun spree for forty-five minutes. (Whether these students were operating on their own initiative or under the aegis of the AAS is not known.) The students pointed toy tommy guns at other students in front of the Straight, at one point trying to confiscate the camera of an *Ithaca Journal* reporter who was present. They proceeded down the street, disrupted traffic, and poked their guns into the ribs of a campus patrolman. (The patrolman did not pursue them, as had become the practice at Cornell.) They strode over to Day Hall, where they walked up the stairs to Perkins' office; when he came out, they walked away. While in Day they tipped over a sand-filled wastebasket for cigarette butts. They continued to Goldwin Smith Hall, the main building for the College of Arts and Sciences, where they overturned two candy machines, discharged a fire extinguisher, and ran down the hallways banging on doors of offices and classrooms. Then it was back to the Straight. On the way there they surrounded a campus patrol car and banged on it. Inside they proceeded to the Elmhirst Dining Room, which was closed, sat down, and demanded service. A waitress went to get help, but by the time she returned they had departed. Four of the seven were identified by witnesses and later charged with misconduct by the brand-new Student-Faculty Board on Student Conduct.[58]

Many individuals in the AAS and the Cornell community would describe the toy gun spree as more or less a prank. On the surface this might have been correct, but the act had a latent meaning much like the comedy scenes that foreshadow danger in Shakespearean tragedy. The spree was part of the serious escalation of threats that was taking place over the week. And the men who played with toy guns in December would be brandishing real rifles in April.

The AAS then held a meeting at 320 Wait, where it debated its next step and discussed the actions that the Garner faction had taken that day. Its members decided to build on what the activists had done by holding further demonstrations, this time with more participants. Garner also presented the AAS with a statement drawn up by Warema that was a reply to Perkins's response to the initial demands. The statement reaffirmed the commitment to an independent program and provided an extensive justification for it, but it also held out the possibility of more negotiations. This meeting, coupled with the demonstrations of that day, brought the factions of the AAS back together. The statement, which was read several times, helped students overcome their confusion and gave them heart to fight on. When the meeting ended at 1:00 a.m., ecstatic activists poured out into the street, banging on cars and jumping in the air. Perkins later depicted the students as "in euphoria." (His information was probably provided by campus security, which no doubt had the meeting under surveillance.)[59]

Leaders then took the new statement over to the *Sun*, which published it Friday in the spot normally allotted to editorials. This was the first time during this affair that the AAS presented an extensive argument for its case to the university community as a whole (other than the simple presentation of its demands earlier). The statement decried "compromise" and "integrated" programs and advocated student control. Building on Dean Brown's mea culpa in the aftermath of the McPhelin affair, the statement declared the AAS the physician designated to cure the disease of whites, which is racism:

> As long as whites design their own programs or define the limits of the Afro-American Studies Program . . . the programs thus implemented are founded on racism and can be of no benefit to anyone. . . .
> Moreover, the Blacks must have the right to define the role of white students in the program, even to the point of their restriction. . . .
> Because we have been led to expect the program which we have defined, we will accept nothing less. There can be no compromise between the physician and patient or between who defines and who controls.

At a news conference on Friday afternoon, December 13, Perkins spoke of his weariness with the AAS's tactics but said he would not seek to restrain these "exhibitions" so long as they remained "peaceful." And he expressed his credo: "I operate on the assumption that the Cornell community will function reasonably if I and my colleagues deal reasonably with these demands." Then he seemed to equivocate: "I am extremely reluctant to accept this idea of a college exclusive to one race, but I am not finally opposed to it. It would involve a rearranging of my own personality." [60]

Meanwhile, the AAS presented Perkins with a timetable, stating it would discuss the constitution with him on December 17. It also said it would announce its choice of a director on Monday and would meet Tuesday evening and promulgate a final "nonnegotiable constitution" for Perkins's approval on Wednesday, December 18.

The AAS held other demonstrations on that Friday the Thirteenth that were designed to dramatize and symbolize the reasons for its other list of demands. At 10:00 a.m. seventy-five students and some small children sat down outside Perkins's office in Day Hall with bongo drums and guitars. They remained about an hour, playing music and conducting a play-reading "seminar" that demonstrated the need for special class space for their program. When they turned down Perkins's offer to speak with them, he had a cart of food delivered to them. The students kicked the cart over, spilling its contents across the floor.

Around 11:00 a.m. students demonstrated for a black psychiatrist at the Gannett Health Clinic. From there they proceeded to the Ivy Room of the Straight, the campus's main public dining room. Thirty students jumped on tables and danced, upsetting several lunches; after the dancing they marched through the neighboring Elmhirst Dining Room, then went to three different libraries (the Uris Library for undergraduates, the Olin graduate library, and the library of the School of Industrial Labor Relations), removed an estimated thirty-seven hundred books from the shelves, and took them to the circulation desks. They informed the library staff that "these books have no relevance to me as a black student," dumped them on the floor, and removed drawers from the card catalogs. The demonstrations ended with the students playing music and conducting mock fights among themselves and with white bystanders at Goldwin Smith Hall. Then Saturday night at Barton Hall, playing African music, they marched in small columns across the length of the basketball court in front of the somewhat dumbfounded audience (most Cornellians knew little or nothing about the affairs under discussion), delaying the game for several minutes.

The administration knew the decisive moment had arrived. As Dean Miller told Perkins in a December 15 letter in which he adopted the militants' logic concerning standards, "The University is rapidly approaching a crisis of decision with ramifications of great academic significance." In Miller's opinion, "The Faculty would forego some, but not all, of its prerogatives in the expectation that your judgments would approximate their own." He spoke of "our well-worn habits" that "would lead us to seek appropriate professors" for the program.[61]

Arranging a Meeting

In moments of crisis, one pulls out one's best weapons. Perkins surrounded himself with the best advisers, holding emergency meetings with Muller, Miller, Davis, LaFeber, and Sindler, among others. Typically Perkins would facilitate and ask questions, letting the people around him contribute the substance. His objective was to see where the consensus of thought pointed. John Marcham noted that people "praise him for his great ability to handle a small group discussion and to draw out intellectual points from people. . . . He's a great committee chairman. It's no coincidence that practically every committee he's on nationally he's the chairman."[62]

Davis was one who received a call on December 15 to attend an emergency meeting. Thus began three days of "very prolonged affairs" whose objective was to draft a document responding to the AAS's last ultimatum. Davis singled out Sindler and Muller as particularly insightful during these pressure-packed marathon meetings. Muller's recommendations were practical and sound, while Sindler was "the one who was most searching in his thoughts and in the exactitude of his criticism . . . being willing also . . . to back down and to concede points to correct ideas."[63] An anonymous source described the sessions as "extraordinary," saying, "We knew that this was a very pressing and important matter, that great mistakes could be made, and thus when criticism was offered it was taken in a way you never see in ordinary committees. In other words, there was a tremendous contrast between this group . . . and every committee and board I've attended in fourteen years at Cornell. . . . Of course, it was sort of wartime conditions . . . but there was a give and take, a willingness to be candid and to back down, which you very seldom see with a group of men together."[64]

The first discussion on December 15 involved working on a memo from Perkins to the AAS in response to its latest ultimatum. The document that emerged reiterated the legal problems associated with an autonomous program in the absence of state approval but then suggested alternative models. If the students wanted a program that operated within the degree-granting structure of Cornell, they and the administration would have to find a way to collaborate with the faculty and the departments. An "institute" with "fellows" could work along these lines, similar to the arrangement of Cornell University Religious Workers. An independent institute or college with its own charter, however, "would involve a direct application to the Department of Education and the Regents. . . . We are sure that these matters can be settled fairly promptly." [65]

At 1:15 a.m. Tuesday, Perkins was awakened by a telephone call from an unidentified student who said he spoke for the AAS. The caller said the president's presence was "required" at 320 Wait Avenue at 11:45 a.m. Perkins told him he did not make dates in the middle of the night and asked that he call Perkins's office in the morning. In a letter he wrote later that day, Perkins expressed his concern about the call and told the AAS he could not rely on the authenticity of such callers (he had been receiving "a great many" calls from individuals claiming to speak for the society). He said that he awaited a reply to his last proposal and that they could meet with him in his office or at Kaufman Auditorium in Goldwin Smith Hall. According to a source, because of the phone call and other information that was pouring in, "it was clear that Tuesday the blacks were going to try to have some kind of confrontation where Perkins would have to reply formally to their demands. But there were all sorts of open questions." [66] The following portrayal of the meeting in Perkins's office is indebted to a source who asked to remain anonymous, corroborated by Miller's observations.

Like officers at war, Perkins's staff was very concerned about the setting for the climactic meeting. Recalling Corson's rude experience at 320 Wait, it was decided by Sunday that under no circumstances would Perkins meet the AAS on its own turf. But the staff also assumed that the delegation from the AAS would not consent to come to Perkins's office. So Perkins suggested Kaufman Auditorium as an alternative. To the staff's surprise, Garner agreed to come to Perkins's office in a delegation of three students.

Showdown in the President's Office

On December 17 a key Perkins adviser received another "emergency phone call" to come to Day Hall. [67] When he arrived, "the whole atmosphere was instantly different from Monday or Sunday." Plaincothesmen with walkie-talkies were everywhere, communicating with patrols around the campus. A student had reported overhearing a black student at a diner saying that Perkins was going to "get it today" if he did not accede to the demands. "There was a feeling of tension and of almost electric excitement here because the blacks were going to come today." Racial paranoia contributed to the mixture of fear and awe.

At 10:30 the AAS sent a message that it would be arriving at 1:00. So the staff (Sindler, who had to leave early, Muller, Davis, Perkins, Miller, and the anonymous source; Corson was in New York at a trustees meeting) had to work quickly on a document of response. They worked on every word carefully. "In fact, I never saw a document improve so rapidly in so short a time as to the clarity of the prose," the source said. [68] They felt pressure to produce a strong statement that was thoughtful and heedful of the political and normative complexities. On the one hand, it had to express the belief in the right of blacks to have a significant voice in the program and to combat racism; on the other hand, it would have to find a way to be consistent with the principles of free inquiry. The final product achieved this balance.

After finishing the document, Perkins asked Miller and another adviser to stay for the 1 o'clock meeting. Soon the third floor of Day Hall was evacuated. Only Perkins, a plainclothesman, and an adviser were present (Miller would arrive later). Perkins was munching on an apple, a meal that his troubled stomach could handle.

Shortly before 1 o'clock, Keith Ferdinand strode in with a tape recorder. He nodded coldly at the adviser. Perkins greeted him in an "overly friendly" manner and started talking about an unusual tapestry on the wall. Ferdinand appeared to be alienated by the conversation, which seemingly contrasted the elegance of the tapestry against his own lack of wealth and power. A few uncomfortable moments passed while Ferdinand set up his tape recorder. Moments later a parade of seventeen students filed into the office's anteroom. Perkins and his adviser were taken aback: they had expected only three, a much more manageable number. Perkins requested that only six come into the office, but before he could do anything, ten students walked into the office, leaving six or seven in the anteroom. (Ferdinand, Jones, Cooper, and Garner were the only ones clearly identified.) It was going to be an incredible two-hour meeting.

My source noted tension and competition between Jones and Garner, though Garner was clearly in charge. Jones's contributions "seemed to be attempts to attract attention, to be militant, to show that he could sass the president to his face . . . whereas Garner went in for none of that. . . . Garner spoke with . . . so soft a voice. . . . He never insulted President Perkins—he was a model of respectable behavior—but there was a kind of almost frightening impatience and about-to-declare-war tone to his very calm voice." Others provided the provocation, calling Perkins a liar and swearing at him. One tall individual was "very nasty, very provocative and aggressive. . . . He wore those sunglasses that reflect . . . and had on dungarees with a long pocket on one side out of which was sticking the handle of a very formidable knife, and he, like a number of others, stood during a good part of the meeting." The three officials (Miller had now entered) assumed that others were armed as well, but this was the only weapon they saw.

Perkins sat on a couch at the far end of the room, before a large round table. Students passed notes and walked around, sometimes back and forth in front of Perkins. At one point the man with the knife walked to the narrow spot behind Perkins's couch. "It was not intended as a place for people to go back of. But he went back in a threatening way, and he also came around and then sat down next to Perkins on the couch, put his arm around toward Perkins's shoulders, leaning over and looking at him in a very snarling, provocative way, and when Perkins would speak he would often come back with some rather insulting remark."

My anonymous source recalls the menace in the scene:

There was a continual harassment and a continual exploitation, which was really brilliant militarily, an exploitation of their power, physical power in that room. So that where two or three students would have felt intimidated by the symbols of authority and of the Presidency . . . of the knowledge in the books on the walls, by the wealth symbolized by the desk and the chairs, they completely surmounted that hurdle in coming in force and were able to take the initiative completely in putting Perkins not only on the defensive but making him I'm sure feel physically insecure since there he was surrounded by a group at least some of whom were armed and who were . . . extremely hostile.[69]

After about half an hour, when a woman student left to go to the washroom, my source went out and informed the plainclothesman in the anteroom of the knife. The officer radioed other security officers, who made themselves available close by in case a problem developed.

What transpired in terms of substance? Despite the pressure, Perkins's performance was praiseworthy, by all accounts. Garner opened the dialogue by holding Perkins responsible for allowing the Cornell Conservative Club and a new organization for racial balance to publish an advertisement in the *Sun* that critiqued racial exclusion in the black college and advocated moderation. The AAS thought Perkins had the authority to stop such actions. Perkins replied that he did not. The AAS also accused Perkins of creating a climate that encouraged the advertisement because of his arguments in press remarks that the autonomous college would be separatist in terms of race (something that the AAS had avoided saying in its charters and statements; it stressed autonomy, not racial exclusion per se). But Perkins had taken the group at its real, not its ostensible, meaning.

According to the source, Garner's opening sally was an "excellent gambit" for the start of the session because "it tended to dramatize the whole meaning of institutional racism and to suggest how a thoughtless remark on the part of an administrator could lead to the publication of an ad that might really exacerbate racial relations on the campus and lead to violence." Then Garner gave Perkins a copy of the latest charter for the black college and a list of the specific demands. He asked Perkins to read the demands to the group (the tape recorder would record Perkins's response, proving to the rest of the AAS that the demands were discussed). Perkins had to decide instantly whether he would read it aloud. What strategic advantage or disadvantage would accrue to reading it or not reading it to the group? Perkins began to read it aloud.

"Now, I'm sure while he was reading it the situation began to clarify in his mind and he saw what a strong hand he had gained because . . . we had spent many hours very, very carefully crafting a document to reply to that particular demand for a . . . Black college."[70] After reading the AAS demands, Perkins responded by discussing the document that he and his advisers had crafted before the AAS's arrival. As mentioned, the reply stated that the university could not establish the college the AAS sought even if it wanted to but that there were many good alternatives available, including innovative approaches within the established structures or creating a college independent of Cornell entirely. This method proved vastly superior to simply handing out the response for the students to read because they would have construed that approach as demeaning, akin to a teacher handing out material:

And they would have killed it right there. Now, by reading their document and coming to a rather eloquent end and then having them say, in effect, what are you going to do about it, he could say, well, I happen to have just exactly my answer, and he could take up his document. They could not stop him from reading his reply which . . . we had drafted. So this gave him the perfect opportunity to make them listen. . . . This was a very great gain. . . . I think they were a bit taken aback by all of the legal and constitutional obstacles to creating a Black college. This was . . . very forcefully put and it was pretty overwhelming when you added it all up, and I think it was pretty convincing that he could not simply sign a document creating a Black college.[71]

According to this source, Perkins stood up to the intimidation and pressure very well, and he defended himself with strength. "Unlike some people who've been called liars of late, he stood up to it with a very steady eye, 'Young man, you better watch what you call me here.'"

Because Miller came to the meeting late, he missed some of the earlier statements. Right away he noted the hostility of the atmosphere. But once Perkins began responding to Garner and the demands, in Miller's eyes he controlled the situation. "The President took charge from that point on. He didn't really allow anyone else to speak unless he called on them. He did all of the talking. He took the document, and he went through it point by point. . . . And he said, now, just a minute, there are some things you are saying here that just won't happen. There is no way that we are going to have a faculty appointed by students. . . . But he said, now there are some things you can do. We can indeed try to recruit a black psychiatrist for the clinic."[72]

Perkins made some mistakes, according to my witness: he was condescending when he should not have been, and his reference to his service on race-related boards came across as patronizing. The students greeted this trumpeting of his credentials with hoots and catcalls. After the meeting, students played the tape of his comments all over campus "and greeted them with hysterical laughter." It was "living proof that . . . here was personified the great white father, the . . . bourgeois liberal, this was institutional racism par excellence and so on. And they had it, they had it on tape."[73] Perkins was also somewhat evasive about how the specific demands would be met. Then there was the continuing problem of dealing in legalisms rather than principle. LaFeber and others argued that Perkins should meet the AAS's beliefs with his own: that the radical program it wanted ran counter to the principles of Cornell and liberal education. Black studies, yes; a black college, no. This concern was valid because the AAS leaders were astute readers of the intentions, beliefs, motives, and emotions of their adversaries. It was a Machiavellian world in which every act and utterance had important implications and consequences.

After the meeting, Perkins was visibly distraught. "This was a shattering episode for him. He was more than limp, he was really shaken to his very core and . . . he did not get over it for quite some time."[74] But there was reason for hope from the administration's perspective. For the first time, the students seemed to grasp the problems associated with an independent college, and after Perkins had laid out the problems and presented his case, the students began to engage in dialogue. For almost a month, right after the Howard conference, there had been no real dialogue, and it had seemed that there was no middle ground between the DuBois plan and a separatist black college. It now appeared the AAS was at least somewhat open to working something out that was radical yet consistent with the structure of Cornell. With the holiday break now upon Cornell, there was reason to hope that a solution could be worked out that would reconcile the interests of activist black students and the university.

Aftermath

Soon changes in the leadership of the AAS in the wake of the December confrontation provided further hope, for the militant faction lost the upper hand at a key meeting in January. The organization's goal of creating a black studies program under its effective control did not change, although its tactics became less confrontational. Fathoming this shift, the administration decided to pursue a policy designed to entice the less militant students toward cooperation. Perkins thus made a bold move: he decided to reestablish a committee dealing with the Afro-American Studies Program, but this time he would make sure that the chair of the committee was an able administrator who could work with both students and the administration. The administration also decided to pursue James Turner for program director, for it felt (and hoped) that Turner combined radical credentials with a sense of responsibility. I will discuss these developments in the next chapter.

The December confrontation in many ways marked the most dangerous time for Cornell and the administration. Though students would arm themselves in the showdown over the Straight, the December period was in many respects more dangerous because of what was going on within the AAS and because the administration had less information about what was happening. Garner's faction advocated "destroying" the university. Indeed, when the deadline for the establishment of the autonomous college passed, Garner considered calling for a violent revolutionary move but demurred, saying he did not trust his constituency, although several of his followers told him that they would have supported him. (Just what such action might have consisted of was never made known.)

Danger lurked over the horizon, however. Militants still had residual power in the AAS, and the newly anointed judicial system had to decide what to do about the students identified as perpetrators of the December 12 disruptions. Indeed, a second coincidence (the first being the assassination of Martin Luther King the same day as the takeover of the Economics Department in April 1968) struck an ominous note on Friday the Thirteenth: the inauguration of the new judicial boards took place that day, the very day that the cases for the December 12 actions were referred to those boards. Board members knew these cases were the beginning of the long-awaited showdown between the university and the AAS (see Chapter Seven). Just when the conflict over a black studies program seemed ripe for resolution, a major conflict between blacks and the administration of legal justice broke out. The conflicts over the black studies program and the judicial system posed questions cut from the same cloth: which is better, a black studies program based on integrationist principles or one based on separatist principles? Which is better, a rule of law for blacks and a different rule of law for whites or a common rule of law for both? If a common rule of law, what assurances do minorities have that their interests will be acknowledged, that they can attain justice? Is knowledge one or separate? Is justice one or divisible?

CHAPTER SIX

PROGRESS OR IMPASSE?

The December actions led to a decline of the radicals' fortunes. In early April John Garner left school to work in the ghetto and Gary Patton and Larry Dickson left for other reasons. During the second semester outsiders such as Michael Thelwell and Cleveland Sellers came to Cornell as lecturers and convinced the AAS that the militants were hurting the revolutionary movement as much as they were helping it. Consequently, a coalition or conglomerate of the AAS's factions shared power, moving the leadership toward the center.

At a meeting in late January, Garner announced that he was going to resign, which some members interpreted as a ploy to rally the organization behind the radicals' leadership. In the past the students had always given Garner a vote of confidence when he threatened to resign, but "the December fiasco had done irreparable damage to [Garner's] image."[1] Before this meeting several students had met at Tom Jones's home to plot Garner's removal. They knew that Jones's candidacy would not succeed because of his unfavorable image with many AAS members.

At the next meeting, near the end of January, Garner again raised the issue of his resignation, whereupon everyone became serious, expecting conflict. After tense debate, a leading activist who was also a possible candidate spoke up and opened the floor to the selection of a president, and Garner nominated Edward Whitfield, a quiet, brilliant moderate. Whitfield was relatively unknown in the AAS, and his ideology was not purely "black." Garner nominated him because he thought Whitfield had no chance of winning, yet Whitfield won with the pivotal support of Robert Rone and others.

In spring '68 the AAS had elected Whitfield chair of its Philosophy Committee. In this capacity he studied revolutionary literature. But like Robert Jackson and Tom Jones, Whitfield had also had meaningful exposure to conservative thought: he had studied with Allan Bloom. Because of Bloom's influence, Whitfield had dreamed of becoming the first black philosopher-mathematician. Long after he had read some revolutionary literature, and indeed, even at the time he led blacks into the Straight, [he] believed that *The Republic*, as taught by [Bloom], was the world's greatest book. . . . He often remarked, with a good deal of satisfaction, that Bloom had taken great pains to co-opt him and to make him aim to become the black Plato. After the Straight [he] would argue, again with satisfaction, that Bloom was one of the few professors on campus who understood the revolutionary implication of the Society's actions and, more importantly, who believed that the black leaders were revolutionaries. He attributed Bloom's insight to the fact that [Jones], [Jackson], and he had studied under Bloom.[2]

Andre McLaughlin portrayed Whitfield in glowing terms. He was a "very brilliant person, great mind. I felt he really understood the society in which we were situated, that particular historical context. And I think Ed has always been determined not to be defined by outside voices, in terms of who he is as a man, a person, regardless of color, that he would shape his own destiny. If I had to say anything about him, that's what I would say about him: a man who is determined to shape his own destiny."[3]

Members of the radical faction who could not adjust to the new order became loose cannons, leading to confrontations that we will discuss. The faction fell into disarray. Eric Evans joined the new controlling coalition, leaving Garner, Patton, and Dickson outside the main action. The AAS then established a central committee to govern its affairs until the end of the semester. Soon this became an executive committee of five leaders: Jones, Jackson, Rone, Evans, and Whitfield as president.

The Kennedy Commission and AAS Pressure

On December 21, four days after the major confrontation between President Perkins and the AAS in his office, several members of the administration's executive staff met with Perkins to discuss what should be done over the holiday break to reestablish "meaningful discussions with our Black students." Perkins turned to Keith Kennedy, the vice provost of the university, and said, "Keith, we need somebody in the administration to really take charge of this. We have decided that you are the individual to head up such a discussion."[4] Kennedy was the perfect choice: he was close to Perkins, he was an insider, and he knew how to get things done. Kennedy had been director of research in the College of Agriculture and then the associate dean of the college. Lean, with short-cut white hair, the sharp Kennedy looked ready for business. Admired as a straight shooter with common sense and administrative ability, he described himself as a "let's get the job done" kind of person in his interview with me. In this respect he was the opposite of Chandler Morse. Over the break Kennedy began meeting with students and faculty and plunged into reading literature on black intellectual history.

By cultivating contacts inside the group all year, Perkins and the executive staff were keenly aware of what was going on inside the AAS. Provost Corson maintained an especially good source whose name he would not divulge even twenty-seven years later. Kennedy remarked that Lisle Carter, one of Cornell's few black professors, had informed Corson and him that the most militant students were so distrustful of whites and the establishment that the administration could not possibly win their trust. "Therefore, it was important that we establish a platform, I think those were the words [Carter] used, that the more moderates could stand on and exert their leadership."[5] They developed a classic divide-and-conquer strategy: appeal to the would-be moderate majority against the militant minority. Dean Robert Miller interpreted Whitfield's election as a signal that most members of the AAS felt that the radicals had taken them "beyond the depth to which they wished to be involved. . . . They wanted to be solid, they wanted somebody they could unite behind and not someone they were afraid they were going to have to disavow. And Ed Whitfield was that man."[6]

The administration and Kennedy made a key move, reestablishing the committee that Morse had chaired, this time under Kennedy's aegis. Kennedy was an able administrator who was not afraid to speak his mind with black students (something they respected) and who understood the university's need for faculty and administrative control. Moreover, the AAS, burned by the experience with Morse, was now willing to work with a strong person in the administration toward a program.

By this time, perhaps because of the stellar help David Brion Davis provided during the December crisis, Perkins had absorbed the fundamentals of the Yale program that Davis championed, in which the administration had taken the lead to establish an interdepartmental program based on the model of a center. A center exists on its own, establishing its own curriculum and possessing the power and resources to bring in speakers and temporary instructors from around the world, but its tenured (and tenure-track) members typically have appointments in other departments as well. In other words, a center combines the qualities of an independent operation and an operation embedded within the established structures of the university.

Nonetheless, faculty members at a meeting in January discerned a more radical thrust to the administration's position. According to Fisher and Wallenstein, Perkins pushed the AAS's case for as autonomous a program as possible. Perkins asked mathematics professor Paul Olum if he considered himself qualified to judge the credentials of a black studies candidate. "You're damned right I am," Olum replied. There was also heated discussion over the inclusion of whites in the program. According to Olum, "Mr. Perkins was trying to sell us the black point of view in this meeting; he really wanted us to accept it."[7] This meeting epitomized the conflict over the black studies program. Although the AAS had abandoned the radicals' tactics and extreme separatist logic, it never surrendered the goal of achieving the functional equivalent of an independent college in the form of a center. According to Irving McPhail, "The whole issue was that as African-American students, we felt very strongly that we should design the program. It was more than we had to be consulted; we should be the principal architects of the program."[8]

On January 7 Perkins sent a letter accompanied by a "Memorandum on Afro-

American Affairs" to the AAS's outgoing president, Earl Armstrong. Perkins said the "unsatisfactory outcome" of discussions in December had led the administration to review its approach. It had decided to make a "fresh start" to work together by appointing Kennedy "chairman of a student-faculty-administration group to make recommendations." (Note that Perkins avoided the name of the old Advisory Committee.) The group would consist of fifteen members, including eight students chosen by the AAS. "Our aim is to bring the Afro-American students into a working relationship that is capable of resolving the questions that have been raised."[9]

The memo included a pledge to ask the trustees to earmark $175,000 for the 1969–70 academic year. It mentioned several other items that were intended only to provide a starting point for negotiations: appointing a director; beginning an inquiry into the development of an urban-based "action-oriented educational institution," possibly in New York City (here Perkins referred to Robert Browne's speech about the black university at the Howard conference); making 320 Wait Avenue available as "the headquarters for Afro-American Studies" as of the beginning of the present spring term; and efforts to increase black faculty and recruit a black psychiatrist or clinical psychologist.

Perkins's overture was greeted with caution and interest. The AAS would work with Kennedy but not appoint the students on the committee as Perkins's letter provided. Instead it appointed a negotiating committee to deal with Kennedy and the program. By establishing its own committee without a single head, the AAS could work with the administration and still maintain enough distance and uncertainty to prevent co-optation. The AAS also pushed to establish the essentials of the program before hiring a director, no doubt sensing that the administration hoped to use the director as a way of maintaining control. Indeed, Government Department Chair Allan Sindler claimed on the basis of several meetings in January that the administration "felt itself to be in a very unhappy bind" and "was hoping perhaps too much that [James] Turner as a person would pull all the chestnuts out of the fire; that is, there was a disposition on the part of the administration to overlook some of the defects of structure that they were proposing on the assumption that Turner, being the kind of guy he was, would work out such effective relations with the administration and the faculty and the rest of the university, that these structural weaknesses could easily be overcome."[10]

The AAS took two actions to return the administration to the defensive. To dramatize the group's headquarters' need for furnishings, six AAS members removed thirty lounge cushions from Donlon dormitory on January 10 and transported them to 320 Wait Avenue. The Campus Patrol quickly returned the cushions to Donlon. Donlon residents identified three of the six students. (The conduct boards later charged them with "fraudulent conduct.") The next day Perkins received a memorandum from the AAS declaring Turner as its choice for director of the program and outlining his salary and terms of employment. Kennedy, Corson, LaFeber, Cooke, and others contacted Northwestern to get more information about Turner. They were troubled by his militancy and by the fact that he had done very little work on his Ph.D. Overall, however, they were relieved, for the reasons Sindler mentioned.

Turner's intelligence and character had impressed them when he visited Cornell in December. Equally important, the evidence suggested that he was someone with whom the administration could work. "All reports indicated that he was militant but highly responsible," Kennedy said.[11] Recruiting Turner became a top priority.

At a meeting with fifty students and Turner in Day Hall during Turner's visit, the students again upped the ante, demanding a black college or university. Kennedy told them this "was unacceptable, was not being considered, and would not be considered." The discussion then turned to other matters. Kennedy indicated that the program should be set up in the form of a department or a flexible "center for Afro-American studies." Kennedy said that professors with professional appointments in the center should also have appointments in an academic department. The students conceded that this arrangement was desirable but objected to making it mandatory "because they could see a department blocking an appointment of an individual that otherwise appeared to be well qualified in Afro-American studies."[12]

On January 21 Kennedy arranged a meeting with several key faculty to get a sense of the faculty's pulse when it came to issues raised by the proposed center and Turner's visit. Sindler, Norman Penny, Olum, Davis, and Stuart Brown joined the group. Kennedy reported that the idea of an outside panel making appointments "ran into considerable opposition" from this group. The next morning Olum, Penny, Sindler, Donald Kagan, and Douglas Dowd met with Kennedy and Perkins in the president's office. Though Dowd was supportive, others continued to resist the structure and logic of the center. Kennedy told Gould Colman, the head of the Oral History Project, on January 29 that "all indications from the students as well as the comments from Mr. Turner to me just prior to his leaving [are] that we have an extremely explosive situation on our hands. . . . Mr. Turner has numerous offers from other universities. At best, we're going to be fortunate . . . to secure him at Cornell."[13]

The situation was explosive indeed. But according to Donald, "James Turner's selection did improve the dialogue between the blacks and the administration. Until he arrived, the administration never quite seemed to understand what blacks wanted."[14] After meeting with Turner, administrators had a better idea of what blacks wanted: as much autonomy as possible, with courses dealing with practice and theory. The problem was that by many accounts, this was not all that the students, or at least the more revolutionary students, wanted. Confrontation was valuable both ideologically and strategically. It is interesting in this regard to compare the militants' impressions with those of Sindler. Both understood the dialectic of confrontation and dialogue in exactly the same light. The AAS understood its dialogue with the administration as a game of constantly upping the ante by making progressively more radical demands. This strategy would give them more control in the end and expose the hollowness at the core of the liberal order. This method was deployed by many radical groups on American campuses in the sixties.[15]

Sindler depicted in similar fashion how the astute AAS took advantage of Perkins's use of concessions to try to gain control of the situation: "And so Perkins, since he was targeted by the black students as the only man with whom they would deal . . . , was always on the spot to respond, at least as he saw it, to respond with letters and memorandums and so forth, which would indicate and demonstrate the good faith of the University, and pry open these negotiation channels. . . . [There was] a consistent tendency to promise . . . to concede in advance . . . more and more details of autonomy in a rather desperate and honest effort to get some discussion going." [16]

The Black Ideology Course

On January 30 Stuart Brown called a special session of the Educational Policy Committee to consider Sellers's course on black ideology and two courses dealing with black literature, one a freshman seminar taught by CURW poet in residence Don Lee, the other a Society for the Humanities seminar called "Black Literature and Its Cultural Roots," led by Thelwell. The EPC consisted of Sindler, Kagan, Robert Elias of English, Ulric Neisser of Psychology, Charles Wilcox of Chemistry, and Kenneth Greisen of Physics. Elias and Neisser already favored approving all the courses, whereas Sindler and Kagan were very critical. (The two others' minds were not yet made up.) Four AAS members—Faye Edwards, Gayla Cook, Robert Rone, and Cleveland Donald—spoke to the EPC in favor of the course and of student control over the curriculum. They asserted that white faculty were incompetent to participate in the process of appointment in the program. Though the EPC eventually voted 4–2 to accept Sellers's course, the debate was heated. Sellers had completed only two years of college at Howard University before joining SNCC. Nonetheless, his work in the field of action was distinguished by serious and often dangerous efforts to organize voters in the South. Sindler even accepted the basic idea of having nontraditional lecturers whose exceptional experience justified temporary teaching appointments, especially given the aims of the program. But Sindler thought that Sellers's particular course was riddled with problems. It was, "in my view, an atrocious course taught by a highly questionable man." The main problem was what Sindler considered the course's overt politicization. "I don't flinch at the word [*political*]," Sindler stated, but this "was a thinly disguised . . . propagandist course for the most militant forms of black ideology." [17]

Sindler also disagreed with the AAS's advocacy of "flexibility" in the program, which he interpreted as a code word for exerting control. Giving such control to students would set "a grossly inappropriate precedent for the emerging center," and approving Sellers's course would make it difficult to apply standards in the consideration of future courses, thereby contributing to setting up "a kind of admittedly inferior education for blacks" at Cornell. To go along would be to act in the name of "keeping the peace" and of "assuaging our own guilt feelings." This would constitute "a kind of tragedy in which we're really acting against our best judgments for a set of reasons which really don't pass muster in a university." [18]

Sindler later defended the stance he was taking on the grounds of the broader purposes of the university and what he considered its obligation to black students.

He claimed his position had nothing to do with "a sort of pugnacious or self-righteous assertion of faculty rights" but rather an "anxiety" on behalf of the university and the black studies program. If the program became an "insulated enclave," it would be marginalized. Sindler wanted something similar to the Yale program, which he considered much more consistent with the principles of liberal education. At Yale, black students and faculty discussed the merits of different programs and agreed that "only an academically rigorous program was wanted." And white students were welcome.[19]

Sindler also explained his stance in terms of the dynamics of equal and mutual respect. "Some degree of collaboration, mutual respect, mutual interaction has to take place." If the center is established for "essentially political reasons" and therefore fails to develop good relations with the rest of the university, it will be perceived as "some second class operation out there which is disrespected by the rest of the university. And I think this would be, if not tragic, at least a blunder to structure the center in that manner."[20] Sindler's position differed from many of those involved in the debate in a telling respect: he believed that the university had something to teach black students, not just the other way around.

Kennedy managed to save the day for Sellers's course by presenting an honest argument: he admitted that the course was not justifiable on intellectual grounds but pleaded that the course be approved for political reasons.[21] Sindler and Kagan respected Kennedy's honesty and forthrightness.

Sellers's course was technically open to white students, but when it finally met at the end of January, all the students were black. "It should be exclusively black," Sellers told the *Cornell Daily Sun*. ". . . Given the black experience and black history, I don't think that there are any whites who could contribute to the course."[22]

Meanwhile, the administration remained in constant contact with Turner. Things were getting more tense by the moment, especially because of what was happening between the AAS and the judicial system (discussed in Chapter Seven). During this time only certain members of the faculty were involved in the negotiations, not the faculty as a whole (consistent with the pattern that went all the way back to the establishment of COSEP). On February 12 the issue of the center was supposed to be discussed at the general faculty meeting. The meeting drew surprisingly few attendees, and the issue somehow never made it onto the agenda.[23]

The Statler Incident

On February 3 Kennedy informed the AAS in a letter addressed to the whole society that "the President is prepared to recommend to the Executive Committee of the Board of Trustees the establishment of a Center for Afro-American Studies and we are continuing our efforts to secure James E. Turner as its Director." Kennedy noted it was "highly desirable" that most, if not all, of the professors in the center have joint appointments. Turner and the AAS objected to this, leading to further discussions and negotiations. The administration scheduled a return visit by Turner from Saturday, March 1, through Tuesday, March 4. In the meantime, the judicial system had started dealing with the students cited in the December disruptions and the January theft of the cushions from Donlon. Then, on the eve of Turner's return visit, a serious confrontation broke out at a symposium on South Africa at the Statler Auditorium.

What happened at Statler would come to symbolize the administration under attack. In the terms of social psychology, it was a "condensation symbol," an act that epitomized the state of things and the thoughts in people's minds in one powerful image.[24] The Center for International Studies had sponsored a symposium on South Africa from February 26 to March 1. The program was intended to achieve a better understanding of U.S.-South Africa relations and to provide a "full opportunity to discuss the complex problems that derive from the controversial policies of South Africa." Among the events were a panel chaired by Chandler Morse on apartheid and a lecture by Allard K. Lowenstein, a major political figure and leader in Senator Eugene McCarthy's 1968 presidential campaign. (Perkins was scheduled to introduce him.)

The evening session on February 26 included a speech by Otto Krause, founder of the liberal South African newsmagazine *News Check*. Krause defended the regime of apartheid, leading to a major standoff over Krause's right to continue speaking during the question-and-answer period. SDS members Jeffrey Dowd (the son of economics Professor Douglas Dowd) and Bruce Dancis shouted for a vote on the question, but law student Bruce Detwiler, who opposed Krause's views, persuaded the audience in the name of free speech to let Krause continue without taking a vote.[25]

On Friday afternoon, just before Lowenstein's speech, Perkins met with black students to discuss the budget for the Afro-American center. The trustees had agreed to commit the $175,000 Perkins mentioned in his letter to the AAS on January 7, but no more because of a budget squeeze. Perkins told the students that he would try to find more money elsewhere. Tom Jones then asked for a greater amount from the budget itself, another $100,000. This request was troubling because the rest of the university was undergoing cuts of 2 to 5 percent. When Perkins mentioned that the university was in a "financial blizzard," one of the students shot back: "You have all that money in South Africa. Why don't you take it out of South Africa and give it to us?"[26] The university's investments in South Africa had been a bone of contention between the university and both SDS and the AAS for quite some time. The main investment was in Chase Manhattan Bank, which had holdings in South Africa. The return on the investments was minimal, but the capital investment was substantial. The Board of Trustees had declined to sell the stock despite pressures to do so.

Perkins promised student critics that he would publicly explain the trustee's unwillingness to sell the Chase Manhattan stock at the Friday night session of the symposium, February 28. SDS and AAS members, acting jointly for a change, decided to hold up Lowenstein's lecture unless Perkins's explanations proved satisfactory.

The elegant Statler Auditorium, in Cornell's prestigious School of Hotel Administration, was filled to its capacity of several hundred as the session opened. Everyone knew some sort of confrontation was brewing, but no one was prepared for what happened. Before Perkins could get to the podium to introduce Lowenstein, Eric Evans took the microphone and announced (according to the *Sun*), "The peculiar thing about this whole damn symposium is it's stacked." With Perkins sitting at his side, Evans told the audience: "We deal with Perkins. If he don't deal with us, we do our thing." As Perkins started moving toward the lectern, Evans called on Bruce Dancis to come to the podium. "I want you to explain to the audience the university investments—and defend them," Dancis ordered the president. "I doubt if I will satisfy you," Perkins replied as he commenced his explanation.[27]

As Perkins spoke, Dickson and Patton stood at the two ends of the stage. Dickson, who was awaiting a hearing in civil court for his assault of the *Sun* reporter in front of 320 Wait Avenue in December, held a four-foot length of two-by-four board at his side. Perkins assumed that the university still had money in banks that did business with South Africa. He said the trustees's main concern was to maximize returns but that no more money would go into South Africa pending further investigation.

Suddenly Patton rushed to the lectern and grabbed Perkins by the collar, lifting him to his toes. With his free hand he grabbed the microphone. Black students in the audience began to beat their university-purchased bongo drums as Patton attempted to speak. Perkins looked flustered and flushed under Patton's grip as the boos of the crowd drowned out Patton. "You just blew it!" cried a black student in the audience. When Lowell George approached the stage to help Perkins, Dickson pointed the two-by-four at his head, deterring him from further action. After several seconds, Patton released Perkins, who hurried off the stage to be driven home in a Safety Division car. Confusion reigned for about five minutes as the students continued to beat the drums. Evans, Patton, and Dickson conferred on the stage before Rev. Gladstone M. Ntablati, a South African liberation leader, stepped up to the lectern and scolded the attackers. Amid cheers from the audience, he continued. "What happened tonight is against all the principles of what we black people in South Africa believe in." Then Cleveland Donald spoke from the floor, stating that "his Black Brother [Patton] had reacted to a very emotional situation and that the community should permit the Black Community to sanction Mr. Patton."[28] As Donald and Ntablati spoke, Patton and Dickson left the hall.

The program continued, albeit in altered fashion. Government Professor Douglas Ashford expressed his disapproval of the students' actions and introduced another speaker from South Africa. Then Lowenstein spoke briefly. Instead of giving the speech he had planned, he talked about the crisis of American society and the universities. "Under these circumstances it was rationally impossible for me to discuss South Africa," he explained.

Though most of the audience was shocked at the treatment of Perkins, some parties had a different reaction. Kennedy's report to the Safety Division of his observations captured the competing moods of the room and the administrator's concerns: "Eric Evans stepped to the microphone and stated 'we blew it.' He went on to say that President Perkins was let off too easily and as a result they didn't receive answers to their questions. It was amazing as well as very disturbing to see the reaction of many members in the crowd change from one of concern about the uncalled-for treatment of the President to one of almost outright anger that the President didn't remain in order that they could criticize him publicly." [29]

David Burak recalled his upset at the collaring of the president:

I was in the audience, and I saw it, and I said, "Oh, no." It was Larry Dickson and Gary Patton. . . . Gary was the brandisher. Larry had a stick but didn't go close to Perkins. They went out the back side of the stage, and I went out the back door because I knew where they would end up. And I was pissed. I thought it was so fucking stupid. What we were trying to do was build a large movement toward divestment, and this is one of the best ways to squelch [the movement]. So there is this little area behind the backstage door, that's where I intersected with them. I looked at them both and said, "You fucked up." I told them they should apologize. Gary said, "Hey, man, I might have fucked up, but I ain't apologizing." [30]

Harris Raynor, a member of SDS's labor committee, had helped prepare the symposium with Bob Jackson and Bruce Dancis and looked forward to exposing the administration's duplicity on South African investments that evening. His hopes exploded with the ill-advised collaring:

We had all the moral high-ground. Black students were all sitting in one area. They had brought the drums and Perkins couldn't answer the questions. We were winning and it was absolutely great. Then Dickson and the other guy got impatient, and instead of letting the university show itself for what it was, they got up and the two-by-four came out. Somebody in the audience yelled, "You blew it!" . . .

Perkins almost had a heart attack. He turned white as a sheet. You had these young black militants and this old man. [31]

Monday the *Sun* carried a front-page picture of the collaring. Strangely, rather than rallying the campus to his side, the picture lent aid and comfort to Perkins's critics, as it symbolized in their eyes the plight of an administration that was failing to protect its interests and those of the university. Strength was needed, not weakness. The *Sun* also carried an editorial by Stanley Chess, headed "Friday Night—Ugly and Stupid." Chess emphasized the dangers of "jostling" Perkins and of the need for equal application of the law for blacks and whites. And in an op-ed piece, Paul Rahe, referring to the Statler incident and the confrontation of Krause on Wednesday, charged that the symposium had created powerful challenges to the principles of free speech and an open university. He asserted that "a stand must be taken, and taken firmly." [32]

The AAS held a meeting right after the Statler affair. Members concluded that blacks should be the only legitimate judges of blacks (an argument they were making in the larger battle over the judicial system), but the AAS decided to wait until the administration or the judicial system took a position before coming to its own conclusions about the disposition of the cases. Near the end of the meeting, Patton claimed that the AAS should support him because "I did a revolutionary thing." Even the radicals, including Garner, were "incredulous" at this claim. "After the meeting, the Radicals took the brother into the hallway and read him out of the group."[33]

The *Sun* also printed an AAS statement signed by Whitfield that presented the group's position on the Statler incident. The AAS had not planned or approved Patton's collaring of Perkins (a claim the evidence supported). But Whitfield said the Cornell community should be careful not to "equate the suffering, destruction, and oppression of millions of our Black brothers with a moment's discomfiture on the part of a university president." Referring to the proper way to adjudicate the case, Whitfield said, "We shall as a group move immediately to see that our brother is properly disciplined. This is our responsibility to him, to ourselves, and to the community. It would be wise of the university to accept this solution." Just beneath the Whitfield-AAS statement, the *Sun* published a statement from Professor Henry Ricciuti, the chair of the Faculty Committee on Student Affairs. The statement affirmed the importance of freedom of speech to the idea of a university. "To acquiesce in the denial of that right is to invite the imposition of one or more orthodoxies which can only be fatal to the freedom of inquiry and expression."[34]

Six weeks later the judicial board summoned Patton to appear, but he had already left Ithaca. Dickson had left school just before the Statler incident, so he was beyond the jurisdiction of Cornell's judicial system. A short while after the Statler incident, Garner left Cornell. By this time he had become disillusioned with campus revolutionaries. His passage meant that the most important person in the AAS's history would not be around for the event that would soon make the group famous.

The Statler incident shook the campus. According to Fisher and Wallenstein, a high-level administrator claimed that "Perkins was never the same after he was pulled from the podium at Statler. He had always considered the blacks his friends; evidently, he was deeply shocked and aggrieved by what happened at Statler Auditorium."[35] The incident need not have happened: shortly afterward the *Sun* reported that unbeknown to the administration, Cornell had already sold its Chase stock! Louis Durland, the university treasurer, had sold the stock and then left on his honeymoon before informing anyone.[36]

Later many professors pointed to the Statler incident as proof of the administration's weakness in defending the principles of free speech and an open university. Yet only Henry Ricciuti wrote anything in the *Sun* that took such a stand. According to Corson, who missed Ricciuti's statement, one of the most distressing things about the incident was the lack of faculty support for these principles in the wake of the incident (perhaps they figured that Perkins was being victimized by forces he had helped to unleash). "The only two people who ever said anything about [the threat to academic freedom] during or afterward, who ever deplored that, were the visiting South African black clergyman and Allard Lowenstein. *Nobody else said a word!* . . . Now, if there ever was a case of academic freedom being violated, there it was . . . , [the deepest challenge to] the whole authority structure of the university. And to have a group of law professors write Perkins a letter after the Straight and say, 'We don't trust you to protect our academic freedom,' that's a real bit of evidence, I think." [37]

Malott Hall

On Monday, March 10, two hundred anti–South Africa demonstrators led by SDS (with AAS cooperation) confronted three Chase Manhattan job recruiters at Malott Hall, the home of the business school. Farther from the scene of the action, several hundred students, faculty, and administrators (including Vice President of Student Affairs Mark Barlow, according to Burak) stood in a peaceful picket line. The recruiters had taken their place at tables inside a suite of offices, only to be confronted by protesters who had gained access by unlocking a service door with a key they had obtained from somebody inside. Demonstrators swarmed into the offices and forced the recruiters away from the suites and into the dean's office. The demonstrators next barricaded the recruiters in this office with Barlow, the dean of students, and the dean of the business school. At that point university officials agreed to call off the recruitment that day and the next, a decision that Barlow said was made under "duress." The recruiters departed. The next day Corson told the faculty, "I believe this is only the second time that a regularly scheduled Cornell University event has ever been completely disrupted and cancelled." [38]

The demonstration involved some violence. In addition to the threats against the recruiters, Safety Division Detective David Wall was cut in the hand when he tried to prevent the demonstrators from unlocking glass doors in Malott Hall. He said it could have been a lot worse:

There came a time when they decided they were going to come in and dump the tables. I was told, "Keep them out." . . . When we got totally overrun, I got pushed, I got knocked down on the floor, and [there was] glass all over the place. . . . There were ten or fifteen students. I mean, they just literally chomped all over tables, literally, everything went flying. It all happened just, whoosh! So fast! . . . I went right through a window, head first. . . . I could have been killed. . . . Several of the recruiters that were there that were sitting in the chairs, I mean, their chairs went over backwards, they just left their briefcases and everything and just walked away. [39]

Detwiler, Chip Marshall, and Tom Jones defended the demonstration. Burak, however, bemoaned the tactics as detrimental to the educational aspirations of the movement. "Free speech was important, sacrosanct to the institution, so I didn't want to compromise that. . . . [Looking through a window] I saw that the numbers were really bad, the protesters really outnumbered the Safety. I told Safety that the interview should end and be done, and they agreed. Two minutes later the door [flew] open, and I was already inside after climbing in the window!" [40]

Sources claimed that the Malott Hall incident was a turning point for the faculty as a whole and that it contributed directly to the faculty's initial unwillingness to accept the deal that got the AAS out of the Straight in April.[41] The demonstration also angered the administration, which vowed to take punitive action. But when it set about to deal with the affair, the administration followed a pattern very similar to the one after the McPhelin incident. After a faculty meeting on March 12 at which Corson in an extraordinary speech addressed the administration's urgent need of faculty support and assistance to deal with the impending crisis, administrators called several professors to Day Hall in the evening to discuss what should be done. They set up committees to consider the three most pressing issues: the judicial system, the black studies program, and Malott Hall.

The Malott Hall Committee, which included Professors Joel Silbey of History, David Lyons of Philosophy, and others, was intended to be a fact-finding board similar to the Williams Commission. Right away, committee members wanted to hear what Doug Dowd had to say about the issue. His son was involved in the action, and he was a leading campus critic of the administration's and America's investments and actions around the world. Silbey considered this request a sign that the committee was more concerned with correct politics than with the legal issues raised by the confrontation.

The committee met with members of the administration and the Faculty Council. Nothing came of the deliberations. No students or nonstudents were referred to the campus judicial boards or to civil authorities for investigations—precisely the result, according to Silbey, that the administration wanted. He claimed he was the only faculty member in the group who was not predisposed to letting the matter drop. To Silbey, the handling of the Malott affair was a rehearsal for the events of April. Most important, by not citing anyone for the Malott Hall demonstration, which was much more confrontational, violent, and threatening to the principles of an open university than what the AAS activists had done in December and January, the administration provided the AAS with a classic weapon for denouncing the legitimacy of the judicial system: double standards favoring whites, for whites outnumbered blacks in the disruption.

Silbey painted a picture of capitulation that had disturbing implications for the near future. His comments offered a rare inside account of the proceedings of an important committee, and the issues he raised are important. Silbey singled out Corson as an exception to many of the following criticisms:

It was clear that the *administrators* who were there . . . wanted some way out. That they were *desperate* not to cause any problems if they could, not to raise any challenge. . . .

There was a group of faculty who I would consider myself equally radical to, who unlike myself were willing to dispense with all sorts of due process and procedures, and the maintenance of the University as a place of—well, an ivory tower beyond participation in politics, if the cause was good. . . .

The other part of it was the absolute weakness and abject fear of the administrative personnel. And here I include the Faculty Council. The people who were supposed to be running the university, who were obviously at their wits' end and who *already* were beginning to develop a conception that what we must have is *peace* at any price. "Somehow we must get out of this. Somehow we must find an easy way out, regardless of what is right and what is wrong in a situation. . . ."

They resented, more than anything else, people raising problems—because it was clear by then that the Malott Hall people were not going to be touched in any way and that this committee was not going to recommend that anything be done to them. . . .

It gave me an insight into the university faculty and people on the Faculty Council which was frightening. That if the University ever had to stand up to defend itself from within, from challenges from within, it was not a very *strong* structure because people had no very clear ideas of . . . why a University has to abide by certain rules or live under a certain code and that the administrative malaise of just brushing everything under the rug was very widespread.[42]

Sounding the Alarm

On March 12 Corson took his case to the faculty in an extraordinary meeting that featured eloquent debate and deep tensions that exposed the irreparable fissures among the faculty and the administration. History Professor Edward Fox called this meeting of six hundred faculty "the largest and quite possibly the most fateful meeting in [the faculty's] history."[43] The agenda called for a discussion of the Presidential Commission on Military Training, which had recommended reform of course credits for ROTC (another committee chaired by Kennedy) and the future of ROTC. After clearing some parliamentary hurdles, Corson made an eloquent personal statement based on "my own grave concerns at the new directions that have emerged recently. . . . The message I wish to communicate today is simple. I am convinced that the period ahead of us is more critical than any we have ever faced." He discussed the university's relationship with black students and the antiwar activists and the recent acts of harassment against Perkins and the university. Corson also addressed the "critical issue of separate judicial systems for white students and for blacks" and noted that differences of opinion now entailed serious elements of confrontation and disrespect. Then he made a plea for more faculty support: "The faculty involvement, however, has been ad hoc, indirect, and sometimes *ex post facto*. If stability is to prevail I believe that the faculty involvement must now become direct and continuous." He scolded the faculty for not speaking out about the Statler incident and urged them to make their presence felt on the judicial boards and in the adjudication of cases affecting academic freedom and free speech. "There are standards of academic freedom and of scholarly behavior which are commonly held and these must be expressed clearly, publicly and frequently."[44]

At the conclusion of his talk Corson proposed organizing five small faculty and student committees to assist Perkins by giving continuous advice. He then proposed a statement of principles affirming that the rights "to speak and be heard are central to the concept of a university and that the faculty is determined that these rights are going to be maintained on this campus"; the university must protect the rights of all who are invited to come and speak or conduct business, and the faculty must uphold the integrity of the judicial system.

Though Corson, perhaps the most respected of the administrative elite, won extended applause and the support of the majority, the subsequent debate revealed rifts that would take their toll over the ensuing weeks. Isadore Blumen, a statistician in the School of Industrial and Labor Relations, a staunch conservative, and a mastermind at parliamentary procedure and strategy, was the first to respond. Though he agreed with Corson, he turned the tables on the administration by referring to a case that the administration had hoped was dead and buried: McPhelin. He told the faculty about his efforts the previous spring to have the administration openly defend academic freedom.

> This had not been done and the failure to speak and to act has been repeated again and again. The Faculty had learned their lesson: each time they yielded, or postponed on the grounds of expediency or vague hopes, they sowed the seeds for a new confrontation which was worse and uglier than the last. It was too late now to depend on appeals to reason alone. It was, perhaps, even too late now to rally Faculty, students and staff to the defense of reason. But the effort should be made, and the defenses had to be manned with determination.[45]

Groups that threatened the freedoms of the university should lose their privileges and be dealt with by the law, Blumen declared to applause.

Feelings were running too deeply across loyalties to allow the faculty to form a united front. Two facts were most troubling. First, despite Corson's pleas, he was a pivotal figure in the administration's ultimately siding with Garner and the AAS in the McPhelin affair. Second, as Silbey disclosed, the advisory group dealing with the Malott Hall disruption would decide to let those demonstrators off the hook, even though what they did cut to the heart of the principle of an open university that Corson was imploring the faculty to defend. In other words, Corson's passionate plea was made in the face of what was coming to look like a mocking fate. But Corson's keen sense of events had not betrayed him. He sensed that the university could crumble unless the faculty and the administration rallied in a serious, sustained way around the principles of liberal justice and liberal education. The politics and psychology of the institution, however, would not allow this.

After Blumen spoke, Professor Frederick Marcham presented a resolution authorizing the Faculty Council to form the advisory groups about which Corson spoke. It passed by a voice vote. Marcham's recollections of his presentation of this resolution also reflected the deep fissures that ran through this meeting. Before the meeting Marcham had received a call from Miller, asking him to discuss the situation with members of the Faculty Council. He met with several individuals and drafted a strong statement about academic freedom and the need for a special council of concerned faculty who could act with dispatch to deal with threats when they arose. Marcham believed that one reason troubles festered was the labyrinthine committee system at Cornell. With the "welter of committees and councils," proposals just "vanished as if washed in quicksand. It seemed as if persons who wished to produce a crisis by violating some well-established rule of academic or social life could do so with impunity." So Marcham advocated "an action group on call six hours a day." But the statement was unacceptable to the council, which no doubt rightly considered it an affront to its authority, and the matter was dropped.[46]

Miller had also asked Marcham to introduce a motion after Corson's speech. Marcham met with Corson fifteen minutes before the meeting, and Corson told him he had to draft a new motion to conform to the last page of Corson's speech (about the formation of advisory groups). Marcham did not like what he saw. Instead of recommending the establishment of a strong action-oriented committee to counter student threats, the proposal left the Faculty Council largely in charge. "The Faculty Council was to be at least minimally in command, even though at every stage up to the present it had shown itself to be inept." The statement also included an affirmation of academic freedom as well as something many could not abide: commending the administration on its handling of the crises: "The Faculty commends the Administration of the University for the patient and restrained responses to recent violations of these principles involving disorders and threats of disorder."

Marcham suddenly realized he had been "played into an impossible position." The motion "ran opposite to my beliefs," and by presenting it, he was indirectly allying himself with the administration. As he walked from Day Hall to the meeting at Bailey Hall, he struggled with his predicament. He took his place near the front of the room, and just before the meeting started Perkins came over, put his arm on Marcham's shoulder, and said in an avuncular way, "Now that you're here, everything will be all right."

As Perkins spoke, Marcham recalled, "more and more I came to see that I was being used to give some sort of authority to what the administration had planned." At the last moment Marcham found a way out of his dilemma: he told the assembly that "he had come to the meeting, not as a person, but as an agency designed to translate the Provost's requests into a motion." Some sources understood that Marcham was divorcing himself from the motion with these words; others did not catch the subtlety. At any rate, to Marcham, the experience revealed that Perkins was maneuvering behind the scenes, in this case using Corson and Miller as agents. Marcham and several of his allies thought Corson could do better. "He was a man for whom we all had deep respect . . . one whose whole outlook and manner seemed much like our own."

Eventually the motions concerning the new committees under the aegis of the Faculty Council and the statement of principles passed, but not without debate. William Friedland, a leftist professor of industrial and labor relations, said everyone agreed with intellectual freedom, "Yet Cornell was reaching the stage during which the question of what were the legitimate University concerns was being raised by the students. Faced with such questions the Community would not simply reaffirm the traditional normative system."

At the end of the discussion, Blumen introduced an amendment to delete the phrase commending the administration for its actions. It carried by a voice vote. Finally, the faculty dealt with a statement by the Faculty Committee on Student Affairs that supported the principles of free speech, peaceful change, and the integrity of the judicial system. Dowd replied that it was time to rethink the "Draconian jurisprudence" the motion represented. Black students "came out of a different past," so "now was hardly the time to demand mechanistic implementation of the existing disciplinary machinery." Sindler responded that Dowd and his supporters had miscast the meaning of the statement; it did not at all foreclose reconsideration of legal principles and processes but simply upheld the notion that no one group was above the law. The idea that a higher law justified lawbreaking "was ominous because, flatly stated, it meant the end of the idea of a community." After intense debate, the motion passed, 306–229. Sindler was shocked that what he considered a "self-evident" statement had generated so much controversy. The controversy was a sign that liberalism was in trouble at Cornell.[47]

More important, the originally concisely worded motion was replaced by amendments that watered down the commitment to an open university and the judicial system. According to Government Professor Peter Sharfman, the "thrust" of the amendments was to "soften the blow": "we're not trying to affront anybody; we're not trying to make a confrontation." As a result, the amendments were contradictory, enabling both radicals and conservatives to leave the meeting feeling fairly secure in their positions. In short, nothing meaningful had been established, other than once again smoothing over differences that were utterly irreconcilable.[48] What began with Corson's clarion call for a clear defense of liberal university principles ended in a political muddle.

Black Studies: Progress or Impasse?

Kennedy and the administration believed that the meeting with Turner over the weekend of March 1 (that disastrous weekend for Perkins) had gone reasonably well, though issues concerning the program's autonomy had not been resolved. Then on March 6 Tom Jones met with Corson and told him Turner was very upset by several things Perkins had said to him earlier that week and that Turner would turn down the offer unless several new commitments were met. In particular, Turner and the students wanted Cornell to increase its support from $175,000 to $215,000 and acknowledge that the black studies center could recruit faculty and develop a program that could lead to a degree-granting unit. "Mr. Jones indicated to Mr. Corson that if the President didn't agree to these items, that Turner would not accept the position, and that we would have a real confrontation on our hands."[49] According to Corson, Jones then spoke with Perkins, and Perkins gave in. Twenty-seven years later, Corson portrayed the meeting with Jones as hostile, reading from the notes he had taken after the meeting itself. (In 1971 Corson started to collect and edit his notes into a volume but gave up the project when "right away I got to the point where I couldn't sleep.")

> We talked a long time about the amount of money that was committed to the black studies program, and I think it was a few hundred thousand dollars. And they were

saying, "That's not enough. We've got to have more." And I said, "There isn't going to be any more. This is it. We've got a program that is a rational program, and it can be supported by that." Jones then went to see Perkins, and Perkins relented and gave him another $30,000. And after that there was no way to say no, to say no and make it stick. That was a big mistake.

According to [Jones], Perkins had not kept his word about hiring Jim Turner to be the director of the Afro-American studies program. And Jones said he was going to pay for it. And there was nothing I knew about where Perkins had not kept his word. We had done everything Perkins had said he would do. . . . So I just listened to Jones. He began by telling me the conditions under which the university was to proceed. The Afro-American Studies Center was to be among the highest of university priorities. The university will move with the assistance of the center to establish an urban component. The university has a commitment to use all possible mechanisms to implement the degree-granting status of the center and to provide for direct recruiting and admission of students to the center. . . . This is Jones telling me what I am to do. . . . Jones said that he was going to raise enough hell to get Perkins in trouble and that he might go to jail for it and that he might take some innocent freshmen with him.[50]

When I asked Corson whether Jones was the mastermind of the Straight takeover, he replied, "I know he was." Jones, however, begged to differ in a later interview, claiming that he opposed the Straight takeover as a tactic.[51]

Kennedy met with Jones a few days later, and something started sinking in. What Turner and the students wanted was not a program within the framework of liberal education but courses that would contribute to "a better understanding of their heritage" and "provide them with the training that would educate them, train them . . . [to] go in and work as community workers." When Kennedy told Jones that this sounded like a new kind of "professional school," he perceived that they "began to really understand what we were talking about."[52] Though there must have been truth to this observation, it betrayed the same lack of political imagination that seemed to afflict other liberals in the administration. Kennedy was grasping for an understanding that he could reconcile with his preconceived notion of progressive liberalism: a "professional school" was comprehensible and nonthreatening. Unlike individuals such as Sindler, Berns, and Bloom, he did not fathom the revolutionary aspects of what he was confronting. Though the students knew they could not win an independent college, they had not abandoned their revolutionary objectives, desiring something more radical than a professional school.

Turner's portrayal of Kennedy—a man he ultimately respected—shows profound philosophical differences in play. Kennedy's understanding was all one could expect from the liberal imagination in the service of social justice.

He, in the best tradition of American liberalism, had wanted to make that [liberal, progressive education] available to the disadvantaged. He understood that America, in his way, his limited, halting way, owed some debt and that the university had to be a socially responsible agent in this period of turmoil and social change. What confounded him was the depth, you see, of the students' objection. He couldn't understand that once they got here, why did they keep raising one objection after another? This is my point: that no white institution was prepared for the presence of these black people. . . . They didn't see them as agents of their own empowerment, of their own self-perception.[53]

As mentioned, Jones soon got what he wanted from Perkins. By all accounts, the meeting Jones had with Perkins and Kennedy went amicably. On March 16 they both scheduled a meeting with sixteen members of the faculty from five different schools who represented different views of the program. Of the sixteen, only three strongly opposed the idea of the center's being a degree-granting unit. Earlier, on March 10, a meeting of deans and department chairs had reached a similar consensus. Nonetheless, as March wore on, the AAS grew more upset at what it perceived to be foot-dragging. It kept getting contrary messages. After the March 10 meeting, Kennedy commented, "We found that the students were most upset that we were continuing to drag our feet on making this decision and expressed the point of view that we had not operated in good faith."[54]

As we will see, by now the main action involved the judicial board and the FCSA. In addition, SDS had turned up the heat concerning low-income housing in Ithaca, forming a committee with other concerned groups to develop a plan for housing and to pressure the administration to build one thousand units to alleviate the shortages caused by students. On March 21 the Labor Committee (LC) faction and the Joint Housing Committee (JHC) held a demonstration of seven hundred students that included a torchlight march down Library Slope and around the campus. SDS's Action Faction wanted more confrontational tactics (concerns about a takeover of Day Hall swept the administration), but the LC leaders wanted to ensure a peaceful demonstration to gain legitimacy for the claims they planned to present to the Board of Trustees at the New York City meeting April 10–12. The board also planned to discuss budget cuts, the sale of the controversial Cornell Aeronautics Laboratory, and approval of the Afro-American Studies Center despite the lack of clarity about its mandate and provisions. The trustees' consideration of the center followed two days of talks between university officials and James Turner. Muller said he hoped to "get this thing buttoned up over this weekend." The trustees initially gave the JHC only part of what it wanted, but threats of disruption caused them to "clarify" their position the next week in a manner that proved more satisfactory to SDS—"a move which ended SDS talk of immediate militant campus action."[55]

The proposal that the administration presented was the other important part of the trustees' agenda. The proposal showed that the administration had moved considerably in the direction of Turner and the AAS (the AAS's tactics were paying off). According to Sindler, "The Center plan negotiated by the administration and endorsed by the Trustees in April thus approached the autonomy clearly rejected in December. The responsibility for this shift and for the approval of the Center fell squarely on the president, who persistently and directly involved himself in handling the relation of black students to the University."[56] The final plan that the administration took to the trustees was not shown to the faculty as a whole or to the Cornell community; its first public appearance was in the *Sun* on April 10, the day it was taken to the trustees. No other program in Cornell's history had ever given students such power in shaping the curriculum and selecting faculty.

The proposal's main features were these: [57]

- A provision of $215,000 for fiscal year 1969–70 (the amount Jones had demanded), with a pledge to seek "supplementary budget items" if unanticipated financial needs arose.
- A statement that although salaries and office expenses would "usually" follow the normal university schedule, "the Center will remain flexible in the determination of appropriate salaries for its faculty, staff, and secretarial assistance."
- A pledge of $25,000 for the development of an urban extension, with more money available through negotiations of needs.
- The power, granted to the director, to recommend academic appointments without the stipulation that they be members of other departments (a major concession to Turner and the AAS).
- A special hiring mechanism for tenured and nontenured appointments until the center had developed sufficient strength and personnel. For tenured appointments, the AAS would provide a list of fifteen qualified scholars in Afro-American studies or affairs, with Kennedy, the vice president of academic affairs, the director, and three students appointed by the AAS making the selections. The plan envisioned scholars consisting of individuals representing "a breadth of disciplines." For nontenured appointments, at least three members of the panel of scholars would have the final say on a candidate's qualifications; the university would seek the advice of an ad hoc committee of five members (two tenured faculty at Cornell and three from the panel of ten scholars). After the center got on its feet, the director would recommend faculty who would be reviewed by the vice president for academic affairs (then Stuart Brown) in nontenured cases and by the vice president for academic affairs and the provost (at that time Corson) in tenured cases. (Because of the Straight crisis that soon followed, non–Cornell personnel were dropped from the appointment decision by administrative fiat.)
- No authorization to grant degrees "at this point." Students would be enrolled in other departments. But the university pledged full cooperation in developing the program so that it could offer a major within Arts and Sciences and a field of graduate study.
- A pledge, to ensure sufficient students for the program, to make at least half a revamped COSEP committee consist of center personnel and students. This was a significant move because COSEP was also deeply involved in admissions. Subsequent events showed that student and administrative activists would have a meaningful say in the admissions of freshmen to Cornell and in steering students into the center and related programs.

As the trustees met, four hundred riot police forcibly expelled several hundred students at Harvard who were occupying the administration building. The incident was important because of the issues it raised concerning student violence and university reaction and because the violence inflicted by students and police sent shock waves throughout campus administrations across the land.[58] The Cornell administrators' fears of repeating the Harvard scenario played a big role in the warlike deliberations the administration would soon enter.

The trustees voted to accept the administration's proposal for the center. Vice President of Student Affairs Mark Barlow told the *Sun* that Turner was the "likely choice" as the first director. Anyone who read the April 14 article would have assumed that the crisis was over. But two days later a *Sun* headline read, "AAS Blasts FCSA Statement; Judiciary Contradiction Shown." The real crisis had begun. Though the judicial board's actions were the direct cause of the Straight takeover, the takeover was also the product of the seemingly ineluctable disillusionment of the AAS with the administration. As Irving McPhail said, "The frustration over the drive to black studies, which was being thwarted at every turn, led to the takeover of Straight Hall."[59]

Finally, an ominous event should be noted before we turn to the judicial board. Though the radical Garner faction had been marginalized by March, the AAS was still exerting tremendous pressure on nonconforming blacks. As seen in Chapter Three, Lowell George received a memo from an anonymous source dealing with a report the source had received from a student I will identify as "P." P was upset that Perkins was not able to meet with him on March 17 to discuss the dangers that many black students confronted at the hands of the AAS. P told the source that Alan Keyes and others had been threatened because they had white girlfriends and that on a Saturday evening two black men came to the Residential Club asking to see Keyes, who was not there. "They didn't look like they were there for a tea party." P said that an open threat against Keyes had been made at an AAS meeting. According to the source, "He added that students, Black and White, are living in fear—P is afraid and that some 'nut, on either side' will do something irrational, like a Black Panther did either at San Francisco or UCLA—more particularly, he thinks (fears) that someone might take a rifle shot at Alan."[60]

Eventually Keyes left Cornell and transferred to Harvard, where he completed his Ph.D. It is also known that by this time the AAS was purchasing rifles from stores in the region to use for self-defense, sometimes enlisting the help of SDS members to buy them. These would be the rifles the AAS would smuggle into the Straight.

CHAPTER SEVEN

LIBERAL JUSTICE OR RACISM?

The judicial cases precipitated the takeover of the Straight. Given past experience, the judicial system's status was ambiguous. The decline of student government and the conflicts between faculty and students in previous cases meant the new system would have to earn its reputation. Unfortunately, the very first cases it had to deal with were the most explosive in Cornell's history. By the time of the Straight crisis, most students knew little about the boards and eventually accepted the SDS and AAS contentions that they were illegitimate.

The controversy over the judicial cases reflected the deeper debate over the purpose of the university. The AAS challenged the liberal assumptions of intellectual and legal individualism by advocating the politics and law of recognition; it proclaimed the inability and illegitimacy of the white judicial system to judge black students. At a key judicial hearing the AAS appeared en masse as the representative of the defendants, claiming that the AAS as a whole should be tried, not the individual defendants. A separate educational program run by blacks for blacks would be paralleled by a separate judicial system run by blacks for blacks.

In the end a majority of the members of the judicial boards felt justified in taking a stand on the principles in which they believed. The boards consisted of respected professors and students who worked together in a laborious and conscientious fashion. Even critics of their conclusions praised the quality of their deliberations, and members felt mutual respect. FCSA Chair Henry Ricciuti explained that "these were elected members, and usually the faculty elects people who are not at extremes."[1] But critics charged that all the conscientiousness in the world could not make them fathom the AAS concerns.

The most important figure on the boards in terms of strategy and philosophy was Allan Sindler, who was unwilling to sacrifice what he thought was right in the face of pressure. "He was kind of a cold guy. But we couldn't fault him for the principle he articulated," Ricciuti said.[2] Cornell counsel Neal Stamp criticized Sindler's commission for being more philosophical than practical. "This is one of the things that really disgusted me about the Sindler Commission—there were all these philosophical statements, but it didn't come down to something specific that would give us a road map."[3] Nevertheless, few could argue that Sindler was not a preeminent university citizen. John Marcham put it best. "Of course, this man Allan Sindler, who was a tremendous community person, went on to head the senate at the University of California. [He] had a huge heart. He said he was beaten by the conservatives when he was at Duke as a younger faculty member, and he was beaten by the liberals here!"[4]

According to Philosophy Professor David Lyons, some Jewish professors who had been active in the civil rights movement felt betrayed by blacks as the rift between blacks and Jews started opening up in the late 1960s. Anti-Semitism had arisen within the circles of Black Power. A defining event was the 1968 teachers' strike in New York City, in which the predominantly Jewish union leadership clashed with the black members of the Ocean Hill–Brownsville school board over the issue of "community control." New York City was an important focal point for people at Cornell, especially Jews who hailed from the area. Most of these individuals were bona fide liberals, but they observed the rising tide of Black Power and black nationalism with alarm.[5] As one government professor observed of his colleagues such as Sindler, Berns, and Bloom, "These men were morally committed to treating blacks with the same respect they'd give any other students. What they would not do is treat them *more* equally."[6]

But the AAS was as ready to fight as Sindler. Its members opposed the judicial system's right to try their cases on several interrelated grounds. The prosecutions were selective, based on political retaliation rather than principle. The defendants and the AAS had been treated unequally, for whites and SDS students who had committed disruptive acts had not been punished that year (the failure to act against the Malott demonstrators was clearly on their minds after mid-March). The judicial boards did not constitute a jury of their peers because no blacks served on them. The judicial system was an extension of the university, and since the actions the judicial system cited had been taken against the university, the university was a party to the very cases it was now judging.

One AAS member said SDS members "were clearly treated differentially": "These folks involved with SDS were basically rich white boys and girls who, . . . when they graduated, cut their hair, took a bath, and went to work on Wall Street. Let's not be naive. I think that the white power structure at Cornell understood that this was an adolescent acting out on the part of their young. Obviously, our experiences as African Americans was something that they did not understand, that they found threatening, and that they felt, I guess, needed to be suppressed in a way that the acting-out behavior of their young probably did not require."[7]

Another motive was less political and more traditional: the students did not want the ignominy that, in their eyes, attached to the sanctions. In particular, there was a concern about being humiliated by their parents' finding out. Andre McLaughlin remarked, "These were our classmates, and they represented the collective will, and we knew that their families had as much invested in them as our families had invested in us. And that most of them were first-generation [college students]. And they could not go home, they would be disgraced. . . . They were reprimanded, but . . . [eventually] they were under the threat of being kicked out of school."[8]

Steve Goodwin also stressed that the threat of being suspended or kicked out of school was harsh under the circumstances. And he pointed to the problems that had beset the previous system, problems that, in his estimation, meant the system was "defunct." Part of the problem was the perceptual gap that was opening between blacks and whites:

> The judicial system just had to go. You can't resurrect a defunct judicial system and try somebody and give it credibility with the black students. . . . That's just not going to happen. First of all, any time white folks can't get control or a handle on how to handle things, they come up with a very intelligent way to bow out. . . . You've got to remember that you grew up in a society back then that was the old boys' network. And maybe the students brought down that whole way of thinking. You can't have laws for us to subscribe to that we don't participate in designing and making up.[9]

The treatment of the Malott Hall incident lent credibility to Goodwin's and the AAS's claims. But Tom Jones had resigned as a member of the student conduct board, and no serious black candidates ran for office after he departed. Thus the extent to which the process was racially exclusive depended on the racial lens through which one looked.

Paul Rahe was a member of the old student conduct board earlier that term and a member of the new board until he resigned to work at the *Sun* as a columnist. He had participated in the elections for the newly constituted boards in the fall and had noticed that no blacks had made the final cut. Only two black students had signed up to compete in the elections for the boards, and one had dropped out of the competition. The one left was, according to sources, not an appropriate candidate. Tom Jones had actually helped to draw up the blueprint for the new system in the summer and had served on the Undergraduate Judicial Board until late 1967, when he resigned with other students because the old Faculty Committee on Student Conduct had overruled the UJB and imposed penalties on the many students who had disrupted Marine recruiters in Barton Hall. Jones would later claim (after the Straight takeover) that he resigned because of a racist FCSC ruling, but researchers on this claim could never find the case. The evidence suggests that he resigned because of the FCSC's treatment of the Barton Hall demonstrators. Art Spitzer, a student on the FCSA, was one of those demonstrators, but by spring 1969 he had turned into a "Sindlerite."[10]

Rahe had another observation. He and others involved in the judicial system anticipated they would be targets of confrontation sometime during the year:

> We knew then that they were going to test the system. In September it came up at one of our gatherings that the radicals on campus had recognized that the board

was all white and that they were going to challenge its legitimacy. It was a rumor that got to us. . . . My guess is that the absence of blacks was an accident. But . . . [they knew they had] a lever. They had fought the old system, and Sindler had designed a new system. And then the trick is to delegitimize the new system. . . . And the thinking was coming as much from the SDS people as from the blacks. And we also knew that when the toy gun incident took place, that this was it. . . . This is the crucial incident. . . . And we had meetings to discuss how to deal with the challenge to the judicial board's legitimacy. . . . And we decided as a group that we had to go ahead.[11]

Confrontation in December, Decision in January

On December 13 the new members of the FCSA met for the first time. The reconstituted committee had student members because of the implementation of the Sindler Commission reforms as modified by the proposal for joint membership boards. December 13 was also the day after the toy gun spree—an ominous coincidence.

Later that day Art Spitzer was summoned to President Perkins's office, where he found Perkins and several administrators discussing what to do about the AAS and the demonstrations. Spitzer would attend several of the emergency meetings Perkins held during this time.

On December 17 the University Student Conduct Conference (USCC) met with members of the dean of students' office to discuss the December demonstrations. Associate Dean of Students Ruth Darling attended in lieu of Elmer Meyer, the dean. The dean's office was ambivalent about what should be done. Some individuals, like Darling, openly sympathized with the plight of black students and viewed the demonstrations as a "desperate message" to the administration that they had needs. But Darling and her ilk also appreciated the university's need for order.

Darling was surprised at the intensity of some of the USCC members' concerns. She described the chair of the group, Professor of Entomology David Pimentel, as "extremely upset and angry at the events that had taken place, and highly critical of the administrators,' particularly the Dean of Students [office's], inability to control what had taken place on Friday [December 13]."[12] Pimentel told me his main concerns were that rules should be followed and that attacking libraries strikes at everything the university stands for.[13]

During the December events, members of the dean's office, Lowell George, and Harry Kisker (code administrator) had followed the demonstrators and tried to maintain order with the help of some students who were acting as marshals. At one point they even interceded to prevent a fight between whites and blacks. But based on their judgments at the scene that the demonstrations were sufficiently orderly and that citing the students would only exacerbate tensions, they did not warn the demonstrators that they might be violating the code. (Officials had been able to identify only three or four students after the fact.) The December 17 meeting concluded with the decision to wait for the Safety Division investigation before recommending anything concrete.

Over the Christmas break, administrators and faculty labored over what to do. Then the Safety Division reports came in. The facts—especially concerning the toy gun excursion—pointed to pursuing the matter. Given the obvious implications of the cases, however, the dean's office did not want to decide unilaterally to refer the case to the new Student-Faculty Board of Student Conduct (SFBSC). "We felt that it was such a serious case with tremendous ramifications that we would not alone make a decision as to whether or not to refer to the judicial board," Darling said.[14] So the office asked the FCSA and the USCC to convene to discuss the matter during the January finals study break.

In mid-January the dean's office met informally (there was no quorum, given the time of year) with six administrators and three faculty, including Pimentel, Sindler, Ricciuti, Darling, Gloria Joseph, and Meyer. The long meeting was characterized by protracted discussion and polarization. Pimentel's faction "felt that there was simply no question and that we should stop arguing."[15] Sindler and Ricciuti also supported a law-and-order stand. Others were ambivalent. Darling, though, felt that "one had to remember that law and order as we perceive it has no meaning as far as black people considering their history, that the very system that we have here is a system that has crucified them and subjected them for centuries."[16]

The new code did not have a prohibition that seemed directly applicable to the case involving the expulsion from 320 Wait Avenue (there was no provision for "harassment," and "disorderly conduct" did not seem to fit, at least in officials' eyes). So almost by a process of elimination officials decided to pursue the cases of those cited for the toy gun and Donlon incidents. The fifty to sixty students who demonstrated on December 13 were more orderly, and the demonstrations were symbolic political statements; under the Sindler-inspired code, the political nature of these acts meant that the university should treat them less punitively.

The toy gun and Donlon cases entailed the following charges: three students were charged with "fraudulent conduct" for removing the cushions from Donlon; four students were charged with "disorderly conduct" for harassing people on December 12.[17] Since one student was named in each case, the total number of students was six. By the time the judicial board finally considered the cases on April 17, which was also the first time the board was able actually to see the reports on the cases, one student had dropped out of school, leaving five students facing formal charges.

The December 12 cases were referred to the judicial board along with the Safety Division report. Several questions were attached that dealt with legal issues and the meaning of the demonstrations for the community. Not everyone at the informal January meeting was convinced that the students would appear. Whatever the merits of the case, the manner in which the citations came about posed questions of legitimacy that the AAS would not ignore. Wondering why only students from the most militant wing were cited, it would suspect selective enforcement designed to sever the AAS from its militant wing. Racial claims gained credence when the special committee assigned to the Malott case balked at pursuing charges.

On January 31 Kisker sent notices to the six students, telling them to appear before the SFBSC on February 13. The back of the form listed eight points about the procedures, the eighth of which stated, "If you fail to appear at a hearing or to cooperate in a reasonable manner, the Board may proceed to a judgment." According to sources, this provision had been added to deal with the case of Alicia Scott, who was charged with disorderly conduct in the dorms (see Chapter Three). Scott had failed to appear the previous year, the only case of intentional nonappearance on record, and the judicial boards had added this clause so they could try her in absentia. The clause would play a role in the disposition and politics of the cases.

On February 3 and 5 the students came to Kisker's office for the standard initial interview. Irate and hostile, they threw the notices at the wastebasket when Kisker informed them that they had to appear before the board.

No-Shows

On February 13 the judicial board held its usual biweekly meeting to consider the cases of the six AAS students. Because the students did not appear, the board, following its usual practice in such events, rescheduled the cases for the next meeting, on February 27. Perhaps the students had misunderstood the time or place of the meeting; whatever the explanation, trying a case in absentia was detrimental to the defendants because they could not present their side of the case or contest evidence and witnesses. D. Peter Harvey, the student chair of the board who had studied constitutional law and taken a seminar on Justice Oliver Wendell Holmes with Walter Berns, was most concerned about this issue. The board sent a letter to the students, telling them that not appearing on February 27 would have "serious consequences." At this point the members of the board did not know what to expect; their main concern was simply to get the students to appear before them. Like the administration, members of the board were preeminently concerned with establishing dialogue, believing that reason could settle the differences. But point 8 of the procedures allowed the case to be tried in absentia. Would refusing to exercise this option make the judicial board seem ignorant of its own procedures? Worse, would it create the appearance of racist double standards?

What might have happened had the judicial board gone ahead and decided the cases then and there? Students later told members of the board that the AAS would have accepted, albeit reluctantly, any minor penalties. At this point the legal standoff had yet to be fully staked out. It would be easier for either side to accept compromise (given the ideological and strategic issues involved, this view might have been naive, even at this point). But if the defendants failed to show up a second time, it would constitute a slap in the face of the legal system. Conversely, holding the defendants liable for not appearing would be a slap in the face of the defendants and the AAS. The longer the delay, the greater the stakes for each side. On February 27, the eve of the Statler incident, the defendants again failed to show.

Two days after Gary Patton collared President Perkins at Statler Hall, the FCSA met to discuss the incident and the nonappearance of the six defendants. It produced a statement (influenced mostly by Sindler) that affirmed the necessity of students' voluntary cooperation with the judicial system and stressed that nonappearance was "an implicit denial of membership in the educational community." The statement was firmly worded, but both judicial boards fathomed the potentially momentous consequences of their stance. Most members wanted to find a way to prevent a major confrontation that did not sacrifice the principles of the rule of law in the judicial system, but this very commitment would paint them into a corner if the AAS did not cooperate. The obvious way out was to impose a minimum penalty or to get the defendants or the AAS to voice at least minimal acceptance of obligations to the system; but everything depended on the AAS.

On March 3 the judicial board passed a four-part motion after a tense two-and-one-half-hour debate. Minority and majority reports appeared in the *Sun* on March 7 (along with an editorial that said that the boards had no choice but to take a stand).[18] The majority report encouraged the defendants to initiate discussions with their professors and peers concerning their positions within the Cornell community and in relation to the judicial system; if the students failed to appear at the hearing on March 13, the new date, they would be suspended. The board would lift the suspensions once the students did comply; if and when they appeared, they would not be tried for their nonappearances, only for the actions that originated the cases.

The majority report stressed that its main concern was to support "the notion of a Cornell community, and how best to insure its integrity and viability." Yet it also acknowledged the "political nature" of the noncompliance. "In light of this contention, the board would welcome the initiation of discussion on how the system may be improved, if necessary, to make it appropriate for the entire community." The minority statement construed the majority's stance as a wound to the community, not a healing gesture. "Any attempt to force black students into complying with the conduct board, whose legitimacy has always been tenuous, will only exacerbate, if not assure, destruction of our community. . . . The conduct board has clearly shown a malign sentiment."[19]

Letters were sent to the defendants on March 4, informing them that they must appear on March 13 or face automatic suspension. On March 6, however, the USCC decided that suspensions should not take place immediately in the event the defendants did not show up on March 13. The USCC said that the cases would be reviewed, like all other suspensions, by the Appellate Board. It was important, the USCC emphasized, to have a representative of the AAS meet with the USCC as soon as possible. The USCC contacted Whitfield for a meeting, and he agreed to come. It was a rare ray of hope.

That meeting was scheduled for Wednesday, March 12. But the secretary who made the phone calls gave out the wrong date, March 11. When the error was discovered, she contacted everyone involved to correct the mistake—*except Whitfield!* At noon on March 11 the secretary found Whitfield waiting alone in the appointed place. She apologized and gave him the correct information. The next day, however,

Whitfield did not show up. The USCC proceeded to discuss the cases and the Malott incident and voted to invite Whitfield to its meeting the next day. Not surprisingly, he refused to come. Given the AAS's agenda and its experiences with the Cornell bureaucracy, the mistake about the March 12 meeting could not be forgiven. Whitfield's showing up in the first place may have signified a willingness to work something out; if so, the scheduling mistake certainly did not help matters.

In a March 12 editorial the *Sun* speculated that if the faculty voted that day to support the judicial board's jurisdiction to decide the cases on March 13, that "may mark the end of Cornell University's proud years of relative calm." The *Sun* called for the university to accept SDS's call for a new student-faculty committee to consider the legitimacy of the judicial system, for the judicial system to suspend operations for a month while the new group made its report, and for the different sides to get together and talk. "All of these efforts may fail miserably. If they do, only a month has been lost. If they are not tried, much more may be lost."[20]

But the faculty heeded neither the *Sun* nor SDS. As noted, Provost Corson and the faculty reaffirmed the fundamental principles of freedom and of the integrity of the judicial system, albeit equivocally. Right after the faculty meeting the AAS held a meeting of one hundred to two hundred students at 320 Wait Avenue. That morning the AAS had advertised this meeting in the *Sun*. The half-page ad, which applied the logic of the group-based politics of recognition to the legal cases, was worded ominously:

> Because of the recent pressure to establish a black studies program on this campus, a university's committee of questionable legitimacy is moving to oust six brothers. Although most of us were involved in the efforts to secure our right to a relevant education only these six brothers have been singled out as scapegoats. . . . We must demonstrate that by moving against the six, they move against *All*. The meeting on Wednesday is our last chance to discuss the issues and to decide on a unified response before the committee acts. *All Power to the People. Black Power to Black People.*

March 13: Hope Defeated

At the March 13 hearing the six defendants did not appear before the board at the Ives Hall Conference Center. One hundred and fifty students appeared in their stead and presented a statement that challenged the legitimacy of the board. Ruth Darling described the "famous meeting" as "extremely orderly and peaceful," though members of the SFBSC portrayed a pressure-packed scene as students peered through windows and made some threatening noises. Mario Baeza, a freshman, read the statement, and then the board heard testimony from some COSEP members, the dean of students, and others who argued for sensitivity to the black students' concerns. Art Spitzer expressed the feeling on the minds of many board members:

A lot of people there felt that even if they didn't show we should somehow avoid suspending them if possible. But no one could think of an easy way. Everyone realized that if they didn't show and were suspended it might lead to violence of some kind. . . . What everyone hoped for was for the blacks to appear and ask for postponement of the case for a chance for further study of the judicial system. . . . We also discussed various ways in which we could accept something as appearance, if other people showed up instead of them, or if they just sent a statement . . . a vast majority [was willing to interpret this as] showing up.[21]

The white members of the two boards felt they were trying to be reasonable. But in the view of the AAS, their reason was accompanied by the power to expel, and this power was illegitimate. What the whites saw as an honest attempt to uphold justice the blacks saw as a power play wrapped in rationalizations appealing to justice. The AAS's statement said:

The university has a right, and indeed, a responsibility to maintain the integrity of its procedures. The Black students have their own necessity to represent the struggle against the systematized injustices which occur in even so enlightened a place as Cornell University. At such times, as in the case at hand, it is absurd and unjust to expect that the University or its agencies can in fact adjudicate such matters since they are in fact party to the action. It is clear that some impartial and disinterested group has to be involved as is the case in labor-management disputes.[22]

After the presentation of the statement and the testimony, the board deliberated for two hours. The board was encouraged by the AAS's showing up and happy that the possibility of some meaningful discussion seemed at hand. "In view of the encouraging prospects for mutually beneficial discussions," tired SFBSC chairman D. Peter Harvey announced, the board voted to "hold in abeyance the original charges" until there was an opportunity for such discussion to take place. Harvey also declared that the board would forward the AAS's statement to the FCSA to begin the process of discussing the issues at stake.[23]

As he read the statement, Harvey looked at Baeza, who was watching the board's every move. Satisfied with Harvey's statement, Baeza turned to leave the room. Everyone heaved a sigh of relief. Ruth Darling and Gloria Joseph felt a spark of hope. Darling heard a black faculty member concur that it was "a very statesman-like decision." Joseph and Darling looked at each other with anticipation. "We said, 'let's all get a drink.' In other words, we felt, that for one brief shining moment— you know—that something significant had happened. We felt maybe we were over the hill," Darling recalled.[24]

Suddenly Baeza paused near the door and asked Harvey to read the statement again. Holding the charges "in abeyance" was unacceptable. Darling's joy instantly turned to regret. "I recall my sinking feeling right there, that was what we were going to be hung up on. We did go and have a drink, but not with the same sense of relief that we had had before. And sure enough, of course, that was the problem right there, the word 'abeyance'—what did this mean?"[25] Distraught Cornell citizens left, while the already exhausted board continued to meet through the wee hours of the morning.

The AAS also met in the aftermath of the board's decision. It decided against cooperating with the judicial board unless the board dropped the charges or applied them to the AAS as a whole. The supplemented Faculty Council group decided the next day, March 14, that applying the sanctions to the AAS as a whole was tantamount to dropping them because the university just could not suspend 150 AAS students. During this discussion individuals such as Ben Nichols and Chandler Morse pushed for leniency and the continuation of dialogue. Others, such as Spitzer, were drawn more toward the Sindler position, which was to keep seeking dialogue without accepting either of the AAS conditions. But the AAS continued to see the same sword of Damocles, twisting in the wind over the heads of their brothers. After this meeting, the Faculty Council group disbanded and the action shifted to the FCSA. (Meanwhile, the advisory group recommended not charging the Malott Hall disrupters.) On March 14, however, the dean of students told the AAS that he would accept its two conditions unless the FCSA overruled him. Though Meyer was indeed overruled, his action showed a lack of consistency in the administration's conduct of this business.

The FCSA now embarked on an intense two-week project of writing up a report that responded to the AAS statement presented to the SFBSC and the Cornell community through the *Sun*. All concerned parties knew that the fate of Cornell hung in the balance. The task involved reviewing the entire judicial system's procedures and principles. The key question involved the legitimacy of the SFBSC's deciding "political" cases and whether an all-white board was entitled to judge black students. The FCSA repeatedly asked the AAS to participate in this endeavor, but the AAS rebuffed it because the FCSA did not grant the two AAS conditions. Many observers questioned the legitimacy of the FCSA's conducting this review, as it was a target of the AAS's critiques. Yet even Darling acknowledged that it was the best body to conduct the inquiry because of the quality and seriousness of its members.

Over the weekend of March 14, just as the FCSA's labors were beginning, three white students were assaulted on campus. Michael T. Neal was attacked near Triphammer Bridge, and Winthrop Byers was beaten on the Arts Quad. Though attacked from behind without provocation, both men were able to identify their attackers as black; the victims were not robbed but suffered bruises. Joel H. Klotz fared worse: students found him lying unconscious on the Arts Quad early Sunday morning. His attackers inflicted serious head injuries; he remained unconscious for four days and in critical condition for several more. Even after two weeks in the hospital, Klotz could remember nothing about the attack.[26]

The beatings sent tremors throughout the campus. Perkins denounced them, and the *Sun* proclaimed in an editorial that all of Cornell's 250 black students "were on trial" until the AAS identified or cooperated in identifying the perpetrators. The AAS shot back that the editorial unjustly associated the organization with the attacks. In a letter to the *Sun* the next day, Whitfield accused the newspaper of libel, writing, "We see no connection between these alleged acts and our organization." He said such unjust allegations "may in fact lead to a [*sic*] escalation of violence on this campus." That same day the *Sun* published what amounted to an apology and a retraction, claiming that the editorial was misunderstood.[27]

But the *Sun* published another letter just beneath Whitfield's by a black student who wanted to remain anonymous. Under the heading "One Black's View," the writer denounced the AAS's separatist ideology and actions, claiming that many blacks did not agree with its agenda. The writer expressed "shock" and "shame" that "some of my brothers have found it necessary to attack white students." He or she then claimed that those black students who opposed the AAS's direction of action were afraid to speak out. "Even though I am black, if I signed my name to this letter, I would be intimidated. I have seen it happen to others."[28]

The FCSA Report

The FCSA started meeting to work on its anxiously anticipated report addressing the entire set of issues before the judicial boards. On March 18 it met with a subcommittee of the USCC, which argued three points: the judicial board is as representative of the community as it could be, individuals' sanctions should not be transferred to the group, and politically motivated misconduct should be treated the same as misconduct for nonpolitical motives. As a result of this meeting, Meyer sent a letter to the AAS saying the FCSA had overruled his offer to agree to the AAS conditions. That afternoon the FCSA also met with seven black faculty members and staff, whose views differed completely from the USCC's. Justice cannot be had in an environment of institutional racism, the faculty members believed. Spitzer remarked, "I felt like i was banging my head against a brick wall and as I recall speaking to other committee members we all left that meeting feeling very very pessimistic about race relations in general and about the progress of negotiations here in particular."[29]

The next move on the part of the AAS was to inform the FCSA and Meyer that it would cooperate in reforming the judicial system only if the charges were dropped. Not surprisingly, the FCSA (on March 20) refused to accept this position. Dropping the charges under these circumstances would mean that "anyone could get away with anything if he just put enough pressure on us and so on," Spitzer said.[30] The FCSA thus proceeded to review the system and work on the report on its own. From March 21 to 23 it met seven hours a day.

The FCSA was divided over what to do. Some individuals who met with the committee (Meyer, Wayne Biddle, Edward Donoghue, and Mark Barlow) strove to hold off ultimatums and to keep channels open. Members of the FCSA (among them David Lattin and Robert H. Foote) leaned toward the AAS yet also felt bound by the imperatives of the judicial system. Ralph Bolgiano (also a member of the COSEP committee) and Paul McConkey (also a member of the Human Rights

Committee) appreciated the claims on both sides. Ricciuti and Sindler were probably the staunchest advocates of the judicial system's claims, though they were not unsympathetic to the AAS. They were both integrationists. Spitzer said, "When you finally come down to it, for [Ricciuti] the university certainly takes precedence over the problems of any group on campus." [31]

And then there was Sindler. Like his friend Berns, the more circumspect Sindler had a following among students, though he had earned it primarily in the less visible realm of committee and university duty rather than in the classroom and the public arena, where Berns excelled. Spitzer observed that Sindler understood the AAS more than anyone on the committee, even though he was its strongest opponent (this attitude was another trait he shared with Berns). "Professor Sindler is perhaps . . . able to express the feelings of Blacks better than anyone else on the committee, and then to disagree with them, for better reasons than anyone else on the committee," said Spitzer, for whom Sindler became a role model. "He makes very fine distinctions between things. . . . So his philosophy is very finely drawn." Sindler's racial politics were to the left but were conservative when it came to legality and the rule of law. "A university had to protect itself, and . . . there was really no choice," Spitzer said of Sindler. Spitzer compared Sindler's position with that of Morse, for whom "the problems of blacks are so overriding and so important that just about nothing" takes precedence. [32]

Darling's perceptions were similar. Asked whether Sindler believed that the FCSA report would "resolve" the crisis, she replied starkly: "I don't even think that he would regard that as a relevant question. . . . His feeling was this is a principle which we must hold to, and what happens if we hold to this is not our concern." [33] The meaning of this observation sinks in when one recalls that it was made when everyone feared that Cornell was on the verge of a racial cataclysm.

On Monday, March 21, Sindler presented the FCSA with a thirty-page draft of a statement that became the blueprint for the final report. Faculty Dean Robert Miller appeared at the meeting and asked several times, "What can we do to get out of this?" [34] No one doubted that the administration wanted the boards to avoid setting off a crisis, but unlike the situation when setting up the committee to deal with the Malott case, now the administration's hands were tied because the USCC, the FCSA, and the SFBSC were controlled by people less given to compromise for compromise's sake. (Under the new system the president maintained the authority in special cases to intervene and determine whether to pursue or drop charges.) [35] A debate ensued over whether the boards should give the students the choice of showing up or not showing up. They discussed the issues of individual versus group accountability and whether "political" cases should be treated differently from nonpolitical cases. The most involved discussion lasted two days: whether to require the defendants to show up for the hearing before the board or to authorize trying the cases in absentia.

By March 23 the committee had still not made up its mind on this crucial issue. That day four members, Spitzer, Ricciuti, Bolgiano, and McConkey, brought in drafts with suggestions. They made up a balance sheet of pros and cons and weighed the potential consequences of each decision or position. For example, which decision would strengthen the AAS moderates over the radicals? Should the cases be dropped? They dealt with the problems associated with the fact that the entire judicial system was new. There were no precedents for dealing with nonappearance, so why should students be held accountable when the procedural rules were admittedly unclear? And they wrestled with the problems associated with the university's failure to prosecute the Malott disrupters.

As the meeting wore on into its eighth hour, it dawned on a majority that they were facing a battle over competing principles that they could not escape. But they did not carry through on this crucial recognition, which should have compelled them to engage in public relations to garner community support. (SDS and the AAS, masters of politics and the war of words, would later excel in this capacity and win in the arena of public opinion.) The FCSA confronted the irony of the rule of law: it was incumbent on the judicial bodies to learn the arts of war and politics at the same time that it was incumbent on them to support legal principles that putatively transcend politics.[36] Spitzer stated later: "I think that if we were going to come down finally to a fight, to a disruptive demonstration on the campus by the Blacks, to a crisis, to a confrontation, that the least we could have done was to try to fight it on our own terms, our own grounds, in other words, on a good case where we would be able to get the support of most of the community. Unfortunately . . . [we were] unprepared for battle."[37]

Finally a vote was taken. The vote on whether to drop the charges—the one remaining AAS demand—was 6 – 6 (only two members had changed their minds over the last few days, in opposite directions from each other). Ricciuti asked the members to consider how strongly they felt about their positions. They felt "a tremendous amount of respect and understanding" for each other, so they strove to air their thoughts and reach an agreement. The six who voted to not drop the charges voiced stronger convictions, and so the committee decided not to drop the charges. Over the next two days the committee put the final touches on its report of the cases (Ricciuti wrote the major draft) and its forty-five-page report of its review of the judicial system (based mainly on Sindler's draft and input discussed earlier in this chapter). The SFBSC then met and decided to ask the six defendants to appear at its next meeting on April 17.

One of two student members of the FCSA (the other being Stephen Wallenstein, the coauthor of *Open Breeches: Guns at Cornell*), Spitzer, was moved by the integrity and conscientiousness of his colleagues on the committee. As seen, he had been a leading participant in the antiwar demonstrations at Barton Hall that led to the downfall of the old judicial system. A sophomore from Bayside High School in Queens, the intense, medium-built Spitzer considered himself a "liberal reformer type" who preferred working within the system (hence his reluctance to join SDS when they asked him to assume a leadership role). He and a handful of other students had established Cornell's chapter of the American Civil Liberties Union, the organization in which he would make his future career. His commitment to liberal principles of justice was solidified under fire with his colleagues on the FCSA. Spitzer said, "My main recollection is that the committee spent a great deal of time soul searching and debating internally about what was the fair thing to do here . . . it was certainly not a decision that was reached easily by the committee. Then all hell breaks loose." [38]

The FCSA's report, which appeared March 26 in the *Sun,* stated that the defendants should appear or face suspensions. It answered the criticisms of selective enforcement and touted the primacy of individual legal responsibility over group responsibility. To the AAS's charge that the adjudicative system was the "agent" of the university and an expression of institutional racism, the FCSA proclaimed that "it enforces, not the University's political principles, but the community's rules and constraints as embodied in the Student Code. . . . No administrative officer, including the President and the Provost, has authority over the adjudicative process." (Indeed, if anything, the administration wanted the process to back off!) It asserted that the judicial boards were no more a "party to the action" than the civil authority is to the actions of civil suits.

Finally, the report dealt with the issue of defining a "jury of peers," a question that also involves issues of personal identity, race and justice, and race and objectivity. "The adequacy of any selection method turns on what kind of . . . 'representation' is being sought." Defining the proper type of "representation," the report refuted the assumptions of the politics of identity as operative principles of adjudication. The proper ends of the adjudicative system entail the attempt to weigh evidence fairly, honestly, and objectively. The key to liberal justice lies in each adjudicator's being true to his or her intellectual conscience in applying valid community norms to individual cases. "Each adjudicator is expected to apply individual and independent sensitive judgment to cases involving alleged Code violations. Each is required to uphold the Code's provisions, which constitute the body of common rules for the community, but do so in light of the total circumstances of the particular case." The report acknowledged the potential significance of taking such factors as the student's college, class year, living unit, race, gender, and social class into consideration in selecting members of the judicial boards but stood firmly behind the basic principle that individuals should strive to transcend narrow or tribal commitments when it comes to adjudication. "If a board member perceives his representational commitment to be segmental and tight, such as to his campus political organization, he cannot function properly in the present adjudicative system. Nor is the problem solved by multiplying political diversity on the disciplinary boards, since their function is to adjudicate equitably and not to legislate." [39]

The FCSA report was a powerful defense of the judicial system and its basic principles. It also displayed the links between liberal principles of adjudication and liberal principles of education: individual accountability and thinking over group loyalty; community and universal standards of reason and equity over group-based epistemology. Ricciuti said, "That statement I thought was a very cogent argument. [Sindler] sold the committee on Student Affairs on it. It isn't as though our committee had a lot of disagreement on it, in principle." [40] In Sindler's view, however, the administration did not feel the same way. "The reaction of the administration was quietly adverse; presumably it failed to meet its need for avoidance of confrontation." Perkins did not even mention the report at the April 9 faculty meeting "but did comment favorably on the efforts of unnamed others to effect compromise between the AAS and the adjudicative system."[41]

With the issuance of this report, the die was cast. On the same day it was published in the *Sun,* the conduct board met and voted to ask the six students to appear on April 17 for a hearing. But Harvey did not mail the letters over the spring break, hoping something would happen to make sending them unnecessary. Upon his return, nothing had changed, so he had to send them. The letters reminded the students of the seriousness of nonappearance. "In the language of the FCSA report, by such willful nonappearance the individual separates himself from the University community, and therefore is suspended temporarily, pending his appearance before the appropriate conduct board." When the letters were sent, Darling sensed that "to my mind, that was sort of the final call of doom, that . . . something would happen."[42]

The Showdown

On April 12 the FCSA met with Provost Corson, who informed it of the decision not to pursue the Malott Hall demonstrators. The FCSA was not pleased and considered publishing a statement about the case, although the onslaught of events nipped this effort in the bud. Then on April 14 the COSEP committee and six members of the AAS met with the Faculty Council. The students asked the council to intervene to stop the cases, but the council lacked the power to do so. Then the students pointed out something that proved embarrassing: section 8 on the back of the notices to appear—as well as a section of the similar procedures of the Committee on Academic Integrity—provided for cases to proceed in the absence of the defendants if they did not appear. The judicial board could have heard the cases in absentia all along! Barlow told the FCSA the next day, "We have egg on our face." The AAS and SDS were able to use the system's confusion over point 8 to discredit the system. If you don't even know your own rules, how can you hold us accountable for breaking them? Yet this "finding" also provided the FCSA and the SFBSC with an easy out of sorts. They could say the students did not have to appear, mete out a minor penalty, and let everyone go home happy, without losing face.

Tension built during the two days before the April 17 meeting. Again members of the COSEP committee attempted to persuade the boards to alter course by presenting the FCSA with a response to its report. The response attacked the report's premise, that the black students were full members of the Cornell community. Like the AAS, the COSEP committee called for outside arbitration.

After vacation, a day before the April 17 meeting, the AAS published a statement on the *Sun*'s editorial page. The statement reiterated the AAS's criticisms of the judicial system and called the report "sorry . . . , arrogant, smug, complacent, condescending and totally totally inflexible." The *Sun* also published an ominous AAS advertisement in a special supplement: "We tried to negotiate—that didn't work. Now we must find some other way to support the brothers and assert our right to political [determination] as a group."[43] (By now, though, the Board of Trustees had approved the black studies program.)[44]

The FCSA convened again on April 16 and decided that point 8 meant that the judicial board could hear the cases in absentia and that the students would not be penalized for nonappearance. It made its statement justifying nonappearance available to the *Sun*, but the statement was never published because of the avalanche of events. According to Fisher and Wallenstein, "Most of the campus remained ignorant of its existence under the impression that the FCSA had never responded to the charges against point #8. This turned out to be a crucial misunderstanding."[45]

On April 15 Mario Baeza of the AAS called Peter Harvey and started complaining about the requirement of appearance (this was a day before the FCSA decided to drop this requirement). Baeza asked Harvey whether he could come down to the dorms and talk with him in private. Baeza told Harvey that the AAS wanted the cases to proceed in absentia and that minor penalties would be acceptable. Above all, the AAS wanted a speedy resolution of the issue. Harvey came away believing the AAS would accept a minor penalty. He assumed that Baeza spoke for the AAS— he had been the main AAS representative at the March 13 meeting. Yet Harvey had also learned that factional strife had broken out in the AAS again and that Whitfield was losing a measure of control.

Many individuals in the affair wondered why the AAS might have changed its tune about the cases. Some speculated, on the basis of only less than overwhelming circumstantial evidence, that something was brewing, that the AAS had a plan to use the decisions for a political purpose. That Parents Weekend was coming up heightened their suspicions.

According to Fisher and Wallenstein, an AAS member got in a fight with a white student in front of the Straight over a parking spot on April 16 and bloodied the white man's face. When the student asked campus police to arrest the student, the officers told him they could not do anything. The student felt that the university was unwilling to protect his rights under the law. A similar situation would arise with the taking of the Straight. Comments by many sources, including Fisher and Wallenstein and former security officers, and other failures of the campus police to act in similar situations, including a shoplifting spree in Collegetown, suggest that the administration had adopted a "hands off" policy when it came to potentially illegal actions of dissident students, especially blacks.[46]

The SFBSC Decision

Just a few days before the critical April 17 meeting, the trustees had approved the Center for Afro-American Studies, and earlier on April 17 the USCC decided that the misconduct cases should be postponed a week so that the students could be informed of the FCSA's decision to try the cases in absentia. Once again Sindler was the major force behind the latter move, sensing that Parents' Weekend augured trouble. Fisher and Wallenstein remarked that "Allan Sindler had a premonition [that] something would go wrong." That night SDS met to discuss ROTC and housing. By the time SDS member Joe Kelly spoke, the judicial board had rendered its decision. Kelly said the AAS would be meeting all night and that "sometime tonight, they'll be in touch with us. They know where to reach us."[47] The members were told to prepare for an emergency meeting Friday morning, April 18. Harris Raynor recalled attending the SDS meeting late Thursday night and being informed by AAS representatives of the plan to take the Straight. "They told us that they were going to do this action, take over the Straight. It was decided, even though we didn't necessarily agree with all the political stuff they were doing, that we should support them."[48] SDS decided to convene at Anabel Taylor Hall the next morning to discuss setting up a picket line around the Straight to protect the AAS. This would be the first major joint action for the two groups; at Columbia and elsewhere, black and white activists had separate political agendas that discouraged alliances (indeed, Raynor said he was not committed to the AAS's larger agenda). For the next few days at Cornell, unlike at Columbia the previous year, blacks and whites would act together.[49]

The SFBSC had to decide among four possible penalties: no action, which meant no penalty at all; reprimand, which entailed a sending a letter to parents and the student's dean about the student's serious misconduct but not making the letter part of the student's permanent record or a part of letters of recommendation; suspension, which would last as long as the board deemed necessary; or expulsion, which meant not being able to return to Cornell. The defendants did not appear. In their stead Whitfield appeared with five AAS members and told the board "it would be wise" to decide on no action. COSEP members who appeared concurred with the AAS. The board's first decision was whether to delay the decision one week, as Sindler and the FCSA recommended, but the AAS and the COSEP members asked the board to decide the case then and there. After the AAS and COSEP members left, the board was left alone to reach its decision on the disposition of the defendants.

The board voted unanimously to decide the case then and there. Then the SFBSC turned to the disposition of the cases, which it now opened and read for the very first time (it was the practice to read the materials of the case, which consisted of the reports of the code administrator and the Safety Division and related evidence, only at the actual hearing; all previous SFBSC meetings concerning this case had dealt solely with the issue of nonappearance). Under tense conditions, the board deliberated from 9:30 p.m. until 2:00 a.m.

During the deliberations, according to a USCC document, "approximately 150 members of the AAS arrived, knocked loudly on the doors, and demanded that the Conduct Board speed up its decision." Some members of the five-person board felt intimidated by the regular pounding on the walls and the language.

Harvey went outside to talk with the group and was told that they could not understand why the board was taking so long. The exchange revealed a lack of knowledge about how the system worked and the problem of communication that bedeviled the board—a problem that was about to grow much worse. Harvey then called Whitfield and told him that the board would adjourn for the evening if Whitfield did not attempt to quiet the crowd. The students quieted down but remained in the halls until the decision was reached.

The board went back to its deliberations and at 2:00 a.m. voted 4 to 1 to reprimand the three students charged with harassment for the December actions.[50] The members felt this penalty was justified regardless of the political motivation and the alleged symbolic communicative intent (making it relevant to free speech and the First Amendment) because the demonstration exceeded the bounds of legitimate free speech. In the Donlon Hall case the board decided on no action because the Safety Division returned the cushions to Donlon within an hour, and the intent was not to keep them but to dramatize the need for such items in the students' building. Regardless of the logic, the decisions on the two episodes looked like a compromise.

Harvey informed Whitfield of the decision, and Whitfield passed on the mixed news to the students, who *applauded* the announcement. Harvey, Spitzer, Sindler, and others could not help feeling that something had already been planned. Later David Burak would say that SDS knew of the plans two days in advance.

Within moments Cornell was thrown into a turmoil that no one, not even the AAS or SDS, would be able to control. The student body would come to accept the claims of Jones, Evans, and Burak that the judicial system had been corrupt all along and dominated by reactionary faculty. Many members of the judicial system fell into a kind of shell-shock, feeling they had been used for political reasons.

At 1:43 a.m., minutes before the board rendered its decision, the first of a series of eleven false alarms broke the silence of the unsuspecting night at a dorm. Roughly an hour later someone wrapped a six-foot-high cross made of two–by–two lumber in cloth and burned it on the porch of Wari House, the black woman's co-op, and a rock was thrown through the front window. The overtly racist acts sent panic throughout the co-op. The crisis was at hand.

THE STRAIGHT CRISIS

CHAPTER EIGHT

DAY 1: THE TAKEOVER AND THE ARMING OF THE CAMPUS

Allan Sindler's premonition, matched by authorities downtown, proved correct. Something was brewing for Parents Weekend, when several hundred parents would come to Cornell.

The AAS claimed that certain events triggered the takeover of the Straight, but the evidence suggests it was carefully planned. Students had started coming to the office of Dana Payne, associate dean of the Arts College, two weeks before the takeover, asking to drop courses because the time they should have spent studying they had instead used to participate in marathon AAS meetings (by this time the AAS was meeting virtually every night). An assistant dean, Pearl Lucas, was "told by at least one person that it was being planned for some weeks." Lucas recalled a letter to Payne from a student who stated "that he had not done well, and did not want the committee to take action on his grades because he said that he had been busy planning for the seizure of the Straight."[1] And Tom Jones, of course, had alerted Provost Corson on March 6 that Jones intended to "raise enough hell to get Perkins in trouble, and that he might go to jail for it."[2] (In 1987, however, Jones said, "I wasn't part of the leadership and I didn't want to do it [take the Straight], and I didn't think it was necessary. And I'd been voted down in the meeting that decided on that. But the kids felt they needed to feel they had done something.")[3] Finally, the initial stage of the takeover—simply getting staff and occupants out of the Straight—required significant planning that belies the claim that the takeover was spontaneous.

According to Cleveland Donald, the issue of black studies was "practically dead" by the time of the takeover; the trustees had just given the AAS pretty much what it wanted. So the reasons for the takeover must have been related to the judicial board's decisions, the desire to make the new program as radical as possible, and the escalation of revolutionary dialectics. As Donald said, "The occupation of the Straight was another violation of the rules of the game."[4]

The other objective was to show that the AAS intended to protect blacks on campus. The AAS interpreted the burning cross at Wari House as an assault against black women and an affront to black manhood. Another member of the old Garner faction (Garner's best friend) commented that "the most immediate catalyst for that was that . . . we had a burned cross à la the KKK, and obviously this represented an escalation of the struggle. . . . This cross-burning, this threat on the lives of a group of African Americans living together, studying and attempting to find their place in the world at Cornell, was devastating to the entire African-American community. In my recollection, that plus the frustration over the drive to black studies, which was being thwarted at every turn, led to the takeover of Straight Hall." [5]

Caleb Rossiter, son of Government Professor Clinton Rossiter, maintained in a recent book on the politics of the 1960s that the revolts of black students on American campuses were a function of the liberation of feelings that had been repressed by oppression for centuries: "In the late 1960s, in the safety of college campuses, black Americans were able to, and so had to, vent the anger that they, their parents, and the many generations enslaved or endangered that preceded them had, on pain of death, been barred from showing. Men in particular provided rage to this revolt, spurred by the memory of being unable for centuries to provide even a modicum of protection for the women and children in their families. . . . More than anything else, Cornell's Crisis was a drama of liberation in which black men dared to acknowledge that feeling." [6]

The AAS held a meeting on the judicial crisis earlier in the week of April 14. The members gave the leadership (the executive committee of Ed Whitfield, Eric Evans, Tom Jones, Robert Rone, and Robert Jackson) something with which they had not entrusted it before: a "blank check" to devise a response to the anticipated unfavorable ruling. The members implicitly understood that this meant a building takeover. Ironically, the administration had begun to develop a plan to deal with a building takeover—but based on a takeover of Day Hall. The idea to take the Straight arose from one or two individuals, but it was quickly accepted. What an ingenious move! The imposing, medieval-looking building is the nerve center of student life at Cornell. Taking it over would be an act against the entire Cornell community, not just the administration.

A few days before the takeover, the AAS leadership contacted SDS for help. David Burak recalled hearing from the leaders a number of days ahead of time. He, Joe Kelly, and Chip Marshall were called to a meeting at Julio's, a downtown bar. "They said, 'We're probably going to take over the Straight.' . . . Larry Dickson, Irv McPhail, a third person—it may have been Bob Jackson. . . . [So the cross burning] as far as I can ascertain was a contrivance." [7] Marshall recollected, "At that time they were pretty serious, and they wanted—they definitely knew they were going to need support and help. So they talked to me and Burak and Kelly and we did some prework for them." [8]

Sarah Elbert (at the time known as Sarah Diamant) was another SDS member and ubiquitous campus citizen who shared in the planning. After the meeting at Julio's, Marshall called her and set up another meeting, at her farmhouse, with Whitfield and SDS leaders. "Look—the blacks are going to take over the Straight," Marshall informed her. "We're going to support them. We're going to get together and get this stuff ironed out tactically. We can't do it on campus. What do you think?"[9] Elbert figured that her "rural, shacklike house" in Varna was a perfect, secretive place. "Why don't you all just come over here and we'll all have lunch?" she said. When Whitfield and the SDS leaders arrived, Elbert listened to the fascinating plans. "It was like a poker game—it was like . . . like Robert Redford and Paul Newman in *The Sting*. They're all sitting around the table, right? Ed is dealing and he's not saying anything until he finds out who's holding what cards, right?"

Marshall and Kelly wanted action. Impatient to engineer something revolutionary, such as what SDS had achieved at Columbia the previous year,[10] they volunteered to push the envelope for the AAS. "The white guys, Chip and Joe," Elbert recalled, were "very eager—really. . . . I remember Chip very anxious to convince Ed Whitfield that 'by God—we were in this with them and that there wasn't anything, you know, we weren't going to do.'" The conspirators agreed that SDS would set up a picket line outside the Straight to protect the AAS inside and to publicize the AAS's positions and the reasons for the takeover. Controlling public opinion would prove imperative in terms of campus politics, a role Elbert considered heroic and instrumental. "It meant that our bodies were interposed between anybody who was going to get the blacks. . . . It was a very important thing—physically an important realization in terms of racism and radicalism—that that's what you had to do. You had to become—as many people in Chicago would say—'a voluntary nigger.'"

As noted, just seventeen minutes before the judicial board handed down its decision, a false fire alarm rang out at one of the University Halls. By 5:08 a.m. on April 18 ten other false alarms had sounded at nine dorms and at Goldwin Smith Hall, the main building of the Arts College. Several firetrucks rushed to the first two alarms, their sirens sending an eerie harbinger of things to come across the campus.

At 2:52 a.m. police received a frantic call from Charisse Cannady at Wari House. Someone had thrown a brick through the front window and planted a burning cross on the doorstep! From 2:00 until 6:00 a.m. security and safety officers, Ithaca police, and firefighters would run back and forth between their headquarters, Wari, and the false alarm scenes. According to Fisher and Wallenstein, "All day Friday, rumors about the cross burning and false alarms spread through Cornell. What did they mean? Was there a connection between the cross burning and the reprimands? What might happen next?"[11]

Nothing else happened Friday morning, so the administration proceeded with its preparations for Parents Weekend, hanging the traditional "Welcome Parents" sign on the front of the Straight. Cornell counsel Neal Stamp even called Ithaca Mayor Jack Kiely on Friday and reported that Cornell did not anticipate any trouble that weekend; but Kiely kept his police forces on alert anyway. Saturday morning Stamp called back and confessed, "Gee, Jack, I gave you some bum scoop yesterday."[12] (Just before the start of the 1968–69 academic year, Kiely and his aides had informed Cornell administrators in a meeting that they expected big trouble at Cornell that year, and "the administration was unwilling to admit that they could have trouble up there.")[13] Even the weather seemed to transform the campus: warmth and blue skies gave way to cold, gray clouds and chilly rain—not ideal for Parents Weekend. Then word started spreading that SDS planned a meeting at the unlikely time of 6:00 a.m. Saturday.

The AAS met again the night of April 18. Before the meeting more strange things happened on campus; false alarms broke out at 8:13 and 8:26 p.m. "The wail of fire engines could be heard coming onto the campus."[14] At 8:46 another alarm went off: "possible bomb threat" at the Straight. Officials cleared out five hundred people, including parents who were watching a Parents Weekend play, but no bomb was found. At 8:56 someone called in a bomb threat for the Statler Auditorium, where Perkins and hundreds of parents were about to enjoy a concert. Officials did not empty the auditorium, but they delayed the concert to search for the bomb.

The AAS meeting was full of anxious excitement. Like the meeting in December, when militants had left "in euphoria," a party atmosphere prevailed that combined seriousness of purpose and playfulness. One leader stepped forward to declare it was time to take a stand for manhood: the university must be taught a lesson. Not everyone in the AAS felt the same seriousness about the takeover. Stephen Goodwin, for example, supported the effort but thought it was foolhardy. "I mean, they've got all these kids partying one night and fired up, and then they all march them over there from the party. . . . I'm half whacked out of my mind, I'm going over and 'take over the Straight' at 3 o'clock in the morning? . . . Yeah, yeah. Sure, fine.' But the Straight takeover didn't just 'happen.' . . . There were people who already had in their minds how to get the rest of the people involved: throw a party, get everybody fired up at the party."[15]

So the fateful decision was made. Five or six students went ahead of the others, shortly after 5:00 a.m., to set up the invasion by commandeering the keys from the janitors and the manager and by locking the doors to keep people other than AAS members from coming in. Twenty minutes or so later, forty to fifty others joined them in the second task of clearing and securing the Straight. Few had gotten much sleep, so by the time the situation came to a head, many in the AAS must have been as tired as members of the administration. People would be asked to make crucial decisions potentially involving life and death under circumstances of great stress and exhaustion.[16]

Wari and the Alarms

When the administration found out about the cross-burning the previous day, Perkins issued a public denunciation, expressing his and the community's "deep regret." Later Whitfield told alumni the AAS had to take a stand against the lack of respect blacks had received at the hands of the judicial system and the Wari cross-burners.[17] Many at Cornell, however, harbored strong suspicions about the cross-burning, including many sympathetic to the AAS. The officers who arrived on the scene right after Cannady phoned in the alarm (they were already in the neighborhood) were immediately suspicious: the cloth at the bottom of the cross had not yet burned, so it had to have been set moments earlier, but they saw no one running from the scene. Nor had the neighbors seen or heard anything suspicious. An officer at the scene recalled the event clearly twenty-seven years later. "The speculation was at the time that the cross-burning was an inside job. At the time, it was just two pieces of two-by-two, and they weren't even nailed together. They were sort of put together with rags. And it was hastily constructed right there."[18]

The timing of related events raised further suspicion. Moments after Cannady reported the incident, WINS radio in New York City carried a story about it, which the station had picked up from a national wire service. Within minutes calls from across the country inundated the Ithaca police dispatcher.[19] And the false alarms, which led to the emptying of several dorms, were just too coincidental, suggesting a conspiracy. Several dorm residents spotted blacks around fire alarms that were pulled or running from the scenes.

Corson told me that he was virtually certain that some black students had planted the cross. "I am 99.99 percent sure. I've been told by black people involved and others on the campus at the time." Also, a black admissions officer at the time told Corson that the same students were responsible for throwing the brick through the Wari House window. The evidence at the time was very suggestive, especially because no evidence pointed to anyone else. Corson claimed, "It was part of a plot to stir up the students. This was part of the hell that Tom Jones [threatened] . . . [though] I've been told that Tom Jones was not the one to burn the cross." Corson admitted he could not air his suspicions at the time, as it "would have been terribly incendiary, and I had no direct evidence, not even indirect evidence. And it wasn't until fifteen, twenty years later that I began to accumulate evidence."[20]

Even Ruth Darling, a strong supporter of the AAS cause, suspected involvement by a person or persons associated with the AAS. Darling had a long conversation with Cannady the next day and found her genuinely upset (it is likely that Cannady did not know who committed the terrorizing act). Darling then made further inquiries with security, and the more information she obtained, the more suspicious she became. "It began to seem to me, even then, although I was ashamed of my feelings, that this was all part of a very sophisticated plan. . . . It could be racist, but . . . there was enough circumstantial evidence to indicate that blacks had been involved in some of these alarm pullings."[21] Many others shared Darling's suspicions, but not one public word was spoken about them in public because doing so would have incurred the wrath of the AAS and SDS. Thus at the heart of potentially the most successful revolutionary student action in American history most probably lay a lie, a false representation of the truth that won the activists control over the entire public discourse. (It is not at all certain that the AAS would have been able to win such overwhelming student support had the administration made its suspicions of the cross-burning known in a thoughtful manner.) That so many responsible people were unable to say publicly what they honestly felt about this matter—at an institution ostensibly dedicated to the pursuit of truth—reveals how relatively easy it would be for the forces behind the AAS to sway opinion on campus.

In the *Sun*'s Twentieth Anniversary Supplement on the Straight takeover, Goodwin and English Professor Dan E. McCall (then a member of COSEP) finally went public with their beliefs. Goodwin said, "It was a set-up. I knew of it. It was just to bring in more media and more attention to the whole thing." McCall went further, contending that three individuals planted the cross. "I know the guys who did it," he said. "And they were black." He admitted that the roommate of one of the three perpetrators told him in confidence who did it. "He said another black student, a woman, told him the same story, breaking into tears in his office and saying the three students had 'betrayed' her." McCall said the act was "spontaneous" and that the three students "got in big trouble" with AAS leaders, who "greatly resented" what was done. Nonetheless, the AAS did nothing to counter the lie that sparked the takeover. Jones and Whitfield in 1989 denied knowing of such evidence, but they acknowledged that it "could be true." [22]

In response to the AAS and public demand, the administration appointed a commission chaired by Lisle Carter, a black visiting professor of public administration, including Law Professor Ernest Warren and English Professor Douglas Archibald, to investigate the cross-burning as well as an attack on the Straight by Delta Upsilon students that I will discuss in greater detail. The commission report, issued on May 23, 1969, faulted security and the white community for not taking the Wari occupants' fears and concerns seriously enough. Among other things, the officers had left Wari for a while after 3:00 a.m. because they thought matters were in hand and because there were other fire alarms to which to respond. They eventually returned with a watch team. The women's "request for protection was neither frivolous nor hysterical, and they were understandably indignant when they felt that it was not being taken seriously." [23] The police defended their leaving the scene by referring to the false alarms (they did not mention their suspicions about the burning being staged), but the committee concluded that the police could have explained their reason more clearly to the women. Though the report probably adequately captured the officers' failure to treat the Wari students' fears as seriously as they should have (after all, there is no evidence that anyone in Wari knew about the origins of the cross), its failure even to raise the issue of an inside job challenges the committee's claim that it conceived its mission to "be as concise, crisp and factual as possible." [24]

The Takeover of the Straight

The evidence of the actual takeover and subsequent events reveals some criminal behavior, but the truth must be spoken. Also, be aware that many acts were committed by individuals or small groups on their own, unbeknown to the larger organization, and that different individuals had different beliefs and attitudes toward what was happening. Accordingly, some of the descriptions and observations that follow might appear to conflict with other portrayals, yet that is the nature of a complex clash that involves many individuals in a mass movement. Finally, you are urged to remember that the students were young and angry—Irene Smalls would often punctuate her recollections of events with the exclamation, "We were so young!"— and that one must avoid indulging in generalizations based on race. Many leaders in our society pushed the envelope of appropriate behavior when they were young, so our assessments of young people's acts must possess due perspective. Just as most white students did not belong to SDS, so did most black students remain outside the AAS, and many who did get involved had ambivalent feelings about its ends or its tactics. Nonetheless, acts were committed that cannot be justified in any rational way, especially on a college campus. I am especially indebted to Fisher and Wallenstein's manuscript in this portrayal of the actual takeover. (Fisher's presence at Safety provided him with much information.)

The advance group entered the Straight through the back door in a heavy mist that would soon become a freezing rain. They first encountered employees who had arrived early to ready the Straight for business and to prepare food. The interlopers ordered the employees to give them keys and to leave the Straight. The employees resisted, and a scuffle ensued in which an employee was grabbed and knocked down. A woman employee hit an intruder. The campus dispatcher received a phone call from another employee who shouted that he had been struck in the face and "could not tolerate any more." The dispatcher heard fighting. Eventually the intruders prevailed and began to barricade the door and windows with whatever objects they could find.[25]

Upstairs at around 5:30 a.m. Paul R. Hutchins, the night supervisor of custodians, ran into three students carrying wires, chains, and knives, including one "crude bayonet." The students declared that they were taking over the building and rounded up the custodial staff. Other students started entering the Straight through the elevated terrace in the back, where they had been assembling, and started spreading throughout the building, looking for occupants. Two students remained with the custodial staff. At 6:00 a.m. the AAS released the custodians through the service entrance at the back (they had barricaded other spots). Hutchins reported the operation had been well-planned "and professionally directed. Everyone had an assigned duty."[26]

At 6:15 a.m. students, one brandishing a club, took over WVBR, the radio station in the Straight, so that Whitfield could announce the takeover to the community. The captors remained for a few minutes, leaving when they were informed that they were committing a federal crime. After "truly extraordinary" efforts, WVBR managed to reestablish broadcasting from a location downtown.[27]

Finally, the AAS had to deal with the people sleeping in the rooms upstairs, including the resident manager, law student Lawrence C. Salameno, and twenty-eight parents. Salameno heard the commotion and called security. While he spoke to a police officer, a group of students in Black Panther berets leaped over a balcony and poured into his room. One of the students ordered him to leave. Salameno asked them what they intended to do with the guests upstairs and noticed that they were surprised to hear that parents might be in the other rooms.[28]

After they had rounded up all the employees, the students went to the parents' rooms, pounded on the thick doors, and shouted to the occupants to get up and leave. Parents made various reports to security and the administration about the treatment they received at hands of the AAS. All were shocked and angry, and many were terrified. The official AAS and administration version was that the parents were treated courteously, but the evidence paints a different picture. Treatment varied with the situation. It is also possible that some parents, out of anger, exaggerated the treatment they received, though none of the parents' reports contradicted any of the others'. According to these reports, some students threatened parents and treated them rudely. Several parents reporting seeing weapons (clubs, knives, even one pistol); others did not. Some had to leave their rooms in their nightwear, and most had to leave belongings behind (one couple left $600 worth of jewelry). When occupants did not open their doors with sufficient dispatch, the aggressors kicked the doors in and broke locks with crowbars. One woman was told that "the black man has risen." Some parents were called pigs and warned, "Your lives are in danger; you had better get out fast." Another woman said the students who ousted her from her room were "loud and vigorous and frightening." She exclaimed, "This is Nazism in its worst form." A *Sun* reporter flatly stated, "All the parents involved said they were 'terrified' by the blacks." [29]

After the crisis had settled at the end of April, Perkins wrote apology letters to the parents, promising reimbursement for any expenses related to the incident. He also enclosed letters from alumni who supported his policies during the crisis (a distinct minority of the letters he received). Among the responses Perkins received was one from a lawyer who had spent the night in the Straight. He accepted the president's apology but then unleashed his fury. First, he questioned Perkins's statement that such a takeover "was not anticipated in the manner that it happened." He had noticed that all the doors to the Straight had been shut and bolted by 11:30 Friday night—something that he had never witnessed in his previous stays there. He had heard the commotion before other parents, so he called security for rescue before the students could stop him. He told Perkins of the reply he received:

> The first question I was asked was whether they "were white or black?" I then opened my door to investigate and saw the intruders just as they managed to open the door leading to the hallway. Upon advising the Security Police that I had seen a black man, I was told that there was nothing that could be done for us. It certainly put one in an unpleasant state of mind to hear such a response, and it almost seemed as if the intruders were white the answer would have been entirely different. . . . Just prior to their last threat that they would break down the doors "and carry us out," I again phoned the Security Police for advice. The police stated "Do as they tell you. If they'll let you out, go out. Don't argue with them." [30]

The attorney concluded by saying that his letter was intended to provide a counterview to the favorable alumni letters included with Perkins's letter of apology.

We have seen that the evidence suggests that the Perkins administration had made it known to security (explicitly or implicitly) that student militants, especially blacks, should not be arrested or impeded unless absolutely necessary. This policy coexisted with the policy of keeping local law enforcement officials off campus at all costs. As a result, the university was helpless to defend itself and others from concerted disruptive action.

The students led the parents down several flights of stairs to the garbage room at the back of the Straight, where they waited to be expelled en masse. "One man took ill and began gasping for air, and was released after demands from two other parents. The parents had to jump off a [three-]foot loading dock into the freezing rain. Salameno described them as 'panic stricken.' Security took them over to nearby Sage Hall, where they questioned them and provided them with food." [31]

Meanwhile, Stamp notified the authorities downtown. At 7:00 a.m. the SDS group went to the Straight and set up a circular picket line in front. Soon about seventy-five members were patrolling the area around the Straight for protection. They handed out leaflets that explained what had happened and why and announced a rally in front of the Straight at 10:00 a.m. "Fight Political Repression!! Black Students Have Seized Willard Straight Hall!!" After denouncing the legacy of capitalist and colonialist exploitation and racism, the leaflet said, "The Blacks in Willard Straight Hall Are Fighting Against Much More than a Simple Reprimand. They Are Fighting to Free Their People From a System Which Denies Them the Right to Self-Determination." It then demanded the recision of the reprimands and amnesty for any crimes committed in the Straight takeover. This was the first public expression in favor of amnesty.

Thomas Tobin, director of public information, said that the SDS line was more for show than for actual protection. Sometime during the morning a reporter for United Press International (UPI), Jean Blabey, was stopped in front of the Straight by SDS and ordered not to proceed any further. Blabey just kept on walking through the picket line. According to Tobin, "The press interpreted the picket as pretty much of a publicity or public relations gesture on the part of SDS, an attempt, if you would, to at least publicly involve themselves in the activities or actions of the black students inside the building." [32]

Once they secured the Straight, the AAS sent the women to the kitchen to cook breakfast, and the men took up lookout positions at windows and doors. They took turns going to eat and then held a general session. Whitfield addressed the group about the objectives of the takeover: the plan was to hold the Straight for a few hours to make the point and then leave. Few expected what awaited them. The AAS had already made contact with the administration and was not armed beyond the few weapons spotted by the guests.

Students portrayed what went on inside in various lights. The official word from the AAS and the administration was that the students treated the Straight with respect, but as we will see, they caused considerable damage (unlike the Students Afro-American Society, which had left the building it occupied at Columbia the previous spring in immaculate condition). [33] Also, at some point during their thirty-four-hour stay, some radical members debated whether they should burn the Straight to the ground if Perkins did not meet their demands. And when they brought in arms in response to threats, the situation exploded with tension. Nonetheless, the occupants engaged in a variety of activities, including—according to some sources—studying. McPhail said he and many other students brought their books and studied every chance they had:

> Most of us had books, and in addition to kind of talking about where we were—what we were doing, conferences, that kind of thing—people were booking. People were taking this thing very seriously because we had exams coming up. . . . I think that there's a mythology out there that suggests that all of these movements—be it at Cornell, Columbia, or anyplace—represented kind of a group of black thugs or something from the ghetto that these great universities in their great magnanimous zeal let into the institution, people who couldn't read, write, compute—people who were not good students, who were flunking out, who just came up and raised a lot of hell and took stuff over and then left.[34]

According to Andre McLaughlin, the takeover was festive at the start. Students used the phones to call their roommates and friends who had avoided the party that night and told them to come over and get involved. It was the place to be, and it might be dangerous for others to remain outside on their own. McLaughlin also pointed out, "The first thing we did, without anybody telling us, we went back and started opening freezers and started cooking things for people to eat. Nobody said that this was a women's job; we just said, 'Hey, we gotta eat.'"[35] Students also called their parents on university phones and received the kind of response McLaughlin received. "When I called my mother from there, she said, 'I didn't send you there to be takin' over any buildings. What's wrong with you, girl?' That's the first thing we did, we called our parents. Because we didn't want them to see it on TV [first]. . . . We didn't particularly get the kind of response that we were expecting. We weren't liberators to our parents, right?"[36]

Goodwin did not take part in the takeover per se, but he did go to the Straight and got hold of the tape machines in the WVBR studios (where he had hosted a radio show during the year called "Uncle Tom's Cabin," on which he would interview a black student or person and ask the audience at the end of the interview to decide "whether the interviewee is an Uncle Tom or not"). During the takeover, "I taped conversations and sold them to Reuters or UPI. The black students wouldn't talk to whites, so they talked to me, and I taped it."[37]

Irene Smalls had gone home for the weekend, so she had not attended the party or the takeover. Still, she returned as soon as she could to help the cause on the outside. Smalls scouted out what was going on with campus police and the deputies later:

> I was willing to do whatever it was that I was asked to do to support the black students in the Straight. . . . They would send us out . . . and we were supposed to be keeping an eye on the National Guard and so on and so forth. Now that I think about it thirty years later, I'm like, that is ludicrous! Sending me out to keep an eye on the National Guard! The idea was that these were our fellow students in the

Straight and we didn't want them to, you know, get hit with something that they weren't aware was up.[38]

Fight Back or Wait It Out?

The Safety Division dispatchers were the first to hear of the takeover, in calls from the Straight. They immediately informed Lowell George, who called Vice President Mark Barlow. Barlow hurried to campus at 6:30 a.m. and checked out the situation before he called Perkins and Corson (who was at a medical school ceremony in New York and hurried back as soon as he found out). Meanwhile, campus security officers surrounded the Straight with the few men that they had and stationed people by Day Hall. Eugene Dymek, head of security, made a fateful decision: *campus police would be unarmed and would let AAS supporters come and go but deny entrance to anyone else.* George then notified Perkins and Kennedy at 6:10 a.m. Early that morning Stamp had called Ithaca Mayor Kiely and confessed that he had been wrong about the quiet weekend ahead. Kiely went to work and set up a meeting of Ithaca safety officials in his office. Around 7:00 a.m. Kennedy and Stamp arrived at the Safety Division and were briefed.

At about 7:30 Kennedy began trying to contact the students in the Straight. He asked to speak with Whitfield, but the occupiers kept hanging up the phone. Kennedy and company debated turning off the utilities (someone had seen the students laying out fire hoses to repel intruders) but decided against it because of fears about the toilets flooding. They did turn off the phone lines (after many student calls had been made), except for the pay phones, which they kept open for purposes of communication. SDS started its picket and began feeding equipment into the Straight for the AAS.

Perkins showed up at 8:00. The executive staff (Perkins, Stamp, Vice President of Safety Peterson, and Vice Provost Kennedy), accompanied by Dymek and George, set up the first "war room" in the elegant White Museum study across the street from Day Hall. They had received an intelligence report from SDS about the AAS's demands. Barlow did not trust the report, but it proved reliable. He was in and out, often dealing with student groups who were getting involved around the campus. Stuart Brown covered Day Hall.

What became known as the "war council" (and then "the university in exile," as the staff adopted a strategy of changing the location of its headquarters to avoid capture) confronted two major decisions. First, should Perkins cancel his speech to the parents slated for 9:00 a.m. at Statler Auditorium on the topic of "prospects for stability"? Administrators had information that SDS planned to disrupt the meeting—and who in his right mind would want to give this speech under the present circumstances? They canceled it. Unfortunately, nobody informed the parents. When the parents showed up to find out just what was stable in the university, SDS greeted them. Burak made a speech on the AAS's behalf, only to be met with boos and catcalls from the parents.[39] This incident foreshadowed things to come.

Though Perkins did not show up at Statler, George sent most of his officers

there, just in case there was trouble. This would prove to be another fateful decision. At 9:00 a.m. only five officers remained at the massive Straight (seven policed
Statler, four covered Day, and two remained at Safety Division headquarters).[40]
The Straight's north and south ends remained underprotected. Also, at 9:30 Meyer's
office set up shop at CURW, down the street from the Straight, and formed an intelligence and rumor center.

The other question the war council had to deal with was how to respond to the
takeover. There were four options: calling in armed police and forcing the students
out, charging them with trespass; securing an injunction from a county court that
would order the students to leave by a specified time or face contempt charges (this
method had recently been used with good effect at the University of Chicago); negotiating with the students; and just waiting them out.

The council dismissed the first option quickly. It had failed miserably at Harvard
a few days before, and the melee that resulted in expelling the students from the
building had caused physical injury and damage and won the student militants
unanticipated support. Since the *Trojan Horse* incident—coincidentally, in front of
the Straight—the administration had avoided bringing in outside force at all costs.
"We continued to operate on the principle of not letting outside police on campus,"
Corson told me.[41] Besides, as everyone who was involved stressed, Ithaca and Cornell just did not have the law enforcement resources to accomplish this task.

What about an injunction? It entailed the exercise of authority and decisiveness,
but not necessarily force (that would depend on choices made down the line). Under an injunction, a court tells the occupiers that they may leave freely by a specified
time or they will be arrested when they do leave later. Barlow preferred this approach, which had worked at Chicago and Columbia earlier that year. It put the
onus on the occupiers as lawbreakers while it made the administration look patient
and deliberate. Nonetheless, University Counsel Neal Stamp maintained that no
one seriously entertained the injunction possibility. "Nobody in the administration
would go along with it. Nobody. It was a matter of philosophy. They wanted to control the thing right on campus, not involve the courts off campus."[42]

Nonetheless, Stamp proceeded to get the injunction papers ready and contacted
people downtown, just in case Cornell went that route. But the administrators demurred. True to their modus operandi, they prepared to wait and negotiate, letting
the situation dictate what to do.

According to Tobin, who had assigned himself to cover the executive staff during the crisis, the staff was not at all panicky at this point in time. Tobin would provide some of the most objective observations during the crisis. "The executive staff
seemed to be willing to wait it out. As I recall, there [were] discussions of taking the
injunction route. . . . Parents Weekend would continue. . . . The decision was made
to go ahead with business as usual on campus. . . . There was . . . no sense of . . . extreme urgency in terms of getting the students out of that building."[43]

They could not completely abandon the injunction option, however. Stamp told
the staff they would have to make contact with the occupiers and order them to leave
as the first step in the process. So around 9 o'clock Stamp, Kennedy, and Dymek

went to the Straight and worked their way through the picket line. Dymek, repeating what Stamp had told him, addressed the AAS with a bullhorn and ordered it to leave. When some students leaned out the window just above the Parents Weekend sign, Kennedy asked whether he could speak with Whitfield. Eventually Whitfield came to the window and shouted to Kennedy that the students would be issuing formal demands in a short while. Kennedy shouted back that the administration wanted "to try to reach an early settlement if possible."[44] Dymek thereupon took the bullhorn and announced that the students should evacuate immediately, no conditions granted.

Just then the sounds of a fracas came from the south side of the Straight, in the back. Whitfield left the window to find out what was happening. Administrators and SDS members rushed to the scene.

Attack!

Fisher and Wallenstein wrote that "in retrospect, the commotion around the window on the south side of the Straight marked the turning point of the occupation. Eyewitnesses to the incident contradicted each other. Two distinct versions emerged."[45]

What is known for sure is that twenty-five brothers of the Delta Upsilon fraternity, a leading "jock house," had entered the Straight through this unguarded window. Their motives appear to have been mixed: to liberate the Straight, to confront the AAS in vigilante fashion, and to persuade the AAS members to leave the premises. Yet even if we grant their better intentions, their storming of the Straight can only be interpreted as an attack on the already alarmist AAS. To the DU brothers, however, the AAS takeover during Parents Weekend was the final straw; some of them fancied themselves acting on behalf of the silent majority. It was the first sign of a new and revolutionary situation, a form of "student power" attempting to fill the vacuum of authority created by the administration's inaction.

The confrontation was loosely associated with other fraternities. The DU members had earlier received a phone call urging them to join other fraternities in taking over the AAS headquarters at 320 Wait Avenue, probably as a countermeasure to the taking of the Straight. The administration had to make a major effort to head off what could have been disastrous action from the Greeks.

But Delta Upsilon did not care about taking over 320 Wait: the brothers would act on their own and go to the heart of the problem. According to Barry Stacer, a sophomore and a football player, the brothers "were tired of everyone taking care of the minority and ignoring the majority. . . . Everyone had the right to be there [at the Straight]." Stacer stated the fraternity's case:

> We felt we had as much right in the building as the blacks did; it's a building for Cornell University students. . . . Our entering was a denial of the legitimacy of their seizure. It was purely a political act. . . . Being athletes and competitors, which

usually goes hand-in-hand with a law-and-order philosophy, we just couldn't let anybody get away with seizing the Straight. We lost all faith in the University administration. . . . We wanted to go in and talk to the blacks and see if we couldn't talk them out of what they were doing.[46]

The AAS, however, saw nothing benign in the intrusion. After entering through the unguarded window, a DU group of fifteen made its way up the labyrinth of stairs in the back of the Straight to the main lobby (two members split off on their own). On their way the brothers encountered women who started screaming. In the lobby several AAS members ran to defend themselves and their women, attacking the new intruders with whatever they could get their hands on: cue sticks, wooden chair legs, iron pokers, baseball bats, claw hammers, aerosol cans, fire extinguishers, and squirt guns (possibly filled with "pepper water," a chemical irritant invented by the Black Panthers). Chaos broke loose when the Delta Upsilon brothers announced that they were there to open the front doors of the Straight.

The AAS pushed the intruders back amid fighting, spitting, squirting, pushing, and screaming. At the window the AAS threatened, "We are going to get you at DU."[47] According to SDS leader Chip Marshall, who was at the scene to help the AAS, "As they left, a couple of guys [from DU] were . . . shouting things like we're coming back, we're going to burn it down next time."[48] A flying object cost one fraternity man several teeth, and combatants on both sides were bloodied in the face. A campus police report described the exit scene: "Projectiles were bouncing off the windows and flying glass was imminent. The black students . . . appeared to be very upset, and made several threats about filling the whites full of lead."[49]

To the AAS the DU intrusion was an assault on the organization and an affront to black women. Later that summer, though, Jones made a speech that was intended to defend the AAS posture but also lent some support to the DU claim that it was seeking dialogue, not confrontation. "So we went downstairs. . . . The white boys were standing there; when they saw us coming, they wanted to negotiate, you know, 'Let's talk about it, you know, we can discuss this thing.' It was too late for that, because the sisters had already been harmed; they had no business being in the building anyway."[50] As noted, though, the campus police were undermanned at the Straight because their colleagues were needed elsewhere.

Andre McLaughlin commented on the DU attack. "That was the only time we got nervous. Then we were thinking they might set us on fire. We got kind of paranoid then. . . . Some people . . . had this poker mentality, like they were really in battle. But there were other people that were very overwhelmed with a sense of being isolated from just everybody, the campus, the community. Wondering what was happening. And you find that people have their own thresholds for stress under those kinds of circumstances."[51]

There was some validity to the fraternity's claim that it was there to negotiate. But the campus police had interesting observations about the scene. Sergeant George Taber felt that the administration and security simply did not have enough control over the situation. "People didn't know what they were doing. . . . I had been on the job three days, and then finally [was given] a uniform, or some semblance of a uniform that they threw together, and I was told to just go down and stand there."[52] Current Cayuga Heights Police Captain David Wall, who worked at that time with Cornell security and interviewed the DU students after the fact, said their motives were not pure:

> I think it was a mixed bag. I think they went over there with the full intention of saying, "Look, guys, you don't take over a whole building." . . . The problem is that you had a few hotheads. They went there with the sole intention of saying, "To hell with you, we're going to take it back!" . . . [The AAS] had taken pool cues and taped knives from the kitchen to them. They were very well organized and very well established in the building. . . . There was a tremendous amount of hostility from DU. . . . Even those who went there with a little more low-key, sensible approach came out very disgruntled, very angry, very bitter. To put it bluntly, as if to say, "This is bullshit. We're coming from a college, from a school, a university, and this is like a war zone."[53]

According to Chip Marshall, the officer standing by the window did indeed let the students in. But the officer was alone and unarmed, as were all the campus police on duty at this time, so SDS stepped in, in effect, to do the campus security's job for it.[54] The AAS would use SDS's failure to keep the DU members at bay as leverage when its leaders asked SDS to be ready to take a building on the AAS's behalf later in the controversy. But on Saturday this commitment meant that SDS would perform the job of protection. Here was another glimpse of militant student power filling the vacuum of authority at Cornell. And this was the point when the crisis moved beyond a typical confrontation with authority to become a conflict with revolutionary potential. Soon SDS would play a role in meetings held at Noyes Center with the leaders of various fraternities to quell a potential uprising among fraternities. (Marshall described the fraternity leaders as "tending to be liberal" and therefore opposed to vigilante actions.)[55]

The DU attack was like pouring gasoline on a fire. Kennedy said, "I could string those DU people up by the ears—that broke off everything."[56] Suddenly the AAS considered resorting to arms. At 10:00 an occupier spoke to onlookers from a window, denouncing the "campus clowns" who had broken in, "swinging sticks and hurting people." He then warned that "if any more whites come in, you're gonna die in here" and promised a "reign of terror. We took this building without hurting anybody and we're trying to hold it that way." A student wearing a Cornell football jacket shouted back, "Get your ass out of there."[57]

Though the AAS never threatened to use the guns in any capacity other than self-defense, the presence of guns had serious consequences that will be examined in time: the arming of other groups on campus, a dramatic shift in the administration's posture in negotiating (it would now settle at almost any price), and lending background power and credibility to specific threats that Tom Jones made against individual administrators and professors on Tuesday evening, when danger was at its peak. And to the extent that those who possess guns also possess power over those who do not, by arming itself the AAS gained significant bargaining power over the administration and the unarmed campus security officers.

Another development followed along these lines: the demonization of DU and the concomitant censuring of anyone who spoke out publicly against the AAS. The DU attack gave those who opposed the AAS's posture a bad name. On Saturday night DU was targeted with threatening phone calls and had to post guards for protection; SDS's spin on events was starting to prevail. The administration remained largely silent, and no other groups were talking.

Soon after the DU affair, the Interfraternity Council (IFC), a forty-five-person organization consisting of the fraternity presidents or representatives, met with other interested parties, including parents, in an emergency session at Noyes Center, down the hill from the Straight. The purpose of this meeting was to defuse some of the fraternities that had "had enough" and were talking about storming the Straight. One of Cornell's most popular teachers, Sociology Professor Charlie Ackerman, spoke at the gathering and discouraged the fraternities from taking precipitous action. Ackerman was a noted gadfly who had developed close relations with fraternity men, especially athletes. Over the years he had played a major role in educating the "jock houses" about social and political issues. According to some sources, Ackerman's background and immediate influence were important in keeping fraternities that might be inclined to take action at bay. In addition, his recent denial of tenure had politicized the fraternity jocks to some extent and made them less deferential to faculty authority. A week before the Straight takeover the jock houses had even organized a massive rally on Ackerman's behalf on the Arts Quad, at which Burak spoke, wearing a large snake around his neck. Andrew Hacker told me that "there were a lot of traditional fraternity types at Cornell who could have been a large group opposing the Bailey Hall kind of thing [the action Tuesday night on behalf of the AAS], but because they had become semipolitical—sensitized— because of the Ackerman thing, they didn't cause a rift in the students." [58]

The IFC meeting succeeded in stopping what would have amounted to an act of war, but the truth is that the DU failure had already subdued the desires of those present to mount another attack. Unfortunately, the administration did not pass this absolutely crucial information on to the AAS inside the Straight. An interesting possibility emerges from this vantage point: though the DU attack transformed the crisis into one of extreme danger at one level, it is also possible that it unwittingly served to head off another dangerous move by a consortium of fraternity brothers at another level. Pick your poison.

The first gathering at Noyes endorsed getting an injunction. The meeting featured some antiadministration rhetoric from parents and people such as Paul Rahe, who blamed the predicament on the administration's failure to lead decisively over the previous year. At the second meeting later that afternoon, however, the IFC group voted 43–2 against an injunction and informed the administration of this. IFC student members then met with President Perkins and Vice Presidents Kennedy and Muller. By this time the campus was fully aware of what was happening. Muller had made a broadcast on WVBR informing the campus of the basics and beseeching everyone to stay cool. Meanwhile, the war council had gone back to Day Hall, where it prepared to move everything over to Myron Taylor Hall, the home of the Law School where the augmented Faculty Council, with student volunteers (selected to give advice) whose names had been chosen by lot, was meeting at 11:00 a.m.

New Demands

At noon Kennedy picked up a note outlining three AAS demands: to nullify the reprimands, to reopen the question of housing, and to conduct a thorough investigation of the cross-burning. Another demand would be forthcoming: thorough investigation of the DU attack. At 2:00 p.m. Perkins discussed the demands with Barlow, Kennedy, Muller, and two students, Peter Harvey and Chip Reveal. By then the AAS had dropped the irrelevant housing demand, and the administration had already commenced an investigation of the cross-burning, so that demand presented no problem. The issue of nullification was stickier. When someone mentioned that surrendering principle (nullifying under pressure) was a problem, Muller interjected, "We aren't sacrificing any principle if we save lives." This refrain would be repeated often in the coming days.

The rest of the morning and afternoon consisted of meetings of the Faculty Council, the IFC, the war council, and the dean of students. In the afternoon Muller and Barlow met in secret with a black student named Nat Jones, an AAS member and a brother in Delta Tau, a white fraternity. After Muller left, Jones said things that turned Barlow around. Jones told Barlow that nullification was necessary to resolving the crisis because black students considered the judicial board's action "rank discrimination. . . . And coming from Nat Jones, this moved me very much. . . . We had butchered the whole thing from A to Z." [59] Barlow had been a member of the Sindler Commission and greatly respected its work and Sindler's contributions, but he had thought all along that Sindler's stand on the judicial board's treatment of the sanctions was wrong, even "despicable." (In his eyes, Sindler's influence and position were key reasons that the crisis over adjudication could not be resolved without a showdown.) [60] Barlow went back to the war council and reported what Jones had said. Still, he continued to believe that an injunction offered the best way out of the mess. Meanwhile, SDS arranged to use Bailey Hall that evening at the university's expense.

SDS leaders at CURW (next to where the war council was starting to meet and right next door to the rumor clinic) had engaged in a heated debate over whether they should seize Day Hall in the wake of the DU attack. Gary Esolon, the SDS housing initiative leader, had received an angry call from an AAS member in the Straight, castigating SDS for not preventing the invasion. Burak pushed for SDS to redeem itself by announcing a takeover of Day at the teach-in that evening, yet

Marshall, Kelly, and Jeff Dowd voted him down. They would not commit to a takeover at this point, preferring to "hold the possibility as a trump card."[61]

Throughout the afternoon efforts were made to retrieve parents' belongings from the Straight. Earlier students had passed a heart patient's pills out of the Straight, and from 5:00 to 6:00 p.m. parents came back and picked up their belongings at the back door after students carried them down from the rooms. Only a small radio remained missing. It was a tense scene, for it was the parents' first chance to meet their evictors face to face. Angry parents, especially the mothers, vilified them. Kennedy said, "I had to get the men together and tell them to get their wives out of there or the whole thing would blow up. Black students were perspiring because it was a long hike up there and hauling baggage and bringing it down— I tried to convince them to let the parents go in and get their stuff. . . . But they wouldn't. . . . [Parents] just literally almost attacked them. They certainly did verbally."[62] That these AAS members were willing to retrieve the belongings and expose themselves to such excoriation without responding suggests that they still felt some obligation to the Cornell community.

Earlier that morning the dean of students office set up shop at CURW headquarters at Anabel Taylor Hall. All morning the phone rang off the hook with the calls of curious Cornellians and others. Before long the office had set up Cornell's first official "rumor clinic," which was equipped with nine telephones that at times rang constantly. The clinic was modeled on the smaller-scale rumor clinic formed a year before to handle the turmoil over the McPhelin case and King's assassination. Its mission was to track down rumors and report the facts to the best of its ability. Tobin maintained that the rumor clinic backfired: rather than quelling false rumors, it often helped to spread them.[63] Soon there would be at least three "realities": objective facts (complicated enough), interpretations and opinions about what the facts meant, and rumors and perceptions. Those who wanted to mold public and political opinion drew on all three sources.

Already the rumors—emanating from phone calls and police radio reports— were getting scary: 250 whites on their way to storm the Straight, a bomb ready to go off at Noyes Center, a bomb threat at DU. Later that day callers made two more bomb threats against "right-wing groups," more threats to retake the Straight, a threat to burn down Wari House, and a threat to take over Day Hall. Another rash of false alarms broke out. Saturday evening the rumors swelled, as call after call reported guns and hatchets being smuggled into the Straight, and others sited snipers and other dangerous activities on campus.[64] Similar reports poured into the Ithaca police and fire departments, and the Cornell Safety Division. According to Fisher and Wallerstein, some of the reports were "hysterical."[65]

The AAS was not sheltered from these reports. SDS, supporters, and, surprisingly, even the administration kept the occupiers abreast of what they heard. Interestingly, SDS and the rumor clinic developed what Ruth Darling called a "strange coalition" because they occupied rooms right next to each other at Anabel Taylor (SDS set up shop in the reception room), another sign that the students were starting to run the store. "So we were using the same telephone lines and were in close contact with each other throughout the entire process," Darling reported.[66] At one point Jeff Dowd of SDS and Darling got into an argument because the phones were so busy that SDS had trouble getting access to the lines. Other than showing the emerging SDS attitude that it had as much right of access to key university equipment as the administration, SDS's relationship with the rumor clinic provided the organization with a superb source of campus information. SDS kept the AAS apprised of rumored vigilante actions as well as of the administration's conversations with local officials and the governor's office about sending deputies and the National Guard to Ithaca. These reports helped to convince the AAS, already paranoid after the DU attack (which, amazingly, some AAS members interpreted as university-sanctioned), that it needed weapons for self-defense. Irving McPhail recalled that fears of the National Guard and more fraternity attacks went hand in hand. "Our sources, our contacts on the outside, started telling us about [Governor] Rockefeller having organized the National Guard or something to come in and to forcibly remove us. And now there is a very, very clear threat not only to our movement but a threat to our lives as well."[67]

The rumor clinic was also the scene of an ominous event. At noon a student who was an Episcopal nun ran into the dean of students' new headquarters, out of breath. She had just witnessed one of Cornell's leading militants arrive at the Straight. Someone inside yelled, "What do you want us to do with the building?"—perhaps referring to the debate they had about whether to burn the building. "Give it to them!" the militant shouted back. "Go home and get your guns. We'll shut down the whole university."[68] Meyer and Muller quickly told the campus police what they had heard. Was it simply another rumor, or was it true?

The "Teach-In"

Like most such events on college campuses then and now, the SDS teach-in that night served to advance an agenda rather than to objectively assess the issues. SDS presented its case for the AAS demands. The IFC representatives spoke of the AAS as the victims of a breakdown in the judicial system, presenting a caricature of the system as one of rank injustice. For the AAS and SDS, the fraternities no longer presented a problem. Even Barlow contributed to the disparagement of the judicial system; in so doing he even misrepresented (according to Spitzer) the membership of the FCSA—of which he was a member! After Dowd and Marshall reviled the judicial system, FCSA member Art Spitzer was the only one with the courage to rise and present the other side, but no one wanted to hear his words. Spitzer's observations of the meeting show how successful SDS was becoming in molding public truth.

Spitzer pointed out the significance of the Straight having been taken over on a Friday: the *Sun* did not publish during the weekend (though it would issue a special edition that extraordinary Sunday), and established student groups normally did not meet then. Thus activist groups had an opportunity to beat the "system" to the punch in presenting their own versions of events and influencing the course of opinion. The Economics Department takeover, the takeover of 320 Wait, and some of the key December demonstrations had all taken place on Fridays. Spitzer observed:

> This was the point at which it became most obvious to me, I guess, that a lot of the problem was just mismanagement by the administration. . . . *It's important for the administration or the Establishment or whoever it is to be as forceful in communicating its point of view as the opposition is.* . . . Glad Day Press [the SDS press] is just unbeatable as far as an information distributing network [is concerned]. . . . [At the teach-in] I was taking notes, and I noted a dozen of what I was pretty sure were errors of fact, not to mention large areas of opinion that were, well, greatly distorted . . . and no mention at all would be made of any positions that had been made the other way. . . .
>
> This went on that Saturday night; it went on even more blatantly at the Barton Hall meetings for the rest of the week. I hate to use such a loaded term as the "big lie," but certainly when you hear a story repeated to you over and over again and not hear it challenged, there's little reason why you should doubt its authenticity. And yet those people who could have challenged it and who should have been there challenging it were just not. . . . Barton Hall was the key point where only one side was heard consistently.[69]

Perkins listened to what the speakers at the teach-in had to say, following his usual method of waiting for a consensus to emerge. He defended the decision to forego an injunction by claiming that "campus sentiment opposed the use of force."[70] The sentiment of the teach-ins that week influenced this assessment, as did the thinking of the Faculty Council and the IFC.

Guns!

On Saturday evening the executive staff met at Perkins's home. At 9:00 pm. Dean Miller answered a call from Whitfield, who had just received word that someone had informed the Cornell police of eight carloads of students heading toward the Straight. Barlow immediately checked with DU and the fraternities to see whether they knew anything about the report and was told they were not involved. Miller tried unsuccessfully to calm Whitfield. "There was no doubt in my mind that Ed Whitfield, when he called, was really quite scared. I think he was genuinely frightened."[71]

Mayor Kiely, however, had another view. He spoke with Whitfield and others in his office when the crisis was over, and when Kiely remarked that they did not look scared, Whitfield responded, "Mr. Mayor, we never said we were scared. We said we'd defend ourselves. The university administration is the one who said we were scared."[72]

A rumor that 320 Wait was about to be stormed was also making the rounds. And someone called the campus police and told them that "you have until nine a.m. to get them out of Willard Straight!"

The executive staff agreed to meet the next day at 9:00 a.m. Just as the meeting was breaking up around 10:30, the phone rang. A patrolman had spotted "four students, three black and one white, entering the back of Willard Straight—armed with rifles." Unarmed officers let them enter, pursuant to Dymek's policy of letting the AAS's allies pass in and out of the building. Reporters also saw guns being smuggled in. "Well, it's a whole new ball game," Corson remarked.[73] Learning about the guns, Tobin noted, shoved the administration out of its "wait them out" approach. There is "no question" that "the weapons were the factor that raised their deliberations to a much higher pitch and gave the sense of so little time to get students out of the building." Muller and others felt that an "unfortunate incident" could be triggered at any time. "I am convinced that this is the ogre, if you would, that hung over the executive staff during their deliberations on Sunday morning."[74] The press (which by now had quite a presence at Cornell) already had information about the guns entering the Straight, but everyone decided to hold the story until the next day out of concern for public safety. Everyone instantly recognized that the situation had suddenly been transformed in terms of danger, and the press decided to sit on the story out of a general sense of responsibility.[75]

In fact, the guns had entered the Straight not long after the DU's were repelled that morning (the nun's observations were accurate, as were similar calls to the rumor clinic). Just before the break-in an SDS unit left the Straight to disrupt Perkins's speech scheduled at Statler, yet Harris Raynor remained at the Straight, one of the two captains of his unit. "My recollection is that there was a black guy . . . He's the one I saw with the guns. He came up and was carrying a box wrapped in the blankets, and tried to get that box into the Straight through a window. It fell down and rifles came out. Not everybody knew this at the time, only a couple of us saw it," Raynor recalled. Regathering, SDS leaders held an emergency meeting in Anabel Taylor Hall to debate what to do in the face of the sudden new danger. Bullets could fly with nervous young people barricaded inside the Straight and potentially trigger-happy vigilantes in the surrounding area. "Our people could be in the middle of a cross-fire," Raynor remarked. "It was a fairly dangerous situation, and we had to decide what our responsibilities were." They decided that they should "at all cost prevent violence" by "putting ourselves between the Straight and anyone trying to get it." Raynor contacted the AAS by phone and said, "Look, we're going to get in between you guys [and the outside], so don't shoot us!?[76]

The next morning the campus police issued a public statement about the presence of guns: "Officials of the Cornell University Division of Safety and Security have confirmed that at 10:35 p.m. last night, April 19, a rifle with a telescopic lens, two or three gun cases, and some hatchets were moved into Willard Straight Hall, the student union being held by black students."[77]

After finding out about the guns, Kennedy tried to reach Whitfield again from Perkins's house and was unsuccessful. He, Miller, and others went over to the Safety Division, and Kennedy got through from there. "I told Ed that we'd received a report that they had guns and I asked him if it was true, and he did have them. They were for defensive purposes only, and he hastened to add that members of the white community had nothing to fear if they didn't attempt to drive the students out by force." Whitfield also told Kennedy that the AAS did not trust the administration to protect the black students. Kennedy implored Whitfield to leave the Straight, offering to bring in buses with police protection, and Kennedy suggested the students bring the guns down to the back of the Straight and put them in his car. "He hesitated for several minutes, and I was hopeful that they were willing to do this, but then after apparently a conversation, because it sounded like he'd put his hand over the mouthpiece, he again told me that he was sorry."[78] Kennedy abandoned his efforts. Right after he hung up the phone, sirens whined as authorities responded to another false alarm at a dorm.

Administration sources claimed that the AAS was scared—though AAS members I interviewed and Mayor Kiely painted a more complex picture. But their fear, at least for some, no doubt coexisted with other emotions and sentiments. Human nature remains complex, even in the most trying of times. After talking with Whitfield on the phone at Perkins's house, Miller observed, "Psychologically, I think you can understand some rationalizations for people wanting to believe that they were going to be attacked."[79] This does not mean that genuine fear was not merited. Objective fear and ideology created a volatile mix.

The AAS had decided to purchase rifles earlier that term because of specific threats it had received at Cornell since the struggle of April 1968 and because of its identification with the philosophy and strategy of "self-defense of the black community" that was now an integral part of the Black Power movement, especially the Black Panthers. The ideology of self-defense had arisen in the Deep South during the civil rights movement, then passed over to the Panthers and other militant groups such as the AAS under the now-departed John Garner. Originally it was a response of more militant civil rights leaders to the frequent lack of support they suffered at the hands of law enforcement in the face of racist violence. The late Robert Williams, the pioneer of the practice in South Carolina, chronicled the reasons for his resort to self-defensive arms in his classic book *Negroes with Arms*. Williams's book is a good antidote for those who cavalierly dismiss the necessity of arms for self-protection; so is Cleveland Sellers's *River of No Return*.[80] Many of Williams's appeals are as American as apple pie: when the state will not protect one's rights and existence, one exercises one's constitutional right to bear arms. (When the crisis had ended, Jones proclaimed for all to hear that the AAS would not have been denied its constitutional right to bear arms.)

As AAS treasurer, Stephen Goodwin signed the checks for the gun purchases. "All this had to be authorized through me." They bought the guns at a local gun store. All sorts of people in upstate New York and Pennsylvania ride around with guns in their cars, he pointed out. "But when a black guy got a gun, that was a big thing."[81] Goodwin, who did not participate in the actual purchases, did not recall who in the AAS actually bought the guns and when.

SDS had assisted the AAS in procuring guns. One SDS member who asked to remain anonymous said he and another SDS heavyweight drove around upstate New York purchasing guns for the AAS:

> They asked us if we could help them get some guns. I think it was fairly close [to the Straight takeover], or a few months before. Anyway, we drove around and

bought a few rifles, you know, because black guys couldn't do it. . . . One guy came to us and I think he said something like, "We've been getting these death threats and stuff and we got to protect ourselves, so can you help us out?" I'm sure some of those guns ended up in the Straight thing. . . . I remember when it came out that they had guns in there, . . . I kind of rolled [my] eyes . . . [and thought], "Well, we got chumped on that one." [82]

The administration knew about these purchases, as Corson explained:

We knew they had guns. . . . Gun dealers from all over the area reported that in the weeks previous. . . . I asked [Tom Jones's wife, Stephanie], "Why the guns?" She said it was partly a macho thing, of asserting themselves. . . . And she told me it was also because they were being told by black leaders . . . that there was a plot in the Northeast United States to round up all black people, that prisons were being prepared. And they were buying guns to defend themselves. Now when we talked to the state police and the guy came over, he said, "You don't have anything to worry about. This is being done all over the North; guns are being brought up from the South." [83]

Corson's comment reflects the paranoia and fear that had beset the AAS—a state of mind that was being matched by the largely white campus. But bringing in the guns transferred power to the more ideologically driven members of the AAS. Some envisioned the rise of romantic revolutionary ideology in terms of the famous movie *The Battle of Algiers*. Authenticity was tested by the encounter with death. The ultimate logic of the politics of recognition was moving toward the surface. Yet not all AAS members fell prey to the lure of romantic revolutionary death. Andre McLaughlin told me that when Jones and others first started talking about being willing to die as they stood up in the windows of the Straight, she and others wondered what was going on. "I remember when it came all the way from downstairs, Tom Jones said to the reporters, 'We were ready to die.' We said, 'What's wrong with *him?!*" [84]

Under the circumstances McLaughlin might have been right. But this does not mean that the basic idea is misguided. The ultimate test of freedom is the willingness to die in its defense; otherwise why go to war against Hitler? If one is not willing to die for freedom, one is free only by the grace of God. It was Malcolm X who taught that the black man would never be free until he was willing to die to achieve or defend his freedom, like the white man. The night before an assassin felled him in Memphis, Martin Luther King delivered a speech in which he—not unlike Abraham Lincoln—foreshadowed his own death. A student of Hegel, the subject of King's dissertation, King refused to cower before a bomb threat on his airplane that morning and rumors of death squads in Memphis. "Like anybody, I would like to live a long life. Longevity has its place. But I'm not concerned about that now. I just want to do God's will. And He's allowed me to go to the mountaintop, and I've looked over, and I've seen the promised land. I may not be there with you. But I want you to know tonight that we, as a people will get to the promised land. . . . I'm not fearing any man."[85] King proclaimed his own willingness to face death in the name of freedom.

Thus the willingness to face death to achieve freedom is respected in political philosophy and action. The legitimacy of the idea in action, however, depends on the appropriateness of its context. Williams, King, and Malcolm X confronted danger in the real political world of action. Did the AAS qualify as a member in this elite group, or was its struggle to some extent manufactured? When he left Cornell in disgust, Garner dismissed the university as a theater of revolution, calling campus activism "playpen revolution."

Still, the AAS had received death threats while occupying the Straight and had to take them seriously. And it had a historic mission. The Cornell crisis had assumed a hybrid form of the absurd and the deadly serious in both historical and existential senses. Even though it was only Cornell and even though the AAS had made more of its oppression than the facts merited, as the crisis unfolded it suddenly became treacherous. Before anyone knew it, the forces that propel or influence all powerful events in history paid a visit to Cornell. But this seemed preposterous: Cornell was not Selma or Birmingham. Marx made a famous statement in *The Eighteenth Brumaire of Louis Napoleon* that history is lived twice, the first time as tragedy, the second time as farce. Cornell appears to have been both at the same time.

No one wore the romantic and Hegelian mantles more comfortably than Tom Jones. Later he spoke of the effect of the guns and what went on inside the AAS:

> Now, immediately after that DU thing we started receiving reports—first from scouts that we had on the outside, second, straight from the Dean of Students office—that they were at Noyes Center . . . trying to calm down a mob of fraternity men that were discussing whether or not to attack us. . . . Now our scout on the outside told us that at Delta Upsilon, at the white fraternity, they were loading guns into the trunks of several cars. [Actually, the cars were being loaded with band equipment for Parents Weekend.] . . . We had no choice, so we armed ourselves. . . . A citizen's right to bear arms . . . how inviolate that is, how sacred it is, how that's a cornerstone of this nation. . . . We were putting our lives on the line to defend our women, to defend our own lives, and to defend our political rights. We put our lives on the line with one provision: and this was also a new twist—just one provision—that along with our lives on the line, everybody else's life was on the line, you see? If we are going to die, a whole lot of other people were going to have to die.[86]

Irving McPhail expressed similar, though more sober, sentiments. "I think that people need to realize that this was a serious movement with some serious goals and serious ideals that were organized and led by very serious and courageous African-American men and women. . . . Not only were we talking about our very lives, we also were talking about our very academic careers."[87]

Soon a professor of mathematics would compare the scenario to incidents in Machiavelli. That Machiavelli, the great theorist of political power and symbolism, was relevant to the situation was another indication that the crisis was now wrapped in historical significance. A number of professors would start interpreting the situation through the lenses of their professional training, including history, political science, sociology, psychology, and, yes, classical Greek tragedy. Donald Kagan of the History Department, for example, told me that the crisis stepped right out of the pages of Thucydides and his portrayal in *The Peloponnesian War* of the civil war in Corcyra, in which the darker aspects of human nature and action were exposed.[88] Yet the most relevant classic source of all would be Thomas Hobbes, the great philosopher of the psychological and social implications of disorder.

That Night

That night "hysteria, fear, and paranoia raged throughout the campus."[89] An insulated, tightly knit community in a small, rural town, Cornell was much more vulnerable than campuses such as Berkeley or Columbia, also scenes of strife in the '60s, to being captured by the forces of fear. At Columbia and Berkeley, large surrounding cities absorbed the tensions, alleviating potentially overwhelming pressures. Cornell's setting led to the opposite effect: a magnification of tensions and fears. There was no escape.

Rumors flew like preternatural spirits or the ghosts of Shakespearean prophecy. More reports flooded in of whites and blacks looking for vengeance and of whites and blacks loading guns into cars. At 3:00 a.m. a *Sun* reporter spotted a light in the clock tower that overlooks Cornell, just north of the Straight. He thought he saw a spotlight directed at the Straight and a long-range rifle. Reception of this report threw officers and administrators into a panic, calling up as it did memories of the 1966 sniper killings from the clock tower at the University of Texas. What an apt yet frightening image: a rifle and light targeting students in the dead of night from atop Cornell's famous watchtower, the symbol of knowledge and enlightenment in a benighted world. Campus police checked the tower and found that the sniper was an apparition, just a janitor at work. But by this time it was becoming hard to maintain a rational line between what was real and what was not. What reason dismissed as fiction had taken on subliminal truth.

At 12:30 a.m. a fire broke out at Chi Psi, a fraternity whose black president, Otis Sprow, had played a key role discouraging the fraternities from storming the Straight in the IFC meetings earlier that day. Barlow recalled the two Chi Psi brothers charging into the Safety Division and informing the police. He and Sergeant Graham were just getting ready to go home when "two Chi Psi's came screaming in, one drunk as hell. 'My fraternity is on fire! They've cut telephone wires!' I was just panic-stricken myself because that thing was really ablaze."[90]

As firefighters sped to the blaze, Kennedy called Whitfield to assure him that the sirens were not headed toward the Straight. Firefighters put the fire out and determined that the cause was faulty electrical wiring. They also spotted several rifles inside the fraternity—"show guns" on racks, according to Chi Psi. Remembering the "alphabet fires" in the wake of King's death and the McPhelin affair the year before, many Cornellians assumed the fire was arson. Regardless of the merit of this suspicion, the fire spiced the surrealism that was sweeping Cornell. Then another fire broke out at Chi Psi at 1:20 a.m. This time inspectors traced the fire to the top of a refrigerator inside a closet, but they also determined that the refrigerator could not have caused the fire. Chi Psi was certain it was an arson.

Stuart Brown spent part of the night at the Safety Division. "The campus during that time was extremely tense," Brown said. "There were lots of automobiles being driven around. There were reports coming in over the radio system in the Safety Division of gunshots, and as these reports came in, the Safety Division undertook to check them out. This was very, very jumpy. During my stay there, one very experienced Safety Division person came in and described very vividly and in detail what he had taken to be a rifle shot—the sharp crack that a .22 has." Reports of gunfire in the dorms at the bottom of Library Slope arrived, and "almost simultaneously, there came in a report again over the radio that a black student or some black students . . . had been seen in front of the Straight with rifles inside it . . . inside the Straight with rifles."[91] The reports were confused; one newsman even reported erroneously that students in the Straight were shooting down the hill at the dorms. Eventually the division realized that this particular report was mistaken. By 3:30 a.m. the campus had "cooled down very, very considerably."

Conclusion

Arms had come to Cornell, and nobody knew what to do. As one participant observed, within a day what was previously unimaginable would turn into a commonly accepted reality.[92] In short, it was becoming a revolutionary situation.

The crisis was in many respects the culmination of the interaction of events and administrative policy over the previous year. The administration had more or less given the reins of the black studies program to the students, even though it had struggled desperately to maintain some input and control over the program's development. Now it confronted the next stage of the struggle, and its control over events was even more tenuous.

The key mistake on day 1 (other than letting Delta Upsilon into the Straight) could have been its failure to go to court for an injunction ordering the AAS to vacate the Straight. An injunction, which had worked well enough in similar situations at other colleges, could have provided the right balance of decisiveness and restraint. Given the AAS's fears, the group might well have obeyed an injunction if the timing were right. Perkins and his staff were afraid of surrendering control to outside authorities, but this fear presupposed that they had sufficient control in the first place. Perkins felt beholden to "campus sentiment," yet campus sentiment was uninformed and confused (only the AAS and SDS had plans).

One could conclude that this policy was successful if the only objective was to get the AAS out of the Straight at the cost of no lives. As Muller said, "saving lives" was the one and only "principle." But it is interesting to compare Muller's position, which the administration widely shared, with that of the AAS. Again, we are confronted with the Hegelian insight: those who are courageous enough to risk something important will prevail over those who are not. The AAS was willing to risk more than the administration because it did not have the administration's responsibilities to the campus and because it had a reason to believe and something in which to believe. The only other individuals on the campus who were willing to take risks for what they believed in were the radical faculty and students who genuinely believed in the AAS cause and the faculty on the other side who believed that liberal principles of justice and academic and intellectual freedom were worth fighting for. In their eyes the campus was turning into a tyranny of the majority backed by the threat of force, an ideological boot camp unbefitting a university.

CHAPTER NINE

DAY 2: THE DEAL

The executive war council met at 9 o'clock the next morning at the Law School. By now the national media were on their way. President Perkins arrived with notes laying out the university's options under different scenarios. He did not mention the guns, but they haunted every thought. One concern overrode everything. In Stuart Brown's words, "We were convinced that we should try and get the blacks out of Willard Straight that day and not let them go through another night, and the problems that would be associated with having armed individuals in that building when classes resumed on Monday morning. . . . Another night could . . . be absolutely disastrous." Even the weather seemed to conspire against the administrators, as clear skies and warmth had replaced the cold rain. Now more people would be staying on campus, within rifle range of armed groups. This sense of urgency meant the administrators would enter negotiations in a less than optimum position. "It seemed, therefore, necessary for us to do *everything we conceivably could* to negotiate with the black students and get them out of the building before night fell," Brown said.[1]

The avalanche of calls from the news media posed another problem. Information director Thomas Tobin wanted the administration to prepare an official statement so he could answer the relentless media questions about the guns.[2] VP Steven Muller went off to work something out.

Dean Robert Miller felt the administration had to have a basic plan by 11 o'clock, when the Faculty Council was slated to meet. He knew the AAS would scoff at pursuing the appeals process, and the thought of an injunction seemed frightening. Before Perkins even finished reading his list, Miller interrupted to say that "we were not being realistic as to what the situation was, that we had to deal with the students' demands in some way or we had no choice of arriving at a negotiated settlement."[3]

Miller presented the draft of a three-part presidential statement he had written: (1) the new problem was more serious now than previous crises, (2) the reprimands could be dealt with only by the faculty meeting as a whole, and (3) the president would call a faculty meeting and present a motion for nullification.

The statement caused a commotion because it amounted to giving the AAS what it wanted with nothing in return. Was it advisable to offer this agreement before real negotiations had even started? "We can't do that," Provost Dale Corson said. "I think we can," Miller replied. "But I've just realized that you're right in the sense that the President can't do this. . . . Only the faculty has the power to do anything about those reprimands."[4] But Corson's concerns were not simply about jurisdiction or procedure; they also pertained to the substance of the proposal.

Miller volunteered to ask the Faculty Council to call a faculty meeting in which he would present a relevant motion. Perkins went around the room, asking those present what they thought. No one voiced opposition to Miller's proposal, though Miller did detect "reluctance, in the sense that everybody realized that it was not going to be a popular thing to do, that it was not a stroke of genius in terms of making everybody emerge from this mess in good repute."[5] The proposal would provide the linchpin of the administration position, but in the afternoon the AAS would add demands and accept only one minor concession that it ultimately did not honor. Nonetheless, the proposal carried the day because no one else had a better idea and because the fear of violence was overwhelming. Miller later pointed to the onslaught of media and the "gratuitous arrival of the National Guard" as factors that contributed to the potential for chaos, and he told an ominous story about a neighbor whose son was organizing a vigilante group. "They had guns and they were 'going to go up and take the situation in hand.' And I think if it had gone another night, the odds were at least one in five that we would have some shooting."[6]

Who would go to the Straight with the offer? Keith Kennedy was an instant choice because of his experience with the AAS. But it was thought there should be another negotiator to provide a neutral front and some protection. Miller volunteered, but it was his agreement, and his presence might compromise his role with the faculty. Kennedy then suggested that he and Muller go, and it was agreed. Muller told me he was the "logical choice, as I was the vice president for public affairs" and had not been involved with the AAS.[7]

Muller, forty-two, was born in Hamburg, Germany, and had come to the United States when he was twelve or thirteen. A Rhodes scholar from the University of California at Los Angeles, he received his Ph.D., specializing in government (comparative politics), from Cornell in 1958, the same year he became an assistant professor at Cornell after teaching for two years at Haverford College. At Cornell he received tenure and worked his way up the administrative ladder, assuming the position of Vice President of Public Affairs in 1966. Muller was a well-spoken man and an able administrator who maintained a presence internationally. The Cornell crisis would put him under demanding and sometimes unfair scrutiny.

After Muller's selection as a negotiator, Brown triggered an "anguished" discussion by asserting that the faculty would never go along with Miller's proposal. Still, Miller prevailed. He acknowledged that the proposal amounted to giving in to the AAS demands, although he averred that this was what had happened in the end at Harvard, so Cornell might as well get it over with. According to one report of this meeting, Miller "did not deny that he thought the faculty would rescind the penalties eventually, so they might as well do it sooner."[8]

Based on its understanding of the negotiating problems that had bedeviled such campuses as Berkeley and Harvard, the council thought someone with legal knowledge should talk to the AAS about the legal problems it might be confronting and its legal options and rights. Law Professor Ernie Roberts suggested they ask Rudolph ("Barry") Loncke, a black second-year law student, to meet with the AAS before Muller and Kennedy made their journey to the Straight. Roberts called him and he agreed to help. Ed Whitfield told Kennedy he would meet with Loncke at 11:45 a.m.

At 11:00 a.m. the augmented Faculty Council of twenty-five met in the room next to the war council. Perkins came and went from the meeting, often leaving to talk on the phone with Robert Purcell, the chairman of the Board of Trustees, and with Jansen Noyes, another trustee. Corson briefed the council on the situation. (Neal Stamp thought Perkins's constant talks with trustees distracted him, making it harder for him to maintain consistency and decisiveness.)[9] Support for Miller's proposal was equivocal across the board.

Before Muller and Kennedy went to the Straight, Perkins returned from the phone. Based on his discussions with Purcell, Perkins now insisted on a quid pro quo of sorts: in return for getting the faculty to nullify the reprimands, the AAS had to agree to join the effort to establish a new judicial system. Perkins portrayed this seemingly minor concession as a "vigorous condition."[10]

Meanwhile, Muller told Perkins that the staff had agreed that Kennedy and he would simply discuss the proposals with the AAS staff and react to subsequent events. Key members of the executive staff did not anticipate that an agreement would be struck right away. Miller wrote out the proposal's details, and Muller took notes. There is no dispute about the presence of three parts of the agreement at this point: the AAS would agree to participate in the reform of the judicial system, Miller would call a special faculty meeting and recommend nullification of the reprimands, and the university would investigate the cross-burning.

There was more dispute about whether other parts of the agreement that emerged were included at this point, the most crucial of which was possible university amnesty for the students for damage and crimes associated with the takeover. Corson later said that he and others considered it inappropriate to bring up amnesty so early in the negotiating game. Somehow Muller made it a part of his notes, perhaps reflecting the understandable desperation to get a deal. Speaking of the ultimate decision he and Kennedy made to offer amnesty, Muller said, "This was our decision because nobody had told us not to do it." The key in the end is "that nobody got hurt. And that's the object of the exercise."[11] Muller thought the AAS would be reluctant to leave if not given amnesty.

Loncke met with the AAS at 11:45. He had witnessed violent situations and communal panic while in the military in Vietnam, and he felt an obligation to render what help he could. "I heard rumors that the state police and others were gathering to deal with the crisis, and to me that evoked images of some sort of a slaughter. Not because of ill will, necessarily, but just because whenever you mix the guns and police and black folks . . . it was an invitation for disaster. I've never—and I've been in warfare, been in terrible situations—. . . felt the sense of panic of a community [like that at Cornell]. It was complete, utter panic. . . . I feared that unless something happened quickly to defuse the situation, it was going to explode." [12]

Loncke phoned the AAS at the Straight, and its leaders agreed to talk with him. He went to the Straight without ever having spoken directly with the executive war council; he discussed the legal and strategic situation primarily with Ed Whitfield and Eric Evans. Like Muller and Kennedy, Loncke perceived the AAS leaders as scared but honest about their intentions. They were prepared to make a deal. "It was pretty surprisingly easy, I thought, mainly because the leadership of the black students wasn't interested in bloodshed and wanted to avoid it, and I think they knew how vulnerable they were, or we were, to being the subject of gunfire." [13]

At noon Muller and Kennedy made their way to the Straight. They rattled the back door and were greeted by a student who went to fetch Whitfield. Muller smoked two cigarettes before Whitfield appeared at the door to the Straight theater, then led them into the foyer, where another student stood holding a gun. Muller asked whether it was loaded. "No," someone said. "What I had anticipated was very hostile, very angry black students. What we found was very concerned, and really fairly frightened and almost paranoid students." [14]

The group Kennedy and Muller met with included, at different points, Whitfield, Evans, Bob Jackson, Tom Jones, Bert Cooper, Zachary Carter, and Loncke. Kennedy described Whitfield as the "nominal" head. Muller observed that the AAS was only loosely organized, the leaders interacting constantly with other members to ensure legitimacy. Whitfield and Jones treated the administrators politely, but others were more hostile. For security reasons the negotiators remained in the foyer, which, like the entire Straight, was dark because the electricity had been turned off.

Muller, who did most of the talking, told Whitfield the administration's key goal was to get the students out as quickly as possible. Using the presence of deputies as leverage, Muller said the students had to get out fast because nobody knew what the gathering of deputies foreboded. "How do we know that this isn't just a trick?" someone asked Muller. "How do we know that if we get out of here, we're not all going to be arrested?" Muller sensed that they suspected an ambush but "weren't sure about what would be happening. . . . Our problem was to persuade them that they had nothing to fear by coming out." [15]

The negotiators presented the agreement. Whitfield conveyed two major points: the AAS could not rely on the administration to protect its safety, and it wanted a faculty meeting called immediately. Kennedy and Muller pointed out that the latter was impossible, although they would do all they could to ensure the students' safety. After Whitfield asked what would happen if the faculty refused to go along and nullify the penalties, Jackson asked a key question: "We have a lot on the line, but what does Miller stand to lose if the faculty goes against him?"[16] As to legal issues, the administrators told the students the university would not act as a legal buffer between them and authorities downtown, nor would the university counsel help them; Stamp had been adamant about this point.[17] Otherwise the administrators were open to what the AAS wanted, which included twenty-four-hour protection; legal action against Delta Upsilon, including a list of names of the brothers who invaded the Straight; and protection of 320 Wait.

At some point the discussion turned to another crucial issue: amnesty for the students involved in the takeover. Except for one phone conversation with Corson, Kennedy and Muller had had no contact with the staff at Anabel Taylor Hall during the two hours they were in the Straight. When the students asked what would happen to them when they left, Muller and Kennedy assured them that there would be no harm or arrests. "Would they be punished for occupying the Straight? No. We could guarantee that: amnesty for being in the Straight. Our instructions were, 'Get 'em out before the sheriffs come, if you can.' . . . This was our decision because nobody told us not to do it."[18] While these discussions were taking place, a campus patrolman radioed that he had seen three rifles being taken from 320 Wait Avenue. At the same time a leading militant's car was seen arriving at the Straight, and he and a friend were seen carrying a long fiberglass case and a rifle in a blanket into the Straight.[19]

It is unclear how much of the agreement was accepted at this point. What is clear is that Kennedy and Muller came away with the essentials of the agreement based on Miller's three points and had agreed to the other provisions, including amnesty. They had even agreed to investigate the DU attack and release the names of the brothers involved (a move that might have placed those men in danger). While the AAS prepared to leave the Straight, Kennedy and Muller returned to Taylor to inform the war council of the agreement. What they had to say stunned some members. Mark Barlow, for example, had assumed that the first encounter would be only preparatory, the beginning of bargaining. He was particularly upset at the promise to release the DU names: "This shocked me for two reasons. . . . It had not been my understanding that Steve and Keith had been given *carte blanche* to negotiate and to commit. . . . I thought [Perkins] was aghast. Secondly, I was livid and very upset by the willingness to give the names of the white students who'd gone in."[20]

Corson, also taken aback, criticized Muller's actions: "Muller inserted things in that agreement he had absolutely no authority to do, and some things that damaged us—the 'no sanctions' part, not being held responsible for damage, no prosecution. . . . Keith was shaken by all this. But it was Muller who was responsible as far as I know. There was no leverage. You couldn't bring charges against these people because there was a promise by the vice president of the university not to do it. I sat with Perkins when we got a copy of what had been signed. He read it and said, 'Where did this come from?'" [21]

Back with the executive staff, Muller and Kennedy were optimistic about what they had wrought. They told Miller, "We just think they might buy it. They listened very carefully. But Whitfield wants to get this straight from you, Bob, and I said that you'd call him on the telephone to confirm it." Miller agreed, then paced the floor for a while because he was "very nervous" about what he would say if the AAS demanded amnesty.[22] A native of Omaha, Miller was very respected among Cornell's administrative elite. He received his Ph.D. in soil sciences at Cornell in 1948 after having served with distinction in the Pacific during World War II as a first lieutenant from 1942 to 1945. During his duty he had the honor of being included in a story by Homer Bigart, the famous war correspondent for the *New York Times*. Corson described Miller as "a very sensible, rational man" who had dealt ably with many difficult decisions and events as an officer in the war. The conscientious Miller approached the crisis with the same basic commitment as Muller, Kennedy, and others: give first priority to getting the students and the guns out of the Straight. Some would question his commitment to the broader principles of the university during the crisis, but while some individuals second-guessed themselves, Miller felt secure in the value judgments and choices he felt compelled to make.

At first Miller was reluctant to support the condition of AAS participation in reforming the judicial system, but he changed his mind when he found out from Stamp about what was going on downtown. District Attorney Matt McHugh had interviewed parents forced out of the Straight and was considering criminal charges. Also, parents expressed their desires to file civil suits against AAS members. Under these circumstances, amnesty from university sanctions seemed advisable to show the university's goodwill; and if amnesty were offered, quid pro quo called for the AAS to assist in creating a better judicial system.

Around noon the phone rang at Myron Taylor Hall. It was Whitfield, calling for Miller, just before Kennedy and Muller arrived. Miller was relieved that Whitfield did not bring up the amnesty business, dealing only with the reprimands and the faculty vote. "I understand that you're prepared to call a faculty meeting and support our demands for nullification," he said. "That's approximately right," Miller responded. "But there's a very important difference in the way I'll put it. I'm not prepared to support your demand for nullification. I am prepared to recommend that if you get out, that the faculty for its part nullify on the grounds that this situation has gone from a squabble over procedures into a situation of deadly peril for a lot of people, and . . . that such a squabble can't be allowed to continue with such perils in it. I'll make this recommendation only if you guys get out of there quick with your guns." Whitfield said the AAS wanted a faculty meeting called that afternoon, but Miller said it was logistically impossible and that he would never convene one while the AAS remained in the Straight. "Well, how do I know once we're out that you'll even call a meeting?" Whitfield asked.

Miller made a deal. "Just to show you I mean what I say . . . , if you get out, vacate the building, I'll call the meeting. [And] I will recommend nullification; if the faculty doesn't approve it, I will resign." Miller said that as dean, he could not guarantee what the faculty would do, but he would try his best to persuade them. He also said he would not inform the faculty of his decision to resign until after the vote. Whitfield and Miller understood each other and hung up.[23]

Miller then dictated the terms of the agreement to Muller, who, with Kennedy, went to the Straight with it. When Perkins asked for a copy of the agreement (he had been on the phone with Purcell again), none was available. Muller had not made copies, and soon Whitfield would have the sole original. An agreement had been patched together, but there was no backup copy to serve as a baseline.

Whitfield had to clear the agreement with his own executive staff. All along he had had to cover his left flank as militants pressured him to hold the line against the administration, especially Jones and Evans.[24]

Kennedy and Muller checked things out at the Straight before entering final negotiations. Students were cleaning up litter and garbage, and things looked fine—an estimation that would be important because it made the case for amnesty more plausible. (Kennedy pointed out that the final negotiations took place in areas away from where damage was later found.) Then they sat down to the final discussions in a meeting room near the dining hall. The agreement included the calling of the faculty meeting and the motion to nullify; university amnesty for the takeover; round-the-clock protection for the AAS at 320 Wait Avenue; investigation of the DU incident, including a written report to the AAS that provided the names of the perpetrators; investigation of the Wari House cross-burning; AAS cooperation in the reform of the judicial system; a promise by the university to help the AAS secure legal assistance in defending itself against criminal and civil charges (not university personnel or money); and AAS departure from the Straight. The AAS wanted to sign the agreement at 320 Wait after a procession across the campus from the Straight. The next discussion dealt with how its members would proceed to exit the Straight and what to do about the guns.[25] We will look at this issue in a moment.

At 4:00 p.m. Miller met again with the Faculty Council and briefed its members on the deal. "The Council was outraged. They regarded it as complete surrender and were very much against it."[26] Actually, three members—Chandler Morse, Ben Nichols, and Ernie Roberts—were favorably inclined toward the agreement, but the other nine were strongly opposed. Miller said the AAS had given a quid pro quo in agreeing to leave the Straight. According to Tobin, the press would react to the agreement the same way the council did: as a "complete capitulation."[27]

Downtown

Meanwhile, at 2:00 p.m. local law enforcement officials and two state police captains met in Mayor Kiely's office. They all agreed that Cornell should get a court injunction right away. Kiely considered calling a state of emergency covering the campus, but he and the others were sensitive to Cornell's desire to keep outsiders out. At no time did they consider storming the Straight; they had insufficient manpower, and they were not so inclined in any case. But they were open to calling the governor to bring in the National Guard if an emergency developed. McHugh mentioned that a big problem was "that we didn't always know who spoke for Cornell University and, in particular, the administration." [28] They did not know on whose word they could rely, and they were getting conflicting information and rumors; Kiely got calls from several different Cornell officials. Officials downtown thought Cornell was unprepared for what was happening.

After discussing the possibility of an injunction with Stamp, Kiely got a call from Corson, informing him that the AAS would leave the Straight and walk across campus to 320 Wait. Kiely's main concern was that the students leave the Straight unarmed. Corson told McHugh that students would be carrying their guns in their march. Kiely recalled that when Corson told them the students were coming out with guns, "Everybody went into orbit down here. . . . This was a horrid mistake. There wasn't a soul down here in any one of police agencies that concurred with this and we sent that message up the hill time and time again. Mr. Stamp concurred with it." [29] McHugh and Kiely felt they had enough manpower to protect the AAS from attack, if that was the problem, and they volunteered to provide it, to no avail.

The Last Part of the Agreement: The Guns

Whitfield then called Kennedy and informed him that the AAS was ready to leave the Straight. The AAS wanted Miller and Kennedy to walk with its members in the procession, probably for protection. A handful in the AAS thought that the administration might have ordered an attack. Kennedy said it would be inappropriate for the dean of the faculty to walk with them because he had to present the motion at the meeting the next day, so once again Muller came along. Within ten minutes Muller and Kennedy were back at the Straight. Everyone they encountered was polite, Kennedy said. But "for the first time now they were carrying arms. The individual that met us at the door had a carbine. He escorted us up." They waited a bit in the Programs Office; beyond the door they heard the typing of the agreement and saw students tidying up. They were then taken to the main room of the Straight, where all the students, about eighty, were assembling to receive instruction. There was "absolutely no shouting." There would be "absolute silence while they marched from Willard Straight to 320 Wait." [30] At first Kennedy and Muller were placed in front of Tom Jones and Larry Dickson, but Kennedy objected, saying he would not walk out in front of armed men, so the AAS moved them to the back of the line. They discussed the agreement some more; Muller suggested signing it at 320 Wait, and "Whitfield bought this."

Before they got in line, Kennedy and Muller tried to talk Whitfield into leaving the guns in the Straight. "You're not going to carry them out like that, are you?" Muller asked. "Why not take them out the way they came in?" But the AAS would not give up its arms. Its members were concerned about self-defense and wanted the guns to symbolize their political will, their willingness to protect women, and their power.

Muller said that no one on the staff had anticipated the AAS's desire to exit with the guns, so he and Kennedy did not have a policy on this issue when they went back to the Straight. "At first we said no. And then they said, 'All right, if you don't let us take the guns, we're not coming out." Muller then called Corson, and what would prove a fateful decision was made:

> I said, "Dale, they are willing to come out." He said, "Thank God." I said, "Yeah, but on only one condition: that they come out with their guns." He said, "We don't want that." I said, "I know—but I'm not sure we can get them out without the guns." He said to try it, "and if it doesn't work, try it again." I said, "Dale, what do you want me to do if it doesn't work?" There was a long pause, and he said, "Get them out." I said, "OK, do you want me to call you back?" He said, "Try to get 'em out without the guns. But if the only way to get them out is with the guns, get 'em out." I said, "OK." [31]

Muller then implied to the AAS that Perkins had declared it unacceptable to allow the students to exit the Straight armed. "And their almost immediate response was, 'Forget it! We're not coming out!'" [32]

Thus the university's negotiators had to settle for getting them out "with the guns." But Kennedy managed to get the AAS to consent to a distant second best: he asked Whitfield and the AAS to unload the guns and open the breeches for all to see. He also asked to inspect them himself. Whitfield said the AAS would never consent to this. "Ed, you inspect them and we'll take your word for it," Muller said. So Whitfield conducted what amounted to a cursory inspection and proclaimed that things were in order. As the AAS members walked out, several reporters saw live ammunition in some of the breeches. And as Jones and others admitted later, it would have been simple enough to load the breeches in an instant. [33] Yet Muller observed that many of the students were inept with the guns, and some had the wrong caliber of bullets for the guns they carried. [34]

Neither Kennedy nor Muller fully understood the impact the guns would have until they stepped outside and saw all the cameras. "As soon as you come out and see all those cameras whirring and so forth, you know that this is going to go over the entire countryside," Kennedy said. [35] Shortly after the incident, Kennedy expressed regret about having acted precipitously with both the agreement and the guns. "I wish we perhaps had bargained for a little longer on their leaving the rifles in Willard Straight. I don't think there was a ghost of a chance that they would leave them in." [36] In his interview with me in 1996, Kennedy was even more self-critical:

> It was decided that someone should go along with me, and that's where we made a mistake of choosing Steve Muller along with myself, because both of us were too

imperious and wanted to get things done in a hurry. Dale Corson would have been much better because he would have been more patient. . . . Steve and I both operated pretty much [alike]: Let's get the job done. And that was no time to be eager. I'm convinced . . . that the students would have left without carrying their guns if we [had persisted]. . . . I don't think we used as much care and judgment as we should have.

And we just yielded to everything that they wanted. . . . And Allan Sindler and several of his colleagues were of course very, very, very unhappy because we had not followed the judicial procedures. . . . The next several days were nightmares.[37]

Kennedy also pointed a finger at the president and higher-ups. "I don't think there was much leadership, quite frankly, on the part of the administration," an assessment he applied to everyone—Perkins, Corson, himself, and others. "We sort of moved around, frankly, like we were shell-shocked."[38]

Muller blamed Perkins. From the time Perkins left the executive staff meeting to talk with Purcell until after Muller and Kennedy returned from 320 Wait and the agreement was signed, Muller said, he and Kennedy never spoke with Perkins. "I can say with total confidence . . . I did not have any contact of any kind with James Perkins, nor did Keith Kennedy. The highest-ranking person in the administration that we had contact with throughout this period was Dale [Corson]."[39]

According to Fisher and Wallenstein, Corson should have been one of the negotiators. "He wouldn't have agreed to several provisions of the final agreements (Later, senior faculty rumored that Corson had been too hawkish with student protestors for Perkins's satisfaction; hence, he was relegated to overseeing the faculty council, while the big decisions were made elsewhere)."[40]

Corson considered letting the students leave with the guns "the biggest mistake of all. . . . We would have gotten by the episode with no notice if it weren't for that. . . . I believed we could not go by another night without somebody getting killed. We had a big group of deputy sheriffs, one hundred, two hundred, downtown, itching to [cause harm]."[41]

Comic Relief: The Martinis

At some point on Sunday, April 20—probably at lunch, based on statements by Barlow, but possibly for dinner—the executive staff received a "gallon of martinis" that someone on the Statler Hotel staff sent over to the eight members. The staff considered the gesture "thoughtful but dangerous," so rather than drinking the pitcher, some members of the staff had just one martini. For a moment, at least, the members were able to relieve a bit of the overwhelming anxiety.[42] It is hard to think of a more dramatic contrast between the campus generations than this scene of administrators drinking martinis while student activists strapped on gun belts and planned what to do next.

Once the matter of the guns was settled, the AAS was ready to go. The members lined up in military formation, with women in the center and Jones and Dickson bringing up the rear. The AAS asked Gloria Joseph, who had spent some time in the Straight, to march out with the women, but she said she would prefer to walk with her fellow administrators Kennedy and Muller. "When the shooting starts, they're not going to pay attention to whether you're an administrator or not," one student told her. "They'll be shooting at everyone who's black. So get in line with the other black women." She did.[43] The university provided a police escort of seven uniformed patrol officers (armed with only nightsticks) and two detectives. Whitfield asked Muller and Kennedy to walk far enough behind so it would not appear they were being held captive. Two members of the dean of students' office were also asked to accompany the marchers.

"Breeches open, no ammo!" Whitfield shouted. They were ready. As word that "the blacks are coming out!" spread across campus like wildfire, dozens of reporters raced to the Straight. Figuring the group in front was a decoy, a few hapless reporters thought they would outsmart the others by going to the back of the building. In so doing, they missed the most dramatic scene on college campuses that year.[44] The crowd in front of the Straight quickly swelled from two hundred to two thousand.

At 4:10 p.m. the eighty or so AAS members walked out the Straight, fists held high in imitation of Black Power and Black Panther salutes. They brandished their seventeen rifles and shotguns, along with the knives, clubs, and spears they had amassed. Eric Evans, AAS minister of defense and a hard-liner, led the way with large, loaded bandoliers draped across his chest and a large shotgun in his hand. Whitfield followed, holding a rifle and looking somewhat sheepish. Homer ("Skip") Meade wore a Western-style hat and a poncho: Black Power meets Americana. As marchers left the dark, cavernous foyer of the Straight's front porch, they were met by the light of day and a stunning array of surprised, even aghast, onlookers and the flashes of legions of cameras. "Oh, my God, look at those goddamned guns!" Associated Press photographer Steven Stark exclaimed.[45] But he had enough presence of mind to take a picture of Evans and others right in front of the Straight. What came to be known as "The Picture" won the Pulitzer Prize as picture of the year.

Looking forlorn and sapped, Muller and Kennedy took up the rear of the procession, just behind Jones and Dickson. Jones carried a rifle and had a club at his waist and a knife in his belt. SDS members cheered as the marchers crossed the large porch of the Straight; hundreds of other onlookers stood in stunned silence. The marchers strode across the Arts Quad and to the bridge over the gorge at University Avenue and Campus Road. Onlookers on foot and in cars stopped in their tracks. The troupe marched across the bridge and up the road to Wait Avenue.

At 320 Wait, AAS officers went inside as several men with guns spread out across the porch and took positions around the house. Whitfield produced the agreement as part of a signing ceremony and asked Muller and Kennedy to sign it. The press began shoving microphones in their faces, but the administrators had not yet seen the actual agreement. "I can't sign anything I haven't read," Muller told Whitfield. Muller turned to Tobin and asked him angrily to get the microphones out of the way.

A squabble over some of the terms of the agreement ensued. The AAS possessed meaningful leverage because of the guns and threatened to retake the Straight or some other building. But Muller's and Kennedy's concerns were about minor points, so the parties went into AAS headquarters and worked on the wording. The AAS pushed for what it could get at the last minute. Would the university pay for any incidental damage to the Straight? Kennedy and Muller called Perkins, who acceded to this request, figuring the damage was minimal based on Dymek's quick inspection after the evacuation. The final agreement was struck. Muller described what was going through his mind. He was tired and, according to other observers, humiliated. "Now we wanted to get the heck away from here! They pulled out this cockamamy piece of paper," he said. Muller could have waited and looked at it later, but all he could think was, "Let's sign the goddamned thing and get out of here."[46]

After twenty minutes, Muller, Kennedy, Whitfield, and Carter came out the building, and Whitfield read the agreement to the press. Whitfield wanted a copy, so he deputized a student to follow Muller to photocopy it. As the administrators slipped into a Safety Division car, they heard a call on the radio warning of four men in a Barracuda, carrying shotguns.[47]

In June 1969 Kennedy movingly depicted his state of mind, expressing the thoughts of a good man who did not deserve to be in such a position:

> We were not thinking as clearly as we should have been perhaps under the circumstances. We were doing the rewriting of the document over at 320 Wait, and it was not the most conducive atmosphere [*laugh*] for clear thinking. . . . To attempt to recount . . . all of the things that flashed through my mind during that long walk, which I still wake up at night with nightmares about, and the assembly of the people on the . . . lawn in front of 320 Wait. . . . All I could think of, what a horrible circus this is. . . . Now in retrospect . . . I would not . . . under any circumstances would I execute or negotiate a document after the people had left the building. The whole thing would be done before. . . . I think that hopefully there would be learned a good deal about this and it would be understood and it would be what I would call a much more dignified position on our part. I don't think the students gained anything by subjecting us to . . . the humiliation of this. It hasn't worked out in their best interests as a whole.[48]

After Kennedy and Muller left, an AAS spokesman issued an ominous statement from the front steps: he proclaimed that the AAS had planned a peaceful takeover, but "the campus police saw fit to utilize the fraternity boys from Delta Upsilon to oust us. We only leave now with the understanding that the University will move fairly to carry out its part of the agreement that was reached. Failure on the part of the University to do so may force us to again confront the University in some manner."[49]

According to Fisher and Wallenstein, the first official Cornell news release downplayed the presence of guns, but it was too late. The next morning, "The Picture" appeared on front pages around the world.[50]

The Fallout

At 5:30 p.m. Stamp, Perkins, and Corson got their first full, shocking look at the agreement. One thing Perkins eventually did (I am not sure when) was to order the DU names dropped from the investigative report—but the names had been included in the original version! Earlier, Barlow had even threatened to resign if those names were included. By this time Perkins was completely drained, according to Stamp. "He sat there at the desk in his shirtsleeves, his collar open, his tie hanging down, holding his head. He was a beaten man, really, really beaten. He had reason to be."[51]

That night the Faculty Council (which had already called a faculty meeting for 4:00 p.m. Monday) and the FCSA met separately. At the FCSA meeting Allan Sindler excoriated the agreement. Miller said he and his companions got a "licking." The Faculty Council, too, was upset. Kennedy said, "Steve and I were emotionally bushed, to say the least, but we met with them [Faculty Council and concerned faculty] and were subjected to all kinds of charges and abuses—a chance for them to vent their spleen on us."[52]

The next morning Perkins and his executive staff would get an earful from faculty who were among Perkins's closest advisers, including Philosophy Professor Max Black and Mathematics Professor Paul Olum, two men who would become barometers of faculty opinion over the next few days. Miller recalled that Olum and Black "were beside themselves. . . . I guess the substance of that conversation can be summed up in Olum's turning to me at one point and saying, 'Well, the question is not when you resign, but why haven't you resigned already?'"[53] In an internal document in the president's office in which members of the executive staff recalled their experiences during the crisis, an unidentified executive staff member said, "I do remember now Paul saying that he thought this [resignation] was the only honorable thing for you [Miller] to do."[54]

The problem is that once the guns entered the equation, the administration lost control of events. As the able Kennedy admitted, the administrators abandoned judgment and deliberation in favor of the urgent desire to get the AAS out of the Straight. The AAS, taking advantage of the fear it engendered (unlike the administration, it had no concrete obligations to protect the safety of the Cornell community as a whole), held out for greater concessions. The AAS was winning the game of chicken. In their rush to get the students out of the Straight, the negotiators—backed by the leadership—made two key, all-too-human blunders: they conceded too much, such as amnesty and absolution of responsibility for damage, implying that the judicial system—one of the most innovative in the country—was corrupt; and they acceded to the guns. These concessions would soon prove extremely damaging in terms of public opinion outside of the university, and they virtually guaranteed that the crisis would escalate: the AAS was still armed, and the faculty (as foreshadowed by the Faculty Council and FCSA) was not going along.

Kiely remarked later that the administration lost the ability to exercise judgment once the guns came into play. Officials downtown had a better sense of power and its implications than the executive staff. The former knew instantly that letting the AAS out with the guns would be a monumental mistake, above and beyond the public image. And they thought all along that an injunction was the right move.

Part of the problem was the lack of concerted leadership by the president or a delegate. Perkins never even saw the agreement in writing until after it was signed. Ruth Darling, hardly hostile to the administration and its goals, maintained, "One of the feelings that I had was that there was no clearly defined single person who was leading—in command of the situation. This is not to say that I felt things were completely falling apart, but it was hard to put your finger where decisions might be made."[55] McHugh had a similar problem. "The administrators with whom we were talking about a negotiated settlement themselves did not know what the two administrators inside the building negotiating were in fact doing."[56] Stuart Brown pointed out that there was no unanimity on the presidential staff about what to do. "We discussed in a casual way what some of the limits might be. It wasn't just that we sent them there with a charge to get the black students out under any circumstances. But I can't . . . remember how tightly we tied this down."[57]

The AAS also had its share of inner conflict, yet it managed to act much more decisively. It benefited from the flexible, dynamic interaction between leaders and members that it had practiced over the previous year and from its core beliefs, which it was willing to defend at great cost. The administration, to the contrary, had a heritage of waffling in the face of concerted pressure, and it was not likely to toughen up under such extremely trying circumstances. In an op-ed piece in the *Sun* on Monday, Rahe depicted the crisis as the logical conclusion of administrative practices. The crisis was "the culmination of a series of events leading to the destruction of this University as a viable institution committed to the unfettered search for truth, a series of events involving the use of force by a small minority of students to coerce the University to give in to demands."[58] The path to the Straight led through the Economics Department takeover, the takeover of 320 Wait Avenue, the Malott Hall demonstration, and the assault on Perkins at Statler. But Rahe neglected to point out another culprit: few on the faculty, as Corson stressed, had organized or striven to create a public presence for the principles of intellectual freedom. The times had required commitment, and the faculty did not respond to this need until it was too late.

Many years later Sindler recalled, "Perkins had been traumatized (in effect) by these fast-moving events and was unable to function. Muller, Corson, and others had to make decisions in the absence of leadership by the president."[59] Sindler's account appears true, but one must also acknowledge the extraordinary difficulties of the situation (though such difficulties did not affect Sindler's conduct, as seen in Chapter Seven). Recall Kennedy's assessment: everybody was "shell-shocked." And as Berkeley philosophy Professor John Searle wrote in an insightful book on the up-heavals at Berkeley and other campuses in the 1960s, it was a rare leader who could navigate through the storms that beset universities from every direction. "These crises have exposed two major structural weaknesses in the position of the college president: he has divided and inconsistent responsibilities, and he lacks any natural constituency."[60] Corson pointed to the fact that the university had to grapple with larger issues that were difficult to resolve and that Cornell was not alone. "I want to emphasize again that all this is being fought out against the context of what is going on in the country. It's not Cornell University. It's the Cornell University that is part of a very large pattern of disarray in our society."[61]

The Press Conference

At 6:00 p.m. the negotiators held a press conference. Muller was back in his best form, performing with charm and flair. (Tobin said that Muller was "extremely fac-ile in terms of his ability to speak and explain situations.")[62] He began by justifying the agreement on the grounds of the "growing imminent threat to life" and the many threats. Muller went on to claim that the major damage to the Straight was "not extensive" and that the students had cleaned up before leaving. Then came the inevitable question: Wasn't the agreement a "complete capitulation"? He answered, "I would characterize it as anything but that. . . . The only controversial demand was nullification," and even this demand dealt with "relatively minor infractions" that were "not worth risking the future of the University or the lives of our stu-dents, black and white." The university had won a victory in getting the AAS to agree to cooperate in the project to reform the judicial system, he said. Nor did Muller see a problem in presenting the names of the DU students to the AAS. He concluded by proclaiming that the administration had to act fast before the author-ities downtown sent in troops—even though Kiely intended no such thing. (The remark angered the already disgusted Kiely downtown.) Notwithstanding Muller's smooth press conference, "the press bought very little of it; they especially disre-garded his denial of 'complete capitulation.'"[63]

The press would remain skeptical of the administration's version of events as the crisis unfolded. To most of the world outside Cornell, allowing students with guns (and their SDS supporters) to dictate the terms of agreement was difficult to jus-tify. This was also the posture of a majority of faculty the first two days. But even-tually a political dynamic would take place that separated Cornell from the outside world. Student opinion would overwhelmingly move to support the AAS and SDS interpretation of events, and many of the faculty would change their minds. (For example, on Tuesday, April 22, Otis Sprow, the black president of Chi Psi, told the *New York Times* that "the administration does not understand the 'Afro study pro-gram' and has 'really done nothing in that direction.'")[64] Within Cornell, what was once unacceptable would soon become acceptable.

Damage to the Straight

On Sunday evening reports from crews cleaning up the Straight revealed damage much more extensive than anyone had reckoned. The Students Afro-American Society, which had taken over a building at Columbia the previous year, had left the premises in immaculate shape. (By contrast, the buildings that the Columbia SDS and other white students occupied during that series of protests had been trashed.)[65] Cornell was another story. The list included eleven of seventeen bedroom doors damaged; furniture, mattresses, and other items strewn throughout, some damaged; glass in two corridor doors broken; seventy-five pool cues (some rare and custom-made) broken; locks of coin boxes on vending machines broken; close to $1,000 taken from the machines; the main floor damaged; vast amounts of food rotted; human waste left on the floor; WVBR phone lines severed; scrawling on walls necessitating repainting; damaged safe (it had been dragged to another room and attacked with a steel rod); keys stolen, requiring replacement of locks; and two paintings damaged. According to Straight director Edgar A. Whiting, the total cost amounted to $30,000: $15,000 in actual losses (two-thirds based on damage, one-third on food used or spoiled), and $15,000 in loss of income. The insurance company would refuse to pay because the agreement between the administration and the AAS stated that the university would cover the costs. Working in Herculean fashion through the night and Monday morning, crews enabled the Straight to reopen for service at noon Monday.[66]

The AAS, SDS, and Arms

After the agreement was signed, the AAS was busy with matters of self-defense. Students were seen leaving 320 Wait with guns, and armed students were reported going to and from cars. More threats and rumors arose from various quarters about snipers, bombs, and vigilante groups. Several callers told the Safety Division that armed students were marching from Wait Avenue to Wari House and that arms were being taken into Wari. Some members of fraternities and other whites also took to arms.

SDS was likewise busy, holding meetings on Saturday, Sunday, and Monday. According to many sources, the SDS Action Faction smelled blood and yearned to support the AAS (and redeem itself for not protecting the AAS from Delta Upsilon) with dramatic action. David Burak told me that several members of the faction were genuine revolutionaries who wanted to destroy the system.[67] SDS leaders (including Burak at the time) had their sights set on seizing Day Hall. Such an act would have been increasingly dangerous given the arming of the campus. This situation caused the coolest administrative head, Corson, to call Kiely and request police backup; Kiely would ask for more than two hundred sheriff's deputies to be on call. By Tuesday their presence would dramatically escalate the stakes. Had the involvement of guns not presented such a problem, the deputies might never have been summoned.

At its meetings on Saturday and Sunday, SDS came close to voting for a takeover of Day Hall. Government Professor Paul Marantz attended the Sunday meeting, an experience that was like watching Leni Riefenstahl's portrayal of the Nuremberg rallies in *Triumph of the Will*, he told colleagues.[68] At the meeting on Monday night, attended by twenty-five hundred students and other supporters, SDS was poised for action in the wake of the faculty's refusal to nullify the sanctions, but its members decided to wait a day. According to Harris Raynor, many SDS members dropped out at this point because they believed the danger had passed. "My politics were not there, we were not into it, so the particular struggle they were dealing with was kind of over."[69] This shift left the SDS field largely to the Action Faction, a result that escalated the potential for a major confrontation.

The Media, the Guns, and the Professors

On Sunday evening Perkins attended a concert at Statler, arrived home around 11:00, and found that a copy of the final, typed agreement had been delivered while he was out.

> That was the first time I'd seen the . . . retyped version. And I sat there and I must confess that I was frightened by what we'd all done—me being the responsible party. I'd hardly gotten through that before I turned on the television, and there was a picture, a series of pictures, of Steve and Keith standing in front of 320 in . . . that rather interesting posture. And I went to bed, I remember, feeling that we had one hell of public relations problem on our hands that I hadn't really thought about. I didn't go out to see the parade and I probably should have. . . . I had a vague picture that they had come out with guns, but it didn't really mean something to me until I saw that television picture that night.[70]

According to some sources, Perkins even considered repudiating the entire agreement on the grounds that it had been entered into under duress (contracts entered into under duress are void under law). Purcell was pushing Perkins in this direction, as were some key professorial advisers. Kiely said that Perkins told him in a conversation Sunday evening or early Monday morning that he did not intend to honor the agreement. Perkins "didn't say that he wouldn't implement it, he said he wouldn't honor it. It was a disgraceful document that had been signed under duress . . . [Those were the words he used,] 'shameful' and 'disgraceful.'"[71]

But Miller strongly opposed this. "You can't repudiate it in my opinion. I think that would be fatal."[72] Even Black and Olum agreed on Monday that Perkins was bound by what they considered a disastrous agreement struck by his own negotiators. (Ironically, the AAS would later back out of its sole concession, participating in the reform of the judicial system.)[73]

At long last, Perkins fell into a troubled sleep. Then the phone rang. It was Black. He was at English Professor Mike Abrams's house with a consortium of leading senior faculty (up to seventeen professors at one point), including Cushing Strout, Walter LaFeber, Sindler, Olum, Hans Bethe, Raymond Bowers, and Clinton Rossiter. What would eventually be called the "Group of Forty-One," or the Strout-Abrams group, had problems with the agreement. More than the specific terms, the professors were troubled by the rush to judgment under the circumstances. A faculty vote the next day would be tarnished by duress and ignorance of the situation. Indeed, many faculty had been away from Ithaca that weekend. (Some historians were at the Organization of American Historians meeting in Philadelphia. Many other individuals I interviewed or who gave Oral History interviews had also been away, and the majority were uninformed.) The Strout-Abrams group primarily wanted postponement of the vote. The AAS, however, would interpret any postponement as betrayal.

Black was a man of large ego whom many faculty distrusted because of his close ties to Perkins. Born in Russia in 1919, Black had received his education in Europe (Ph.D., University of London) and had been a member of the Cornell faculty since 1946. He was a prolific author of books on the philosophy of math and science and a Fellow in the American Academy of Arts and Sciences. Black told Perkins the faculty had just read the agreement and "we were terribly upset." In addition to the concern about duress, they disapproved of amnesty and the proliferation of guns, thinking they and others could not teach in the face of these dangers. After about half an hour, Perkins and Black hung up. The conversation had been amicable, and Perkins appeared to have appreciated being forewarned about the faculty's resistance. He tried to go back to sleep but gave up at 5:00 a.m., went downstairs, and "scratched some notes about some kind of public statement on the business of guns and disruption because it had come through loud and clear to me that we now had a very concerned faculty and campus on our hands."[74]

The Group of Forty-One formulated four resolutions in Abrams's kitchen; the key resolution recommended against nullifying the reprimands while duress persisted. The eloquent Strout was selected to present the motions at the faculty meeting Monday afternoon. Reflecting on the task that lay before his group, Strout had a "sinking feeling." A keen student of American intellectual history, he had a sixth sense about the inner meanings of passionate moral and political movements. He sensed that he and his colleagues were stepping into something bigger than any one individual could fathom. He believed in what he was about to do, but he feared the law of unintended consequences that seemed to loom before them.

Black's call on behalf of the Group of Forty-One was a barometer of overall faculty sentiment. The faculty were revolting against nullification. As he sat awake deep into the night and early morning, Perkins must have been aware of how serious the situation was. Everything pointed to escalation: the AAS had spread arms to its locales, other groups on campus remained armed or were arming, vigilantes were organizing, the faculty were likely to refuse to accept the agreement, SDS and the AAS threatened further action if the agreement fell through, and public opinion was beginning to condemn the agreement as a capitulation and to condemn the decision to let the AAS remained armed. No wonder the beleaguered president could not sleep.

Gunshots in the Night

Though Darling's rumor clinic and the Security Division had received numerous reports of gun shots over the previous two days, no concrete evidence existed of any actual gunfire. Yet at 10:30 p.m. an underpublicized shooting took place at Hollister Hall, an engineering building near where the war council and SDS held court. According to the *Ithaca Journal* three days later, "Six shots were fired . . . into the south side of Hollister Hall on the Cornell campus, one of them crashing through a window above the heads of two students who were studying in a lighted room on the third floor."[75] Was the shooter trying to hit the students or just scare them? The administration asked the Safety Division to withhold the information because of concern that it might cause panic or ignite gunfights. This incident, with the spread of arms, convinced Perkins to issue a "decree" against arms early Monday morning. As Fisher and Wallenstein remarked, without taking the Hollister shootings into consideration, "The recent muggings on campus (one student was nearly killed), the fire Saturday night at Chi Psi fraternity, and the dramatic display of arms on Sunday had brought the campus to the brink of mass violence."[76]

Eric D. Evans '69, Afro-American Society Leader, addresses the press on April 20, 1969 (Archives picture collection, #13-6-2497). Courtesy of the Division of Rare and Manuscript Collections, Cornell University Library.

Cornell University President James A. Perkins being shoved away from a podium during a symposium on South Africa on February 28, 1969. (Courtesy of the Division of Rare and Manuscript Collections, Carl A. Kroch Library, Cornell University, Ithaca, NY 14853-5302)

Students picketing in support of the takeover of Willard Straight Hall, early the day of the takeover: April 19, 1969. (Courtesy of *Cornell Alumni News*)

SDS leader David Burak addressing picketers in support of the takeover. (Courtesy of *Cornell Alumni News*)

Delta Upsilon students attempting to expel the occupiers of Willard Straight Hall were repulsed; the flying object at right is a large ashtray. (Courtesy of *Cornell Alumni News*)

A parent expelled from the Straight's lodgings by the Black students is a lone picketer in protest of his expulsion. (Courtesy of *Cornell Alumni News*)

The occupiers of Willard Straight Hall marching across campus following their agreement to leave. (Courtesy of *Cornell Alumni News*)

Vice Presidents Steven Muller and Keith Kennedy signing the deal over the AAS exit from the Straight with Edward Whitfield and another AAS leader. (Courtesy of the Division of Rare and Manuscript Collections, Carl A. Kroch Library, Cornell University, Ithaca, NY 14853-5302)

Afro-American Society leader Eric Evans reading a statement concerning the agreement soon after the conclusion of the takeover of Willard Straight Hall. (Courtesy of *Cornell Alumni News*)

Economics Professor Douglas F. Dowd, supporter of SDS and an early advocate of a Black Studies program at Cornell, addressing the Barton Hall Community in the aftermath of the Straight takeover. (Courtesy of *Cornell Alumni News*)

The Barton Hall Community voting on Tuesday night against the Faculty's initial decision to reject the deal negotiated between the Afro-American Society and the Cornell administration that ended the Straight takeover. (Courtesy of *Cornell Alumni News*)

Supporters of the initial faculty vote convened on Wednesday morning outside Bailey Hall, site of the Cornell faculty's meetings, in advance of the vote over whether to support anew the Monday deal between the administration and the occupiers. (Courtesy of the Division of Rare and Manuscript Collections, Carl A. Kroch Library, Cornell University, Ithaca, NY 14853-5302)

A demonstrator exhorts the faculty to stand firm against the pressure to reverse course. (Courtesy of the Division of Rare and Manuscript Collections, Carl A. Kroch Library, Cornell University, Ithaca, NY 14853-5302)

Student protestor exhorting the faculty to stand firm. (Courtesy of *Cornell Alumni News*)

Cornell professors Clinton Rossiter and Walter LaFeber are leafleted on their way to attend the second faculty meeting. (Courtesy of the Division of Rare and Manuscript Collections, Carl A. Kroch Library, Cornell University, Ithaca, NY 14853-5302)

In Barton Hall, SDS leaders Charles ("Chip") Marshall and David Burak confer with Tom Jones, leader of the Afro-American Society. (Courtesy of *Cornell Alumni News*)

An exultant Cornell President James Perkins greets the Barton Hall Community following the faculty's vote to reverse its refusal of "the deal." (Courtesy of the Division of Rare and Manuscript Collections, Carl A. Kroch Library, Cornell University, Ithaca, NY 14853-5302)

Provost Dale Corson, who would replace Perkins and become Acting President soon after the school year ended. (Courtesy of *Cornell Alumni News*)

A weary James Perkins in the midst of the ordeal. (Courtesy of *Cornell Alumni News*)

Vice President for Student Affairs Mark Barlow. (Courtesy of the Division of Rare and Manuscript Collections, Carl A. Kroch Library, Cornell University, Ithaca, NY 14853-5302)

Government Professor Allan Sindler was the architect of the new judicial system and a ubiquitous campus citizen. Sindler was the first professor to resign in the wake of the Straight crisis. (Courtesy of The Cornellian)

Arthur Spitzer was an anti-war and student government activist who defended the principles of the judicial system on the Faculty Committee for Student Affairs. (Courtesy of The Cornellian)

Tumultuous vote on Tuesday, April 22 by faculty of the College of Arts and Sciences to reverse the university faculty earlier refusal to accept the Straight agreement. (Courtesy of the Division of Rare and Manuscript Collections, Carl A. Kroch Library, Cornell University, Ithaca, NY 14853-5302)

Eric Evans, David Burak, and President James Perkins standing before the Barton Hall Community. (Courtesy of *Cornell Alumni News*)

CHAPTER TEN

DAY 3: A "REVOLUTIONARY
SITUATION"

Monday morning broke with the world's press carrying front-page stories of the agreement and pictures of the AAS exit with guns. The *New York Times* carried "The Picture" on page 1, under the headline "Armed Negroes End Seizure; Cornell Yields" (the headline on an inside page read "Armed Negro Students End 36-Hour Occupation after Cornell Capitulates"). John Kifner's report described the agreement matter-of-factly as a "capitulation."[1] It was in the context of this widespread interpretation that the administration began meeting again early that morning.

Decrees and Morning Meetings

Students were still basically in the dark about what was going on. Most were shocked by the guns and the rumors, but many others were leaning in the AAS's direction because of their normal sympathies and SDS's influence on the public forum. Regardless of where individuals stood, though, most assumed that the agreement had ended the crisis. Few could have anticipated the brewing faculty revolt.

As faculty learned of the agreement, rebellion began to grow. Max Black said that when he and Paul Olum "saw the terms of it, we were very shocked."[2] The Sunday evening SDS "teach-in" (discussed in Chapter Seven) revealed that few Cornellians knew even the most basic facts about the matter at the heart of the dispute, the judicial system. Nor did they grasp the faculty's concern about making important decisions under coercion. That campus opinion was still undecided, however, meant that the administration had an opportunity to shape people's impressions according to its interests. To do that it would have to take a stand against certain groups and assert power on behalf of what it believed. Would it be up to the task?

James Perkins began the day utterly exhausted. Robert Miller observed, "The pressures on the President that day were simply incredible. He was in the midst of a scene of turmoil. From the early morning until the moment that he went on stage [3:00 p.m.] I don't think he had as much as a minute by himself."[3] According to Steven Muller, Perkins "was visibly, totally exhausted." He said Perkins did not sleep for three days.[4]

At 9:10 Perkins took his first strong stand by issuing a "decree" over all local radio stations (followed by an official university news release) that banned guns and disruptive demonstrations from campus.[5] He acted on his initiative, though Mark Barlow helped him draft the language. The decree stated that any student found carrying a gun outside his or her room would be suspended automatically, and any such nonstudent would be arrested; and that any student who entered a building to occupy it for a coercive purpose would be automatically suspended, any such nonstudent would be arrested, and any group or organization that provoked such an act would be disbanded. Arrangements had been made with the Safety Division and city and state police to enforce these rules. According to Barlow, Perkins was under "fantastic pressure publicly" to show strength.[6] In addition, Perkins ordered the Safety Division to rearm itself.

Flush with the feeling of authority, Perkins even considered making a strong statement by going to 320 Wait Avenue and Delta Upsilon to round up all the guns. He would have had to procure the support of local police, but such help was available. Keith Kennedy and Barlow talked him out of it, contending that the proctor should be the one to initiate such a move. The administration failed to understand the perquisites of power. According to a doctrine at least as old as John Locke's *Second Treatise of Government* (1690), executive power by its very nature grows in times of true emergency, thereby creating its own justification within reasonable limits.[7] By talking Perkins out of making a strong, principled move to protect public order in the name of the flimsiest procedural nicety, a chance to regain executive control of Cornell was squandered. Though the executive orders were in effect, the campus remained armed, and the stakes were escalating. As the next two days wore on, Perkins would miss more opportunities to retrieve authority.

The war council reconvened at 9:00 a.m. Amid various meetings, Perkins established a "Law and Order Committee" consisting of Ithaca Mayor Jack Kiely, District Attorney Matt McHugh, and Ithaca Police Commissioner Louis Withiam, who had come to meet with the administration. Ithaca officials were hopeful because they assumed that Perkins was not going to honor the agreement. McHugh said so quite clearly: "At that time it was my distinct impression that the President's position was that he was not going to honor the agreement made on Sunday with the black students because it was entered into under duress."[8]

But Perkins did not follow through on this inclination because he did not want to compromise his negotiators and because he was worried that taking this stand would usurp the discretion of the faculty at the upcoming meeting. Once again procedural concerns and sensitivity to the feelings of others encumbered the exercise of executive authority.

As part of the Law and Order Committee, Ithaca officials called in eighty deputy sheriffs that night as part of a "training exercise" (by Tuesday night the number would exceed 250). They called the assembly a training exercise so that they could keep the group downtown, off campus—a policy that everyone desired. Because Monday night was quiet, Kiely sent the deputies packing, only to recall them in greater numbers Tuesday afternoon in response to an anxious call from Provost Corson (see Chapter Eleven).

At noon Perkins issued another decree, declaring a "situation of emergency" until further notice. He assumed full authority to maintain safety and declared that regulations would be drafted to control firearms and illegal demonstrations. He also announced a "convocation" at 3:00 p.m. at Barton Hall, at which he would address the situation for the entire Cornell community.

There was much debate on whether Perkins should hold the convocation that afternoon. Some staff members, such as Muller, opposed the idea, sensing the dangers of a false step. Barlow and others saw it as an opportunity. "I was pounding the table to get him there, and well . . . he went. And I said, 'Here's your chance to tell ten thousand people what happened, . . . what we've done, what we must do now to put ourselves back together.'"[9] Though he was ambivalent, Perkins decided to hold the gathering, hoping to bring the campus together as a community. "I hoped and prayed that somehow or other I would think of the right things to say when the time came if people gave me time to think about it, which I never got," he said.[10]

During the morning Perkins also met with student activists. He called Ed Whitfield, Eric Evans, and Faye Edwards to discuss the decrees about the guns and the emergency. The 9 o'clock radio message was "dead serious business," he said, and anyone caught with a weapon would be arrested or suspended, or both. Evans asked, "Does this apply to whites and to faculty?" Perkins said the order covered "persons," meaning everyone. When he told the students the Safety Division had rearmed, they were *pleased*. "Oh . . . that will be helpful too, because our great fear is that if we disarm and the whites don't and the Safety Division isn't armed, we're sitting pigeons," Evans replied.[11] Evans grasped the logic at stake concerning the importance of sovereignty and maintaining a monopoly of force.

A few minutes later SDS leaders Chip Marshall and Joe Kelly paid a visit to Perkins. "We support your efforts to disarm," Marshall said. But they opposed the ban on disruptive or coercive demonstrations, which was like holding a red flag in front of a bull. "That's just martial law as far as we're concerned: it's just provocative," Marshall declared. Perkins was up to the challenge, saying, "For this tense period, this is an emergency. I'm going to treat it as such. And you just better act on the assumption that this is the way it's going to be." The orders, he said, would be in effect until at least the end of the week.[12] After the students left, Perkins continued his marathon of meetings and discussions, speaking with James Turner, more trustees, and others. After his noon radio address, he had lunch with Jansen Noyes and Robert Purcell.

It is noteworthy that Perkins, in a final attempt to forge a consensus, asked Marshall and Whitfield to serve on his Law and Order Committee and to escort him to the stage at the convocation scheduled for 3 o'clock. They refused on both counts, unwilling to be seen as complicit with the administration.[13] Marshall was incredulous at Perkins's request. "We expected him at the convocation to come down very hard. He was very afraid we were going to disrupt the convocation . . . [yet] he wanted us to walk in with him. Just incredible. I couldn't believe he asked me. . . I mean, this is appalling, but that's the way he was."[14] Perkins made a similar request to Olum and Black, who told him Corson was a more appropriate escort.

Meanwhile, news and rumors about what had happened over the weekend and what loomed on the horizon surged throughout the campus. The viability of authority hung in the balance. The majority of Cornell was struggling to comprehend the predicament and looking for authority in both the narrow and broader senses: Who was in control? Who should be in control? Whose interpretation of events and justice should prevail (or be most authoritative)?[15] These were really different sides of the same question. Authority would pass to whoever combined strategic power with the most convincing (and conviction-based) normative argument. The university was now its own laboratory in how to gain power and moral authority in a highly charged, potentially revolutionary situation. But because authority was up for grabs, fears of disorder lurked beneath the surface. In the rumor clinic Ruth Darling and her aides worked in "an atmosphere . . . of deep gloom because we could not see how a reasonable solution could be reached under the present circumstances."[16]

The Government Department Meeting

On Monday morning, April 21, Assistant Professor Peter Sharfman received a call from the Government Department secretary, Lois J. Rolley, informing him that Allan Sindler had called an emergency meeting for 10:00 a.m. and had canceled Government classes. The call alerted Sharfman for the first time that the Straight crisis was not a run-of-the-mill Cornell conflict.

At the meeting Sindler summarized the events and the discussions of the Faculty Council and the FCSA. The thrust of his remarks was that the administration—by its own account—had changed its views about what should be done because of the students' threats of bloodshed and that this reaction set a "terrible precedent." According to Sharfman, "The crucial factor for me was not the guns on campus, it was the . . . fact that a university administration was prepared to abandon a reasoned policy, abandon a vote of the faculty [in March the faculty had voted support of the judicial system], abandon what they themselves still maintain they believed in, because they were afraid of what students might do."[17]

History Professor Frederick Marcham described in haunting words the growing dread that had come over many members of the Government and History Departments during March and April, especially after the unprovoked beatings on campus. Their fears seemed to be coming true.

For many days faculty and students organized nightly fire watches to protect the academic buildings. Members of the history and government departments thought themselves particularly vulnerable to attack because in their lectures and discussions they dealt with political, economic, and social topics that bore upon issues that concerned the black and white radicals. . . . Almost from day to day Walter Berns, Allan Bloom, or some other member of the government department came to me and asked me to draft a petition denouncing violence and intimidation. The student who had been beaten [unconscious] was, I believe, for these persons and others, evidence of the last and worst challenge to the world as they had known it. . . . [That world had] now become a place of fire and bodily danger. I myself said that one day we might see a corpse hanging from a tree limb. All of us had looked into the pit. Certainly the members of the government department had done so.[18]

Reflecting on the crisis twenty-eight years later, Muller (a member of the Government Department) maintained that key members of his department had made matters difficult for the administration. "Our situation was complicated by something that most people knew nothing about and cared nothing about, and that is that I was a member of a small department of which at least four members were in flagrant hostility against President Perkins—Bloom, Sindler, Berns, and Rossiter. . . . These people regarded me as a tool for an evil president."[19]

The Government and History Departments were distinctive at Cornell, at least in terms of this issue. They were housed in the same building, West Sibley Hall, and possessed an esprit de corps, a common commitment to the principles of liberal education. The departments were nationally ranked and had some of the best and most committed teachers on campus. Many members, such as the liberal Walter LaFeber, the conservative Walter Berns, and Donald Kagan, who is hard to label, had won the Clark Award as the outstanding teacher of the Arts College, and several others were in the same league. During the Straight conflict, the History Department, with members on both the left and the right, was almost unanimous in its opposition to the administration's handling of the crisis (LaFeber said that the department was 25 to 1 against the administration).[20] The Government Department had some younger members such as Eldron Kenworthy who would take the other side (Andrew Hacker, somewhat older, would stay uncommitted until the crisis ended), but its heavyweights were united in opposing the administration's deal. This relatively united front made the departments a kind of localized clique that had not existed, at least to this extent, in the crises at such schools as Berkeley, Columbia, Harvard, and Wisconsin, where energetic faculty resistance to the students was less concentrated.

After Sindler spoke at the start of the April 21 Government Department meeting, someone (probably Bloom) passed around a resolution stating that the department would abandon teaching if the faculty voted to nullify the penalties that afternoon. Some department members thought this resolution constituted a form of coercion in its own right, but fifteen of the nineteen members present signed it (Hacker, Paul Marantz, Arthur Rovine, and Kenworthy did not). After some modifications, the resolution read, "We declare that the University cannot function when decisions are reached by negotiating with armed students." If Miller's resolution passed, "we pledge ourselves to cease classroom instruction and to undertake a review of our relationship to the University in the light of this intolerable and, one would have thought, unthinkable situation." The signers responded to claims that the resolution was coercive by pointing to the fact that coercion was all the administration now understood. Furthermore, the situation had changed. Though principle was at stake, everything had turned political on the campus. "The integrity of the University was at stake," Fisher and Wallenstein wrote.[21] With this meeting the forces of West Sibley assumed the role of counterinsurgents.

On the other side, the thoughtful Kenworthy described the meeting Monday morning as "almost something of a cabal . . . a psychological atmosphere already generated." Though he did not sign the resolution, Kenworthy was moved by what he considered the articulate and impassioned arguments of his senior colleagues, "whose minds I very much respect." But he also thought the declaration was precipitous, amounting to "painting yourself into a corner too soon."[22]

Problems in the Government Department

Before we return to the sequence of events, it is instructive to look at a conflict that had broken out between the Government Department and the administration that ultimately involved issues related to the larger crisis: the philosophy of education, in this case the philosophy of the teaching of politics. Interestingly, the philosophical debate mirrored the political debate at Cornell.

For over a year the department had been enduring a conflict over the growth of a faction dominated by the so-called Straussians, students who had studied at the University of Chicago under the famous political theorist Leo Strauss.[23] Though a minority of five (Berns, Bloom, Werner Dannhauser, Myron Rush, and Abram Shulsky), the Straussians possessed some key allies and the ability to set the tone of the department. Sindler and Berns were close, but as department chair Sindler strove to balance the sides.

As explained in Chapter One, Strauss taught that the path to political and moral wisdom lay in the teachings of the ancients, especially Plato and Aristotle, who taught that there was a natural law or truth by which political society should be organized. The ends of politics should be intellectual and moral virtue, to which liberal education and academic freedom are indispensable, especially in liberal democracies, which are prone to self-interest and the tyranny of public opinion.[24] In Alexis de Tocqueville's terms (to Berns and Bloom, Tocqueville was, with Lincoln, among the most important thinkers on American democracy), the university's purpose in a liberal democracy is quasi-aristocratic: to instill the intellectual virtues that help to counteract the passions of self-interest and the "tyranny of the majority."[25] So understood, the university helps to foster constitutional citizenship by making individuals more deliberate, thoughtful, and just. From this perspective, the overt politicization of the university has undemocratic and anticonstitutional implications, as Berns and such better-known thinkers as George Kennan maintained in the 1960s.[26]

In many ways Straussianism appealed to student activists looking for deeper meaning in their education: it is no accident that Tom Jones and Ed Whitfield had been close to Berns and Bloom, respectively. Indeed, Bloom argued that a proper part of liberal education is satisfying the thirst for justice. Political philosophy addresses the most fundamental questions: What is justice? How should we live? [27] But the fundamental disagreement over the politicization of the university led to an irreparable break between student militants and the Straussians during the crises of 1968 and 1969, and Straussianism did not carry much moral weight with many professors who were not part of the camp (many considered some of its practitioners severe and dogmatic).

During the '60s, normatively based political science was being replaced at most universities by a scientific approach (the behavioral revolution that accompanied the rise of the multiversity). Steven Muller was a representative of this approach to scholarship, and he lamented the impact of the Straussians on the Government Department. In a secret June 1968 memo to Perkins, Corson, and two others, Muller said that the "desperate" situation in the Government Department required "drastic measures." He called for the dean to publicly declare the department "a disaster area" and appoint himself as temporary chair, after which the dean should be given immediate authority to bring in several new hires.

The problem in Muller's eyes was that the Straussian emphasis on normative principles and values stood in opposition to the trend toward value-free scientific inquiry in the social sciences. Straussians wanted to revive the community of liberal education that Clark Kerr said no longer existed. (Indeed, Bloom was at that time playing a major role in attempting to revive the classics and liberal arts at Cornell.) "In its present state, the Department is an embarrassment to the University and a significant obstacle to a strengthening of the social sciences," charged Muller, who advocated his rather drastic recommendation in the name of promoting science in the department and at Cornell. [28]

Muller's memo reflected the battle over the meaning of education in political science—a battle that was a microcosm of the conflict between the traditional notion of the university and the new notion of the multiversity that had swept the country. Bloom made much of both these debates. "Aristotle said that political science is the architectonic science, a ruling science concerned with the comprehensive good or the best regime. But real science does not talk about good or bad, so that had to be abandoned. . . . But there are irrepressible, putatively unscientific parts of political science . . . , various aspects of justice in action," he wrote. [29]

Muller's memo also revealed a background aspect of the hostility that had developed between the Government Department and the administration. Muller told me the department held the administration in contempt and was out to damage it. A dispute had long raged over support of the Arts College and classics (Stuart Brown, tied to Perkins, was seen as indifferent to the arts, as dean of the college), and the administration's response to the McPhelin affair alienated the department. In interviews almost thirty years later, Sindler and Berns pounced on the McPhelin affair as an essential issue. By the time the Straight crisis hit, little love was lost between the department and the administration. In a confidential memo to Corson written in May 1968, Brown addressed the Government Department's concern about the access one of its professors, Douglas Ashford, enjoyed with the administration that provided the administration with damaging information about the conflicts in the department. "It looks like another episode in the tragic and disastrous decline of the Government Department," Brown wrote.[30] A year earlier, Sindler had submitted a report to Perkins and Brown in which he addressed conflicts in the department and concluded, "There are some in the department who are most anxious to protect what they view as the special teaching mission and competence of the department, which they see as being threatened by growing trends in the social sciences and in the changes in Cornell University."[31]

It is interesting to ponder the relationship between educational principles and reaction to the Straight crisis. More than any individual, Muller was responsible for the deal that was struck in the Straight. Saving lives was the overriding principle. In his 1979 book on capital punishment, Berns would argue that a policy based on security and nothing else lacks a credible moral foundation; criminal justice cannot be justified only on grounds of survival.[32] Muller said such a view was unrealistic and irresponsible, and protecting the lives of others (Muller's moral concern and administrative obligation) is certainly not the same thing as only being concerned with one's own life. It is a moral objective in its own right. Nonetheless, the Straussians at Cornell were ready to fight for what they believed (a logic they shared with people they had taught, such as Jones and Whitfield), and when the dust settled, Berns, Bloom, and Sindler (a non-Straussian) gave up their tenured positions in the name of what they considered justice in the university context.[33] At any rate, the educational controversy over the Government Department mirrored the controversy over how to handle the Straight incident, in terms of both the principles at stake and the individuals involved. Both sides had different moral codes calling forth different commitments.

The administration did not pursue Muller's recommendation of drastic intervention in the Government Department. The crisis in the fall of 1968 rendered such a move impossible (and would have alienated Sindler, then a key adviser to the administration and generally a force to be reckoned with). Then the resignations following in the wake of the Straight crisis made the point moot. Cornell was free of the Straussians and their antiquated ways.

Finally, it must be stressed that most members of the Government and History Departments who joined the counterrevolution were not Straussians. What they shared with the Straussians was the belief that the fundamental principles and processes of academic freedom must never be compromised. Almost thirty years later such liberals as Walter LaFeber, Richard Polenberg, and Joel Silbey still spoke of Sindler, Berns, and Bloom with deep respect.[34]

The Concerned Faculty

Early Monday morning another, mostly younger group of about one hundred faculty met at Kaufman Auditorium in Goldwin Smith Hall to express their support of the AAS and SDS. The Concerned Faculty, as they called themselves, was led by such heralded figures as Doug Dowd, Kenworthy, David Lyons (Philosophy), and Doug Archibald (English). The group formulated a statement pointing to the cross-burning at Wari House and the invalidity of the judicial system. Defending the Straight agreement on the grounds of the prevalence of racism in American society and history, it said that "fears and emotions generated by the occupation of Willard Straight Hall should not prevent us from understanding the struggle of black people throughout the country against persisting racism." If the faculty failed to nullify the reprimands, it would "abdicate its responsibility to the needs of justice." [35]

Members of this group epitomized the emergent notion of the university as an institution dedicated first to the pursuit of social justice. Referring to the COSEP program and the movement toward a justice-based university, Lyons said, "I don't see any problem about the university being committed to certain social values, to social reforms. The university is committed to values anyway." [36] A graduate of Brooklyn College (1960) and Harvard (Ph.D. 1963), Lyons was a young, idealistic philosopher of political and human rights and a master teacher (he would win the Clark Award in 1976). His first book, published in 1965, was a normative analysis of the limits of utilitarianism. [37] Like the AAS and the Straussians, Lyons was willing to fight for his beliefs. Sheila Tobias, an administrative secretary and activist on campus who also had interactions with the members of the Concerned Faculty, adopted a similar logic. She remarked that she had increased her campus activism over the past year because the university "was becoming a microcosm of society and . . . if we could somehow alter the university we might indirectly be able to change the society." [38] Historian Richard Polenberg (a member of the History and Government opposition to the takeover who was one of the few to change his mind in subsequent years) told me a story about Kenworthy that highlighted the new orientation toward teaching and scholarship:

He once invited me to come into a course that he was teaching, to talk about Japanese-American relocation and what I thought about it. . . . I went through this whole explanation for him. I had just written a book, or was writing a book, on the U.S. and World War II, and I sort of looked step by step at how the process to evacuate the Japanese had come about and how in February 1942, when [the Americans] decided to evacuate the Japanese . . . , no one at that point even knew that there would be relocation centers or concentration camps. Everything sort of developed because options became closed. . . . When I finished this whole elaborate, week-by-week analysis of the administration, of ways in which policies developed over several months, and what the forces were at each stage that moved them in the direction they moved, Eldron sat back and said, "But isn't America a racist society?" Well, that was the lesson that he wanted to come out of this. All the historical specifics were not the things that he cared about. [39]

Kenworthy came to Cornell in 1966 from Yale, where he had received his Ph.D. Though idealistic and progressive, he struggled to ascertain where he stood in the crisis with a thoughtfulness that was a trademark of his character. "Here I am teaching politics without having myself worked out my own positions on many of the clear political issues of the day. So part of that ambivalence I think came from the kind of person I was at that time," he said. The students who were taking such stances had, in his eyes, "more authority, intellectual authority in a certain way." [40]

As events unfolded, the Concerned Faculty would come to play a key role, and Kenworthy's ambivalence and thoughtfulness might have saved Cornell from massive violence.

The Convocation

On Sunday night, April 21, members of the administration had contacted all within reach, including militants, to get their thoughts on whether Perkins should hold a convocation. One student said, "I only know the radical people that he contacted. And everybody said, 'Of course! This is the time to say something.'" [41]

But Perkins was unsure whether he should do it. And if he did, what would he say? While pondering the question between frantic meetings, he received a telephone call from "an unidentified black male" who asked him what he intended to say at the convocation. "Well, I'm trying to put together the ideas, as a matter of fact," Perkins replied. Asked whether he was going to speak about the crisis in detail, Perkins said he could not because he did not know all the facts. The caller then informed Perkins that he hoped Perkins "wouldn't put it in a way that would require the black students to ask for time at the microphone to state their side." The startled president replied, "Well, I haven't even decided I'm going to do that at all. As a matter of fact, I may not deal with this particular issue because it may be premature." [42]

Perkins construed the call as a threat to take over the podium in the event he said something about the issue that the caller and whoever he represented considered counter to their interests. He claimed the call did not fundamentally alter his plans, but it "confirmed the kind of instinct I had that it was going to be too soon to go over the details of that. I also remember thinking that if I had to do it all over again with the advantage of hindsight, I would not have called the convocation." [43]

Though Perkins denied it, memories of the Statler collaring must have rushed through his mind. One person present said, "There is little doubt that Perkins was frightened at the specter of being forcibly dragged from the microphone again." [44] So Perkins went to the convocation resigned to avoid the issue that had brought ten thousand people to Barton Hall—perhaps the only meeting of its kind in the history of the American university. He gave a vapid speech about the future of the university in the face of adversity. Some audience members claimed that the speech was the one he had prepared to deliver to parents on the "prospects for stability." Perkins spoke of the importance of "humane studies" and of struggling for progress in the face of tribulations. He concluded with these words:

> If while looking at ourselves we see people who at least will try to be sensitive to the agonies of others, who will be patient with the process of resolving individual

differences, because they know we have the right to be different; if we see people who are courageous enough to see the pillar that leads to the future, as opposed to wanting to sit on the beaches of the past; if, in short, when we look at ourselves we see the prospect of humane men and women, believing that this is a great university and will be one for decades to come—and that whatever the trials and difficulties, we will be determined that we will act in the large way of which I have come to discover most, if not all, of the people in this room have acted in similar circumstances . . . If we approach this complicated path as humane men, all is possible, as this afternoon, I firmly believe to be the case.[45]

The audience had to pinch itself. Perkins had just squandered his last real chance to lead Cornell out of the crisis. Had the president made a case for or against the agreement by combining principle with a compelling recitation of the facts, he could have gained renewed power. He could even have repudiated the agreement; to do so he would have had to take on SDS and the AAS, but the politics of the situation could have played into his hands. The audience was aching for credible leadership. Of equal importance, student opinion had not yet crystallized. What other American university president ever had the opportunity that was now before Perkins— ten thousand students in the palm of his hand? Had the activists taken the podium or disrupted the meeting, they would have lost credibility with mass opinion at Cornell and thereby lost the basis of their ultimate power. (Tom Jones recognized, as we shall see, that mass white student support was crucial to achieving victory over the faculty.) Yet such a move required the willingness to risk alienating groups to whom the administration had consistently been responsive and to risk being collared once again. Had the president been manhandled, though, any organization associated with the act would have instantly lost the public support needed to prevail in the politics of the time. There appear to have been several reasons for Perkins's failure. He was exhausted and tense, he had had no time to prepare what amounted to the most important speech of his career, and he was unable to tap whatever reservoirs of conviction he possessed.

By virtually all accounts, the speech was a disaster. Even Perkins's closest advisers were stunned. "I was absolutely . . . incredulous," Miller said. Barlow confided, "Of course it was a disaster. Not in the way Steve Muller predicted, but for other reasons I shall never understand, the President chose not to do what I felt had to be done. . . . All I could say was, 'Well, let them try it. Let the black students try to take that mike away under these circumstances.'" . . . Joel Silbey was "appalled": "These thousands of kids had turned out for some sort of guidance and he was not giving it to them."[46]

Perkins had asked Corson to sit with him on the stage, and the provost complied. Corson said Perkins gave a speech he had written for an upcoming event but no one really knew what the president intended to do ahead of time. It turned out that Perkins's failure to address the crisis was "a terrible mistake." As they walked out together, Corson asked him why he had failed to face the crisis and got an unspectacular yet unsurprising answer. "There hadn't been any chance for anybody to prepare a speech for him. . . . He told me when I brought up the issue that just getting the campus together was the most important thing. . . . He'd had no chance to prepare."[47] The fact that there was an understandable explanation does not mean that the president and the administration should be relieved of criticism. The situation dictated what was needed, and that was all there was to the matter. Cornellians poured out of Barton confused and searching for answers. Angry conversations erupted all over campus in classes that met right after the convocation, as well as in less formal settings. What happens to anxious groups when their thirst for order and understanding is thwarted?

Fisher and Wallenstein provided the best insight into the implications of the speech. The convocation was indeed a turning point, just not the turning point Perkins wanted: "In retrospect, the convocation stands out as a turning point in this history. Probably less than a quarter of the students had already taken a firm position—either in support of the blacks or against the administration 'capitulation.' At this point, the great majority of students were undecided and confused. They still had much respect for Perkins and good will toward him. They were hungry for leadership and guidance. . . . *As it turned out, Perkins helped create a revolutionary situation.*"[48]

Like so many others dedicated to the new conception of the university, Perkins never fathomed the threats to academic freedom that loomed within the university. To him the only meaningful threats came from outside, where the government and conservative America resided. Similarly, the main threat to administrative control lay in surrendering control to authorities downtown or in the state. "All weekend and throughout the Monday morning meetings, Perkins had seemed paranoid about losing control to civil authorities. It seems he never considered the possibility that he might lose control to internal forces—the SDS, the blacks, and their radicalized supporters among the faculty and students," Fisher and Wallenstein wrote.[49] The convocation was not the ideal platform from which to proceed to the faculty meeting.

The Faculty Meeting

At 4:00 p.m. an estimated twelve hundred faculty members poured into Bailey Hall, the largest attendance at a faculty meeting in Cornell's history. It was a time for those faculty who "cut ice" to speak, Barlow said.[50] Cushing Strout, who would introduce the substitute motion, called it "a very discouraging meeting," four hours of intense debate punctuated by parliamentary maneuvering. He and others came into the meeting distrustful of the administration, due to the fact that "the whole development of the black studies program had been carried on hugger mugger behind the scenes with no systematic faculty involvement, just ad hoc groups called in here and there."[51]

Corson presided over the meeting. He recognized Perkins, who opened by discussing the evolution of the judicial system dispute and the events associated with the Straight takeover. He justified the administration's efforts. "To allow the occupation to go on invited some untoward accident which could trigger an unparalleled tragedy." He also mentioned the meetings with state and local authorities. "The situation seemed now to have achieved some kind of state of equilibrium," but the administration needed faculty backing to gain stability.[52]

Corson then recognized Miller, who had prepared a statement. After telling the faculty about his promise to Whitfield to introduce the nullification motion, Miller presented the motion, which was seconded. Immediately Strout announced he was going to propose a substitute motion on behalf of himself and several other faculty (members of the Strout-Abrams group). He declared that "he and they had no authority for this motion other than their love for Cornell." An attempt to appeal to and organize the political center, the motion consisted of four parts that boiled down to rejecting Miller's motion under the circumstances of coercion. First, it condemned the Straight takeover and the use of guns without judging the merits of the judicial cases and stated that to reverse the judicial outcome in the face of coercion would set a dangerous precedent. Second, it condemned the cross-burning at Wari House and called for bringing the perpetrators to justice. Third, it called for the expulsion of any student who used weapons in a demonstration. Fourth, it affirmed the faculty's desire to cooperate with the AAS and other groups in perfecting the judicial system. (Strout omitted a fifth part expressing "sympathy" for the difficulties black students had in adjusting to Cornell, recognizing that the language was "patronizing." But such language would reappear in troubling form almost behind his back.)

After some motions to change the language of Strout's motion were defeated, Miller rose to speak against it by presenting his own substitute. He felt "honor bound" to the AAS to get the faculty to vote on his motion. What followed was much "confused and confusing debate," according to Fisher and Wallenstein.[53] Henry Ricciuti spoke and informed the faculty of the FCSA vote on Sunday evening against acceptance of the agreement, 5−3−1.[54] To vote for Miller's motion "would really say that the present judicial system and the Faculty's own recent statement of principles had no meaning whatsoever."[55] (Recall, however, that the faculty had watered down their motion supporting the judicial system in their March meeting, thereby creating confusion on this point.)

One of the biggest debates addressed an ambiguity of Strout's motion: Did it mean that the faculty should reject the agreement because of the conditions under which it was wrought? Or did it say that faculty consideration of the motion simply should be postponed until the present coercive circumstances ended? This debate separated the hard-liners from the softer-liners in the large resistance camp. Individuals presented various motions dealing with this question.[56] The second motion to soften the Strout resolution failed by a close voice vote.

Peter Sharfman broke down the factions that were becoming evident at this point. About two hundred faculty "simply wanted to give in" on the merits, roughly the same as the 228 or so who voted against the resolution that reaffirmed the judicial system at the March faculty meeting. Some believed in the justice of this position, whereas others were simply "giving way to fear." But Sharfman noted, "It became clear there was another body [of faculty] in addition to this who didn't like the idea of a *flat* refusal, who wished to make some sort of gesture of willingness to keep an open mind, to reconsider. . . . And I had an uneasy feeling that . . . they would swing a balance, they could make a majority together with those who simply wished to nullify." [57] Sharfman scribbled some notes about what he would recommend if he had a chance: reopening the question of the judicial system if the black students agreed to be bound by some sort of judicial procedure.

After intense debate filled the hall for over two hours, Perkins spoke "as a private member of the assembly." He had been sitting on the stage, scribbling on an envelope, talking with Corson, and, as always, gauging the consensus in the room. The debate had centered on the judicial system, but the crucial issue the AAS raised was "How do we relate to the white community?" Concentrating too much on the judicial system debate ran the "great danger lest the black and white segments of the community never get to discuss the underlying problems keeping them apart." [58] Perkins thus offered to introduce (through someone else, as the president may not formally introduce motions) a new seven-point motion conceding that Miller's motion would not carry the day but addressing the larger question Perkins raised. Max Black attributed this move partly to the fact that Perkins, "like certainly the majority of the faculty, very much regretted the agreement that had been signed." [59] The seven points—based on Perkins's understanding of the points that had emerged out of the discussion—represented a compromise.

Strout had to make a quick decision: to go along or stick to the motion he and his allies had worked on so painstakingly the night before. That night they had made a vow to stay committed to their motion. Then Corson stopped the meeting and asked Strout whether he would agree to Perkins's motion. Though there was confusion about what exactly the new motion meant, Strout agreed to withdraw his motion, figuring that the new motion would possess more power than his own because it had Perkins's imprimatur. Yet like many others, he second-guessed himself because he had so little time to decide—thirty seconds! Engineering Professor Herbert J. Carlin tried to introduce the new motion but could not read Perkins's handwriting. Corson called a five-minute adjournment, and Perkins wrote it out in full on the back of another envelope.

Walter LaFeber (who thought that even the original Strout motion was "some weasel stuff" rather than a strong statement of principle) interpreted Perkins's intervention as less of a rejection of the original Miller motion than Black did. Perkins understood that the Miller motion would not pass, but he felt that Strout's motion did not concede enough, so he introduced a compromise that he hoped would be less objectionable to the AAS. During the recess he talked with Strout and others in an effort to enlist their support. [60]

Upon reconvening, the faculty voted 540–360 (there were many abstentions) to amend Strout's motion with the seven Perkins points: [61]

Resolved that: 1) The Faculty expresses its sympathy for the problems of the black students in adjusting themselves to life at Cornell; 2) the Faculty condemns the seizure of Willard Straight Hall; 3) the Faculty condemns the carrying and use of weapons by anyone except those officially responsible for maintaining law and order on the campus; 4) the presence of arms and the seizure of Willard Straight Hall make it impossible for the Faculty to agree at this meeting to dismiss the penalties imposed on the three students [slated for reprimands]; 5) the Faculty is prepared under secure and non-pressurized circumstances to review the political issues behind the Afro-American complaints; 6) therefore, the Faculty directs the Faculty Council to meet with representatives of the Afro-American Society tomorrow and to report to the Faculty by Friday at 4 p.m.; 7) the Faculty supports, in principle, the President's action taken today to preserve law and order on campus.

The motion finally carried by an overwhelming voice vote, although it had omitted a crucial part of Strout's motion, the one that condemned the cross-burning at Wari House. The faculty quickly added it rather haphazardly as point 8.

Walter Berns then spoke. He wanted it made clear that the faculty had not, "even obliquely, approved the Dean's original motion."[62] Black responded that the motion did no such thing. LaFeber felt betrayed by the abandonment of the Strout motion, which he considered barely acceptable in the first place. He had wanted a clear statement that the judicial system would be upheld: "When we reconvened after the ten- or fifteen-minute recess, the resolution had been modified. And Perkins had essentially gotten his way. I think Perkins must have argued [during the recess], 'Trust me, this [the Strout motion] is going to lead to really bad stuff if you insist on passing it.' And I think a number of faculty accepted Perkins's word on that. I remember watching this and deciding that at that point I was going to leave Cornell because it was pretty clear what was happening. . . . The other thing that happened was pure fright. People were scared."[63]

At the end of the meeting, Miller asked to read his statement. He informed the assembly of his promise to Whitfield to resign if his motion were defeated. "I shall offer my resignation to the Trustees effective immediately." He then named Acting Dean Ernie Roberts to the deanship. Rossiter then moved that "the Faculty supports the Dean and does not want him to resign." To applause, the motion passed by "emphatic voice vote."[64] Miller still felt honor-bound to step down; unfortunately, the procedural confusion made it uncertain as to whether Miller had been reinstated. Even Roberts appeared to be unsure about this point at the crucial press conference he was about to hold. The AAS and SDS would not be amused.

As 8 o'clock approached, the last major event was a personal statement from Muller. Though he acknowledged that he bore primary responsibility for the agreement, he reminded the audience that the situation was "not of his making." The meeting notes stated, "Approximately one hundred persons in a state bordering on the paranoid were locked into a fortress where a single thrown rock could have precipitated a bloody slaughter. He [Muller] had acted to avoid bloodshed. Cornell could recover from exactions extorted by force, but it could not live down murder. He would not have changed his actions because they allowed him in his own conscience to know that he had acted as a whole man."[65] Muller recalled that this speech was met with "a big hand" and that it "drove a wedge between President Perkins and myself which really has never quite lifted. . . . Perkins was furious . . . because it made him look bad. . . . I didn't say I was sorry or anything."[66]

The meeting adjourned at 8:15. Feelings were mixed. Many faculty appeared comfortable with the Perkins resolution, but their hopes were soon dashed. Parts of the resolution—which had not received much attention from the exhausted assembly—would not hold up to scrutiny. Anyone with any experience with such meetings knows the dangers of settling on a position with a complex compromise at the end of a long, laborious process; wanting to go home can become more important than doing the right thing. Why would the faculty be willing to adopt the complex resolution of the president who had just—in virtually everybody's estimation—failed at the convocation? The product of compromise rather than clear statements of conviction, the new resolution, unlike the Strout motion, was disjointed and poorly phrased. It made the faculty look more cynical and less committed to justice than it was. Moreover, militant students were not prepared to argue over the fine points of a resolution that in the end went against what they wanted.

Of all the commentary I have seen, Sharfman's was the most astute: "It was, of course, a horrendous motion. But I don't think people realized how bad it was until well after the meeting was over. And I'm certain people didn't realize what they were voting for when they voted for it. And it was simply an example . . . of faculty as a legislative body behaving very stupidly and subsequently being punished for it. You should not pass seven motions [and then an eighth] without being very clear what the motion says and debating whether it's phrased well and so forth."[67]

A bad feeling crept over Strout, the key player. "I felt that the situation had become confused and the faculty had in fact shown itself rather unable to come to a coherent conclusion without the intervention of the President."[68] Silbey was typically sardonic about the process. During the brief discussion of Perkins's resolutions, a physicist came in and sat next to Silbey and his friends. He told Silbey that he planned to vote whatever way Perkins wanted because "in times of crisis he must follow the leader." Silbey told him "that people had been hung at Nuremberg for believing things like that, but we dropped the subject." Silbey and his History Department colleagues left the meeting feeling that "the faculty had in a somewhat weak way stood up for principle against coercion. And that was it."[69]

As the faculty limped out of Bailey, hundreds of SDS students strode in past them, ready to attack the shaky edifice the faculty had built. According to Fisher and Wallenstein, the entire resolution was suspect in students' minds because its very first point typified the "great white father" mentality: the problem at Cornell was not discrimination but a "failure of adjustment." (This point was similar to the patronizing motion that Strout had had sense to omit from his list.) At the SDS assembly after the faculty vote, Douglas Dowd read the first provision "in a mocking voice. The students jeered."[70] There were two other problems: the provision about the cross-burning was seen as an afterthought, even though it had been a major part of the Strout resolution that had been discussed at length, and the impression arose that the faculty had paid no attention to the Miller motion that had been such an important matter of trust between the administration (especially Miller) and the AAS. On the other side of the conflict, faculty such as Sindler (whose prescience had not abandoned him) read the compromise to mean that the faculty were actually preparing to nullify the sanctions later in the week.

The Press Conference

Dean Roberts's press conference immediately following the faculty meeting was another disaster, as even the administration later acknowledged. "But for this ill-fated news conference, reason might still have prevailed on the torn campus," Fisher and Wallenstein wrote.[71]

In the face of urgent questioning, Roberts spoke in circles, unable to clarify the multitude of resolutions that had been discussed. It was unclear whether Miller had actually resigned. Students, already baffled by the convocation, felt further betrayed. Many students knew or cared little about the principles that underlay the faculty's decision, but the confusing nature of the resolutions and the public explanations did not win the faculty much sympathy.

Roberts's performance "gave the impression that there was something to cover up," Fisher and Wallenstein wrote.[72] Thomas Tobin, who understood the intricacies of public relations, was generous toward Roberts, pointing out that he did a credible job explaining the conclusions of the meeting under trying circumstances. The faculty meeting was confusing, and the notes pertaining to it were unavoidably jumbled, so Roberts had to follow a poor script.[73] In addition, Fisher and Wallenstein charged that Roberts was upset at the faculty's rejection of Miller's motion.[74] Others saw problems. For example, Roberts said point 8, about the cross-burning, was added "at the last minute," even though it had been an important part of Strout's original motion! When he returned home from dinner and the faculty meeting around 10 o'clock, Sharfman got a phone call from a friend who taught at Ithaca College and was unusually perceptive about such things. The friend had just seen Roberts's press conference. "And he was appalled, and he said . . . , 'What could possibly have possessed you to pass a motion like that?' . . . He realized immediately this was going to be a political disaster."[75]

The press conference further dramatized the evaporation of administrative authority and control taking place at Cornell. Fisher and Wallenstein captured what was coming to pass by quoting a young mathematics professor who had just returned to Cornell after being out of town that weekend. Upon seeing the pictures of the students with guns, "I told everyone I knew that the marines should be called in and stationed all around where everyone can be seen. It's impossible for this unarmed faculty to stand up against armed students. Can't people realize that? As Machiavelli said, 'It is impossible for one who is armed to respect one who is not.'" Fisher and Wallenstein state that "the campus was hysterical that evening."[76]

The SDS Meeting

The SDS meeting was the only public session about the crisis. Twenty-five hundred students showed up at Bailey Hall after the faculty meeting. It was like a war party: attendees chanted, raised clenched fists high, and shouted for revolution. The inner circle of SDS was still unprepared to take decisive action because it had not worked out what to do in the event of a faculty revolt against the agreement; nevertheless, SDS leaders were ready to declare war against the faculty and the administration. Dowd kept assuring SDS leaders that the faculty would soon fall in line, but Marshall and others did not (or would not) believe him.

SDS decided to talk it over on Tuesday with the AAS, which was sending representatives to the SDS meeting that night. The AAS wanted SDS to be willing to take a building, which the AAS had decided to do on its own if necessary. The AAS interpreted the faculty vote as an insult and a rejection of the agreement. Before the discussion, AAS member Skip Meade addressed the assembly, proclaiming that blacks had been oppressed by capitalism and institutional racism for hundreds of years but were now fighting back. "We achieved a great revolutionary victory here" with the Straight affair, said Meade, who denounced the judicial system and accused particular individuals, such as Sindler, of being racists. When he finished, people stood up, clenched their fists, stomped the floor, and chanted, "Fight racism—meet the black demands NOW!"[77] After this speech, faculty members presented reports of the faculty meeting and the decisions; the basic line was that the faculty voted on the basis of its own interests and privileges, not justice. Then the assembly passed two resolutions, one supporting the demands of the AAS and one expressing a vote of no confidence in the faculty for their actions. Only about ten members of the audience voted against the resolutions. The assembly decided to begin formulating what specific actions to take the next day, when SDS leaders planned to meet with AAS leaders.

One unidentified AAS member made the most memorable speech during this meeting. It was the first true call for uniting blacks and whites in a militant common front. The *Ithaca Journal* quoted his speech at length:

> The faculty voted tonight to have a showdown. . . . They can do us in, but they go too. . . . We and the others who were inside the Straight have our rumps on the line now for one real reason: because we dared to challenge a historic concept that black people are supposed to be impotent, that black men are not supposed to take care of black women. . . . Now there is a broader issue. First, they were talking about blacks. Now they say anyone who enters a building for coercive purposes will be automatically suspended. That's a funny thing: You better be careful what you are thinking when you walk through a door. The issue affects all of us, black and white, in a very direct way. It is important to preserve for ourselves the right to act to remove the contradictions in our society that place limitations on our lives.[78]

During this time Tom Jones was responsible for making a key decision: it was time for the AAS to reach out to the larger community of white students if it wanted to forge a mass movement against the faculty. At Columbia a year earlier the Students Afro-American Society had steadfastly refused to align itself with Mark Rudd and SDS (true to the separatist doctrine of Black Power).[79] But the AAS confronted a different situation: blacks were much more isolated at Cornell than at Columbia, and Cornell had greater revolutionary potential. Michael Miles wrote that most successful student movements in the sixties had had to rely on enlisting the support of the sympathetic yet nonmilitant student "center," and Jones decided on a similar strategy.[80] (Jones's personal situation may also have influenced this decision, as he was experienced and adept at working with whites. Jones's ideological zeal was matched by a political and strategic intelligence for dealing with whites that his more alienated cohorts lacked.) As Jones explained in 1987:

> I knew that our chances of success depended on involving the white students, and here one of these absurd arguments developed where the militant leaders wanted to have nothing to do with the white students. This was *our* struggle. I argued that we can't count on people at the university to give a damn what happens to *us*, but I know they care what happens to the general white student population, and to the extent that the white population stands between us and them, nothing happens to us. And so I became involved in what was probably the turning point of the whole crisis.[81]

Moderate members of the audience at the SDS meeting realized that something important was happening: two thousand students appeared willing to take militant "revolutionary" action. Barlow had entered the meeting thinking that most students would support what the faculty had wrought. He left with a different impression, called Perkins, and said, "Look, we got a problem on our hands . . . and we better get together in the morning because my judgment at the end of that meeting is that there's not much support for what the faculty did this afternoon."[82]

Government Professor Paul Marantz was also present at the meeting. It was around this time that he began to view the situation through the lens of his knowledge about historical crises. Such crises are usually not caused by the cynical plans of malevolent people but by "misunderstanding, misconception, or simply the fact that each group is doing what it perceives as logical and sensible. The two protagonists are locked into a situation which resembles a Greek tragedy; neither character can do otherwise, and the end result has to be a crisis. Here, I think very much of *Antigone* and the struggle between Creon and his daughter. So then in voting against nullification I felt that had to be done."[83]

Historian Donald Kagan—a scholar of ancient Greece—likened what was happening at Cornell to the Corcyran civil war depicted in Thucydides' *Peloponnesian War*: "It's the most interesting thing in history. It's what draws history and fiction together. A really good work of fiction also wants to know, how do people behave in tough times, and why do they behave that way? [The Cornell crisis] really had an impact on me because I realized that I had either been thoughtless or wrong in my understanding of people and that I was very much more impressed by Thucydides because he understood this."[84]

Despite the high stakes, others were simply distraught, including Kenworthy, who sided with the students. After the SDS meeting, he was "really desolate." He sat alone, pondering the situation and bothered by the "elation" that took over the SDS leaders when they realized they could mobilize thousands of students for a confrontation. The SDS meeting indicated that "we are kind of engaged in the psychodrama in which . . . the merits of the positions taken by people no longer mattered [and] various groups . . . were placing their own interpretation on events and on words without really . . . examining [them]. . . . I remember leaving the SDS meeting that night feeling that the University was clearly on a collision course."[85]

The SDS meeting convinced the administration that a large number of students had started to turn against the judicial system. The meeting "was the first we realized that . . . this issue had gone well beyond the hard-core two hundred."[86] Perkins went home to get some desperately needed sleep, but at 2:00 a.m. he was awakened by a call from Whitfield's father, Moses. The elder Whitfield had called his son and scolded him for what he and the AAS had wrought. When he made fun of his son for carrying a gun he did not know how to use, his son replied, "I had to carry a gun because I was President of the Society, but I never want to touch a gun again as long as I live."[87]

CHAPTER ELEVEN

DAY 4: STUDENT POWER

Tuesday began in symbolic fashion. Stuart Brown recalled "how dark and threatening the weather was." Cushing Strout had "a nightmare day." By midafternoon much of the faculty was giving in to collective fear.

It was a day of countless meetings among faculty, administrators, and students. Hoping that talk would heal, the administration had urged professors to use their classes to discuss the crisis. Law Professor Norman Penny recalled the dismay that his colleagues in the school felt "at the turn of events, particularly in reference to the leadership and how things were disintegrating, and here we were being asked to do this." The Law School set up the Moot Court room for "marathon discussions."

Many faculty who did meet with students in classes and less formal settings were stunned at the student reaction to the vote. To Penny's shock, virtually all twenty-five of his students, especially the best and brightest, sided with the AAS and SDS. Even Larry Salameno—whose room in the Straight had been broken into and whose father was suing the AAS—took this position. "The general attitude was let's wipe the slate clean and see if we can't rebuild," Penny said. "It was very influential. . . . I suppose I was swayed as much by that experience with my students that morning as I was by anything else. And so I changed my vote." Penny heard similar reactions from his professor friends around the campus. "They thought that the stakes were too great to adhere to rigid principle on what was essentially a minor penalty."[1]

Clinton Rossiter, whose colleagues in Government and History would not be as forgiving as Penny's, also had a conversion experience. Student concerns won him over on Tuesday. "I made up my mind by Tuesday evening that I would switch my vote."[2] Unlike people such as Strout, who changed their votes but not their minds, Rossiter had a change of opinion. His conversion was important for two reasons: first, Rossiter was a member of the Strout-Abrams group and a weighty force on the faculty; second, he had stood out as the most adamant supporter of a hard line on

Monday. After the Monday meeting, he had made a statement that was quoted around the world as the essence of the faculty's stand: "If the ship goes down, I'll go down with it—as long as it represents reason and order. But if it's converted to threats and fear, I'll leave it and take a job as a nightwatchman at a local bakery."[3] But apparently his words were not backed by firm conviction; two days later he even introduced a motion to reverse the vote. Now, to his most cherished colleagues in the Government Department, he was about to become persona non grata.

Not everyone who met with students encountered such opposition. Joel Silbey, for example, tried to explain his vote when students questioned his stance. He found his students willing to listen and ultimately receptive to his hard line. Silbey's report, however, was in the minority.

At noon Tuesday Penny attended a meeting of the deans of Cornell's various colleges as the Law School representative. At this gathering the administration asked the deans to hold meetings in their colleges to discuss reconvening the faculty as a whole. Three students attended this gathering, including Ezra Cornell III, the great-grandson of Cornell's founder, Ezra Cornell. They presented a proposal to suspend classes for the rest of the term so that students could discuss the governance and mission of the university. By the time of this meeting, rumors of an SDS move against Day Hall were rampant. Penny observed an administration in panic and reduced to following students' leads:

> I can remember being appalled . . . at what I viewed as the panic on the part of key members of the administration. . . . [It was] one of the most unsettling meetings that I've ever attended because it was all the top brass. . . . They were literally frightened and, I thought, acting in somewhat a state of panic. And it was to me extraordinarily disconcerting because I've lived in situations where people . . . had reason to be in a state of panic, and I look for a . . . little more balance and coolness . . . and [the administrators] were listening to all these kids seriously about what to do. . . . The thing that panic-struck me was that there was no ability . . . or no inclination on the part of the people sitting there to sort out very carefully the good [ideas] from the bad ones. . . . They were desperate to try anything.[4]

(Provost Corson was an exception; he averred that he did not panic during the crisis, and sources confirmed this claim.) The deans decided to ask departments to meet to decide what to do about classes, and several deans called for college meetings later that day.

Another student at this meeting, Chip Reveal, informed the deans that the Interfraternity Council had decided to hold a teach-in on racism and the crisis on Wednesday afternoon. Perkins and others encouraged Reveal to move the meeting up to Tuesday evening to provide a counterforce to the SDS meeting that was being planned (and that surely involved a mass movement against Day Hall). But administrators let Reveal talk them out of this move because he thought it would be wrong to preempt SDS and "further polarize militants and nonmilitants." (Of course, this was precisely the intent of Perkins's suggestion.) Deferring to Reveal was another sign of the passage of authority from the administration to the students and an indication that Penny's reading of the meeting was fairly accurate. In fact, as economist George Hildebrand observed, many administrators and professors seemed to behave as if students possessed a moral authority that exceeded their own.[5]

Earlier that morning Chandler Morse had called Penny "in desperation," fishing for a solution. He invited Penny to a meeting of the Concerned Faculty at Kaufman Auditorium. Penny did not go but wished he had once he found out what they intended. Their plan pretty much guaranteed "a disastrous turn of events."[6]

The Concerned Faculty

The Concerned Faculty reconvened at noon. The several dozen members of the group, mostly younger progressives, varied in their militancy. According to David Lyons, after the events of Monday they were "more desperate than ever and more concerned than ever to do something."[7] Eldron Kenworthy joined the group because he was looking for a "middle way" that might bridge the gaps between groups that were widening into gulfs. They met until the Arts College meeting slated for 4:00 p.m.

The Concerned Faculty discussed options and circulated petitions. The main options were taking over a building themselves, joining students in whatever action the students endorsed, or surrounding a building that students took over and interposing themselves between the students and the troops that everyone expected to show up. This last position appealed to many faculty, even such hard-liners as Strout. (At other universities many otherwise unsympathetic faculty felt obligated to protect their students from outside force in this fashion. Force by outsiders against students raised concerns that cut across ideological and strategic lines.)[8] But the most vocal wanted some sort of revolutionary action, and they carried the day.

Graduate student Harry Edwards, who earlier that year had led the black athletes' protests of the 1968 Olympic Games in Mexico City, gave a chilling speech that advocated confrontation. He castigated the faculty for saying that the cross-burning was a "childish prank."[9] Strout—who had attended the meeting after a progressive friend had convinced him to admit that he felt obligated to interpose himself between students and troops—was shocked at Edwards's professions. He asked to speak, but the assembly voted to deny him the opportunity to respond. According to Henry Alker, an assistant professor of psychology, "It was clear that this was not a forum in which equal time would be given to an opposite point of view. I was amazed by the votes taken. You merely had a chance to vote 'yes.' There was never a 'no' vote taken. If you disagreed, you simply weren't 'concerned.'"[10] Doug Dowd spoke and spun some fine distinctions, saying he opposed violence but favored coercion and disruption. Morse declared that the faculty who presented Strout's motion had been dishonest. When Max Black tried to defend himself against this charge, he was not allowed to speak. It was the first time in his twenty years at Cornell that Black had been denied the right to speak at a faculty gathering. He considered the ensuing discussion about whether a takeover should be violent "quite abnormal and extraordinary." [11]

By the end of the meeting more than thirty faculty members had pledged to take whatever action was deemed necessary, including taking over a building. Their statement proclaimed: "Because we find that our normal participation as faculty members of Cornell University is incompatible with our responsibilities as men and women, we resolve that until the judicial proceedings against the five black students are dismissed, we shall refuse to take any further part as teachers or scholars, in the education process at Cornell and shall go on strike. . . . And we shall occupy some university building to make clear the seriousness with which we consider the issue." [12] Kenworthy did not sign the document, considering it "not at all appropriate" for faculty to engage in such action; he felt that his colleagues "were being duped." [13] Now, though, the administration and faculty had to factor the intentions of the Concerned Faculty into their thinking.

After the meeting, Black went back to the Philosophy Department and made contact with members of the Group of Forty-One (the Strout-Abrams group). "They were in a state of great anxiety and felt that something simply had to be done or there would be an absolute catastrophe." The group decided to ask the Faculty Council at its 4:00 p.m. meeting to call another faculty meeting to reconsider the vote. It was a "desperate situation." [14]

SDS and Day Hall

Toting sleeping bags, the members of the SDS war council met for four hours that afternoon in Kaufman Auditorium to plan a building takeover. About this time Strout visited the office of Philosophy Professor Norman Krentzmann. The phone rang; Krentzmann answered it and turned "white." Trembling, he said, "I just learned from the SDS that the blacks intend to take another building and burn it to the ground if the police interfere." [15]

Day Hall flew into a panic. At 3:45 Corson hurried into Perkins's office, out of breath, and whispered in his ear that "word has just come out that the SDS is going to seize Day Hall. I think it's imperative to get out of here because this building . . . may well be taken over. They're just having a vote." [16] Perkins was sure SDS was on its way to capture "little old me." [17] While the staff prepared to leave, Mark Barlow came in and assured them that SDS was not going to take over Goldwin Smith or Day. Steven Muller told Barlow he was wrong. Then somebody came into the office and yelled, "They're on their way, get out!" Perkins jumped to his feet, struggled with his raincoat, stuffed papers in his briefcase, and headed down the stairs and out of the building. He and his entourage stopped in front of Perkins's "handsome Buick," decided that the car was too conspicuous a target for those with disruptive designs, and jumped into Corson's less elegant vehicle. "So I went down to Carpenter Hall down in Engineering," Perkins explained, "thereby leading to a panic in Day Hall which I hadn't intended, with everybody leaving the building apparently shortly thereafter."[18]

After Perkins left, Thomas Tobin gave the order to clear the building.[19] Ruth Darling, a hardened warrior of the rumor clinic, recalled the staff's swing between comedy and alarm at Day Hall. The rumors of the takeover "helped us to get a good laugh." She spotted secretaries running down the stairs with arms full of folders and documents. "We were all rats leaving the sinking ship." Darling preferred to confront the raiders if they came, but she also sympathized with those who were afraid. In the end she gave her staff, now eleven in number, the choice of going or staying. She stayed. "So we sat and waited." Nothing happened.[20]

As soon as the Perkins party arrived at Carpenter, Corson called Mayor Kiely, telling him the situation had "really deteriorated" since the morning. (That morning they had met in Kiely's office, at which time Corson had told him that he expected the faculty to reverse their vote soon.) He also told Kiely that SDS had seized Goldwin Smith and that Day Hall was next. Kiely then made a fateful move: he recalled the deputies to Ithaca (the governor had to make the final decision but listened to Kiely). When Kiely found out that Corson's information was wrong and that SDS had not seized these buildings yet, he sent his own investigators to the campus. He respected Corson as the coolest head in the administration, but even Corson was getting emotional.

Corson was right about the larger picture: SDS did have its sights set on Day Hall. It planned to capture Day with a mass student action following on the heels of the meeting it had called for that evening, only now there would be more than two hundred deputies on hand, ready to pounce. (In addition, several representatives of the state police were on campus as observers in case the state police needed to be called in—a situation that did not come to pass.)[21] Chip Marshall said that SDS met with the AAS, which around this time changed its name to the Black Liberation Front (BLF), "all day Tuesday . . . and we planned what we were going to do and we thought . . . we would really take Day Hall. And we made plans for this." SDS contacted professors to plead its case and sent out leaflets all over campus announcing the meeting that night at Bailey to vote on what action to take. Bruce Dancis was going to chair the meeting. "He was going to get up and explain that people had met all day with the BLF . . . and that we had come to a decision; then someone from the BLF was going to get up and talk and say, 'All right, now let's move on Day Hall.'" Those who wanted to take militant action would join this group; those who preferred a less militant way of showing support would plan something else, such as a mass meeting. "What we wanted to make very clear was that there were different kinds of supports," Marshall said.[22]

The Arts College Meeting

By the time the pivotal Arts College held its meeting at 4:00 p.m., Cornell no longer resembled the community of "reason and order" that Rossiter had depicted twenty hours earlier. Dozens of student activists invited themselves in (the first time students had ever been let into an Arts College faculty meeting, except by special invitation) and set the tone for the agenda while the panicky faculty could do nothing to stem the tide. The inversion of authority—with all its psychological and emotional implications—was near total. Early on, in the midst of a statement about Cornell's being on the brink of disaster, someone introduced a substitute motion to hold the reprimands in abeyance until further discussion with the AAS; it lost overwhelmingly. Only outright nullification would get the faculty out of their unbearable states. The faculty (with the sometimes indistinguishable mix of students) no longer seemed like a faculty. In certain respects the gathering resembled the SDS meeting of the night before, except that it was reacting rather than leading. Silbey observed, "There was a fantastic atmosphere at that meeting, like a Munich beer hall, or a Nazi party rally. One was cheered if he said the right thing. Hoots and hollers greeted one if he said the wrong thing. Men got up and said, 'I'm scared, frightened—I'm changing my mind.' The facade of rationality and calmness was stripped away."[23] Only seven faculty members (four Government and three History) voted against the motion to reverse the penalties. It was "an atmosphere of fantastic coercion," Silbey said. "That was the meeting that I think was the most frightening because there you saw in nakedness . . . what the University was coming to. . . . I've always looked back to that Tuesday meeting as the fulcrum of everything that happened."[24]

Walter Berns and Walter LaFeber watched the proceedings from the back of the room. Neither one had any inclination to say a word, as "it would have been absolutely futile," Berns reported. "And to see my esteemed colleagues . . . to see those with great European [background], it was just disgusting."[25] According to sources, LaFeber was profoundly affected by the hysteria and passions around him, recoiling from the lack of composure and reason.

Stuart Brown was supposed to chair the meeting, but he arranged for Stephen Parrish to substitute for him because Brown thought he "might be more useful outside than inside," especially in the wake of rumors about an SDS plot to take over the building where the Arts College met.[26] The meeting was supposed to be in Kaufman Auditorium but was moved down the hall to Lecture Room A in Goldwin Smith Hall because of the crowd. So many students flooded into the room that the assembly had to hold a vote to determine whether the students could stay; the students won, 106–92. Peter Sharfman introduced a motion to restrict students from voting or speaking; it lost by three votes. Observers saw several students vote on this and later motions.

Eventually the faculty (and, by default, students) passed four resolutions overwhelmingly. Two involved stopping classes to discuss racism and related issues and calling for the restructuring of the judicial system, and two called on Perkins to use his emergency powers to end the current judicial proceedings and to nullify all judicial decisions since the beginning of the spring term. Other colleges, including architecture, home economics, and business and public administration, passed similar resolutions.

Fred Marcham noted that "quickly the opponents of reversal found themselves a tiny minority."[27] One professor made a speech that was an emblem of sheer desperation: he would vote for violence six months from now rather than now because the fear was unbearable. Despite their stance just less than two days before, Strout and his Group of Forty-One supported the Arts College move. Silbey stated that the Strout group and others said that the vote had to be reversed "*regardless* of whether they [the AAS] are right or wrong, because the University is not worth fighting over this, over this principle, over principle of due process and so on." The Arts College faculty, which the AAS had earlier determined was its most formidable obstacle to the establishment of its program, had become a "mob," making a reasoned discussion impossible.[28]

Strout sized up the key factors to be considered: the AAS was still armed and had threatened to retake a building; SDS was ready to seize Day Hall; the Concerned Faculty were also prepared to capture a building; and more than two hundred armed deputies were poised to strike. Necessity called for the relinquishment of principle. But for individuals such as Strout who were honest with themselves, such relinquishment must have been hard to bear.

The first call Perkins received after fleeing Day Hall and finding security at Carpenter Hall was from Max Black. En route to the Faculty Council meeting following the Arts College affair, Black asked Perkins what he thought of the council taking the initiative by reversing the vote on its own. "I wanted no part of it," Perkins said. He could not be a party to such an action because only the day before he had led the faculty into adopting the resolution that would be reversed. Perkins then called the council himself and said, "It would be an absolute disaster if the council did on Tuesday what the faculty would not do on Monday under the circumstances that then prevailed." It would "split the faculty absolutely down the middle."[29]

Though he had pursued agendas that circumvented the faculty, Perkins remained leery of openly challenging them. He lacked their intellectual credentials and felt it would be politically ill advised to cross them openly. When someone asked Perkins why he gave the lectures that led to his book *The University in Transition* at Princeton rather than at Cornell, John Marcham pointed out, "He said he had been told by Arthur Dean [then chairman of the Board of Trustees] or someone else that any time he got the idea that he should tell the faculty what to do or lead the faculty, that he should take a cold shower. That was said as a joke, but unfortunately that was the philosophy he appeared to be working under."[30]

Had the faculty stuck with their vote, as Perkins believed many would, he would have found himself between a rock and a hard place. But Black's phone call held out a ray of hope. Black's request was "the first intimation about the shift of faculty," "the first . . . clue that the faculty was in the process of changing its mind."[31] Then the votes of the various colleges started rolling in.

Had the faculty been able to meet right then, the revolutionary situation created the day before would have not have been born, for the cradle of revolution—the Barton Hall Community—had not yet come into being, and the established order had not yet died. On Tuesday evening the first student (not a militant) turned in his gun pursuant to a retrieval system that Corson had set up. There was a chance that revolution could be averted. But nothing authoritative was done, so SDS, the AAS, and the mass student movement they inspired continued to act. The new Cornell began with "The Speech."

"The Speech"

Early that evening WHCU, an off-campus radio station, broadcast an extraordinary speech by Tom Jones. Perkins heard the speech just as a meeting with Corson, Muller, Barlow, Kiely, McHugh, Tobin, and representatives from Ithaca, county, and state police was ending. Other faculty and administrators heard it on their way home from an already tumultuous day. Jones's speech was heard by people who were already at their wits' end.

When Stuart Brown arrived home a bit after 7 o'clock, "My wife asked me if I had heard a speech that had been given by Tom Jones." Brown said no. "Well, it's going to be rebroadcast and you'd better listen to it," she replied. Brown listened. His wife was tough-minded and not frightened by the speech, but she was concerned. People's reactions varied, depending on their makeup and their sense of vulnerability. Soon calls, frightened or curious, poured into the Brown household.

Given the situation, it was astonishing—and surely irresponsible—for WHCU to have broadcast the speech. But it happened by accident, and once broadcast, the speech had to be rebroadcast because the rumors it was spawning were even worse than its actual content.

Don Martin, WHCU's manager, had asked the AAS whether it wanted to send someone for interviews in response to Perkins's law-and-order speech on Monday morning. The AAS sent Jones. Before he arrived, "unnecessary whites" were told to leave the studio and listen to the interview in an office down the hall. Jones entered the studio with a "menacing" demeanor. It is not known whether the AAS helped him prepare the speech, but Jones, Eric Evans, and Ed Whitfield were now the leading public spokesmen for the AAS, and the AAS did not dissociate itself from the statement. Also, the AAS was remaking itself into the Black Liberation Front, a more overtly revolutionary group. Some members—though not most— were swept up in romantic revolutionary ideas and rhetoric, willing to die for the cause, as the revolutionaries in the Battle of Algiers had done. Jones's speech was thus consistent with the direction in which the AAS was moving. The irony is that anyone who knew what was going on also knew that the AAS had already won.

Rather than answering the interviewer's questions, Jones kept speaking from what sounded like a prepared statement. The engineer neglected to turn on the tape recorder because of the stir that had accompanied Jones' arrival; the first statement that came across the speaker in the office down the hall was, "The faculty has stated that this principle must stand even in view of the fact that the probable consequences of that principle standing will be the death of students, white and black, probably policemen and faculty and administrators as well." Then the tape started recording the most memorable speech in Cornell's history.

Jones proceeded to say things that so alarmed Martin that he ordered the tape recorder turned off. According to Fisher and Wallenstein, Martin told Jones, "I believe that part where you list those people and say they are going to 'die in the gutter like dogs' is illegal. It would be illegal for us to broadcast that on the air." Jones agreed. Martin turned that part of the tape over to Jones and gave Jones his word that what Jones said would remain a secret. "But it was too late. The engineer had failed to cut off the speakers" to offices down the hall.[32] What Jones said had been overheard by others who were not privy to Martin's nondisclosure promise.

An engineer said, "I heard the son of a bitch say it, and I'll swear to it." A "terrified" reporter called Martin later and told him he was going to tell the district attorney and the Safety Division about the threats. He was not a party to Martin's nondisclosure promise. (Indeed, Martin was relieved that word would get out.) When Martin called Jones to inform him that his statements would be sent to the police, Jones said, "Well, they'll be out to get me tonight. I better get out of here."[33] The speech was broadcast around 7:00 p.m. and was rebroadcast with the threats intact a while later. It set the tone for the entire evening:[34]

Jones: Now President Perkins has said that people involved in particular kinds of actions will be suspended. Other people will be arrested. Now, we're going to see just where President Perkins is at. See, Mr. Perkins might end up having a university with nobody but his faculty here. And many of them will be gone—very many of them will be gone.

The administration in the person of President Perkins has shown its true colors in terms of his suppressive tactics in declaring martial law. . . . There is nothing further to talk about. Everything that could be discussed with them has already been discussed in the last four months. The only violence that occurred over the weekend was when black students were attacked. Why didn't the faculty reprimand *that?*

The time has passed when black people give up their right to bear arms, which is a constitutional right and which President Perkins has seen fit to usurp. [*screaming now*] And this man calling himself God at Cornell University is going to throw somebody out of that school for doing something which is sanctioned by the Constitution of the United States, which when practiced by black people has become "violent intimidation." Now, we're not going to deal with that any longer. We do see reason now to stand up as black men and black women and deal with our destiny. To deal with what even the society represented by this University is going to throw at us. And we're going to demonstrate that maybe we will die in the process, but by God, we're not going alone. . . .

Martin: Is there anyone left in the administration of the faculty of Cornell University that the Afro-American Society has faith in?

Jones: There are isolated faculty people who have shown strong support for our position. As for the administration, no. James Perkins is a racist. Keith Kennedy is a racist. Dale Corson is a racist. Mark Barlow is a racist. And as racists they will be dealt with. Allan Sindler is a racist. Rossiter is a racist. Walter Berns is a racist. And as racists they will be dealt with. . . . Before this is over James Perkins, Allan Sindler, and Clinton Rossiter are going to die in the gutter like dogs.

Martin: Is there anything Cornell can do?

Jones: I would suggest that the faculty have an emergency meeting tonight and, if they can do so by nine o'clock, nullify this decision. After nine o'clock it's going to be too late. . . . Cornell University has three hours to live.

Martin: [*faintly*]: Thank you.

With this speech, Jones had come a long way from his middle-class roots (his father was a physicist and his mother a teacher). In his predominantly white high school class of 1965 in New York City, he had been voted "most likely to succeed," and he had encountered little trouble in adjusting to Cornell. As a freshman he joined a white fraternity and was elected president of the freshman class. But, as the *Wall Street Journal* reported in a 1997 front-page article on Jones and his brother Ed, "Cornell was changing and so was Tom. Many blacks at the university didn't share his familiarity with whites. They formed their own student association and pressured Tom to withdraw from mainstream campus activities. He also left ROTC. Tom read widely in sociology and black history, undergoing what he now calls a 'crisis of identity.'"[35] Though Jones attained radical consciousness and militancy, observers pointed out that he kept a foot (or at least a toe) in the white world. Described by many as "Machiavellian," he had always been a shrewd operator, aware of his self-interest. Some felt that he "went off the deep end" over the next several days, an assessment with which even he would concur not long after the crisis.[36] Whatever the merits of this assessment, it is clear that Jones, by rhetorically deploying the images of guns and death, is the figure who cast a revolutionary spell over Cornell that night.

At Carpenter Hall, Perkins and the staff, who had been meeting with local authorities and police, heard about the speech from Muller. "There's a bad, bad interview of Tom Jones on the radio. I've heard it and he threatened you, Dale, I don't know who all, and some faculty."[37] They listened on a small radio that happened to be in the room. "Isn't somebody going to answer this guy? Don't you think we ought to go on the air to answer him?" Perkins asked. But Corson, Barlow, and Muller said, "No, that was silly."[38] Tobin—who had heard of the speech from his contacts at the radio station and who had picked up a radio at Statler in case the executive staff needed one—observed that the listeners engaged in wisecracks to break their nervousness. "I had the interesting observer's experience of listening to the Jones broadcast and watching the reaction of . . . people like the President, Corson, Kennedy, Miller, Mayor Kiely. . . . The Sheriff was there and so on. . . . There was a certain amount of wisecracking . . . you know, 'Were you named?' 'I was named, why weren't you named?'" But Tobin maintained that the wisecracking was only to break the tension. After this session, Tobin went to the Safety Division and met with Eugene Dymek and others. Clinton Rossiter (whom Jones named) was there, "in a rather high state of dudgeon." George Fisher, Tobin's assistant, replayed a tape of the speech so that they could list the men Jones named. "I remember the fantastic level of . . . tension that was building in the room" during the playing, Tobin reported.[39]

The first broadcast of Jones's statement was heard all over Ithaca and repeated to thousands. The second broadcast seemed to have been heard by everyone.

Around 7:30 word came that the Faculty Council had decided in emergency session to call a faculty meeting at noon the next day and to urge nullification. By now SDS was meeting in Barton Hall, so Ben Nichols, a member of the council, hurried over to Barton to announce the council's decision. Meanwhile, Perkins had left the meeting in Carpenter with the police and Ithaca authorities to go to a dinner party with a local banker. This act angered Kiely, who felt betrayed after sacrificing so much time and effort to help Cornell. "It's his university, not my university, and if dinner appointments are more important when I've got four hundred people in here at his request and eight thousand students are over in Bailey Hall and so on and so forth, that's pretty discouraging and, in my opinion, shameful."[40]

Ithaca authorities could not understand how Perkins could leave for such a dinner when his university was under an unprecedented threat to its existence, the single most dangerous night in its history. "The moment Perkins walked out the door to the banker's dinner party, civil authority lost all remaining confidence in Cornell's ability to run its own campus," Fisher and Wallenstein wrote.[41] Kiely decided he had no choice but to sign the emergency proclamation in his file, and he lifted the policy of not permitting Ithaca police to act on calls from the Cornell campus.

Reactions to Jones's speech varied. Doug Dowd downplayed the danger to the individuals Jones singled out by pointing out that he and other radicals had received several death threats in recent years.[42] Dymek notified the families of top administrators, an act that Barlow considered unnecessarily provocative, believing the speech was but an "idle threat." But Perkins and other administrators moved their families away from home for protection. Indeed, Ithaca hotels and motels were filling up with fleeing faculty. No doubt friends of frightened or concerned Cornellians were also receiving requests for shelter.

The Security Division had less success in reaching the families of professors who were threatened. It never made contact with Sindler's family, though the Sindlers were home just across the street from Perkins's house. Tobin, who was present at Safety when Rossiter arrived, asked Dymek what he intended to do to protect the individuals named and their families. "Well, I can't do anything. I've only got so many men," Dymek replied. Tobin said that Safety was working with local police and that at least they could notify the relevant parties. Dymek still hesitated. But then Corson, who was also present, ordered Dymek to offer protection and to encourage the families to leave the campus for the evening.[43]

Eventually the Sindlers and others received protection from the Cayuga Heights Police Department on the basis of an order by Cayuga Heights Mayor Fred Marcham (the history professor who was in the Sindler camp). The Cayuga Heights police were also stretched to the limit, however, so all they could do was keep a "close surveillance" on the house, not assign individuals to the Sindlers' home per se. The Sindlers then decided that Lee Sindler and the two children should leave, but they could not find a hotel or motel room. Everything was already full of people fleeing Cornell! Fisher and Wallenstein presented Lee Sindler's account:

> I couldn't get in the first two motels I tried. The clerk at Howard Johnson's told me he was all filled up; for the last two hours he'd been directing Cornell families to a motel downtown. Then I called the Sheraton—they were filled. I explained our situation and said, "Haven't you got a place, any place, where a mother and two children can spend the night?" Finally, the clerk agreed to give me and my children a single room, provided we'd vacate it by 7:30 the next morning.[44]

Allan Sindler spent a sleepless night alone, refusing to be chased from his own home. All alone with the family dog on this dark and rainy night, he wrote his resignation letter. To this day he takes pride in being the first member of the faculty to resign.[45] (The next day Perkins denied at a press conference that any faculty members had had to leave their homes.)

SDS and the Barton Hall Community

The meeting planned for 7:30 was SDS's opportunity to step into the vacuum of authority. In the previous days the "silent center" and other more active groups had tried to influence the course of events but had failed to avert the showdown that had arrived Tuesday evening. The IFC had done a good job controlling the fraternities but a less good job defining the terms of the crisis. As noted, student government had dissolved earlier that academic year, and what was left of it had been more or less wrapped into the FCSA, the very body under attack. The mechanisms of the center were nonexistent or marginal. The Oral History interviews of such participants as Art Spitzer show that the traditional sources of student power and influence had slipped into political irrelevance. Other issue-specific groups had arisen; many, including the Coalition for Rational Action, Students for a Democratic Alternative, the Committee for a Nonviolent Alternative, and the Student-Faculty Ad Hoc Committee for an Open University, had distributed leaflets at the Monday convocation and elsewhere. Most of these groups were conservative and opposed to the militancy that was taking place. Yet the plethora of groups was confusing, none enjoyed the organizational and publicity power of SDS, and their active opposition was too little and came too late. In the days that followed the AAS and SDS victory, however, they would make something of a comeback.

The meeting had been moved from Goldwin Smith to Bailey Hall. As soon as he stepped into Bailey, Marshall knew SDS had a problem on its hands: Bailey was packed at 6:30, an hour early! SDS had done ingenious work in influencing student opinion at Cornell, but its strategizing for action was much more spontaneous and unorganized. By now it seemed that everybody was losing control. Marshall said, "We were just flipping out, we didn't know what we were going to do, you know, 'cause we can tell it's going to be a disaster. . . . Fifty people are coming up and saying, 'We have presentations to give.'" [46] SDS leaders had to confront several questions. Should they take Day Hall? If so, what if the troops downtown storm the campus? What would SDS do then?

Bailey was a tumultuous scene. One participant said, "The tension at the beginning of the meeting was close to unbearable. Fears of violence and the end of Cornell University were very strong." [47] Students—ultimately six thousand of them—turned out for several reasons: to support the AAS, to counsel caution and support of the faculty, to share in the excitement, to observe, and to take action. The dynamic of the evening would turn many surprised students into temporary revolutionaries. One student at Bailey, though, stood up to berate the audience for its plans. "In the real world outside you wouldn't be taken seriously at all!" she scolded. She was met with boos but also some applause for being willing to speak out. One student geared for action nodded his head in approval of her willingness to speak, then launched into cheers at the next set of speakers advocating dramatic action. The crowd continued to swell, so the decision was made to move to Barton Hall.

Several thoughts must have charged through the minds of students who were undecided as they marched in the rainy night over to Barton. What should I do? Are we "taking over" Barton? What if they decide to seize Day Hall? Do I go along? What if I am arrested? What if there is violence? (The presence of the troops was now well known, and some speakers were even challenging them.) Am I in danger? Is it worth taking big risks without really knowing all the facts of the debate? If I go along, will it be out of conviction or conformity? Do I have enough strength to do what I think is right rather than following the lead of others? If I don't go along, will it be out of fear or a lack of convictions?

In the literature on moral choice, one truth stands out: the window of moral opportunity in conflict situations is very small. One often has little time to choose what is right in the face of conflicting pressures. Everyone is upright after the crisis has passed; what counts is what one did in the moment when the decision was on the line. [48] (How many faculty, famous for their lofty thinking, were struggling with this problem at this very moment? If the Arts College meeting was an indication, many were having a very hard time of it.) Among other things, this moment brought certain individuals—faculty, students, and administrators—face to face with important and troubling questions about conviction and commitment. It also showed the dangers of going through life unprepared for dealing with such questions. Those who knew where they stood and why—mainly the activists on both sides of the issue—possessed an enviable authenticity. As some in the AAS had learned, danger (even death) is somehow less fearful—though never without fear—when one has convictions. It is easier to face censure and danger when you are sure of your values. A greater fear is standing for nothing genuine—of being nothing in the moment of truth.

As psychiatrist Howard Feinstein pointed out in an essay on the psychological aspects of the Cornell crisis, "As in any revolution, there were accidents which helped the radicals succeed." [49] One was that Barton Hall was already set up for a huge gathering. In an act of foresight, the dean of students' office and other administrators had set Barton aside for students that week, free of charge, for teach-ins and the like. Barton was ideal because of the number of participants and because it was raining outside, making the Arts Quad a poor place to hold the meeting. In another stroke of luck, the massive sound system that had been used for the convocation on Monday was still operational. "By this fortuitous combination of circumstances the crowd had a warm, dry, spacious place to meet on a rainy evening and a superb amplification system to hear the radical orators vie for its leadership," Feinstein noted. [50] But the scene was also chaotic, Marshall recalled. "We really didn't know what to do. We didn't know where our people were, they were scattered all around, you know, just in a mob." [51] He estimated that at this point 60 percent of the crowd was sympathetic to the AAS and the rest opposed.

Emotions and objectives ebbed and flowed, depending on the speaker, although the psychologies of mass behavior and racial accusation held sway. Several speakers, including Marshall and Dancis, addressed the need for action. They "whipped the students into a near frenzy, preparing them for militant action," Fisher and Wallenstein reported. [52] Then Jones took the podium and made a speech similar to his now famous radio address. But his physical presence allowed him to deploy his rhetorical skills to even greater effect. As Feinstein observed, he bobbed, weaved, and spoke in a soft voice that reassured even as it frightened. Jones's voice rode the crest of such words as *community, principle, freedom, self-determination, racism,* and *slavery*. The AAS was ready to die for the cause, but so must others. "The University will die at 9 p.m. Now the pigs are going to die too. When people like J.P. [James Perkins] . . . are going to be dealt with. . . . We are moving tonight. Cornell has until 9 to live. It is now 3 minutes after 8." [53] Jones affirmed that the AAS did not plan to use its weapons or hurt anyone, but he wanted the assembly to do something to support the AAS. He asked for a show of hands, and two-thirds to three-quarters of his listeners raised their hands. Some students hesitated, waiting to see where those around them stood; others shot their hands up enthusiastically. [54]

Like his radio address, Jones's speech at Barton had a stunning impact on the audience, triggering primeval reactions in some. Paul Marantz said, "After hearing Tom Jones say that racist faculty members would be 'dealt with,' I was so terrified that images flashed through my mind . . . of machine guns being trained on the balcony and, as a demonstration of political terrorism, some people in the balcony being shot. This was a completely irrational image, of course, but it was something that just jumped into my mind, indicative of the way I was thinking." [55] Another young faculty member said the speech "left me afraid, yet marveling at the rhetoric" that slid so adroitly from reassurance to shock. Another had images similar to Marantz's: "At one point a picture flashed through my mind. A machine gun was pointed at the people in the bleachers because we were opponents. It was a grand gesture, a political action which was justified because the ends justify the means." [56] An anonymous source identified an undercurrent that ran through that cavernous hall: the irrational yet symbolically validated feeling that the forces of the new moral order (almost Jacobin in inspiration) could see into one's innermost mind to detect politically incorrect thoughts. One student had an image of being dragged to the podium and being forced to admit his racist thoughts in front of the angry mob. Such visions mirrored the visions blacks used to have about whites, especially in the South: don't step out of line because whitey is watching. The politics of confession was at hand.

David Lyons spoke. He read the statement signed by more than thirty members of the Concerned Faculty, castigated the faculty, and advocated taking a building. Faculty on the other side of the divide would echo his words the next day: "At this moment I am ashamed to be a member of the faculty of Cornell University." Lyons's speech further electrified the audience (if a faculty member is willing to take a building, why shouldn't we?). Afterward, other faculty seconded his position. Skeptical faculty, such as Marantz and Sharfman, thought Lyons was irresponsible for essentially telling the students that they had the faculty's permission to take a building. Some spoke up to stem the tide. An anthropology professor beseeched the throng to "have compassion" for the faculty and to give them a chance to change their minds, a speech that calmed the crowd momentarily.

Then Marshall took the stand and reignited passions. Leading a discussion about what action the group should take, he said, the Action Faction of SDS that organized the meeting had grown concerned that the assemblage would not act with sufficient militancy. "There is no way they [the administration] can ignore this many people, if this many people stand up in their different ways and move!" Marshall exclaimed. He was trying to "fire them up," but it was "like a bad dream," he recalled. What Marshall, Kelly, and the leaders wanted was forceful action. Everything—the war, racism, the duplicity of the liberal establishment, the SDS success at Columbia the previous year—all came to a head at this moment. "By that time we had become pretty hard-core, and we were in that mentality that liberals are worse than conservatives, that kind of thing. So no, we wanted a confrontation; we felt it was the time that a statement had to be made and what we were afraid of was that this whole thing was just going to be blown away and that they [the administration] were going to finesse their way through it. Because at that stage the ideology was that you had to take a stand." [57]

At this point several members of the Action Faction started talking about walking out of Barton and going to Bailey to plan a militant move, probably a takeover of Day Hall. It is unlikely that a majority of students would have followed them out, though the dynamics of mass behavior cannot be predicted. Many no doubt would have, given the responses of many to militant advocacies and the spread of "revolutionary consciousness." A paper written after the crisis by an anthropology student (one of many class papers written about the crisis that substituted for normal course work) discussed the student's conversion experience. He had always been a "middle-roader," but "that night" made him radical. One SDS student said, "It is clear that some of you are just interested in talking, while the rest of you are interested in acting. Well, then, those of you who are ready to act come on over to Bailey." [58]

Marshall continued to rouse the crowd to action. As he spoke, Marshall noticed

Eldron Kenworthy edging his way toward the podium from out in the audience. Like Lyons, Kenworthy subscribed to the notion of the university as an agent of social justice, but he was indisposed to demonizing the other side, and he had more respect for the judicial system than his colleagues on the Concerned Faculty (being Sindler's colleague was a factor in his position). He drew back from the Concerned Faculty "feeding the SDS mania for having a complete confrontation."[59] As Marshall spoke, an image of thousands of students, some with arms, occupying buildings as hundreds of deputies stormed the campus flashed across his mind. "Quite likely we would have something approaching a blood bath in the middle of the night."[60]

Earlier that evening Kenworthy had urged the assembly to consider that the various colleges had voted to nullify. With this statement a "wave of relief swept through the hall" as students noted that there were alternatives to violent confrontation.[61] Now Kenworthy moved to the dais to counter SDS's next round of incitement. Joining the speakers behind David Burak made him third or fourth in line to speak. Before his turn came up, however, Burak asked Kenworthy if Dancis could speak. Dancis took the microphone and announced, "Okay, now those of us who are really serious about doing something tonight, about moving tonight, let's go to Bailey." Kenworthy considered this a rare act of "bad faith" on the part of SDS leaders, designed to head off what they anticipated he would say, so he pushed his way to the microphone. By now a student was weakly challenging the SDS move. Kenworthy went to him and said, "You're not being very effective, move over and let me talk."[62]

Students were already moving toward the doors when Kenworthy grabbed the microphone. He had to speak quickly and to the point. "If you're really serious about getting the change rather than simply playing out some psychodrama confrontation for confrontation's sake, then wait until tomorrow. Wait! Now is not the time to move. . . . A rational revolutionary would not move now. The faculty meeting is tomorrow at noon; if they don't vote to nullify, then I'll be with you. But let's not move now."[63]

By saying he would join the students if the faculty did not change their mind, Kenworthy gained credibility and stopped the flow toward what in all likelihood would have been a violent confrontation. The act also turned Kenworthy's colleagues in the Government Department against him, for they now linked him to the students. Unfortunately, they did not know the entire truth. Kenworthy's colleague Marantz did. "I must say that this was literally one of the most dramatic moments in my life. I saw an instance in which thousands of people were intent on doing one thing and all of a sudden, just through a few sentences coming at the right time, they were dropped dead in their tracks."[64] Doug Dowd then spoke and told the crowd that those who left planned only to hold further discussions, not to take action on their own.

In Marshall's eyes, chaos still reigned, however. Some SDS members split and went to Bailey. As he was walking out, Marshall looked back and saw confusion. He thought, "I can't leave this, this would be a disaster. All these people here and . . . everyone was flipped out. . . . Fifty, sixty people were standing there, were chanting, saying, 'We're going to take the building anyway,' and then no one knew what to do. . . . It was just like a nightmare."[65] Some SDS leaders did leave Barton and go to Bailey and Anabel Taylor (they shuffled back and forth). But after about thirty minutes they abandoned their plans for a takeover and decided to join what was becoming the Barton Hall Community. They also decided to redirect their energies to changing admissions and housing at the university, though these two issues would take a backseat to what was happening at Barton.

Burak was still concerned about what could happen. He differed from other SDS leaders, who were also his roommates, in his reluctance to engage in violent confrontations (though at the King memorial the previous year he had counseled violence, as many others had). He was upset at the violence at Malott Hall and at the Statler in previous weeks, and he had advised Perkins on occasion. He also had knowledge of something that his colleagues in SDS (who had already purchased chains and locks to use at Day Hall) lacked: he had been in contact with the administration (including Perkins) about the situation with the deputies downtown. According to Kiely, that night the number of deputies swelled from 180 to about 400 by 6:30 p.m.[66] Burak knew their presence was extremely dangerous:

I stayed in touch with [Perkins], even during the crisis. Once I used the phone in Barton Hall to call him. . . . I had to report that there were hundreds of sheriff's deputies down the hill. I was lucky that I was able to figure things out fast enough. A guy named Steve Telsy, whom I knew from CURW, had done a little scouting job downtown on his own . . . and he came back and said, "I was downtown and I went by Woolworth's parking lot and there were hundreds of deputies, two or three hundred. I did this counting thing. . . . I don't know what they are there for, but it doesn't look good." I'm feeling some responsibility because I'm an older student here, an older member of the community. And I don't want to have this blood on my hands. . . . [I was a] more responsible radical. I wasn't revolutionary. I wasn't for armed insurrection in the United States. Some people were. . . . Some of them weren't as haunted by this as I was, because I had become so identified with the whole community and the takeover and everything else . . . so I had to continuously scrutinize everything that I did.[67]

Burak's fears of the deputies were not hyperbolic. Security Officer Hauser also went and checked out the deputies who had assembled for the night. His observations were chilling:

If those guys came up here, they were fully equipped. . . . They were in the parking lot down at Woolworth's—it was totally full. There were just cars coming in from Buffalo, Rochester, Minnow County, . . . deputies from all over the state; they were brought here under an emergency order by the governor. . . . These guys had sawed-off shotguns. They were completely riot-equipped police, and if they had gotten the word to go in and arrest these people, I'm sure that there would have been bloodshed.[68]

A month or two after the crisis, Burak attended the Ithaca Police Department ball and ran into three officers who had been present with the deputy assembly downtown that fateful night. What one of them told Burak confirmed the wisdom of Burak's intervention:

> Even us old-timers are glad you guys decided to stay in Barton Hall. . . . We were getting a little worried. Even though we had been around law enforcement all our lives, they had allowed the young rednecks from the hills to be deputized on the Woolworth's lot. And they were loading their shotguns with double-0 buck and saying, "Tonight we're going to get us some niggers and them Jew commies." . . . Because there had been perceived a breakdown of law and order on campus, . . . if there was mass movement out of Barton or any other hall toward Day Hall, that would be time for outside enforcement to come on and use any force they felt necessary to quell it. The Rubicon.[69]

Given his information and fears, Burak decided to reinforce Kenworthy's position. Together he and Kenworthy clinched the case for waiting. As SDS leader Mark Rudd had done at Columbia the previous year, Burak made a deal with the less militant forces in order to forge a broader coalition.[70] He told the throng that he had just changed his mind about going to Bailey because such a move was unnecessary: *the assembly had already taken a militant action by occupying Barton Hall!* (Burak knew that the administration had set Barton aside for the assembly. Later, when Ben Nichols announced that Perkins had given his blessing to the assembly, the crowd booed heartily.) "I think we have just taken Barton Hall. How many are prepared to stay until the demands are met?" The crowd roared its approval. It was a brilliant strategy: the students could claim they had taken a militant action on behalf of the AAS, but the deputies would not storm the campus if the students stayed at Barton! The assembly quickly relaxed and started engaging in festivities, though the faculty vote hung over it like Damocles' sword. The students prepared to spend the night.

The speeches by Kenworthy and Burak turned the tide and inaugurated the Barton Hall Community, a revolutionary community based on three fundamental ideas: participatory democracy and community, student power and restructuring of the university, and redemption through racial reckoning. Aspects of this community were festive and celebratory, manifestations of the release of nervous tension and joy, and the potential triumph of a form of justice. Still other aspects were authoritarian and intolerant of intellectual freedom. Dissenting voices would not be allowed.

Burak's action made him the leader of the Barton Hall Community, much to the chagrin of his friends and roommates, who felt betrayed. He related the story of their reaction and his reception when he returned home to fetch some gear for spending the night in Barton. On the way home his car ran out of gas, and when he got home, "My friends weren't even talking to me." The chill lasted for several days. "They felt that somehow I had betrayed their right to be militant, that I had opted for a middle-of-the-road course."[71]

An observer noted how Burak rose to the occasion and assumed an impressive position of leadership. Despite his reputation for egoism, Burak

> displayed high intelligence, brilliant oratory, and a shrewd understanding of the crowd. He became a leader because of the circumstances and would retain that position through his own skill. He identified with the desires of the crowd and soon became the spokesman for the entire group. Soon the crowd turned to him for the final say on any matter and he was able to exert considerable influence on the discussions. . . . So great was his influence that when a moderate student attempted a "coup" against the SDS, he was soon booed off the stage in favor of Dave Burak. The crowd wanted to stay with someone they could apparently trust. Dave Burak had come up with an ingenious solution at a critical time.[72]

Soon after Burak spoke, students began passing around boots to collect money for food and drinks. People left to pick up sleeping bags, clothes, Frisbees, basketballs, beer, marijuana, playing cards, and other items. As word about the Barton "takeover" spread, many students who had stayed home changed their minds and joined the assemblage. One scene dramatized the extent of the SDS victory on behalf of the AAS—or perhaps the tenuous status of the revolutionary moment: one student, an avowed racist seen earlier that week brandishing a gun he intended to use in the event that the AAS "got out of hand," joining the community with his girlfriend. Sitting on their sleeping bag, the couple cheered many of the speakers who took the open microphone as the night wore on.

As Barton settled down to its festivities, speeches, and anxious waiting, Tom Jones, Eric Evans, and Skip Meade returned to AAS headquarters to plan strategy. The 9:00 p.m. "deadline" had passed, so the university was now in violation of the Jones-AAS ultimatum. The AAS decided to link its fortunes to those of the Barton Hall Community. It, too, would wait and see what the faculty did. "The Afro-American Society has decided unanimously not to move. . . . But let me make it clear that this is the *last* time!" a spokesman (Jones or Evans) announced. The crowd roared. Jones later explained that "the Afro-Americans had taken that position because they valued human life and because the students in Barton Hall represented a new coalition of black and white students who were going to move together to change the University."[73] But when Evans took the podium, someone threw a cherry bomb that sounded like a gun, a grim reminder that danger lurked just beneath the surface.

The assembly also decided on a "policy" toward the press. To many leaders, press coverage of the entire crisis had been inaccurate and biased, focusing on the guns at the expense of the underlying issues of racial justice and student power. Some outrageous examples were at hand. While the AAS was in the Straight, one ABC radio reporter announced that the AAS planned to attack Ithaca with thousands of students. Earlier Tuesday evening a student reporter ran into the press room at the Statler Hotel and told a major radio network reporter that there were "four thousand armed blacks" in Barton, with "five hundred of them copulating in the aisles."[74] Amazingly, the network reported the unverified story, which was as good an example of hysteria and racist fears as one could find. Of course, the account was played back to the Barton crowd, further radicalizing the students. The Barton Hall Community therefore formed an official press committee and established a policy of not granting the press access to the hall. The committee wrote up an official press release presenting its interpretation of events; unfortunately for the SDS and AAS, the press largely ignored the release.

Tobin and his associates in the press corps treated the "self-appointed press representatives" who came to the newsroom set up at the Safety Division with contempt. When this "rather ridiculous" delegation tried to hold a press conference while the reporters were busy writing up their stories that night, the students were ignored and "finally left in disgust." [75] This scene symbolized something important: whereas SDS and the AAS monopolized campus sentiment at this point, the press from the outside world was not buying their interpretation of events. This split between student activists and seasoned reporters ("the people inside" versus "the people outside") meant that Cornell's interpretation of the events would not enjoy success beyond its borders. (Tobin, however, had great respect for the *Sun*'s coverage. The *Sun* headquarters was also the place where the *New York Times*'s reporters were stationed.)

Meanwhile, the administrative executive staff continued to meet deep into the night at Carpenter Hall. It maintained a liaison with the three law enforcement agencies (city, county, state) until around 11:30, when the AAS and SDS announced the suspension of their plans to seize buildings. The staff refused to honor a request to have the four hundred deputies spend the night at the ice rink, the only building other than Barton big enough to hold so many people. It was also just up the road from Barton, making it a dangerous location for the deputies.

As the night wore on, many students left, planning to return the next morning. By 3:00 a.m. three thousand students and one hundred faculty, administrators, and staff remained. Individuals kept making speeches, and the group deliberated what stands students should take. Dowd gave a speech about the transformative experience of becoming a radical, emphasizing how it changes one's entire relationship to the world. The community debated several resolutions and passed five that went into the 4:00 a.m. press release: a demand of nullification, the elimination of the judicial system and the implementation of a new one, a demand that Perkins meet with the assembly before the faculty vote or be subjected to a "no confidence" vote, an invitation to the deputies to join Barton Hall for discussion (disarmed, of course), and a demand that students be included in the making of any decision that had an impact on their lives at the university. At 4:30 the lights went out and people attempted, mostly in vain, to get some sleep. Some stayed awake to keep guard in case of an attack.

By this time many harbored the hope of a nonviolent resolution, but everything hinged on the faculty vote, and the faculty felt more coerced than ever. If the faculty took a false step, all hell certainly would break loose. The events of the day and evening had pushed Cornell to the precipice. Any early joy for the Barton Hall

Community was matched by its opposite on the part of anguished faculty. It was a zero-sum game. Later Industrial and Labor Relations Professor Milton Konvitz, an expert in constitutional law, portrayed his state of mind that night and during the faculty vote on Wednesday in the *New York Times Magazine*. His statement captured the psychological and political implications of the evaporation of authority, a rare Hobbesian moment. The statement was one of the most memorable to emerge from the controversy, and Cornellians refer to it to this day: "Tragically and unbelievably the campus had suddenly, in a matter of hours, reverted to a State of Nature, as described in Hobbes. . . . We knew, from the temper of thousands of our students and perhaps three score members of the faculty, that in a matter of minutes the campus might become an armed camp. . . . Between 2,000 and 4,000 students in Barton Hall were ready to throw the campus into utter turmoil if the faculty did not nullify. . . . We could have a state of war. . . . A society can be destroyed in hours, but it takes years to build one."[76]

Meanwhile, Ruth Darling sat in the rumor clinic, surrounded by the press and inundated with calls from all over the area and the nation. Clinic members knew Jones's speech was rhetorical, "but we had a sense of profound uneasiness" knowing just how much hinged on the faculty meeting, scheduled for noon Wednesday.[77]

Finally, late Tuesday night Silbey, LaFeber, Sindler, and Richard Polenberg talked about what had taken place. They agreed "that the ball game was over" but that they would attend the Wednesday meeting. A little later the Concerned Faculty met in Barton and planned a strategy to ensure the right result at noon. If the vote turned out wrong, James Matlock was picked to seize the microphone at Barton and proclaim that the Concerned Faculty would join the students in whatever action they took. The group also issued a statement similar to the Barton Hall Community release.

As the faculty prepared to vote the next day, they did so in the face of the political challenges and threats that the SDS and AAS had succeeded in creating, despite many stumbles. By a combination of shrewdness, pluck, and luck, everything the militants wanted lay before them. As usual, no one articulated the stakes for everyone so forcefully as Tom Jones. It was a matter of courage that lay at the heart of the politics of recognition. Everything amounted to a showdown over who had the most courage in the face of danger:

> Either you've got to change your rhetoric, or you've got to change reality. . . . It would have destroyed us psychologically to have changed our rhetoric after the faculty vote on Monday night, which meant that the only choice we had was to change reality. So what did we do? We recognized first of all . . . that the reality for most of these faculty people has always been a *peaceful* reality. They have never been threatened. They've never had to put their homes, their lives, their children's lives, on the line for anything. See, they're always fond of spouting principles. . . . But they've never had to put their *lives* on the line for a principle. So the first step we took in changing reality was . . . to make it clear to them they were in danger. We

said it over the radio; we said, "You're a racist and you're going to be dealt with. . . . You put *me* up against the wall, you back *me* into a corner, you're trying to destroy *me*, well, if you believe in your principle so much, then be ready to die for it." The second reality we changed . . . was the reality of the black people being the isolated minority. . . . We made the *faculty* a minority.[78]

How would the faculty react to this challenge? After the key decision was made to stay at Barton, Sharfman went back to his office at West Sibley Hall and called his department chairman, Sindler. The only person able to reach Sindler at home that night, Sharfman asked where the thirty-one signers of the Government and History Departments' letter stood, for it was clear to him now that the faculty would reverse their vote. He told Sindler they should call a department meeting Wednesday morning before the vote. Sindler said no; organized response was now futile. It was all up to individuals now, and he would no longer lead. Sharfman suddenly realized that Sindler must have already resigned. He felt alone and vulnerable with the abdication of his chairman, perhaps the most pivotal faculty figure on campus. It was time for the younger generation to make its own stand.

While the Barton Hall Community flexed its muscles late that night, Sindler had indeed written his resignation letter in the name of academic freedom and contempt for Cornell. "Publicly, at least, only a few faculty members understood that issues fundamental to Cornell had come to a head in the crisis of the Straight seizure: the protection of academic freedom, the threat of an increasingly politicized university, excessive student power, and the defective vision and leadership of the President in defining and sustaining the essentials of a University," Fisher and Wallenstein wrote.[79]

CHAPTER TWELVE

DAY 5: A NEW ORDER

Barton Hall came back to life around 7:30 a.m., and the assembly discussed what students could do to affect the upcoming faculty vote. Students were urged to attend classes that were meeting (many were not) and to encourage professors to nullify. At 9:20 the gathering issued another "official release" that urged students to join the Barton Hall Community in the name of student power. "We will continue to hold Barton Hall until such time as the faculty and the administration of Cornell appropriately reconsiders the black demands. . . . *All* concerned students are welcome to join us in this seizure and engage in the relevant and meaningful discussions that are resulting. Barton Hall now belongs to the students—so should the University. Please join us."[1]

As the morning wore on, thousands of people made the pilgrimage to Barton Hall to discuss the restructuring of the university and the elimination of institutional racism. Several professors ascended to the dais to announce their decision to vote for nullification. One observer noted, "What was significant was that these were some [faculty] members who were going to do so out of fear and lose some of their self-respect. To them, the survival of the university became more important."[2] By 1:00 p.m. the crowd reached nine thousand; some came to attend the teach-in that the IFC, SDS, the AAS, and the president's office had arranged. The Barton Hall "seizure" melded with the Barton Hall teach-in to form "the crux of what has been labeled 'the spirit of Barton Hall.'"[3]

Meanwhile, faculty and other students held meetings in anticipation of the faculty meeting. Three hundred students and faculty met at the Industrial and Labor Relations School; the ILR faculty was stunned to discover that the students overwhelmingly favored nullification. Once again Milton Konvitz felt despair. "The students were in no mood to listen to argument. With few exceptions they had made up their minds firmly and immovably. . . . 'If you don't do as we want, death to the professors.' I had seldom in my years of life felt such deep bitterness of soul, as if all my thinking and working and teaching and writing had been nothing but vanity of vanities."[4]

At 10:00 a.m. most members of the Group of Forty-One met at Mike Abrams's house, pursuant to a plan worked out between the group and the administration. Sometime that morning, Perkins said later, "it became clear to me . . . that I really had no choice but to support the notion of reversing on the penalties."[5] Others believed that the administration had been working for reversal as early as Tuesday (when calling for the colleges to meet).[6]

The Group of Forty-One, which had already decided on reversal, discussed strategy for the meeting while Nobel laureate Hans Bethe, another of Perkins's inner circle of faculty supporters, manned the phone (the "hot line"), transmitting points and questions back and forth between the administration at Day Hall and the group at Abrams's house. The two key concerns were about strategy and the statement Perkins should make endorsing the reversal. Max Black, who was with the administration during this session, cut to the heart of the matter in a stunningly revealing way: the statement should dilute responsibility—and, concomitantly, memory—as much as possible. "The chief policy decision was to present this as far as possible in terms of 'wiping the slate clean.' To try to get everybody to agree that the responsibility was shared by students, faculty, the administration . . . and if possible try and start again and do better."[7]

Perkins created a drafting commission of Steve Muller, Stuart Brown, and Black. The centerpiece of the statement was the desire to "expunge" what had happened from the university's collective memory and reckoning (with the exception of the agreement with the AAS.) When asked by an Oral History interviewer who had also been a student member of the judicial board if such wiping away of the past was feasible (to say nothing of its psychological and ethical implications), Black responded, "No, I think it was politically a good idea." Yet it did not hold up subsequently because of the ill will of "people who showed every temptation of not wanting to forget any iota of the past, and showed a good deal of resentment, desire for revenge, and so on."[8] We will deal with these matters in Chapter Thirteen.

During these deliberations Perkins established a special advisory commission of three students, three administrators, and three faculty (Paul Olum, Ian MacNeil of Law, and Dick O'Brien of Neurophysiology). The students—who had been at Barton—asserted that more was at stake than the reprimands, that students demanded more power in the university. So Olum wrote a preamble that he read at the end of the upcoming faculty meeting: "We hear you, we care, we are trying to understand you, and we would like to do something together with you." Black would read the statement at Barton that day.

During his numerous meetings that morning, Perkins confided to many individuals that he imagined his statement would constitute his "last official act" at Cornell. "The heavens will open once I've done it, but I see no choice for the community except for me to do this. I'll have to use my office to get this through, and if I don't, we're going to have a civil war on our campus here of no mean proportions."

Members of the executive staff concurred with his assessments. "We all agreed we were helping you sign your death warrant," an unidentified source said. Perkins then said, "So I want the record to show that I was completely open-eyed although I really didn't guess the full level of onslaught that would come, particularly from outside. But at least I went into that meeting knowing . . . that once I'd started that role you couldn't stop it. I mean I had to play it right through to the Barton Hall thing."[9]

The Faculty Meeting

The meeting of eleven hundred professors was not open to the public, but two reporters managed to sneak in. The reporter for the *Albany Times-Union* observed, "Deep divisions showed in the words of the faculty meeting in beautiful Old Bailey Hall."[10] The meeting was anticlimactic compared with the meeting on Monday, mainly because most minds were already made up, but it was a time for eloquent statements and feelings of depression or joy, depending on where one stood.

Dale Corson ran the meeting, but it was Perkins who pulled everything together at long last. Thomas Tobin witnessed the proceedings from the balcony. He had a "very distinct recollection" that Perkins made "no attempt at concealing the fact" that he had engineered "the development of the final resolution" and that the faculty as a whole were "somewhat appreciative" of this fact.[11]

The meeting opened with Perkins analyzing, to "extensive and vigorous applause," the nature of the crisis, which, he said, had to do with black students' adjustment problems and the difficult governance of the modern university. He accepted some blame for the crisis but averred that the nightlong assembly in Barton offered grounds for hope. Then he read his statement, which had the full authority of the Board of Trustees.

> I speak to you believing that Cornell and all of us who care deeply for it are involved in the most serious crisis in our entire history. . . .
>
> I hope that those actions which have most deeply divided this community can be set aside. . . .
>
> I hope that we may be able to expunge to the fullest extent possible the seizure of Willard Straight Hall from the records of this University and the incidents connected therewith. . . .
>
> I hope that all of us together can clean the slate so that we can all move forward together.

Perkins then reaffirmed his executive orders and urged a conscientious reexamination of the judicial system. He closed by calling on "each and every one of you to join me in the effort to move this University from the edge of disaster toward a new and more harmonious community. . . . The challenge before us now is to survive together as men of reason." The faculty rose and gave what Tobin called a "rousing ovation."[12]

Corson then called on Roberts, who presented the motion for nullification. It was a simple motion compared with those of Monday: "BE IT THEREFORE RESOLVED, that the Faculty nullify judicial procedures (4/17/69) taken against five students as a result of incidents last December and January." Roberts entreated passage and provided a rationale, saying, "If the Faculty votes yes, it would vote not only out of fear but out of a sense of justice." He received a partial standing ovation.

Vance A. Christian, a professor of hotel administration and one of the few black faculty members, urged passage in the name of racial justice. Law Professor Robert Pasley then countered Christian by recounting the duress and threats of the previous day. "The Faculty was still under threat . . . [that] certain members of the Faculty 'would be dealt with.' . . . It was said there was no choice but to yield. But free men always had a choice: to leave the hall as free men or as cowards." No applause followed Pasley's words. Robert H. Innis, professor of philosophy of education, followed with a warning about capitulating to the "totalitarian Left," thereby inviting a reaction by the "totalitarian Right."

After an unimportant substitute motion failed, History Professor James John rose to his feet. He was a quiet, soft-spoken man who specialized in medieval intellectual history and paleography, but beneath his modest demeanor was a determined man willing to face adversity. John delivered perhaps the most famous and at the time most provocative speech on the other side. He had been working on the speech since Monday and had discussed it with Joel Silbey, Fred Marcham, and others. In his mind the faculty should stick to its position because the main reason it voted against nullification on Monday—the refusal to decide in the face of coercion—was all the more powerful today. John also broke the unwritten rule for faculty meetings that statements should not be read from prepared notes.

I say that if we had a good reason for not dismissing the charges on Monday, the only conclusion that can possibly be drawn from the new situation, if the description of it can be believed, is that we have a stronger reason for not doing so today. The guns are still in the Afro-Americans' hands and Mr. Tom Jones has had the politeness to inform us that he and his accomplices will destroy the university if we don't relent.

If Mr. Jones is going to destroy this university, I say let him try it. President Perkins has promised to preserve order and I have no doubt that the means are available to do that if there is a will to do it. . . .

This university, I believe, can survive the expulsion or departure of no matter what number of students and the destruction of buildings far better than it can survive the death of principle. My particular field of study is the history of universities. In the nearly eight hundred years that they have existed, many eminent universities have come and gone and the world has survived their departure. But those that have departed because they stood for nothing have not even been missed. . . . Let us defeat this short-sighted measure, and thereby set an example which other institutions of higher learning in this nation can proudly emulate.[13]

While John spoke, Clinton Rossiter made "disruptive noises," according to Silbey.[14] Black grabbed the stage, worried that the tide might be changing. He complimented John on his speech and then slid the knife in John's back: it was a shame that John had violated the ancient taboo against reading prepared statements at faculty meetings. For the second time in two days, Black was subjected to an unprecedented indignity (recall the Concerned Faculty's denying his request to speak the previous day): "I was roundly booed by a segment of the audience. The chairman, Dale Corson, then suggested that perhaps such demonstrations were not appropriate. And I told the faculty that this was something that hadn't happened in over twenty years of experience, and that I was ashamed. After which I got a profound silence."[15]

In *The Lives of the Noble Grecians and Romans,* Plutarch related Alcibiades' legal but tabooed biting of his wrestling opponent to ensure victory. The incident symbolized Athens's breaking of traditional forms and limits in favor of the agonistic ambitions that ineluctably led to empire, war, and ultimate decline. The outbreak of hissing at the faculty meeting at Cornell was similarly telling, as it signified the decline of traditional forms in the face of revolution. The faculty were losing their power to students who had threatened them in the most elemental way—akin to war. Corson observed that the hissing represented something new:

> I remember Max Black making some comments and people hissing him. I remember stopping the discussion right there and saying: "We're not proceeding this way. Members of this faculty do not hiss other people when they are speaking their resolves." This was part of the decline of academic freedom . . . during the McCarthy era, [when there were] some pretty tense faculty meetings. . . . There was none of that irrationality at that time. Somebody who felt very strongly about an issue could make an eloquent argument, somebody else would make an eloquent argument one hundred eighty degrees away. But it was all civil and structured. None of that here [at the nullification vote].[16]

Black concluded by asserting that Cornell needed "to say to the world we wish to forget what happened in the immediate past: 'I want to forget, I give you my hand, I don't need to be intimidated.'"

Next Rossiter spoke. Before ascending to the dais, he went over to Cushing Strout and plucked a substitute motion out of Strout's hands. At the dais he pointed out that he was one of the professors Tom Jones had said would be "dealt with." Now, though, he disagreed with John's contention that to nullify would be to abandon principle; his rethinking was a matter of logic, not fear. Then he moved for a substitute motion that he and others construed as dealing more adequately with the issue of duress, but in a conciliatory way. After some debate and a break, Rossiter and Roberts presented a revised motion that eventually passed. It resolved to nullify and stated, "We affirm our strong desire to cooperate with the Afro-American Society and other appropriate groups in an atmosphere of peace and mutual respect to develop immediately a judicial system that all our students will consider fair."

Rossiter's performance was an eerie combination of effectiveness and buffoonery. Fred Marcham's observations on the speech pinpointed the difficulties Rossiter was soon to encounter with his colleagues in the History and Government Departments. After declaring that his vote was based on reason, Rossiter

now became conscious that he had made a stir, and it intoxicated him to be the center of attention. "You may think," he shouted, "that I'm witless or gutless or topless but I don't care!" The audience buzzed and Rossiter was about to sit down, satisfied, among the [Max] Black crowd when his fondness for attention brought him to his feet again. He reached out his hand for the microphone and got a mild shock. He did a little mock dance, as if he had been badly hurt. "I thought they were getting me already," he said. It was all a great joke. I knew that when Rossiter supported reversal of the cause our side was lost. This I suppose influenced my judgment of Rossiter's performance, which I regarded as obscene.

Rossiter's antics could not help but alienate Marcham, who was deadly serious about what was at stake and who felt that "these days brought me nearer to complete despair than any others in my life."[17]

Even after the Rossiter-Roberts motion passed, there was still time for some memorable speeches before adjournment. Gwen J. Bymers of Home Economics and a member of the FCSA said that she was ready to move over to support reversal as part of the large "middle group." Bethe intoned that reversal was necessary because "now the choice was whether the University would continue to exist." William T. Keeton spoke for perhaps the majority when he asserted that his vote was purely due to pressure and duress and that he resented being put in this situation.

Toward the end of the ninety-minute meeting, Assistant Professor of Government Richard T. Hofferbert made a plea for the administration to "make clear the principles of freedom and openness. . . . The Administration was still failing to clarify what the sanctions and the standards were." No response was made to this request. In addition (though it is unreported in the official minutes), Hofferbert directed a question to Perkins, who was sitting on the stage. He asked Perkins what he proposed to do about the professors in the Government Department who had been threatened and about preventing a repetition of such threats. Peter Sharfman reported:

Perkins sat there with his hands folded in his lap and did nothing. And as far as I'm concerned personally, that's the moment at which I decided I could no longer have any respect for Perkins. *Not* in the afternoon when he told the Barton Hall meeting that they were the greatest, or on Monday when he did nothing at the convocation . . . and led the faculty in the passing of his disastrous resolution. . . . Now, in some sense I could forgive a man for making a mistake, but I could not forgive a man for simply sitting there and doing nothing, when he has a *manifest* obligation to do something. . . . If a man can't do anything, he has no business being head, president, of *anything*.[18]

The Rossiter-Roberts motion had passed overwhelmingly, by a margin of about three to one. Despite the strong dissenting voices, Fisher and Wallenstein observed that "tyranny of opinion seemed to prevail at the faculty meeting."[19] Olum then presented his "We hear you, we care, what can we do?" resolution, which passed easily, and the faculty moved—with only three clear nays—to "'occupy' Barton Hall" with the students.

In the end the faculty reversed for several reasons that no doubt coexisted in more than a few breasts. There were those who favored reversal all along, based on conviction or related reasons (such as the Concerned Faculty). David Lyons expressed this position, saying it was time to vote in favor of a university devoted to social justice. "I don't see any problems about the university being committed to certain social values, to social reforms. . . . It could be committed to values . . . [such as] justice to black people. I don't see any problem about that."[20] Then there were those who had honest changes of mind. Norman Penny appears to have been in this category, for he openly admitted his reservations, thereby suggesting honesty. Many reversed for the reason that Hofferbert and others were honest enough to admit: the danger of mass destruction to Cornell as an institution, as well as to the lives of possibly a large number of students. Others voted to reverse simply out of fear. A few of these professors admitted this, as Konvitz did in his *New York Times* article; others constructed rationalizations. (Penny and others recalled colleagues who either lied about their vote or "could not recollect" how they voted.) "They were voting because they were frightened," Silbey remarked. "That was the great beauty of the Konvitz article to me. He wrote it the day after Wednesday, when he could admit that what he had done was out of fear and for no other reason, not for any set of principles, but because he was frightened."[21]

Donald Kagan depicted the bottom line in Hegelian fashion, as a contest over who would cave in to the fear of physical confrontation. A feisty, physical individual brought up on the multicultural streets of Brooklyn, Kagan felt comfortable with minorities and with the prospect of physical violence that lay, at least psychologically, at the heart of the showdown at Cornell. He said that professors who were afraid of blacks or afraid of physical confrontation were the most likely to vote out of fear.[22] Tom Jones, of course, also understood the point that Kagan articulated. After all, courage in the face of death is a linchpin of the politics of recognition: respect me and my cause because I am willing to die for what I believe. Jones's speech the night before put this logic on the line at Cornell, brilliantly, if mischievously, drawing the connections between courage and credible commitment to principle. It was up to the faculty who believed in the principles of the university to resist Jones's challenge by putting their lives on the line against the AAS, whose members had risked their own lives. James John and those for whom he spoke also understood what was at stake.

For those who switched their votes out of fear, it must have been a humiliating time. The evaporation of administrative authority was compounded by the faculty's surrendering to threats. Psychological truths could not be denied, however much the supporters of reversal shouted for "expunging" the memory of what had happened. On Friday, April 25, History Professor Fred Somkin would deliver a funeral oration on the death of the university at a new teach-in at Barton Hall. He was not fooled by what had happened.

Those who voted against reversal did so for the reasons John expressed (no capitulation to force and threats). In addition, there was the commitment to the underlying principles of liberal education. Silbey spoke of the dangers of the university as a political instrument, of the overt and direct politicization of the university in the name of any cause. "I don't think a University can survive if it is in any way an instrument for the politicization of social whims of the moment."[23]

Those who lost the vote or voted for reluctant or shameful reasons then went home or to small gatherings of allies to lick their wounds. Rossiter, though, spoke to the press and explained his vote. "I feel not only that we corrected what was a doubtful action . . . but we moved immediately to restore peace and harmony on campus. . . . I feel assured that an atmosphere of peace and mutual respect will prevail on campus."[24]

The "Barton Hall Spirit"

After the vote, celebrating or curious faculty went to Barton. Ben Nichols arrived first and announced the decision. Nine thousand to ten thousand students cheered and shook their fists in the air. A standing ovation greeted the faculty representatives when they arrived. Perkins had remained at Bailey, unsure of what to do, but Corson, Barlow, and Miller told him he had to go to Barton and "add his blessing to the notion of community to that of the students."[25]

Perkins's entrance to Barton incited a mixture of cheers and boos. Once again Dave Burak came to the rescue. "There has been too much emotion directed at one man when we know the problem is the whole system," he told the crowd. The students on the stage (Evans, Whitfield, and Burak) and in the audience were elated, buoyed by the feeling of victory and the narcotic release of emotional tensions. Evans and Burak beamed on the stage before the world's cameras. Almost thirty years later Burak would say it was the most exhilarating moment of his life. "I had trouble balancing my life for many years, just figuring out 'what do you do?' It's a tough act to follow. It's also corrupting. I had a standing ovation. But I finally came to grips with the fact that you just have to work in a different way. You just can't shoot for this incredible euphoria of a standing ovation of ten thousand people."[26]

What happened next is open to various interpretations. Many observers believed the students on the stage (especially Burak and Evans) humiliated Perkins, who claimed this was not the case. But it is clear that the students knew they controlled Cornell at that moment and that they did not surrender the stage to the university president. As usual, Tom Jones grasped the truth of the situation. The nullification decision, he said, "was made in this room—right here." The faculty "was told by this committee in this room to nullify that act. . . . The old order has ended."[27]

Then Evans took the microphone before Perkins could reach it and started talking about the judicial system. After a while, Perkins made another effort to speak, gently shaking Evans's hand and whispering in his ear. Evans tore himself away and told the crowd: "J.P. shook my hand and put a fatherly arm on my shoulder. Then he said, 'Sit down—I want to talk.'" The audience cheered when Evans refused to give up the microphone. Perkins then sat down and drank from a can of soda. Burak came up, asked whether he could have a sip, and then took one in front of everyone. Meanwhile, Evans was decrying institutional racism. When Evans had finished, he called Perkins to the microphone and asked the president whether a state of martial law still prevailed. Perkins said it did, but "there is nothing I have said or will say which will not be modified by changing circumstances."

Perkins's account of what seemed to be student rebuffs was more benign. He maintained that Evans politely asked whether he could continue to speak and that Perkins consented. Still, Perkins admitted to being "astonished" when Evans called him "J.P." He also said he realized that Burak was extremely thirsty, so out of consideration he let the student leader sip from his drink. Perkins had a jocular and somewhat condescending image of the students on the stage: "There was Eric Evans shaking hands with me. Poor Burak, about to be left out of the act [cameras were flashing all over the place], came up and stood . . . between us, and there we were, a happy little threesome. Once again, you know, having to play the role of the great white father bringing the children all together into a happy Thanksgiving dinner, there I was stuck [*laugh*] with these three guys." [28]

Regardless, the image of the head of the university sitting on the stage at a moment such as this with a student taking a sip of the president's soda was symbolic of the shift of power. Numerous press accounts interpreted it in that way. For example, *Newsweek*'s famous cover story on the crisis included a picture of Perkins seated onstage, looking forlorn. The text noted, "As Perkins sat on the stage, black student leader Eric Evans mocked him publicly because the president had put his arm on Evans's shoulder in a 'grandfatherly' gesture. Then one SDS leader picked his way across the crowded stage, grabbed a can of Pepsi-Cola that Perkins had been drinking, and lifted it high for all to see." [29] Perkins maintained that such accounts were exaggerated, although even he admitted that "I did not feel at my best on the stage." [30]

After these incidents, Perkins gave a memorable speech: "I came first to listen, then to talk. . . . [Barton Hall] is one of the most constructive, positive forces which have been set in motion in the history of Cornell. . . . My optimism for the immediate and long-run future of Cornell has enormously increased. . . . It is perfectly clear to me that we have failed in the recent past to surface how black and white brothers and sisters are to work out in dignity and equality their respective values and missions." [31] In addition, Perkins used Black's point about expunging the memory of the crisis from Cornell's memory. But Whitfield would have none of it, declaring that it was important to remember what had happened so that the past could influence the future. [32]

The speech combined concessions with an attempt to turn capitulation into victory. But it was the students' moment. It was indeed a revolutionary moment at

Cornell, a victory perhaps more complete than at such campuses as Berkeley, Columbia, Wisconsin, or Harvard. The faculty's capitulation was complete, and thousands were assembled to celebrate the win. The image of students with guns and scared faculty and administrators remained vivid in the minds of many—an image only enhanced by the manner in which the president and prominent faculty paid tribute to the students and their leaders at Barton.

Other faculty spoke after Perkins, including Black, who read Olum's statement. As Peter Sharfman watched the procession of speakers, however, he suddenly realized that the revolutionary opportunity was passing away before his very eyes. At the end of the faculty meeting, Barton Hall possessed unmatched authority at Cornell. No one—faculty, administrators, or nonradicalized students—had any plan of action. Had the militants demanded major change, such as a totally autonomous student-run black college, who would have stopped them or said no? Everybody was overcome with relief or anguish and the release of great tension—precisely the moment when a true revolutionary smells opportunity. Sharfman suddenly appreciated the Bolshevik Revolution of 1917 and Lenin's "grasp of the fact that there was suddenly a situation in which if they just went and seized power nobody would stop them." The Cornell revolutionaries failed to carry through, at least at a level consistent with their goals. Their legacy would be a radical Afro-American studies center that was good (but not as good as a program based on the Yale model would have been), a diminished SDS, a restructured and more democratic form of governance that went out with a whimper in 1977, and a tyranny of opinion in questions of race. Sharfman observed, "Perkins had told them they were the University. The faculty had just capitulated to their very presence. And I don't see that there is any force at all that would have had the courage to resist or to deny or to oppose any sort of motion that came out of that body on that day. And nobody had any motions to propose. There were just a long series of congratulatory speeches."[33]

This inertia aside, the supporters of the Barton Hall Community reveled in the fellowship and possibilities of the moment. In an interesting article, "Moments of Madness," Ari Zolberg analyzed the extraordinary and uplifting emotional effects that often follow in the wake of a successful revolutionary movement (he focused on the 1830 revolution in France, which was admittedly less violent than some others).[34] At such times human contradictions and limits seem overcome, at least to the victors. Gould Coleman, Cornell's archivist, had such a reaction to the Barton Hall Community. "Oh, we're going to put the past behind. We're going into a new age. . . . It sort of reminded me [of when] I was a member of the United World Federalist after [World War II]. In the forties we thought nationalism was gone. That's right. Euphoria!"[35] A radical faculty member portrayed the atmosphere of Tuesday night:

> When the air was sufficiently electric and you did not know where things were going but you were simply keeping your antennae up to take part in and to understand what was going on, people looked different. It seems to me that it is only at moments of crisis that people have that look. . . . There is a glow over people. They look like figures in a frieze or a historical painting. I now see why Delacroix painted

that way. People take on the appearance of romance. Actual events have become historical, romantic.[36]

In a letter to his parents, one student exulted: "This body was the most incredible meeting and coalition of every type of person you could think of—from long hair to fraternity athletes. The conduct of the thing was dumbfounding. Parliamentary procedure, order, patience, rationality, openness. There were six thousand kids, a stage, a microphone, and a purpose. . . . I'm sure the University would have been blown sky high were it not for this thing."[37]

Many departments began meeting and discussing restructuring their decision-making hierarchies and giving more power to junior faculty and graduate students. In Economics, this move led to a counterrevolt. Other departments made modest changes or jumped wholesale into the new spirit. Forty-nine members of the Anthropology Department, faculty and graduate students, signed a statement of "The Cornell Community of Anthropologists" that championed intellectual and political solidarity. The statement consisted of seven points, including the claim that Cornell had overreacted to the guns, as well as the assertion that the majority at Cornell did not understand the issues at stake and was complicit in the violence being perpetrated against blacks across the country. It concluded by declaring that "white hypocrisy" was a discredit to Cornell, and although it conceded the necessity of banning weapons, the group expressed the "sincere hope" that this measure "will be matched with equal speed by measures designed to eliminate the very roots of racial injustice. This is absolutely necessary in order to create an academic community based on reason and mutual respect."[38] To the advocates of intellectual freedom, the call to "eliminate the very roots of racial injustice" was alarming, given the context. After all, even Allan Sindler, a civil rights marcher when he lived in North Carolina, had been targeted to be "dealt with."[39]

The Dark Side of Revolution

Some observers were less sanguine about the meaning and implications of Barton Hall. Art Spitzer and some members of the judicial boards walked around Barton in a daze, feeling "had." In their eyes the Barton Hall Community had run roughshod over the judicial system, misconstruing what the boards had really attempted to do.[40]

Cushing Strout viewed the community in historical terms: it was like the Great Awakening under Jonathan Edwards in the 1730s. Edwards would inspire moral upheaval and regeneration by traveling to various towns with his message of God's judgment in the context of the predestination of souls. Most sinners are condemned to hell, but a few can find salvation through moral and spiritual renewal. For the several days that Edwards captivated them, entire communities would be swept up by his message, sometimes reaching manic states of exaltation mixed with fear—only to be followed by inevitable depression.[41] At Barton, Strout observed, "I felt that the radical leaders were like Jonathan Edwards, convicting the students of original sin. And I felt that by that time racism—institutional racism, unconscious racism—had become terms as unempirical as original sin. And I felt that the liberal guilt that was so manifest among the white students was being exploited to the hilt by a technique of demagoguery that was quite transparent. But it was frustrating that it worked so successfully. But it also seemed to be out of control."[42] Strout wanted to speak up but realized his thinking was "shockingly inappropriate" to the context. He recalled Madison's famous comment in *The Federalist No. 55:* if every Athenian were Socrates, the Athenian assembly would still have been a mob. And the students at Barton were not exactly Socrates. Norman Penny had a similar reaction, observing that some of his students reported the happenings at Barton "in almost religious terms . . . It's as if they had stood up for Christ."[43]

In these senses the Barton Hall Community signified the beginning of the "political correctness" that took off in the 1980s, when the activists of the 1960s—the heirs of Perkins—began to hold positions of power in universities. To the extent that the movement promotes awareness of racial injustice, so much the good. But ritualistic emotionalism raises questions when it takes place in institutions ostensibly dedicated to more reflective reason and empirical evidence.[44] As sociologist Alan Wolfe concluded in a perceptive article that links political correctness to the accession of '60s activists to administrative power in academia, the university has been torn by the clash between those who believe the university should be about "ideas" and those who believe it should be about "suffering and redemption." He wrote, "The demands of those who want the university to acknowledge the contributions of once-excluded groups take on the character of psychodramas; it is not what you say but how you 'really feel' that matters. The period when political correctness achieved its high point was a period of emotion, not one of reason."[45]

As René Girard and other imaginative students of mass movements have divined, movements of moral upheaval often need scapegoats.[46] Jonathan Edwards needed Satan and sinners; Robespierre needed reactionaries; the new moralists need racists and sexists. The need for such scapegoats extends beyond the empirical reality of racism and sexism that most people oppose. At Cornell not even activists who had committed themselves to social justice and civil rights were immune from becoming scapegoats. Sindler's family had to flee its home. If Sindler was not safe, who was? And what manner of racial understanding and equal respect can come out of such a state of mind? To what extent do respect and equal citizenship (as opposed to therapeutic equality) require attributes of intellectual virtue that Cornell was now forsaking? And what is the relationship between intellectual integrity and justice? These were important questions that lurked behind the scenes at Cornell, and they beset the university to this day.

Gunnar Mengers, a research associate, wrote an op-ed piece in the *Sun* in which he pinpointed the problem. The cudgel of racism was a new form of McCarthyism and a direct challenge to academic freedom. The process of this new notion of political justice "bypasses the brain"—something that is antithetical to the traditional being of the university. The charge of racism, he wrote, has a mindless, gut-reaction hiss to it; a skilled manipulator can make it whatever he wants it to mean. Repeated as many times as it has been this week, it becomes a ritual chant, an exorcising spell. It takes a shortcut through the nervous system that bypasses the brain altogether. How will the Barton Hall mob eradicate racism? Easily. It will eradicate racism by going directly to the source and eradicating racists. Racism may be a little vague, but racists are concrete. They occupy locations that mobs can march to. They have ears into which it can screech threats. They have faces in which the mob can shake its fists. . . . Radicals, who now hold the leadership surrendered to them by the frightened faculty, and who can outlast anyone at the microphone, will extract the judgment of the mob to close each case.[47]

As we will see, Cornell was not the French Revolution, but enough of that revolution's logic prevailed to alter the terms of academic freedom and liberal education. Henceforth it would be extremely difficult to question, seriously and honestly, the claims and tautologies of the social justice school of thought or the AAS. Liberal education's cardinal tenets are intellectual freedom, intellectual honesty (expressing what one thinks in good faith), and a commitment to the standards of evidence. All three principles became suspect under the spirit of Barton Hall, which was dedicated to a new vision of the university as a vehicle for moral regeneration.

Many professors involved in bringing this change about downplayed the threat to intellectual freedom that the new community presented; Nichols, for example, said such concerns were exaggerated.[48] Others took it seriously, however. In a jointly authored article in the *Sun* in which they explained their decisions to resign, Berns and Sindler asserted, "The Cornell environment is no longer supportive of the kind of academic freedom a first-rate faculty requires. An intransigent moralism promoting the cleansing of the campus of 'institutional racism' and of the 'military-industrial-complex' undercuts the freedom of inquiry and the profession of honest belief a faculty requires. . . . We are free men now, but we would cease to be free men if we had to accommodate our teaching to the orthodoxy of the New Order."[49]

Andrew Hacker, who stood on the sidelines until the very end, appreciated the effect of the crisis on Berns, Bloom, and others. "Berns and Bloom have a very important point, that at many universities there are either no conservatives at all—you can point to whole colleges, whole departments that have no conservatives at all, or very few—and they are surrounded by 'P.C.' [political correctness]. Did this have a chilling effect for conservatives? Yes, it did. [But] *I* could say anything *I* wanted."[50]

Even some members of the Concerned Faculty had second thoughts about the new environment. Howard Feinstein quoted a member of the Concerned Faculty who also had a hard time dealing with racial issues in the new environment. During the spring term he was simply unable to generate an honest, open discussion about race and what was happening at Cornell. "I wanted to say something about the blacks, and they said, 'You can't understand blacks.' I found the whites in the class discussion were all getting meek. It finally occurred to me one night, 'We might as well fold up and move on somewhere else if we can't talk anymore.'"[51]

In the aftermath of the crisis, Perkins rather half-heartedly established a committee, headed by Penny, to investigate the problem of academic freedom. We will look at this committee in Chapter Thirteen.

In addition to the political aspects of the crisis, it was a time for existential confrontation for many individuals. In some respects these situations represented extraordinary educational experiences, something beyond the normal contours of college education. One black student wrote in the *Sun*, "It is seldom that a people [are] called upon to question their identity, while at the same time to question even the existence of that identity." He went on to explain how he strove to balance his racial identity with his intellectual integrity, racial solidarity with academic freedom. "Can there be a university in the absence of academic freedom? By the same token, complete equality in the absence of black manhood?"[52] One black student had a nervous breakdown, and many others experienced intense emotional turmoil. Many professors and students experienced manic or depressive states, or a heightened sense of awareness. A few professors grew afraid of students, and their careers waned. Some were riven by the feeling that something had died.

One graduate student had the same nightmare three nights in a row. She dreamed that someone she knew, but not someone close to her, had died. "But other people were making me responsible for this dead person—for washing the corpse and getting it ready for burial—and I was very angry at this."[53]

THE AFTERMATH

CHAPTER THIRTEEN

REFORM, REACTION,

RESIGNATION

I n this chapter we will look at the immediate and short-term aftermath of the Cornell crisis. The key issue was the fate of President James A. Perkins, though other issues, such as restructuring, were also important. The most significant events took place in three broadly defined realms. First, activists used the crisis to reform Cornell or to further their own objectives. More moderate reformers pushed for democratization of departments and the establishment of a constituent assembly that would devise a governing body based on proportional representation of various campus groups. The assembly was led by professors appointed to the reorganization committee, including Norman Penny, Ian MacNeil, Henry Ricciuti, and Clinton Rossiter, as well as younger individuals who were emerging as key players in the new environment. Radicals accused the assembly of being counterrevolutionary, and to some extent they had a point. Key administrators, among them Mark Barlow and individuals in the dean of students' office, encouraged more moderate students to assume control, thereby deflecting more militant influence.[1] Penny ultimately accepted the role of speaker despite his strong doubts about the efficacy of the assembly.[2]

In addition, many departments underwent change in the name of equality. Anthropology incorporated a version of a commune system between faculty and students, and Economics established an "economics community" based on a manifesto that younger faculty and students composed. After several long meetings, Economics (unlike Anthropology) broke into open conflict when its chair, Tom Davis, agreed to demands to give students and faculty more say in hiring and curriculum matters and to limit the power of the tenured faculty. Older faculty had consented to more modest changes, but Davis's new plan went too far for several senior faculty members who construed the new demands to mean that Davis and those he represented no longer considered them a "legitimate body" within the department.

A group of eight senior faculty members, including George Hildebrand and John Fei, then attempted to replace Davis as chair, without success. After efforts to improve the situation failed, senior faculty, profoundly alienated, started looking for jobs elsewhere.[3]

Among campus radicals, the Concerned Faculty remained active in support of change. Members largely supported Perkins, but they lacked the access to the trustees and the press that more senior professors enjoyed. SDS and the BLF (formerly the AAS), however, dropped out of the limelight. By the end of the week the BLF declared that it had removed its guns from 320 Wait Avenue and agreed to an inspection of the premises (the administration accepted the BLF's assurances that the guns had been removed from the campus).[4] Then the BLF concentrated on developing the black studies program. By the end of the crisis week, Tom Jones had proclaimed that the BLF would not participate in the reform of the judicial system, thereby reneging on the only substantive condition the group had accepted in the Straight agreement. SDS's Action Faction relinquished the power it had won in the preceding days. Although David Burak continued to influence the Constituent Assembly, his estranged cohorts drifted into demands that alienated the student body, including a demand for "open admissions" on behalf of the working class and a May Day demonstration in Barton Hall against ROTC that led to prosecution. The other SDS factions went back to their previous agendas.

The second arena of activism involved professors working independently or jointly to undermine Perkins by networking with trustees, newspaper reporters, and others. The trustees established a committee to investigate the crisis that heard testimony from disgruntled faculty.[5] The third arena consisted of professors and students organizing for academic freedom and against the administration. Some key faculty forged ties with the noted *New York Times* reporter Homer Bigart, whose stories would turn the tide against Perkins.

Perkins, of course, did not stand still. He and others in the administration mounted a campaign to convince the larger Cornell community and the world that the university was emerging stronger despite its tribulations. The next month would feature a furious battle between the president's allies and his enemies. Eventually Perkins resigned, and the Constituent Assembly combined conservative and progressive forces, but the crisis had a deeper impact on Cornell. James Turner accepted the directorship of the black studies program, in the newly named Africana Studies Center, in June; the program was established on ideologically separatist grounds, and though it broadened the intellectual horizons of the campus, it remained dedicated to this narrow line of thinking. In addition, within a few years Cornell adopted a policy based on the more modest examples of Wari House and Elmwood House: a separate residential program based on race, named Ujamaa. Ujamaa launched Cornell's programs of separate residence halls for other groups based on identity politics, a policy that has stirred controversy ever since. In these respects the Cornell crisis institutionalized identity politics as an important feature of the university. Before examining these developments, however, we should look at the more immediate aftermath of the Straight takeover.

Events moved swiftly at Cornell in the wake of the faculty reversal. On Thursday the BLF and the augmented Faculty Council moved in their different ways toward reform: the council recommended establishing the Constituent Assembly and convening a constitutional convention "explicitly charged with identifying and eliminating institutional racism at Cornell University." The BLF, however, held a press conference at 320 Wait Avenue at which Jones declared that "a state of both overt and covert racist oppression" remained, preventing the BLF from accepting the "invitation to join a university community." [6]

Thousands poured into Barton Hall on Thursday for a teach-in on racism that featured strong denunciations of racism by Cleophus Charles and Harry Edwards. Walter Slatoff announced that it was time to end the rigidities that had polarized the faculty and for Cornell to accept political engagement. "Reasonableness can be a hindrance to change for the blacks because it can lead to endless talks and endless committees which maintain the status quo," he said. [7] Sheila Tobias, who presided over the assembly, announced that the Government and History Departments had scheduled a teach-in on academic freedom the next day at noon at Barton, a "sincere effort" to explain the professors' position. "This is a good step in covering the breach which has developed," Tobias opined. [8]

Meanwhile, a counterrevolt was brewing in History and Government. Donald Kagan of History had accepted a position at Yale starting in the fall (as David Brion Davis had several months before the crisis), but the Wednesday vote shook Kagan so deeply that he and his family fled the Cornell campus. "I was absolutely so miserable that I just couldn't bear being there. And so I packed my family into the car and we just drove off to New York to get the hell away from it." When the stocky, rough-hewn Kagan joined the History Department after obtaining his Ph.D. from Ohio State (1958) and teaching briefly at Penn State, he was the first Jew in the department. His family had moved to Brooklyn from Lithuania when he was two (in 1934). His comparison of the Cornell crisis to the Corcyrean civil war depicted by Thucydides in *The Peloponnesian War* was based on expertise, as his second book, published in 1969, was entitled *The Outbreak of the Peloponnesian War*. Like others in his camp, he was an excellent teacher, having recently won the Clark Award.

When on Friday morning he read Homer Bigart's article in the *New York Times* on the brewing faculty revolt—including the resignations of Walter Berns, Allan Sindler, and Walter LaFeber (LaFeber did not resign from Cornell, only from his position as chair of the History Department)—he decided to come back and fight. "And suddenly, everything seemed the opposite. I now wanted to get back and be with those guys. There's a very important lesson here—it shows the importance of heroism, because one hero can enspirit a thousand people. . . . I wanted to be there." So he joined his like-minded colleagues and began planning the counterrevolt, which began with Allan Bloom composing a letter stating that the signers would not teach until safety was assured. Earlier Bloom had been so distraught that he was temporarily emotionally incapacitated; Kagan and his wife told Bloom to pull himself together and fight rather than cry. Kagan described the action:

> We all felt . . . as though we were in a crusade. And the only target that we could sort of fix on, that looked as though it might be of some value but would certainly be of wonderfully psychic value to the rest of us, [was Perkins]—we had to get Perkins.
>
> The next thing I know, Bloom has composed the letter, which will be the sort of petition that the resistance would sign on to. . . . Maybe twenty of us . . . we all signed it. This is critically important. Now there was an open, official opposition, and Bloom was the author of it.[9]

On Thursday morning sixteen members of the Government and History Departments signed the letter, vowing to cease teaching until firearms were removed.[10] LaFeber told the *Sun* that he was resigning as chairman of the History Department and that he was considering resigning from Cornell. "I do not have any confidence in the administration with the exception of the Provost [Corson]. I probably will not be at Cornell University after this year."[11] Many students who had shrugged their shoulders at dissenting faculty the previous day found it harder to disregard the statements of the popular LaFeber.

Then late Thursday afternoon fifteen Government professors attended a meeting held by the undergraduate students of the department (chaired by William B. Broydrick). The students had lined up those who stood on the academic freedom side of the debate. As many as 450 students jammed the lecture room in the basement of Goldwin Smith Hall to hear what the professors had to say. Rumors of resignations had been flying around the campus, but no one knew whether they were true. The room was charged with tension. As he entered the room, Peter Sharfman noticed something unexpected in the immediate aftermath of "the great revolution and everything": though the crowd was sprawling out the door, "people somehow pushed aside to make room for me to get to the aisle and then pushed themselves aside so that I could get down the aisle to the front of the door. . . . At least with the Government Department students, the faculty were still in some sense a different and privileged group."[12]

Sharfman would be surprised to find a similar response in other encounters with students over the next couple of days. On Thursday evening an SDS student of his was disappointed to find out that he would not have a chance to present his term paper to the class because of the crisis. Earlier that night the usually "very cocksure" student reporters of the *Sun* and WVBR had listened thoughtfully and expressed concern when Sharfman told them that the university had come close to being destroyed.[13] On Friday Eric Evans told the Barton crowd that an Ithaca High School student, Cooper Johnson, had been the victim of police brutality the previous night and urged the assembly to march downtown to challenge the police. Instead, the assembly sent a special delegation, which discovered that the charges were untrue. When the delegation returned to inform the three hundred people remaining at Barton, "this was the closest the Barton Hall community came to falling apart. Many whites began to suspect they were being taken," Fisher and Wallenstein wrote.[14] And on Saturday BLF member Bill Osby was booed at Barton when he castigated the students for having applauded the Government and History professors at the academic freedom teach-in.

At the Government students' meeting some professors were poised to announce that they were leaving. Sindler had stayed up late the night before, composing his resignation letter. In announcing his departure, Sindler asserted that the faculty decision of Wednesday was based on coercion, not conviction. Then Berns spoke, his voice broken by emotion. "You know me as a man who stands up against the popular priest Dan Berrigan, when all sentiment is on his side. . . . We had too good a world; it couldn't last. . . . I am speaking to assure you this is a very sad moment for me. I love Cornell. My best friends in the world are here." [15] In the future Berns would treat Cornell like a lover spurned, excoriating it in his writings.[16]

Some students were upset; some were shocked; others felt abandoned. "If you love Cornell, please stay and help us!" one pleaded. "Cornell and we need you more than ever." A less sympathetic student said to those around him, "He's a coward. He leaves when the going gets too rough." Other students, however, admired Berns for taking a typically strong stand on principle. In the years after the crisis many former students told Berns his resignation meant a lot to them because such a drastic act was needed to convey the seriousness of the problem. Years later Berns said that his decision to resign was instinctive rather than deliberate, motivated primarily by the "contempt" he felt for his colleagues at Cornell.[17] (Many others in this camp, such as Sindler, Kagan, and LaFeber, expressed similar feelings.) [18] Later professors from other departments would resign or consider going elsewhere. In June came the resignation of Thomas Sowell, the conservative economist, who had been considering the move for quite some time. Other professors spoke at the gathering. Andrew Milnor, who stayed, asked, "If there are some questions you cannot ask, why have a mind, why live?" Bloom predicted correctly that more resignations would follow. Then Clinton Rossiter spoke. Rossiter, already trying to justify his role in reversing the faculty vote, said, "I did the best I could to bring a restoration of peace and respect to Cornell. [My action] was a moral and practical gamble of the future of this university as an open place." [19] Rossiter's alienated colleagues turned their backs on him after this comment.

At noon Friday the Government and History Departments held their teach-in on academic freedom at Barton Hall. It was arranged at one of the Government Department's meetings on Thursday with graduate students. Someone had to counter the SDS–BLF–administration revision of events. Eldron Kenworthy, who was working with the Barton assembly, assisted Sharfman and his department in getting the teach-in on the Barton agenda—another sign of Kenworthy's balance and sense of obligation to his fallen colleagues despite his role in bringing on the revolt. They decided to include interested members of the History Department, as the two departments were in the counterrevolt together.

Sharfman urged George Kahin, one of Cornell's two leading antiwar professors (the other being LaFeber), to speak at the teach-in.[20] Kahin asked him what he should say, and Sharfman told him, "If I were a student, I would like to hear how somebody who had been in opposition to the majority view in a political matter for years and years felt about the university. And I would like to hear that it was because Cornell was a free university that he had been able to hold an unpopular view until it became popular."[21] Rising to the challenge, Kahin went home and labored for hours over his speech.

Up to seven thousand students and others attended the teach-in. Speaking first, Kahin set the tone by hitting the university head-on.

> I come here as a man deeply worried over the sudden discovery of what I thought was impossible—amazed to find that something I have always taken for granted as a matter which all members of a university understood without question to be basic and absolutely essential to its functioning was not comprehended by large numbers of students. I speak of that basic premise of a genuine university—academic freedom. Perhaps a generation which has never seen this challenged cannot be expected to be aware of it, or at least to perceive its absolute importance. . . .
>
> When I came here to be interviewed for a job in 1951, I came as a man already well smeared by McCarthyism. . . . And with respect to McCarthyist tactics, let me assure you that calling a man a racist does not make him so, any more than McCarthy calling him a Communist made him a Communist. . . .
>
> We voted for the maintenance of academic freedom, believing that without that essential quality there can be no relationship of any kind between blacks and a university, because without that quality you don't have a university.[22]

After the audience cheered Kahin's speech, historian Fred Somkin, sensing the end of the university as he had known it, recited the Kaddish, a Jewish funeral prayer, for what he designated the "death of Cornell University." The usually low-key former lawyer told friends that that was the speech he used to give to juries when he knew they were going to convict his client.[23]

Then Rossiter rose to speak. He was not scheduled to do so, but he felt the need to address the crowd. Earlier David Burak had revealed that Rossiter had some time ago ordered him to "get out of town." Rossiter stormed the stage and grabbed for the microphone until someone restrained him, whereupon Burak apologized and the two shook hands in front of the bewildered audience.[24] Rossiter now talked about his reasons for his vote on Wednesday and his desire to save Cornell. He concluded by answering critics who were accusing him of cowardice. "I am as yellow as that red flag hanging over there," he shouted as an almost ritualistic cheer erupted from the crowd.

Fisher and Wallenstein maintained that the Government resignations and the academic freedom teach-in had an effect:

> Many still couldn't quite see any connection between the Barton Hall events and a threat to academic freedom. But word had gotten around that Berns and LaFeber and Sindler were resigning; students began to think they must have good reasons.

Afterwards, many students said that these resignations were their first indication that something might be wrong. So much euphoria had exuded from Barton Hall that students were in a self-congratulatory humor. They had been victorious, the faculty had reversed its decision, had come to Barton Hall and been applauded— "and really what was the harm?" The Government Department teach-in made many realize that grave issues concerning Cornell's future were at stake.[25]

A letter Alfred Kahn wrote to two friends on April 27 discussed the seriousness of the resignations, stressing that "the most serious blow is that of Walter LaFeber." In another note, he said keeping LaFeber was the most important task the university had and that his leaving would break the dam holding back resignations.[26]

On April 30 Perkins sent a letter to Dean Robert Miller, asking the Faculty Committee on Academic Freedom and Tenure to investigate the problem of academic freedom. Penny, the chair of the committee, heard about the charge to the committee over the radio, not from the president. When he contacted Perkins on the phone, the president said trustee Robert Purcell had pressured him because Purcell had been bombarded with faculty concerns. According to Penny, Perkins just did not grasp the meaning of academic freedom because he was not a teacher and researcher. Indeed, Perkins's letter to Miller implied that Perkins expected the investigation to find no problem. "Neither you nor the Faculty Committee on Academic Freedom and Tenure nor any dean nor indeed any member of the faculty had ever made any report to this effect to me."[27] Penny said:

> This is like not knowing what the black experience is. You have got to have been in the firing line, you've got to be a teacher, and Mr. Perkins was never really a teacher. . . . You've got to have been exposed to the kinds of pressures and recognize the potential for . . . harm to academic freedom in teaching in the teaching-research activities of a full-time teacher to understand what these guys are worried about. . . . And it was quite apparent that he didn't appreciate that.[28]

Rossiter's Ordeal

Of the several victims of the crisis, none was more prominent than Clinton Rossiter. On the evening of July 10, 1970, his son, Caleb, found him in the basement of the family home, dead of an overdose of barbiturates. He was fifty-two. It took his mother, Mary Ellen, twenty years to show Caleb the brief suicide note his father had left. The note, printed in Caleb's book *The Chimes of Freedom Flashing*, stressed that he had given way to feelings of despair and worthlessness.[29]

Rossiter had long been one of Cornell's most illustrious professors. In 1953, at the age of thirty-six, he had won the most respected book awards in both political science and history, the Woodrow Wilson Award and the Bancroft Prize, respectively, for his book on the thinkers who presaged the American revolution, *Seedtime of the Republic*. When he was appointed to the prestigious John L. Senior Chair at Cornell, he was at the peak of his powers, utterly captivating his interviewers; other important books were to follow. But slowly his research and his public persona unraveled. According to Berns, Rossiter had been enormously popular but changed "when the world began to get serious—'68, '69."[30] By 1970 he was a shell of the man he once was.

Though his fall was probably the result of personal problems unrelated to the Cornell crisis, Rossiter's decline did parallel the fall of the traditional American dream in the late '60s. He "was a leading practitioner of the celebratory, optimistic treatment of American government and history I so mistrusted," Caleb remarked.[31] According to John Marcham, the Straight crisis "finished off Clint Rossiter . . . [and] his kids didn't help. They were rebelling, cutting cane for Castro. He was trying at the time he committed suicide to finish one of his books. He could not reconcile his life, which glorified the American experience and process, with what was happening."[32] But Caleb also praised his father in the book and in our interview. "Unlike the professors of the 1990s, my father and his friends were scholars, not academics. They were broad in their knowledge, not limited in their specialization. They too wrote books and articles at a fevered pace but gave far more energy and time to teaching. It was a simple matter of honor."[33]

Caleb's book revealed that alcoholism and clinical depression led to his father's decline. Caleb's account, though compelling and no doubt valid, did not analyze problems his father encountered on campus that could have contributed in some way to his emotional state. Fisher and Wallenstein wrote that Rossiter became the "clown" of the crisis. His own actions, press focus on him as the spokesman for the faculty, and public perceptions conspired to set Rossiter up for a fall. The man himself would attribute this special attention to his "moral standing" at Cornell.[34] But his vote on Monday and his reversal on Wednesday were witnessed around the world, a world that overwhelmingly opposed what he and the faculty had wrought. As noted, Fred Marcham, a bellwether opinion maker for Government and History, considered both the form and the content of Rossiter's performance on Wednesday "obscene."

Rossiter received four or five letters a day during the first days of the crisis. After Wednesday he received an avalanche, split evenly between support and opposition. The opposition was often scurrilous, containing "such violent and obscene language" that Rossiter's secretary began to open the letters to shield the beleaguered professor. One friend of thirty years sent a telegram, on yellow paper, that showed no mercy: "The color of this telegram is the color of you," began the friend, who castigated Rossiter for lacking "moral courage."[35]

Rossiter dreaded going to the Government Department meetings that week, but he went as the good citizen he always tried to be. Berns, Sindler, and Bloom made "very emotional" (Rossiter's words) speeches at the Thursday meeting, after which Rossiter "once again made a tactical error—I sort of blew my stack." Those who really loved Cornell intended to stay rather than leave, he told them. "And this was a very nasty moment, I thought. Afterward I tried to speak to Mr. Berns and to Mr. Bloom and to Mr. Sindler and all three turned their backs on me, which several of them have continued to do since that time," he reported months later. (Sindler said he decided to forgive Rossiter because of how he was suffering.)[36]

Rossiter persisted in going to the offices of his estranged colleagues and asking for a renewal of respect and friendship. One of them said, "Clinton, I am a hard man. And when I decide no longer to have anything to do with a person, he's dead as far as I am concerned." Rossiter reflected: "So to one of these . . . people, I'm dead. I can honestly say that in all the years I've been here there's been nothing to resemble this. No polarization of this kind."[37] Economist Alfred Kahn reported being present when Rossiter called a colleague on the phone to ask for the renewal of their friendship; several feet from Rossiter, Kahn could hear the colleague's phone slam down.[38] Rossiter's relationship with his History colleagues was not much better. At a later meeting concerning the election of History's representatives to the Constituent Assembly, one acerbic colleague declared that Rossiter should be elected to both positions so he could vote no and yes at the same time.[39] Rossiter's relationships with graduate students also declined.

Elected to the steering committee of the Constituent Assembly, Rossiter continued to play an active role on campus, but his professional life grew darker. He would show up on campus in the morning in a drunken state and hold his hand out to colleagues, beseeching them to shake his hand and be his friend.

In May 1970 Kahn (who was also dean of the College of Arts and Sciences) and Arch Dotson, chair of the Government Department, asked Rossiter to take a year's leave of absence because students were reporting that he was showing up in class drunk. Rossiter refused to accept their advice because he feared that doing so would make Cornellians aware of his problems (sadly, they already were). As Dotson left the Rossiter residence after making his leave proposal, Mary Ellen Rossiter confided to him, "I'm afraid he's going to kill himself." Dotson replied, "So am I." A short while later Rossiter was dead.[40]

Shortly after the crisis Sindler made an effort to reconcile things with Rossiter out of concern for a colleague, a gesture that must have been difficult for Sindler because he took what happened hard. On Friday of the crisis week Sindler took Kenworthy aside before a department meeting and asked him whether he had taken the opportunity to defend Sindler against charges of racism before the Barton assembly, especially on Tuesday night. Kenworthy had not done so, and Sindler felt betrayed. Kenworthy was astonished at Sindler's comment: the request showed that Sindler just did not grasp what had transpired that fateful night (indeed, what Kenworthy did just might have saved the university from physical destruction); but the incident also showed how sensitive Sindler was to the charges.[41]

Silbey had an encounter with Allan and Lee Sindler that showed how Lee still thought of the conflict in terms of "us" and "them." Attending a Cornell function at the Hilton on Fifty-Seventh Street in New York many years later, Silbey had gotten up early to take a walk and go to a nearby delicatessen. When he walked in he spotted the Sindlers, the only other patrons. "I walk in and sit down—it's early, it's seven in the morning—and there is Allan Sindler and his wife, Lee. And I look and say, 'Allan, I'm Joel Silbey.' He says, 'Hello, how are you?' with the reserve that he still has, and he turns to Lee, 'You remember Joel Silbey.' And she looks at him and says, 'Which side was *he* on?' And he says, 'Ours,' and she begins speaking to me. That's the feeling I had with people. Before I had anything to say, I remembered where they stood."[42]

Media and the Battle over Control of Cornell

The days following the "resolution" of the crisis were full of internal interest group struggles. We have seen that SDS and the BLF more or less dropped out of the main events as the Barton Hall Community held center stage. I will not devote much time to the Constituent Assembly or the senate that emerged from it because they were tangential to our story and because the senate ultimately proved an uneventful entity, as more experienced and hardheaded individuals predicted. The senate was given the power over such important issues as athletics, housing, dining, and scheduling of certain events, but the faculty held on to power in key academic areas. In 1977 Corson dissolved the senate as his last official act as president:

> It was a poor form of government. But given the circumstances, the distrust of authority, the demand for participation in decision making that existed at that time, it might have been the only sensible way to proceed. People had a lot of hand in discussing issues and exploring issues, employees, administrators, faculty. . . . It was participatory democracy; it was awkward, and it didn't work well. As soon as things quieted down, interest in it faded, after three or four years. By 1975 it was obvious that it could not survive. Finally . . . I went to the Board of Trustees with the recommendation that it be dissolved—back to normal university operations, with ordinary faculty committees, student-faculty committees.[43]

The first weekend after the crisis a group of faculty and students ("self-appointed," according to Fisher and Wallenstein)[44] put together 150 restructuring proposals and advocated setting up a constituent assembly consisting of representatives of various groups on campus to restructure decision making in some key areas of the university. By the end of the weekend word had spread that the Barton Hall meetings were open, and professors from various departments started attending. Student interest was waning, so a few faculty members, administrators, and students who were not SDS sympathizers were able to exert unexpected influence. These people accepted the need for reform, some more reluctantly than others, but they were not radical.

Sheila Tobias played a pivotal role as secretary, as did such students as Richard O'Brien, Michael Wright, and Randi Loftsgaarden. Tobias's vast knowledge of how the university worked proved especially valuable, and her twin beliefs in progressive reform (indeed, the experience helped to launch her feminist career in education, which brought her national recognition) and the harmony of goodwilled interests guided her. According to Peter Sharfman, who was also a key player, Tobias represented the views of the steering committee "composed basically of those earnest sorts of people who believe deeply, devoutly that if people will only talk and listen to each other with open minds, all the problems in the University will go away."[45] Thomas Tobin praised Tobias's great energy, independence, and knowledge, saying, "Sheila Tobias is one of the real great people around here." He also observed how Tobias and other administrators encouraged more moderate student reformers to stick it out in Barton's grinding deliberations, thereby co-opting militant influence.[46] The establishment of the Constituent Assembly represented the taming of the Barton Hall spirit. Indeed, Sharfman soon found himself, a self-described "conservative government faculty member," being treated with deference by students in the assembly.[47]

One student group that competed for power in the pre–Constituent Assembly phase of Barton was Students for a Democratic Alternative (SDA), a conservative-leaning group that was attempting to organize a broader student coalition around the issue of academic freedom. SDA was important because it was the first group to call officially for Perkins's resignation. The group cited the intimidation against speaking freely and openly about political issues on campus and the "atmosphere of fear, coercion, and confusion."[48]

Meanwhile, the Group of Forty-One decided to commit itself to saving Cornell, and published a statement in the *Sun* declaring its members' intent to "stand together" and stay unless "the freedom to teach and to learn without intimidation" is restored.[49] Paul Olum announced the group's motives: "We thought that a group of leading professors—important, recognized, respected people around the university—should say 'what's done is done. We're willing to stay now. But from now on things have to be done in a certain way. If there is another threat of this kind to the functioning of the university, we will leave and we will leave together.'"[50] Whereas the threat to resign if the crisis were repeated was a warning the administration could not ignore, many critics of the group considered Olum's self-flattering language to be another sign of what was wrong with the Group of Forty-One. (Berns said, "We called them the Forty-One Finks!")[51]

Perkins and the administration were beginning to create their own version of events. Perkins issued a lengthy statement to "The Cornell Family" that highlighted the importance of his commitment to COSEP and racial understanding in America. He also laid out plans to address the Tower Club, Cornell's most prestigious and generous group of alumni, in May in New York.[52] Steven Muller prepared to write his own account based on addresses to alumni at Buffalo and Rochester. Before we look at these efforts and those of the administration's enemies, we should look at the public reaction that poured into the administration's mailboxes.

Public Opinion and Letters

The administration was jolted upon hearing the outside world's response to its handling of the crisis. From the Wednesday faculty vote until graduation in June, letters, alumni, and the press consumed Muller, who was a front man for reaction because of his job as vice president for public affairs and because he had recently appeared on the cover of the *New York Times Magazine* when it ran a piece on Cornell. Of some two thousand letters, only about 5 percent were supportive. Some were thoughtful; others were emotional, even vicious. Some were overtly racist. "I had to deal with hate mail that came in to me personally in unbelievable quantity. I think to this day there are some I never opened. It kept me preoccupied for days." [53]

Not surprisingly, Perkins also received an avalanche of over two thousand letters. Some praised his handling of the crisis and his vision of the university. One letter from an alumnus from Tarrytown, New York, stated, "I have never been prouder of Cornell than during this past week. . . . You have taught the whole country, if not much of the world, a great lesson. Your vision that higher education is on the threshold comparable with the transition from classical to practical pursuits, in which Cornell led a century ago, seems to me a correct observation." [54] A federal judge wrote to express the "deepest feeling of sympathy for you in your varying situations." Twenty-five professors from the Section of Neurobiology and Behavior, Langmuir Laboratory, an area that Perkins had enhanced earlier in his presidency, praised Perkins for his handling of a potentially explosive situation. Throughout the crisis, professors in the natural sciences were less upset at what happened than those in the liberal arts, perhaps because their teaching and research were less threatened in the new politicized climate. [55]

But the vast majority of letters were critical (Fisher and Wallenstein wrote that only thirty out of two thousand were favorable). A perusal of the dozens of letters in Perkins's files reveals three major themes: the administration capitulated in the manner of Neville Chamberlain at Munich, the administration had forgotten the link between freedom and responsibility, and the administration relied on double standards in admissions and enforcement of the rules. A letter to the president of the Cornell Alumni Association from one woman captured these themes in denouncing Perkins for his "total surrender," an act that "filled me with disgust, anger, and overwhelming shame for the school I once loved":

> President Perkins, in his own overzealous and self-righteous attempt to appease "social injustice," has completely forgotten his responsibility to thousands of fine, law-abiding students who are seeking a good education. . . . His permissiveness and toleration of intrusions on academic freedom have led to a total breakdown of discipline, and the disintegration of authority. . . .
>
> There is indeed a great and urgent need for more social justice. . . . But to be at all meaningful, it must be accomplished within the framework of democracy and rights for *all*. . . . President Perkins has illustrated to the nation . . . such an appalling lack of courage and judgment [that he] raises great doubts as to his qualifications for the responsible job of running a great university. . . . I have loved Cornell, but the Cornell I respected and loved is no more. I want no future association with the school that exists today. [56]

Tobin said there were up to eighty reporters at Cornell during the crisis; he set them up with telephones and typewriters in Day Hall and in the theater lounge at the Statler Hotel so they would not be scattered all over campus. Tobin also assigned Cornell Public Information Office (PIO) staff such as George Fisher to key areas of the campus, including the Safety Division and the executive staff (Tobin took that key position himself; Fisher took Safety, from which he derived inside information for the manuscript he wrote with Wallenstein). *Times* reporters, however, eventually operated out of the *Cornell Daily Sun*'s headquarters; the *Sun* was another nerve center of information, with Safety and the so-called rumor clinic. Tobin and the PIO developed a kind of symbiotic relationship with the press, feeding each other information. According to Tobin, the administration did not try to influence what the PIO did or said during the crisis.[57]

For its part, the *Sun* carried stories from a variety of perspectives. Its reporters and editors were divided about where to stand. Paul Rahe said, "At the *Sun* we fought over everything, tremendous fights." But everyone benefited from exposure to America's newspaper of record. "The other thing is that the *New York Times* used our office, our phones. So one got to meet these people as they passed through," Rahe said.[58] Stan Chess, the *Sun*'s editor until right before the crisis, was among those whom Perkins had courted (the president had taken him to a football game and kept in touch). Though Chess was critical of how things went, he expressed sympathy for Perkins because of the difficulties he had to confront. During the events of December and the spring, Chess had observed Perkins at close hand and felt that "President Perkins was trying as hard as he could to find a solution. He was committed to finding a solution."[59]

Media commentary around the country and the world was as negative as it was voluminous. The administration asserted that such coverage missed the facts, which was true to some extent, for outsiders could not fathom what it meant actually to be subjected to the pressure that the administration faced. But critics claimed that the administration consistently missed the forest for the trees.

Syndicated columnists such as James J. Kilpatrick, Rowland Evans, and Robert Novak excoriated the administration; Kilpatrick spoke of "McCarthyism" at Cornell, and Evans and Novak wrote of "anarchy" in the wake of the Straight crisis and of "Cornell and anti-Semitism" in a later article. The *Pittsburgh Press* published an editorial titled "Cornell's Disgrace." A *New York Times* editorial compared the guns at Cornell with the rise of jackbooted students in pre-Nazi Germany. A letter in the *London Times* dealt with Black Power and violence at Cornell. The *Wall Street Journal*, the *New Republic*, and the *London Observer* bemoaned the rise of thought control and force in the place of reason (a *WSJ* editorial was headed "The Abyss of Chaos"). Civil rights leader Bayard Rustin castigated Cornell's substitution of "soul courses" for courses of greater intellectual substance.[60] Yet the most damaging coverage came from Bigart. Trustee William Robertson, who considered Bigart's accounts biased, said that Bigart "just murdered Cornell."[61] Berns saw the other side. "Bigart was a savior to us. He sought us out and had a helluva lot to do with Perkins's demise."[62]

John Kifner had covered the Straight takeover for the *New York Times*, but Bigart arrived to help cover the faculty revolt and the aftermath. A Pennsylvanian and forty-year veteran of the *Times* and the then-defunct *Herald-Tribune*, Bigart had won two Pulitzer Prizes for his reporting on World War II and Korea. He wrote front-page articles about the crisis of academic freedom and the conflicts among the faculty that did more than anything else to crumble the ground beneath Perkins's feet. According to John Marcham, himself a master reporter, Bigart was "known as the best investigative reporter in the country."[63] *Times* publisher Harrison E. Salisbury's portrayal of the first time he met Bigart in London in 1943 captures the figure Bigart cut in words that observers would repeat at Cornell. "The glimpse of Homer transmitted the essential characteristics of the man who would become *the* war correspondent of his time. He was alone, a slim, almost frail figure hunched over his Olivette, slowly punching with two or three fingers . . . when the answer [to his painstaking questions to interviewees] mortised together into the plain but intricate structure of Homer's prose his edifice of words stood out like a tower on a treeless plain." Bigart harbored a deeply ingrained suspicion of the honesty of authority figures, especially in times of crisis, and a firm commitment to social justice. But his preeminent commitment was to disclosing the truth as he saw it.[64] He took almost personal offense at what he considered Cornell's camouflaging of the truth. According to Tobin, Bigart might also have been offended at the fatigued Perkins's dismissive response to a question Bigart asked him at a press conference the president convened on the spur of the moment after his Barton Hall appearance on Wednesday. "I wonder to this day if having, you know, been treated almost like a cub reporter for an instant there might not have turned him a little bit," Tobin said.[65]

By the end of crisis week Bigart had become a fixture in West Sibley Hall, the home of the Government and History Departments. Like Salisbury, Richard Polenberg spotted him sitting in Fred Marcham's office, hat tipped to the side, cigarette hanging out the side of his mouth as his fingers poked on the keys of his battered manual typewriter—the classic image of the probing, unbowing reporter.[66] Bigart's instincts as a prizewinning war reporter told him that the war at Cornell was not over and that he should be suspicious of information provided by authorities. According to Fisher and Wallenstein, Bigart became "visibly angry" when Perkins told the press on Wednesday that no families had moved off campus Tuesday night because of the threats. As we have seen, the hotel and motel rooms were filled to capacity with families fleeing Cornell.[67]

All week the Cornell crisis dominated the front pages of the *New York Times*. (Often the stories were accompanied by other articles about campus upheavals. It appeared the sky was falling on American higher education, with Cornell leading the way.) The *Times* was important because it was America's paper of record and because so many Cornell alumni lived in the New York area and were faithful readers of the paper. What it reported bore a strong presumption of truth, especially when one was inclined to agree with its conclusions in the first place.

The first two paragraphs of Bigart's April 24 article reported the faculty reversal and how Perkins "hailed" the vote, but the next four registered the "disgust" of several senior professors at the "abject capitulation" and "surrender to intimidation." Bigart proceeded to pinpoint Rossiter as the leading apostate of the Government Department and portrayed Perkins's humiliation upon his entrance to Barton after the faculty vote. He had been "kept waiting, red-faced and discomforted, while Eric Evans, a leader of the Afro-American Society, mocked him." [68] Though Perkins's critics were still a minority on campus, as another article that day by Kifner indicated, Bigart gave the isolated critics equal billing and then some.

Bigart continued his barrage Friday, the day of the academic freedom teach-in and the day that the New York Legislature was passing an antigun law for college campuses. The front-page article, highlighting the Bloom-inspired letter, was headlined "Faculty Revolt Upsets Cornell: Charges of Sellout Made—Many Won't Teach Until Assured Guns Are Gone." Bigart reported the resignations of the previous day and quoted James John, Sindler, Bloom, LaFeber, and Myron Rush (of Government) to devastating effect. Sindler said he could have accepted the faculty reversal had his colleagues had the "integrity, guts, common sense, and dignity" to admit their reversal was due to coercion rather than principle. Bloom claimed the crisis was something "entirely new. . . . A complete capitulation under threat of firearms to a group of students who have a program for transformation of the university." LaFeber said he was looking for another job because he had "no confidence in the administration." [69]

Finally, the article juxtaposed the comments of the outgoing and incoming chairs of the Board of Trustees, Arthur Dean and Robert Purcell, respectively. Purcell had just bequeathed $1 million to the black studies program and was more in tune with Perkins's vision of the university than the recently retired Dean. Purcell had undergraduate and law degrees from Cornell (1932, 1935) and had served as chairman of several companies and boards. He stated in the Bigart article that the events at Cornell had "constructive aspects" and that Cornell could now "go ahead with a spirit of unity and forward thinking. Progress is in evidence." Dean drew a starkly contrasting conclusion. "I am opposed to granting amnesty merely because you're threatened by students with guns. Any society that gives in to violence is a decaying society, and it has nothing to do with whether students are black or white." [70] Dean had come to harbor doubts about Perkins. Informed of the Straight takeover, he told an anonymous interviewee, "I guess that's what we get for appointing a Quaker!"

On Saturday Bigart reported that fifteen professors had sent a letter to the trustees charging the administration with undermining academic freedom and stipulating that steps had to be taken to protect the university from a faculty exodus. [71] According to John Marcham, who worked closely with many of the key reporters who came to Cornell that week, Bigart got the essentials of the Cornell story right, although he made some factual errors. Marcham thought that the administration failed to realize how the typically superficial coverage of the issue would look to the public, especially the guns coming out of the Straight, and that it faltered badly in the face of Bigart's more sophisticated presentations.[72]

Not everyone shared Marcham's praise for Bigart. Robertson accused him of distorting the truth in favor of a relatively small number of professors who were giving him their perspectives. "Homer Bigart was just an SOB as far as Cornell was concerned. Every article he wrote just tore Cornell down, and he got this information from four or five faculty members, all of whom left Cornell. . . . Those fellows just fed the stuff to Bigart, and he just murdered Cornell." (Perkins later told Robertson that *Times* publisher Arthur Sulzberger had apologized to him a year later for Bigart's "lack of balance.")[73]

Faculty Response

Although many on the faculty still supported Perkins (including the Concerned Faculty) and promoted change in their departments or in the Constituent Assembly, numerous prominent members were disillusioned and started to organize. In addition to the Government and History Departments, a group of senior professors led by George Hildebrand of Economics moved against him. This "Group of Ten" (otherwise known as the Professors for Academic Integrity) consisted of Robert Pasley of Law, Isadore Blumen of Industrial and Labor Relations, Walter Galenson of Economics, Richard Gallagher of Civil Engineering, Wesley Gunkel of Agricultural Engineering, F. M. Isenberg of Agriculture, Richard Phelan of Mechanical Engineering, Charles Sayles of Hotel Administration, Francis Saul of Architecture, and Hildebrand. The group's objectives were to affirm the principles of liberal education and to overthrow Perkins.[74] Like Sindler and others, Hildebrand was distraught over the administration's year-long handling of student lawlessness. In his Oral History interview he decried what he called "the incredibly naïve and romantic permissiveness that prevailed over the last three years" and what he called "psuedoliberalism," which is liberalism unhinged from the commitment to personal responsibility and the willingness to back up the principles of liberal education. In his eyes, "the explanation [for the administration's failure] lies in psuedoliberalism and one element of this psuedoliberalism is what I will call misplaced faith in youth," the belief that the youth of the sixties was wiser and superior to any generation before it. "So it is psuedoliberalism to say that the law does not hold when certain groups challenge it if they feel their grievances are deep enough."[75] The group operated on several fronts: it campaigned among key alumni, trustees, and such ex officio trustees as Governor Nelson Rockefeller; it testified before the Robertson Committee investigating the Straight crisis; and it went to the press, especially the *New York Times*. "We sought to tell our story, we reached some of the editors of the *Times* and we pleaded with them that there was another side to these events besides the one that Vice President Muller and his public relations office was giving out." Hildebrand maintained that the group found it "distasteful" to attack Perkins this way, but "it is a measure, I think, of the extreme conditions that had finally emerged at Cornell that we were put into this situation."[76]

Other behind-the-scenes action broke out almost immediately after the crisis ended. Perhaps most notable were the maneuvers of LaFeber, Fred Marcham, Berns, Silbey, Bloom, Sindler, and a few others. Each was assigned people and departments to call to present their side of the issue and to undermine the administration. Berns called his friends in the Law School (he was rebuffed: "Walter, we don't want to cause Jim [Perkins] any more trouble than he already has," he was told). The group contacted Governor Rockefeller, who was "sympathetic," and Daniel Patrick Moynihan in Washington.[77]

Unlike Government, the History Department stood almost totally against Perkins. On Friday morning of crisis week Provost Corson called Fred Marcham to his office; Marcham went there with Silbey and Polenberg. The provost was concerned about holding the department together. Marcham told him that only five of the twenty-five members were "sure to stay." When Corson asked him what could be done to save the department, Marcham exclaimed, "Denounce Jones's speech!" Corson seemed taken aback and said only that another faculty meeting was set for that afternoon. The group alerted Corson that such a meeting would be a disaster, and Corson called Robert Miller to cancel it. At this point Marcham and his allies had three goals: to save the department, to "oppose all threats to freedom and learning," and to seek Perkins's removal.[78] As for LaFeber, he had begun speaking with trustees as early as Monday of crisis week. He first called Austin Kiplinger, an important member of the board, and told him he should come to Ithaca right away, but Kiplinger refused. So LaFeber called Dean, who was very responsive and started contacting trustees. LaFeber was deeply impressed by Dean. "Dean was, I think, the single toughest guy I've ever met in my life," LaFeber commented in an interview more than twenty-five years later. "He was quite extraordinary."

The seventy-year-old Dean was a native Ithacan, with bachelor's and law degrees from Cornell (1921, 1923). His impressive résumé included numerous honorary degrees (mostly law), general counsel positions and directorships of several major companies, ambassadorships and involvements in important international conferences and negotiations (nuclear disarmament, weapons treaties, and so on), and many national and international honors. He had been a leading senior partner of the prestigious New York law firm of Sullivan and Cromwell, where he succeeded John Foster Dulles as a partner. Dean was tough-minded and dedicated to Cornell. Though a graduate of the Law School, his extensive contributions (often procured by his agents in New York City) all went to the university library and archives. Cornell counsel Neal Stamp's praise was fulsome. "I always thought that Arthur Dean had a better philosophical understanding of the place of the university in society than any other trustee I encountered—that it was the most valuable asset in society."[79]

On Sunday, April 27, Marcham's wife called him while he was attending yet another meeting with Polenberg, Silbey, LaFeber, and others, and told him to return a call from Robert Purcell. By this time these professors had become more concerned with saving the department—to hell with the university. But Purcell's call renewed their hopes for Cornell. Purcell informed Marcham's wife that he had been a student of Marcham's as an undergraduate. She said, "You don't need my husband—I'll tell you what's happening. First of all, he's heartbroken to see a life's work vanish in a week." When Marcham and Purcell finally connected that day, Purcell said there was a Board of Trustees meeting set for Thursday, May 1, at the Cornell Medical School in New York City and that the trustees wanted a statement about academic freedom from Marcham and his closest allies. Marcham wrote the statement that day.

That evening LaFeber called Marcham and told him Purcell wanted Marcham, LaFeber, Sindler, and Kahin to fly to New York the next day to talk with a select group of trustees to prepare them for the May 1 meeting. They booked a 6:30 a.m. flight. Sindler decided not to go because he still felt too emotional to attend—he would talk to the trustees later.

Marcham took an extra drink and fell into a deep sleep. Then the phone rang. It was LaFeber, bearing bad news: he had just heard on the radio that Purcell had issued a statement supporting Perkins. Feeling stabbed in the back, they canceled their reservations, but the next morning they read Purcell's statement in the *Sun* and discovered that Purcell had carefully avoided praising Perkins—they had overreacted! LaFeber managed to book a flight out of Syracuse, so Marcham, LaFeber, and Kahin made their way to New York in the afternoon. Key trustees meeting with this bereaved yet earnest group had to be the administration's worst nightmare.

Purcell met the professors at the airport in a limousine and took them to his office (he was the head of the Rockefeller Enterprises in Latin America). At 4:00 p.m. six or seven trustees, including Dean, greeted them. Marcham delivered his statement, which was a general defense of academic freedom and freedom from force and threats. He asserted that a university should be "free from pressures by the one or the few or the many, free above all from those who cannot trust the causes they advocate to open discussion and rational persuasion." Kahin espoused the position he presented at the teach-in a few days before, that Cornell had fallen into a new form of McCarthyism. LaFeber was the most effective because the trustees wanted facts, and the master historian was able to give them all the facts they needed in response to each question. He knew how to home in on his prey—something students who took his courses on American foreign policy witnessed with each lecture.

After this meeting the group dined at Dean's residence, a magnificent apartment overlooking the East River. According to LaFeber, "Dean essentially told us to keep calm and not give up because there would be some changes made. He didn't specify what they were . . . [but] we came away knowing that Dean (and I don't know who else—Purcell) knew that there was something fundamentally wrong and they were willing to take responsibility. To me this was very important. There was somebody there who was essentially willing to counter what Perkins was doing. . . . If Perkins is going to stay, we're going to lose some faculty." [80]

Three days later the trustees held their marathon meeting at the Medical College. Bigart covered the affair in a front-page article in the *Times*. (The headline that day dealt with the expanded investigation of college disorders by Congress and the

Nixon administration. "SDS Is Singled Out," read the subtitle.) Dean's position prevailed over Purcell's, as Bigart had presented them in his previous article. The trustees issued a ten-point declaration against "tactics of terror," saying that such acts would be met with a "firm and appropriate response." They also issued a statement through George Eager, the president's assistant, that fell short of endorsing Perkins's handling of the crisis. It merely stated that Perkins has "our full confidence in implementing the 10-point declaration adopted by the board today." Bigart reported that the trustees were divided over supporting Perkins.[81]

According to Tobin and others, at this time Perkins asked *Times* editor John B. Oakes to take Bigart off the story; the *Times* refused, but James Reston wrote a column favorable to Perkins.[82] Bigart had left Cornell but was planning a final piece that would be his "blockbuster" (Tobin's term).[83] The *Sun* reported that Perkins would not give an interview. The problem was that this refusal left Perkins's voice out of the single most authoritative public interpretation of the crisis and its effects. Perkins also refused to follow Tobin's advice and let Corson speak with Bigart. Instead Perkins recommended that Bigart talk to Cushing Strout, whom Perkins mistakenly thought was still a supporter. Strout would help Bigart present his next blockbusters on May 28 and June 1.[84]

The Administration's Counterattack

Sindler observed that in the aftermath of the crisis, "Cornell officials had an immediate and major public relations problem," so they "developed what may fairly be called the 'official' account of the handling of the crisis." *New York Times* columnist Tom Wicker supplied the first version on Sunday, April 27, in a column headlined "Humanity vs. Principle at Cornell." He praised the administration for avoiding bloodshed and depicted the evacuation of the Straight as an AAS surrender.[85]

Perkins and Muller began speaking with alumni and others. The weekend after the dénouement of the crisis, the administration, in particular Perkins and Eager, attempted to put together a major statement or interpretation to be sent to alumni across the country and to the major newspapers, such as the *New York Times*, the *Washington Post*, and the *Chicago Tribune*. Muller called Tobin to come over to look at what had been drafted. Muller and Tobin found the statement to contain "some gross inaccuracies" and "some very weak statements," so they managed to talk Perkins out of sending it. Instead Muller started delivering talks to alumni clubs that reiterated his claim that avoiding loss of life was a more important principle than any other, and he made appearances on national television and radio. Muller had his detractors in terms of what he had to say, "but the University needed a spokesman, and Steve did it and did it very effectively," Tobin said.[86]

Perkins had his public relations people work on a "chronology of events," which, according to Fisher and Wallenstein, went through several versions and was never released. (I found it in the Cornell archives, however, and used it often in the discussion of the crisis days.)[87] At some point the administration also made a transcript of an executive staff discussion of its actions during the crisis; this discussion and transcript were made "to set the record straight," though there is no evidence that the transcript was ever released. At the same time, Perkins began preparing his speech scheduled for May 14 at the Tower Club in New York, before an assemblage of Cornell's five hundred biggest donors.

Muller shone in his more familiar role as vice president of public affairs, but many observers thought the administration was painting too positive a picture of the crisis's aftermath. In one rather remarkable instant during the crisis week, Mayor Kiely was watching Muller assure the country on national television that Cornell had calmed down—at the very same time that Perkins was on the phone telling Kiely that things were once again "in a state of uproar." Kiely alleged that administrators would not deserve respect "until they tell the truth." [88]

The Tower Club Speech

The Tower Club speech on May 14 was a classic Perkins performance, justifying the president's actions along the lines that Muller had emphasized in Buffalo and stressing the justice of his vision in grand language. Perkins maintained that the public did not know the real truth and cited the praise he and the COSEP and black studies programs had received in Ernest Dunbar's *New York Times Magazine* article that appeared just before the Straight takeover. The AAS, he said, had made "very significant concessions" to participate in the new judicial system (in truth, Jones had already announced the AAS's refusal to honor this concession). Perkins concluded on a note of hope, saying, "I believe we can all muster the compassion, the patience, and the courage to go on with the important work our nation so desperately needs from the modern American university community. We at Cornell have been through the fire, for which we were not fully prepared." [89]

Meanwhile, three students—Paul Rahe, Karen Novick, and Ellen Schatz—showed up on a mission to counter the president's claims. Rahe, the most outspoken critic of the administration on the *Sun,* had written a negative article for the *Cornell Alumni News,* but Editor John Marcham had turned it down because of its vehemence and because he had his own plans, which we will discuss shortly. Rahe and his allies then decided to act on their own by publishing a sixteen-page pamphlet, *Cornell in Crisis: A Documentary Analysis.* The booklet covered the events from the inception of COSEP and the McPhelin affair to the Straight crisis itself. With the Cornell seal on its front, it looked like an official Cornell publication, but it read like a radical rant. The students accused the administration of appeasement and a cynical manipulation of student groups. Schatz's father, a Tower Club member, had invited the students and resisted pressure to withdraw the invitation once the administration had gotten wind of their plans. According to Fisher and Wallenstein, one administrator told the students they would be disciplined for "disrupting a university activity." ("*Now* they're going to enforce the rules!" Rahe said.) Fisher and Wallenstein also claimed that Muller made a last-ditch effort to dissuade them from showing up and offered to give them a list of Tower Club names so they could send the members the booklet. Rahe refused because he wanted to take the matter into his own hands. The students remained and handed out several hundred copies of their report.[90]

Despite the efforts of Rahe and his conspirators, Perkins's speech was generally well received (though one table of rather inebriated guests periodically interrupted the speech with rude and disrespectful remarks).[91] The speech gave Perkins and the administration new hope. In an interview with the *Sun* on Friday, May 16 ("Perkins Says He Has Better Support Now"), he was aglow with optimism, saying he had received an "unbelievably sympathetic" response and that he had no intention of resigning: "I feel less negative pressure today than I did two or three weeks ago." Perkins also took the opportunity to criticize Bigart, admit he had asked the *Times* to remove Bigart from the story, and confirm that he had refused Bigart an interview on May 15. "I didn't think I could say anything to him because I wouldn't have any idea what he might do with it," he said.[92]

Perkins and Muller also began to attack their leading critics. Perkins alleged that Sindler, by resigning, had violated the terms of his sabbatical, which required teaching for a specified amount of time to repay the university for the leave.[93] Unfortunately, he had the facts wrong; Sindler had postponed part of his sabbatical so that he could work on the judicial system. Answering the president in a stinging letter to the *Sun,* Sindler stated, "It is most regrettable that Mr. Perkins now seeks to discredit and silence faculty who on principled grounds oppose him."[94]

In addition, Perkins began to circulate letters from supportive alumni to the chairs of departments and started telling the press that his only true opposition came from people such as Sindler. Strout read these statements to mean that Perkins thought he was "back in the saddle again. . . . I suddenly realized that he fully intended to come out on top."[95] Finally, in a wrap-up interview in the *Ithaca Journal,* Perkins advocated student participation to counter the privileges of academic freedom. Student power, he said, was being thwarted by "a variety of banners: academic freedom, faculty privilege, administrative privilege, proper distinction between teacher and student."[96] Strout and others interpreted these remarks to mean that Perkins considered academic freedom as nothing more than a privilege of "feudal barons." "I didn't get any sense from him [*laughter*] that he realized that there was something more at stake. He couldn't articulate it."[97]

New Moves against Perkins

Perkins's crusade to turn the tide gained steam at the same time that the professors' behind-the-scenes organizing against him was starting to bear fruit. One arena in which anti-Perkins forces were able to mount an attack was in testimony before a trustees committee set up at the emergency May 1 meeting to investigate the crisis. Trustee William R. Robertson led an eight-member panel that interviewed about sixty-five people from across the political and ideological spectrum. He was assisted by Jackson Hall, who was praised by individuals involved with the committee.[98] The sessions were usually intense, often passionate, and utterly draining. It "tore your heart out," Robertson said, to hear "these good people speaking out against the university, and most of them loved the place and they were doing it for the good of the university. It was tough. We'd go back to have dinner after a full day of that and we were just washed out. . . . But we had a fine committee. . . . We really had no conflict."[99]

The committee enabled the trustees to acquire the information they needed to make sense of the extraordinary situation. The committee report, issued on September 5, was surprisingly critical of the administration's handling of the crisis and Cornell, but by then its findings were moot, at least in terms of Perkins. It criticized the administration's handling of the development of the COSEP program, the lack of preparation for the crisis, the "lack of visibility of the leadership of the University" that played into student militants' hands, the threats to academic freedom, and the concessions made in the agreement with the AAS over the Straight (though it acknowledged that the deal may have saved lives). In addition, the report praised the judicial system established under Sindler's aegis, stressing the importance of individual responsibility. "[It] is not only sound, but represents a model of judiciary and student participation and should be continued."[100] Sindler considered the report a thorough vindication of the system and the stance he took.[101] Critics charged that the report unfairly downplayed black students' laments at Cornell.

Several of the professors who testified before the Robertson Committee, including Berns, Sindler, and Blumen, were enemies of the administration. In addition, several members of the Group of Forty-One made their last stand before the committee rather than taking their case directly to the trustees, as LaFeber, Fred Marcham, Kahin, Hildebrand, and others had done. The group had rallied in response to Perkins's claim that he had no enemies other than Sindler. By now most members felt Perkins had to go in order to "save Cornell," but they were unsure how to proceed. For some reason they believed they had no authority to take their case to the trustees (yet again a lack of decisiveness clinched a group's fate). Six of the Forty-One testified before the Robertson Committee, two of whom (Bethe and Black) were favorable to Perkins. As one more perplexing sign of their lack of resolve, like Perkins at the Monday convocation, they spoke about the fate of the university but never specifically mentioned the Straight takeover.

The Faculty Committee on Academic Freedom and Tenure had been sent letters and other information on the status of academic freedom. Such concerns had found their way to the trustees and the Robertson Committee, whose report stated that although traditional threats to academic freedom had come from outside the university, the recent threat "has been from within the Cornell community (faculty, student, and administration)."[102] On May 11 the faculty unanimously adopted a statement advocating broad academic freedom principles. The faculty balanced such freedom with the responsibility of a member of the learned profession to seek and respect the truth and to make it clear that one's own views were not those of the institution—points probably drawn from the American Association of University Professors' Statement on Academic Freedom.[103]

Three letters to the Faculty Committee on Academic Freedom and Tenure or to Perkins captured how many faculty felt. James A. Gross of Industrial and Labor Relations, who had developed a course on the history of black labor, wrote:

> I must say that I cannot teach that course now because, at this great University, I do not believe that I could objectively criticize Blacks without being called a racist and being intimidated—and if that happened, I know that I would not have the support of your administration.
>
> This abdication of authority and [the] failure to find a principle without which University life is not worth living . . . have resulted and will continue to result in violence, intimidation, and coercion. This University will not be destroyed by fire, it will be destroyed by fear, by hatred, by appeasement and by coercion. The University is no less prostituted because it satisfied the desires of the poor than the rich.[104]

Richard Hofferbert of Government talked about censoring his lectures:

> Many of us who teach subjects which do touch on the political, social, and economic questions of most relevance to blacks in American society were left feeling that we had no support—unless we adhered rigorously to the current party line. I am afraid of a few people who might disrupt my classes. I would be willing to face that if I thought I had the united moral and administrative support of my colleagues in the faculty and of our administration. . . . Under these circumstances, I have considered carefully what I say in class. *And I have edited my lectures. . . . Self-censorship is taking place at Cornell now.*[105]

And Arthur Rovine, an assistant professor of government, wrote a letter to the committee telling of the problems he had encountered. He alleged that he had found more true freedom of thought during his days as a dissenter on Wall Street than during his short stay at Cornell. "On the issue of apartheid I felt freer to speak and write as I wished on Wall Street than at Cornell University. There I could praise or attack, defend or criticize, and no one called me racist or red—the arguments were always on the merits. At Cornell, the arguments are sometimes on the merits, and that is a vital difference indeed."[106]

The Coup de Grâce

On May 28 Perkins presented a letter to the entire faculty in which he anticipated the challenge of the upcoming year and wished the faculty a good summer. "I look forward to seeing you in September," he said.[107] Perkins's words alarmed his foes on the faculty, and they intensified their efforts to undermine him. But that morning what Tobin called the "blockbuster" appeared on the front page of the *New York Times*. Bigart's article blew the first big hole in the president's armor.

Headlined "Cornell Bears Scars of Conflict: Faculty Is Divided over Perkins,"

Bigart told the full story from the side of the disenchanted faculty rebels. It chronicled the genesis of the crisis from the time of the McPhelin incident (Bigart discussed the McPhelin case at length, including the claim that the administration had essentially buried the Williams Commission's report) to the defections of faculty from the left and the right in the aftermath of the crisis. He wrote:

> Here at Cornell the battle lines are sharply drawn. A group of ten senior professors has started a campaign to remove the president, Dr. James A. Perkins. . . . The ten professors make up a small minority of the faculty, but it is regarded as unusual that a group of senior professors should publicly call for the ouster of their college president.
>
> At least a dozen other senior members of the faculty have announced their intention of leaving this hauntingly lovely campus for less scenic but calmer universities. Others in the 1,300-member faculty are job-hunting. Cornell is threatened by a wide erosion of faculty members, especially in the College of Arts and Sciences, where two departmental chairs are resigning.[108]

However much it ignored the other side of the story, Bigart's article exploded the administration's claims that Cornell was gaining strength from the crisis. A drain of senior faculty indeed appeared imminent—a problem from which no major university can quickly recover.

Another blow to Perkins came with the June edition of the *Cornell Alumni News*, which came out at the end of May. The narrative, pictures, and essays about the Straight crisis cast the administration in an unflattering light. Editor John Marcham, a Bigart-like figure in his own right, devoted the entire news section to the crisis, twenty-six pages in all. He and his staff thought hard about whether to publish the material but concluded that the publication's forty thousand readers deserved an objective accounting rather than a whitewash. The coverage included a statement from Steven Muller that presented the administration's position. He conceded that mistakes had been made but maintained that the administration had to act quickly under great pressure. His conclusion could not have contrasted more with Bigart's:

> Firmness surely is a virtue. It is not the only virtue. Blind firmness is no virtue at all. Reason is also a virtue. Prudence, particularly when devoted to the preservation of life, is a virtue. . . . It is not necessarily true that force is the best and only way to meet force. . . .
>
> Cornell unhappily is only one of scores of universities that have confronted force. In our recent movements of greatest trial, we in fact had no mass violence, no riots, and no serious bloodshed. We were nevertheless wounded, but our wounds are beginning to heal with a rapidity so astounding as to constitute the most welcome and blessed aspect of our situation.[109]

Marcham countered with a piece, "Blood-Free Campus Yes, but What Really Happened?" Though he paid heed to both sides, he raised many points that challenged Muller's conclusions:

Emotion, not reason, controlled much of what went on. Universities have tried to operate on reason, and this university fell apart when faced with unreason. In the cauldron of Cornell from Saturday to Tuesday night, a consensus of feeling but not reason was won by the blacks. A secondary feeling that supported nullification was fear. . . . The Wednesday vote, viewed elsewhere as total surrender, appeared to many present as more a vote of confidence in President Perkins to solve a problem than judgment on the merits of the nullification case.

Asserting that "very little of what went on during the week stands up under scrutiny as 'reasonable,'" Marcham discussed some of the more embarrassing facts of the crisis: that two key leaders of the revolt, Jones and Burak, were on Perkins's list as advisers; that the faculty allowed the judicial system to crash by not using it against the Malott Hall demonstrators; that white students had been "savagely attacked" on March 15 and 16; and that SDS knew about the takeover ahead of time. He concluded by declaring that revolutionary reform is "not a bad idea, if you know where you are going." [110]

Marcham received an unprecedented number of letters (three hundred to four hundred) from alumni in response to the edition. Of all the reactions received, only two were "adverse" in terms of being "all encompassingly condemning": from Muller and Perkins. Marcham was "rather amazed" that these were the only two entirely negative replies, though he did receive criticism from several trustees. [111] Normally Marcham would get the university's comments and input before sending the *News* out (the administration organ *Cornell Reports* often accompanied it), but this time all he did was show galleys to Tobin, for he knew he had to act without the administration's input. Tobin, who thought that the coverage was accurate, according to Fisher and Wallenstein, showed it to Muller and Perkins. In Marcham's words, Muller "felt it was a personal attack on him or badly distorted his role in the thing and he was in quite a tussle between him and Perkins through that time." Fisher and Wallenstein wrote, "Distraught, and deeply wounded, Muller pleaded with Marcham" to not publish it as it was written. [112] Marcham refused to budge but decided to let Muller write a response in the *News* as a gesture of fairness. The following Monday Marcham received a "very bitter" handwritten note from Perkins. "He thought it was a terrible job. He couldn't imagine I would do such a thing. He hoped I enjoyed the consequences. . . . [He wrote,] 'Dear Mr. Marcham' . . . [despite our] having been on a first-name basis for quite a number of years. . . ." [113]

In late May Perkins received yet another blow: a letter expressing a severe lack of confidence from fifteen faculty in the Law School, dated May 23. The letter— which did not call for Perkins's resignation but pleaded for radical change on his part—was written in reaction to Perkins's claim that a majority of professors backed him (and perhaps to other statements he made on that date, reported in the *Ithaca Journal* the following day). Ian MacNeil, the lead writer of the letter, stated that two concerns in addition to Perkins's statements motivated the group: academic freedom and the "destruction of law and order on campus" (more signers were concerned about the latter than the former, MacNeil said). [114]

As noted earlier, Perkins had always cultivated the support of prestigious senior faculty. (John Marcham and others considered this policy flawed, especially because some of these individuals did not enjoy as much respect from their colleagues as the president imagined. Others, including Rudolph Schlesinger of the Law School and LaFeber, certainly did command respect.) Perkins had made a special effort to solidify ties with the Law School, perhaps because he felt more comfortable around intellectuals who tend to be more practical and connected to power than other professors. He considered Schlesinger, who had a reputation for integrity and exquisite intelligence, one of his closest friends. But the Law faculty also tended to be more conservative than their Arts and Sciences colleagues, and they were deeply concerned about the threat to academic freedom (indeed, MacNeil served along with Penny on the Faculty Committee on Academic Freedom and Tenure). Schlesinger had fled Nazi Germany with his family in the late 1930s and experienced flashbacks of that ordeal during the Straight crisis. People who knew him described him as profoundly upset. (The anti-Semitism that broke out in June only added fuel to the fire, as we will see.) "This whole thing shattered him," MacNeil said.[115] Schlesinger's name was conspicuous at the end of the list of signatures. The signers pledged their support "of all progressive and reasonable reformation" at Cornell, "consistent with academic freedom and arrived at through free inquiry and peaceful discourse," although they announced, "We are not convinced that you have given the highest priority to the preservation of free inquiry." The signers, who asserted that none of them would be willing to teach at such a university, sent copies of the letter to the trustees and to major committees on campus.[116] This letter, in conjunction with the edition of the *Alumni News*, Bigart's "blockbuster," and the developments discussed earlier in the chapter, pushed Perkins to step down.

The Resignation

The Constituent Assembly, benefiting from a $50,000 grant from the Ford Foundation, was set to open officially with a highly publicized ceremony on Saturday, May 31, at Bailey Hall. Perkins had touted the opening as a watershed in American higher education. Several speakers were slated to address the assembly, including James A. Allen, U.S. commissioner of education, who was a good friend of Perkins's. But this day would be known for something less celebratory: Perkins's request that the trustees find a successor. Perkins spoke at the ceremony, although he had already given his resignation letter to Tobin, who was told to release it at 4:00 p.m.[117] The Law School letter had apparently delivered the coup de grâce. After meeting with James Turner, who still had not formally accepted the directorship of the Africana Studies Center, Perkins hoped to have lunch with Robertson and the committee.

The committee was involved in a tense and heated interview with Douglas Dowd, whom Robertson described as "a rather tough customer," when Jackson Hall, the committee secretary, motioned to Robertson to step outside the room. "I just got a call from President Perkins," Hall said. "He wants to have lunch with you fellows." Sensing that something unusual was about to happen, Roberts canceled the lunch he had planned with Douglas Williams, who was working on a poll of campus opinion about the crisis.

> At the end of this interview [with Dowd] . . . I hurried out . . . and went over across the hall, and there was Perkins. God, he was so nervous. . . . Perkins saw [Williams] and said, "I want him out of the room. I just want to talk to the trustees." Hall had to get out. . . . Then he said, "I've received word from a reliable source that I've lost the support of a good group of faculty, and this afternoon, at four o'clock, I'm announcing my resignation." And boy, that was tough. We were all pretty good friends of his; the board and president have a very close relationship with Cornell.[118]

Earlier that morning Perkins had informed Purcell and trustee Jansen Noyes of his decision. They were the only other ones to know about the resignation at this time, though Bigart would soon find out as well. The formal request would be presented to the trustees at their meeting the following Saturday and Sunday.

The next day Bigart's story about the resignation appeared on the front page of the *New York Times,* the assassin given the pleasure of writing his victim's obituary. The story reported Strout's statement that Perkins should resign, discussed the present situation at Cornell and the work of the Robertson Committee, and reviewed the genesis of the crisis.[119] According to Fisher and Wallenstein, Strout's comments in this article enraged many of the almost defunct Group of Forty-One, and the group dissolved for good.[120]

Perkins's statement to the Board of Trustees did not contain any form of the word *resign,* and some professors attempted to rally to his side. Nonetheless, the board proceeded as if the statement constituted a resignation. Purcell wrote a letter to Perkins accepting his resignation and a letter to Corson naming him interim president effective July 1.

Perkins's last major act at Cornell was his commencement address on June 9, in which he lashed out at his critics, especially faculty who represented what he disdained. He faulted black students for being too militant in conveying needed truths to the white community, although he directed most of his wrath at his white enemies, whom he once again portrayed as ivory-tower recluses. "Only a few among us, I am happy to say, recoil in pious horror from the ugly realities to which our intellectual work may often lead. Only a few seek to purge the university of contact with the real world and reenter the sterility of a dead scholasticism. . . . Discipline by force is always a last resort; the society that is driven to it is simply paying the very high final price for the failure of its members to capture each other's attention and therefore loyalty."[121] (On the same page next to Peter Kihss's story on the speech was the newspaper's "Quotation of the Day," from the National Commission on the Causes and Prevention of Violence: "Our colleges and universities cannot perform their vital functions in an atmosphere that exalts the struggle for power over the search for truth, the rule of passion over the rule of reason, physical confrontation over rational discourse.")

Perkins also warned America about the race problem he had striven to ameliorate. Of all the pressing problems the modern university must deal with, the most important "is the black American's demand for equality in fact as well as law." The next day he gave a lengthy interview to Kihss in which he elaborated on the themes of his address and discussed what led him to resign. The trustees had not pressured him, nor did alumni pressure compel him, he said; it was a faculty action—the letter from the fifteen law professors—that dealt the fatal blow. Finally, Perkins admitted a sad fact, given his commitment to racial justice: though many students had expressed concerns about maintaining COSEP, "I have not had a single black [undergraduate] student express regret" at his resignation.[122]

Disposition of the Criminal Cases

The district attorney charged seventeen AAS members with criminal trespass (a misdemeanor) in mid-May. Plea negotiations took place during the 1969–70 academic year, postponing the trial. Eventually the court dismissed charges against fourteen of the individuals, and in September 1970 three leaders, including Tom Jones, pleaded guilty to fourth-degree criminal trespass and received unconditional discharges, meaning the cases were ended and they did not receive jail time.[123]

CHAPTER FOURTEEN

CORNELL AND THE FAILURE

OF LIBERALISM

Dale Corson's ascension reassured most Cornellians. He had kept the coolest head during the crisis, and he was an institutional man who had spent almost all his time on the campus for the past twenty years. But the Straight crisis left indelible marks on Cornell for better and for worse. In this chapter we will look at some of the most salient effects.

The Hatchett Affair, Tom Jones's New Speech,
and Jones's Change of Heart

Within a year of the crisis, Tom Jones began to harbor second thoughts about what he and his colleagues had wrought. During the summer of 1969, however, he continued his attack on the university. Meanwhile, James Turner accepted the directorship of the black studies program on June 1. An issue that arose regarding Turner's acceptance concerned the hiring of John F. Hatchett as an instructor in the program, as Turner and many in the BLF wanted.[1] Hatchett (who was being considered along with J. Congress Mbata, who would become an institution at the center) had been a director of New York University's Afro-American Center, a graduate student in the Ph.D. program at Columbia, and a teacher in the New York City public schools, playing a major role in the teachers union disputes of the 1960s that pitted blacks against Jews. At first Hatchett's credentials impressed those involved in the hiring decision, but soon questions emerged when word reached them that Hatchett had sparked racial controversy at Columbia and NYU. Keith Kennedy contacted individuals at these institutions and discovered that Hatchett had been fired from his position at NYU for publicly calling President Nixon and others "racist bastards," had been fired from the school system for making anti-Semitic statements during the school conflicts, and had been dropped from the graduate program at Columbia for poor performance (something not mentioned on either his curriculum vitae or his application). Hatchett, Turner, and Hatchett's defenders raised legitimate concerns about his academic freedom.[2] But Hatchett had failed at Columbia, and he embodied many professors' worst stereotype of the unqualified ideologue who would anchor the program.

The university declined to hire Hatchett. Turner reluctantly conceded and then himself accepted the directorship of the center. But the Hatchett affair incited another famous (at least at Cornell) speech by Tom Jones at the Straight. The lengthy speech was memorable because it presented Jones's and the BLF's interpretation of the events of the last year and because it represented a new threat to the university. Jones explained why the BLF would not participate in the reconsideration of the judicial system and the Constituent Assembly and then launched into what some construed to be an anti–Semitic attack. Those inclined to paranoia interpreted a part of his speech to be a veiled threat of arson in the coming year if the BLF's demands were not met (he did not explicitly make such a threat, but his remarks were open to this interpretation). The speech was broadcast on the radio and disseminated across the campus.

> You know, I think all of you realize that it would have been simple enough to begin . . . with real terrorist activities. I'm sure you all read about the Res Club fire last year—do you realize how simple it is to do something like that? Do you realize how dinky the Ithaca Fire Department is? But we didn't do that. . . . We moved to seize a building. . . .
>
> I'm sure you've all heard of Walter Berns about to resign, and Allan Sindler about to resign. Yeah, I'm going to be brutal with you now. Allan Sindler wants to resign, right? Over the issue of academic freedom. Allan Sindler is Jewish. We wanted to hire John Hatchett to teach in our Black Studies Program starting next year; John Hatchett's field is African Studies. . . . Supposedly he's anti-Semitic. Which has nothing to do with his academic expertise and competence to teach African history and African culture. . . . Some of the Jewish faculty members, like Allan Sindler, got on the phone, called over to the Administration, told them over there that if John Hatchett was hired, they were resigning. So what [did] the administration do? . . . They dropped the man. . . . John Hatchett's going to be the issue in the fall. . . .[3]

That summer Jones received one of the highest student salaries to serve on a committee in the Constituent Assembly, and he remained at Cornell to earn a master's degree in city and regional planning. After receiving his degree, he moved with his family to Boston, where he took a job with the accounting firm Arthur Young, leaving behind not only Ithaca and Cornell but also his radical past. Soon he began to regret his and his colleagues' deeds. From his new vantage point the administration had been sufficiently responsive to the AAS, and all the militancy had been unnecessary. As time passed, Jones's business career began to blossom. In 1980 he wrote a letter of apology to James Perkins, having spoken with him a short time before:

The circumstances of our having had this opportunity to talk are such that you may, understandably, question the sincerity of my regret for the events of April 1969. I have thought of you many times, and I have been pained and shamed that a friend of Afro-Americans paid the highest price for that confrontation. . . . I give you an apology for not having stood with you against the tide of emotionalism and racial fear, and for using my talents to mobilize forces which intimidated the faculty and, in turn, led the faculty to vent their anger and resentment upon you. . . .

I am confident that you are yet going to be extremely proud of me. . . . I believe that I can make an important contribution to America during this ten to fifteen year period we are now entering—a period which may be decisive in the ultimate history of America's interracial relations.[4]

Perkins wrote a short yet characteristically generous response:

Let me say immediately that your letter to me met my real expectations for you. Your basic intelligence and sense of fairness come through in full measure. Thank you for saying what you did and the way in which you said it.

I suspected at the time that someday I would be proud of you and satisfied that the tough decision to admit the greatly increased number of blacks into American higher education was a social priority of the highest importance.[5]

In 1995 Jones donated $100,000 to Cornell to sponsor a student prize—the James A. Perkins Prize for Interracial Understanding and Harmony; Perkins returned to Cornell to shake Jones's hand at the ceremony commemorating the donation. Somewhat earlier Jones had been named to the Cornell Board of Trustees, by which time he had ascended to the presidency of TIAA-CREF, the retirement fund for teachers that is the largest mutual fund in the world. (Established by the Carnegie Foundation, TIAA-CREF happened to be an area of expertise for Perkins when he worked at the foundation before coming to Cornell. Upon hearing of Jones's position at TIAA-CREF, Walter Berns, who had been threatened by Jones that fateful Tuesday evening, quipped, "First he threatens my life, now he is in control of what happens after I die!")

In 1997 Jones left TIAA-CREF to assume the leadership of the Smith Barney Asset Management division of Traveler's Group, at a salary of $2 million a year. According to the *Wall Street Journal*, he was now among the most influential African Americans on Wall Street.[6] On November 21, 1997, the *WSJ* featured a lengthy front-page piece by Jonathan Kaufman and Anita Raghavan that contrasted Jones's views on racial advance with those of his brother, Ed. Tom endorsed individual initiative and optimism, as opposed to relying on claims of racism. He had decided it was time to "transcend race" and "tribal politics." The reporters wrote that upon leaving Cornell, Jones quickly "shed signs of his radical past. While many other black professionals in Boston were sporting Afro hairstyles and dashikis, Tom wore suits and ties. He rarely talked about the events at Cornell."[7]

A week or two after the Straight crisis Berns ran into Jones outside of Sibley Hall. "I hope you know I didn't mean it," Jones said, referring to the threats he made in his infamous speech. Berns pointed his finger at Jones and said, "Bang, bang!" to which Jones replied, "You are the professor who taught me that power ultimately stemmed from the gun."[8]

Around the time he was named a trustee, Jones wrote to Berns, apologizing for threatening his life and for betraying his trust. Jones had taken Berns's course on constitutional law and had engaged in numerous blunt discussions with the provocative professor, and Berns took the relationship seriously. Cut from cloth that differed from Perkins's, Berns left Jones's overture unanswered. Later, after Cornell announced the establishment of the Perkins Prize, syndicated columnist Clarence Page wrote an article about Jones's gift and his rise in life, praising Jones and defending what happened at Cornell as a social breakthrough.[9] Distraught, Berns sent Page a long letter in which he chronicled a litany of Jones's and the AAS's sins. "I thought of Jones as *my* student; we talked frequently, and not only about his course work," wrote Berns, who added that he had talked him into staying in school in the fall of 1968, when Jones, like others in the AAS, was considering leaving to work in the ghetto. "I asked him why he had changed his mind, [and] he said I had persuaded him. A couple of months later he threatened to kill me. I can never forgive him for that."[10]

The Arts College Meeting and Max Black's Rejection

In July the Arts College held a special meeting to respond to Jones's alarming speech the month before at the Straight and, belatedly, to threats made during the crisis. Max Black used the occasion to take a better-late-than-never stand, offering a resolution condemning Jones:

> Toward the end of the last semester, threats were publicly made and broadcast on the Cornell campus against designated members of the faculty and administration. Recently, these threats have been cited by the same individual, without apology or retraction, in a public speech given and broadcast on campus.
>
> We wish to express our abhorrence and moral outrage at such utterances. We condemn the use by anyone of ethnic, racial, or religious slurs. We condemn any resort, by words or deeds, to threats against individuals or groups.[11]

The majority rejected Black's resolution, and angry colleagues asked why Black had decided to take the stand now, rather than when it would have mattered. According to Peter Sharfman, the meeting amounted to a ritual of post hoc justification for faculty who felt bad about the stands they had taken (or not taken) in April.[12]

The Pearl Lucas Affair and the Problem of Black Dissenters

Over the summer and the following year a split developed between Pearl Lucas, a black assistant dean of Arts and Sciences, and individuals associated with the BLF, including Gloria Joseph and BLF leaders. The rift reflected tensions between militants, on one side, and black students and advisers who were reluctant to side with the BLF, on the other—a split that reflected the national conflict between integrationist and separatist ideologies. Lucas worked closely with the white deans of the college, in particular Dana Payne and Barbara Hirshfeld. An advocate of integration—Payne and Hirshfeld described her as a "militant moderate"—she strove to integrate black studies as much as possible with other programs and advisers on campus. In her Oral History interview Lucas painted a picture of diversity in Cornell's black student community that contrasted with the solidarity the AAS sought to foster (see Chapter Three).

Over the summer Lucas decided to pass out to COSEP students a *New York Times* article that was critical of the politicization of black studies programs. The writer argued that such programs did not prepare the students to deal with life, thereby contradicting the goal of advancement to which such programs allegedly aspired. Like David Brion Davis, Sindler, and others, Lucas favored Yale's program, which she considered a more appropriate balance between liberal arts and black consciousness. Lucas used the article to supplement the COSEP reading list, which was overwhelmingly militant. Her act angered Turner, Joseph, and some members of the administration, and Turner wrote a memorandum criticizing Lucas. "It turned out that quite a lot of people in the administration thought that it was very wrong for her to pass out an article that was contrary to University policy. . . . It was a criticism of black studies."[13] Over time the tensions among Lucas and more pro-BLF administrators intensified.

The Africana Studies Center, Ujamaa, and Racial Pedagogy at Cornell

The Africana Studies Center opened its doors the following fall. In its first semester it offered ten courses, in black consciousness, black resistance, and other subjects. Of 250 students who applied, 160 were accepted. Only two white students applied, and both were rejected, but eventually the center would admit more white students and would draw on major scholars in the field. Soon it would offer a major and a master of arts degree.

For Irving McPhail—who, with Andre McLaughlin and others, never harbored the second thoughts that beset Jones—the center presented intellectual challenges and experiences that changed his life. He loved working with Gloria Joseph, who taught courses in the center, and learned from other instructors and from the social engagement the center fostered.

> By the time we survived to my senior year, a lot of good things were happening there. The program had Turner, we had a black presence in the faculty, we had courses on the African and African-American experience. I partook fully of all of that.
>
> The other thing I will point out is that I created and directed the Ithaca Black

Community Tutorial Project. It was my major lasting legacy to the Cornell days. Cornell United Religious Workers, the Berrigan brothers, became our sponsors. And by the time I graduated in 1970, we had well over fifty African Americans from Cornell tutoring young kids and adolescents in Ithaca. . . .

My activism at Cornell, again, was more than the struggle for black studies and the struggle for respect and legitimacy. For me it represented a kind of total academic and intellectual transformation that really sent me in a totally new direction that has propelled my academic career since that time.[14]

Despite these noteworthy gains, some observers alleged that the center would have been stronger had it been less separatist and political and more like the programs at Yale and later Harvard. That Africana would seek someone like Hatchett suggested that political pedigree competed with intellectual seriousness at the center, as did the important role that undergraduate students had in formulating the policies on which the center was based.

Even in 1996 Turner emphasized that although the center was open to a variety of perspectives on race, certain ones were still taboo. When I asked him whether the viewpoints of such black conservatives as Clarence Thomas or Thomas Sowell would be welcome in the center, he said they would not.[15]

Turner brought energy, skill, and motivation to the center, but it remained outside Cornell's mainstream. Professors from other fields on campus told me that the center made few overtures to them or to visiting professors in their fields, even though they were working on questions that should have been of interest to the center and encouraged contacts. One professor who was well known in his area of research told me that the center "is still quite a separate organization; it is not integrated into the rest of the university." He mentioned the case of the center showing a surprising lack of interest in a prominent scholar his department sought for a joint appointment.[16] Turner defended the center by emphasizing the importance of autonomy and deepening the inquiry into racial and ethnic consciousness.[17]

Two major controversies arose in the years following the Straight crisis: race-based residential study programs and COSEP's alleged steering of students in the direction of these or related programs. Isadore Blumen said that numerous parents in the early '70s complained to the Executive Committee of the Faculty (which Blumen chaired) that COSEP and students associated with it were pressuring their children to enter race-based programs. (In a memo the new provost said eight of sixteen COSEP members were to be "decided by Turner and the black students.")[18] COSEP issued a handbook that some observers interpreted as an assertion of control over COSEP students. "Students would be brought together and kept together and told what to do while together . . . for their political and economic advancement," Blumen said. After controversy erupted, the administration revised the handbook.[19] Though there were different interpretations of the matter, the evidence reveals politicization of the program.

In addition, in 1970 Cornell authorized the establishment of Ujamaa, a residential study program based on African-American identity. According to a statement about the meaning of Ujamaa when it opened in fall 1972, Ujamaa is a "concept that has its roots in traditional African society, roughly meaning 'familyhood and community, cooperation, and participation.' The concept of Ujamaa expresses ideals of equality, i.e., equal distribution of resources and equal distributions of responsibility— everybody works."[20] Eventually Ujamaa would have over one hundred residents, mostly first- and second-year students. At the time of Ujamaa's inception, Cornell had two other residential programs based on common academic interests, Ecology House and Risley House, but these programs were not based on identity politics or race.

Ujamaa sparked controversy from the start, for some administrators doubted the wisdom of further entrenching separation of the races.[21] In addition, Ujamaa posed legal problems, as state, federal, and constitutional law prohibited excluding individuals on the basis of race. In 1976 the Regents of the State of New York issued a formal complaint against Cornell for violating Section 19.4 of the Rules of the Regents, which prohibited racial discrimination in the state colleges. The "Complaint and Notice of Hearing" and the accompanying "Bill of Particulars" accused Cornell of delegating admissions decisions to administrative staff and students who excluded whites. A background paper from the state education commissioner (based on claims of the New York regional director of the Office of Civil Rights of the Department of Health, Education, and Welfare) concluded that "Cornell's policies and practices do not comply with Title VI Regulation in certain major areas . . . among other things, that 'the initial invitation for applications to Ujamaa was directed only to students enrolled in the COSEP Program, thereby establishing the residence as a residence for black students.'"[22]

Corson and the university strongly contested the commissioner's use of statistics and his interpretation of the evidence, but the state claimed that from 1972 through 1976, no white student had resided at Ujamaa (out of 107 slots per year). After much legal maneuvering the regents and the university settled, with Cornell pledging to make efforts to bring in more whites. But the settlement dissatisfied many individuals on both sides of the issue.[23]

The debate over race or ethnicity-based residential programs is still alive at Cornell. Today Cornell has ten "program houses" that serve as residential colleges based on certain themes: ecology, music, foreign languages and other specialties, American Indian, Latino, and African-American. About one thousand students, or 7.6 percent of Cornell's enrollment, live in such dorms, and only about 10 percent of undergraduate minority students live in them (the lack of an Asian residence program probably skews these figures somewhat, as Cornell has a substantial enrollment of Asian students).[24] The race-based houses have recently survived two legal challenges brought by Michael Meyers (a self-described "militant integrationist"), executive director of the New York Civil Rights Coalition. In spring 1995 the state cleared Cornell of new charges of racial discrimination in the theme houses based on claims similar to those of the 1970s; the state investigators expressed doubts about the "desirability" of the programs but concluded that they were legal because they did not exclude students based on race. In September 1996 the university survived Meyers's suit, brought by the Office for Civil Rights of the U.S. Department of Education. Meyers castigated the decision, saying it was "politically correct" and accusing Cornell of "capitulation to racism." Professor Jane Mt. Pleasant, director of the American Indian Program, by contrast, "credits the Indian House with keeping the Indian graduation rate at 80 percent, as compared with 10 to 30 percent at other schools." She and Professor Thomas Hirschl (who lives in Latino House) contend that the houses provide resistance to the homogenizing influences of a large noncommunitarian campus and promote cohesion, greater interaction with faculty and upperclassmen, and higher levels of intellectual and moral seriousness.[25]

The houses also survived a challenge by Cornell's new president, Hunter R. Rawlings. In April 1996 Rawlings proposed prohibiting freshmen from living in program houses. "New students arriving at Cornell should have an experience that demonstrates that they are entering an academic community, first and foremost," Rawlings said. Opposition erupted immediately as supporters of the houses contended that the policy was an attempt to phase out the houses altogether (roughly half of all program house residents are freshmen). In May students went on hunger strikes and tied up afternoon rush hour traffic by obstructing crosswalks. Rawlings had to put the plan on hold. This student action had precedents. In 1992 student resistance forced Cornell to withdraw plans to achieve diversity in residence halls by assigning freshmen randomly; and in 1993 Latino House was established after seventy-five students occupied Day Hall. According to a *New York Times* report, "At the heart of the debate is whether the ethnic program houses heighten separatism and further divided Cornell or make the large, predominantly white campus friendlier for many minority students. About 70 percent of Cornell undergraduates are white."[26]

The effects of such policies are an open question. On the one hand, such policies do, as just noted, give students a kind of "safe ethnic harbor" in an otherwise often intimidating university setting. The programs associated with the dorms and identity politics can deepen understanding of one's ethnic identity, and this can serve as a bridge to opening the mind to knowledge in the broader sense. In this ideal case, the pedagogy of identity is a means to the broader end of liberal education. On the other hand, such policies can undermine these goals by encouraging balkanization rather than the opening of the mind.[27] Cornell law graduate Paul A. Batista related an illuminating experience in a letter to the *Wall Street Journal.* Batista had just enrolled at the Law School in 1971 after serving in the army and had sought out a quiet place to study (away from the noisy student housing) while his son took his afternoon nap. He had found "a common room" in "a classic Cornell building," only to be confronted by three undergraduates who told him that he had to leave because the building was Ujamaa and whites were not welcome. He felt aggrieved because of the brotherhood he had felt with black soldiers in Vietnam: "We ate together, trained together and lived together. . . . When I was asked to leave Ujamaa in September 1971, just weeks after having shared with black soldiers all the insanity and inspiration of Army life during wartime, I felt that the Ivy League undergraduates who confronted me that night were sincere but wrong, and that the university policy that created Ujamaa was fundamentally at fault." [28]

Most relevant to the issues at the heart of this book, such policies can exacerbate tensions and lead to a decline of university and constitutional citizenship, at least if they are not accompanied by a strong institutional commitment to liberal principles of education and law. An example occurred in spring 1997 when two hundred students reacted angrily to a *Cornell Review* article that parodied Ebonics in a very unflattering way. The students held a protest that included burning about two hundred copies of the *Review*, blocking traffic at the main exits to the university from 4:30 until 9:00 p.m., and taunting Tom Jones, who had given the *Review* an interview, as a racial traitor as he emerged from the Johnson Museum of Art after having presented the Perkins Prize for Interracial Understanding and Harmony. One graduate student told the press that "Black and Latino students who are not here with us are enemies of our people." A former president (and present board member) of the *Review* who at the time was a reporter for the *Syracuse Post-Standard* attempted to speak to the protesters, but she was physically prevented from speaking, and protesters threw burning newspapers at her face.

In response Rawlings issued a statement condemning the lack of civility on all sides, although he failed to condemn the burning of newspapers and directed most of his wrath at the *Review*, a conservative paper that frequently published unwelcome and offensive articles (its board, however, was as ethnically diverse as any student group on campus). Nationally syndicated columnist Nat Hentoff pointed out what appeared to be a hidden cost of the university's condemnation of the *Review* on behalf of ethnic protectionism: "Cornell—rather than attending [to students'] capacities for intellectual independence and due process—is indulging [students] in its belief that they are not up to the challenges of being citizens of the university. The administration proudly considers itself racially enlightened, but would it have treated white students—committing arson and blocking the streets—the same way? These abandoned students ought to get a tuition refund because they have received a diminished, patronizing education at Cornell." [29] Hentoff's words were distant echoes of 1969.

Conclusion

The confrontation with history at Cornell '69 brought forth the best and the worst in individuals across the board. Heroism and decency coexisted in the same breasts with cowardice, thuggery, and the inability to forgive. Ethical neatness is not to be expected when such dividing lines are crossed. Caleb Rossiter proclaimed that the AAS stand was the product of centuries of pent-up anger. "In the late 1960s, in the safety of college campuses, black Americans were able to, and so had to, vent the anger that they, their parents, and the many generations enslaved or endangered that preceded them had, on pain of death, been barred from showing. . . . More than anything else, Cornell's Crisis was a drama of liberation in which black men dared acknowledge that feeling."[30] Andre McLaughlin added to this logic by stressing how significant social change, especially on the part of minorities, sometimes has to break through barriers supported by conventional norms:

> There really are no blueprints for social change, in terms of real social movements. And what works for one may not work for another. We could take lessons from history. All of us feel that, probably on both sides of the issue, . . . we were doing the right thing. The academic felt that he was protecting the integrity of the curriculum and principles of academic freedom. And the black student population, we felt that we were part of an important part of the struggle for human rights. A very important part of that struggle. And so what happens with change is, because there are no blueprints and you can't foresee outcomes, there's confusion, there's panic, and things happen because of that.[31]

There was another side, to which Sindler gave voice in 1971. He predicted that Cornell '69 "comprised a watershed event because of the introduction of firearms" and because it represented "the malaise of higher education, the declining self-confidence of academic men, the shattered consensus on academic values and the relation of the university to society, the bias of faculty in favor of the political Left, the conversion of white racial guilt and empathy to blacks to a quite different posture of abdicating judgment."[32]

The Cornell crisis and its aftermath raise a fundamental question: Can racial understanding and sensitivity exist without forsaking the intellectual freedom that is necessary to both the pursuit of truth and constitutional citizenship? The experience at Cornell reminds us of the teachings of the civil rights movement: that freedom, the commitment to truth beyond politics, and justice go hand in hand. When freedom and justice claims pry themselves too far from respect for truth and the right of others to disagree, drives for power are loosened from their moorings in morality. It is precisely here that the university, dedicated to the principles of liberal education, offers hope for a society that stands in need of honest discussion. As Ellis Cose said in a recent book on race relations, "Something tragic is in the offing unless Americans learn to connect with one another and talk about race in an intelligent way."[33] Such discussion cannot occur if groups can veto or restrict what is said about them in the name of the politics of identity or recognition or any other worthy end, for such moves represent concessions to power or empowerment rather than to the process of discovering or debating the truth. Such pedagogy thwarts understanding by making controversial (and therefore often innovative) thought taboo and by undermining the assumptions of ultimately common reason and common ground on which discussion and moral appeal can take place.

Censorship in the name of the self-esteem of individuals and groups throttles the drive for justice in three fundamental ways. First, it limits our intellectual options. Second, it reinforces cynical complacency by freeing us from the strenuous task of reasoning together in the presence of our differences, which is the very basis of democratic politics.[34] Freed from having to engage in the give-and-take of democratic politics, we retreat behind the shibboleths of our respective camps, growing intellectually lazy. "Identity politics makes life easier for everyone," Tamar Jacoby writes. "Black students live in black dorms—and life goes on as usual on campus."[35] Third, this process undermines the intellectual rigors that are essential to sustained equal constitutional citizenship. Hannah Arendt once taught that the Enlightenment had the relationship between equality and citizenship backwards: rather than equality being the basis of citizenship (as the Enlightenment taught), it is citizenship that bestows the right of equality.[36] And citizenship entails accepting provisionally the common standards of legal obligation that balance rights with such responsibilities as respecting the rights of others and the integrity of the democratic-constitutional process. Liberal education is one important means to this end, as its best practice develops individuals who think for themselves with broad yet critical minds.

From this perspective the Perkins administration got the racial issue half-right. Opening Cornell's doors to new black students was a historical imperative, and Perkins deserves credit for being a pioneer in this domain. Yet the administration was betrayed by its own loss of faith in (or inability to defend) such cardinal principles of liberal education as intellectual freedom, the commitment to truth above all other endeavors, and common standards of reason and law. Failing to uphold basic principles of the rule of law was both patronizing and counterproductive, to say nothing of what it meant for those (especially minority students) who dissented from the militant agenda. Given the tensions of the time, perhaps no one could have fared any better; criticism is easy for those who have not had to make responsible decisions in the face of such pressure.[37] But the stunning collapse of liberal principles at Cornell was paradigmatic for its time and ours.

In the name of morality, Cornell forgot the subtle yet inescapable connection between morality and the commitment to the open-minded pursuit of truth that is the university's distinctive obligation. As Jonathan Rauch argues in *Kindly Inquisitors,* governments and universities have special obligations to protect freedom of speech and inquiry—"governments, because their monopoly on force gives them enormous repressive powers, and universities, because their moral charter is first and foremost to advance human knowledge by practicing and teaching criticism. If governments stifle criticism, then they impoverish and oppress their citizenry; if universities do so, then they have no reason to exist."[38]

The dragons of racial hatred and the fear of challenging ideas have proved hard to slay in everyone's breast, regardless of race. After all the historical congratulations have ended, we remain beset by parochialism, racism, racial polarization, and, above all, by mutual misunderstanding. Too often must we suffer the smallness of angry minds, such as those on both sides of the divide who crossed swords at Cornell in April 1997 in the dispute over Tom Jones and the *Cornell Review.* To move forward, the fostering of equal respect based on intellectual and moral integrity is imperative. But progress is stillborn, killed by a lack of faith in our ability to find common ground within our profound differences. Universities can help only by nourishing what is best within our intellectual consciences, that which seeks to understand the true nature of the world and our embattled lives. David I. Grossvogel, one of the most acute commentators on the Cornell crisis in its immediate aftermath, fathomed how a black studies program based on empowering the minds of all Cornell students rather than the claims of some could have revitalized the university and, therefore, the multiracial society it putatively serves:

> The infusion of a new force—the black—might once have represented rebirth . . . in the kind of stored-up agony out of which awareness of self and others starts. An understanding of black culture, black history, the suffering and the songs born of them, the insights, would have swelled measurably the ever under-nourished humanities that grope as painfully as a late summer stream across the parched lands of the practical university. The black would have been a gainer—but only to the extent that the university would have gained, through the assertion of its most legitimate and most difficult quest: the investigation of the human quandary.[39]

The Cornell story beckons us not to abandon recognition and identity but to pay much greater heed to the liberal and constitutional principles that began their descent in the university at Cornell. It shows the dangers of ignoring racism and racial claims and of severing the quest for racial justice from the moorings of liberal education and freedom. The races must listen to one another, but this cannot and should not happen in the presence of balkanization and intolerance of dissent, as such conditions allow victory only to those with situational power as opposed to those who would persuade.

Two key lessons emerge from Cornell in this regard: (1) the principles of liberal education need strong, publicly proclaimed support from campus leaders who actually hold such principles dear, and (2) professors, administrators, and students must have the courage to speak out against the forces that would compromise these principles in the name of whatever moral vision holds sway. But such voices must do so in racial good faith, lest their preachings be exposed as insincere and therefore unworthy and unable to provoke meaningful change. Liberalism must maintain its racial conscience, but it must also regain confidence in its commitment to individual freedom if the drive for social justice is to recapture the moral authority of the constitutional order. If liberalism remains silent through guilt, embarrassment, or simple historical exhaustion, we are lost. The university can lead us out of our respective caves only by being true to itself.

CHRONOLOGY

1963

James A. Perkins becomes president of Cornell and begins instituting the Committee on Special Education Projects (COSEP), which will bring more minority students to Cornell.

1965

May: Students and the Ad Hoc Committee to End the War disrupt a speech by Averell Harriman, U.S. ambassador to South Vietnam. The act is the first major threat to intellectual freedom on the Cornell campus since the McCarthy era. Several days later the Ad Hoc Committee disrupts a Reserve Officer Training Corps (ROTC) review at Barton Hall.
Summer: Joe and Pat Griffith establish Glad Day Press.

1966

The Afro-American Society (AAS) is founded by students to respond to the needs of new COSEP recruits.
October: Phi Delta Theta is charged with discriminating against blacks at a dance held at the fraternity house. The fraternity is eventually placed on one year's probation. The case highlights the racial tensions afflicting social life at Cornell.
December 14: Bruce Dancis, a Cornell undergraduate, is the first SDS member in the nation to destroy his draft card to protest the Vietnam War. His act galvanizes resistance to the war throughout the country.

1967

January: Ithaca authorities attempt to arrest students outside Willard Straight Hall for selling an allegedly obscene student magazine, the *Trojan Horse* (a court later found the magazine not obscene). Student power, with the support of some key faculty, beats back conservative authority. The case leaves Cornell administrators reluctant to have outside authorities deal with student unlawfulness on campus.

March: The Spring Mobilization to End the War organizes a national movement to obtain pledges to destroy draft cards, sparking controversy between the Scheduling, Coordination, and Activities Review Board (SCARB) and student activists.

May: A commission to review university policy concerning student conduct is established. Allan Sindler becomes its chair.

October: The Sindler Commission issues its report, recommending major changes in the policies and procedures governing student conduct. The commission's policies are based on the liberal principles of freedom and responsibility, and its procedures enhance student input and power. After extensive debate and some modifications, the Faculty Council recommends adoption of new student conduct procedures in February 1968. A new adjudicative system is approved by the full faculty in May 1968.

October–November: Faculty vote for a resolution opposing a directive of General Lewis B. Hershey in which Hershey announced that local draft boards may revoke the student deferment status of students who allegedly interfere with the draft or military recruitment.

December: Anti-ROTC demonstrators are cited for sitting in at Barton Hall. The Faculty Committee on Student Conduct (FCSC) imposes penalties after the Undergraduate Judicial Board (UJB) decides to issue no sanctions, precipitating a crisis of legitimacy for the judicial system.

1968

March–May: Efforts to develop a black studies program intensify. A struggle emerges between those in favor of a program more consistent with traditional notions of liberal education and those in favor of a more militant program.

March 19–April 4: Black students take over the Economics Department, protesting alleged institutional racism in a lecture course on economic development taught by Father Michael McPhelin, a visiting lecturer from the Philippines. The McPhelin incident inaugurates the politics and pedagogy of racial confrontation at Cornell.

April 4: Martin Luther King Jr. is assassinated in Memphis just hours after resolution of the Economics Department takeover at Cornell. King's death sounds the death knell for the politics and pedagogy of integration at Cornell.

April 5: Separatist politics emerge at a memorial for King. Fires break out at several local establishments, including the Cornell chapel.

April 6–8: Many meetings of administrators, faculty, and students are held to discuss the McPhelin incident. Rather than relying on established procedures for complaints against a professor, the administration decides to form a special commission chaired by Professor Robin Williams to look into the affair and to make recommendations.

April 18–25: The Williams Commission holds hearings, conducting interviews with various individuals involved with the McPhelin incident and the takeover of the Economics Department.

April 22: The Cornell chapter of the American Association of University Professors (AAUP) charges that the administration ignored normal procedures protecting academic freedom in the handling of the McPhelin case.

April 26: The Williams Commission issues its report on the McPhelin affair, concluding that the professor's academic freedom and students' right to proper consideration of their claims had not been honored. The report is largely ignored by authorities; Dean Stuart Brown's letter to faculty on institutional racism is given more credence.

September 5: President Perkins sets up a new committee to create a black studies program based on the model of a black graduate student, Paul Du Bois. Chaired by Chandler Morse, the Advisory Committee has a balance of faculty and black students representing a variety of views.

September–October: Factional strife breaks out in the AAS over the nature and politicization of the black studies program. The AAS grows more and more confrontational, especially as the Advisory Committee fails to achieve clear progress.

Fall: The Student Executive Board dissolves, ending a meaningful structure of student government at Cornell.

November 13–17: Several members of the AAS attend a conference, "Toward the Black University," at Howard University. Students conclude that only a separate college will meet their needs. They meet James Turner of Northwestern University and decide he should be the director of the new black studies program.

December 6–7: Forty AAS members confront Morse, declare that the old Advisory Committee is now defunct, and form a new committee consisting of themselves. The next day the students evict personnel from 320 Wait Avenue, the building the administration had slated to be the home of the new black studies program the following fall.

December 10: The AAS meets with Morse and Provost Dale Corson and issues an ultimatum for an autonomous black college along with related demands, such as hiring a black psychiatrist and exclusive use of the Elmhirst Dining Room in the Straight.

December 12: Black students hold demonstrations with toy guns and overturn vending machines.

December 13: The AAS holds more demonstrations for an autonomous black studies program. AAS members sit in at Perkins's office, dance on tables in the main dining room of the Straight, remove hundreds of books from shelves at libraries and dump them at circulation desks, and run through the medical clinic. The conduct boards will cite students for improper conduct for the Deceember 12 actions.

New members of the reconstituted Faculty Committee on Student Affairs (FCSA) meets for first time, unaware of the AAS demonstrations.

December 17: A showdown occurs between Perkins and the AAS (led by John Garner) in Perkins's office after several days of maneuvering on both sides and excruciating pressure. Provost Dale Corson later describes this period as the most dangerous time of all that academic year, more dangerous than the takeover of the Straight the following April. Perkins manages to convince the AAS that a totally independent college is not possible. A blowup is averted for the time being.

At same time, the University Student Conduct Conference (USCC) meets to discuss what should be done about the AAS disruptions a few days earlier.

December 21: Perkins asks Vice Provost Keith Kennedy to head a revamped administration committee on black studies. The AAS later agrees to deal with Kennedy as the administration's chief spokesperson.

1969

January: The Garner faction in the AAS loses support due to the results of the December actions. The AAS elects Edward Whitfield its new president, hoping to unite the organization behind a less confrontational posture. The AAS and Turner begin a series of intense negotiations with Kennedy and the administration over the nature of the black studies program.

January 20: AAS students take cushions from Donlon Hall to the Wait Avenue building. The cushions are eventually returned.

January 31: After deliberations by the dean of students' office and the USCC, Code Administrator Harry Kisker orders five AAS students to appear before the student conduct board on February 13 for adjudication of their citations for the December disruptions and the taking of the cushions on January 20.

February 13: The AAS students fail to appear before the conduct board; the board rolls the cases over to its next meeting on February 27.

February 27: The cited students again fail to appear before the conduct board.

February 28: At the start of a symposium on South Africa at the Statler Auditorium, Perkins is grabbed and shaken by the collar by AAS militants Larry Dickson and Gary Patton. The AAS kicks Dickson and Patton out of the organization.

March 3: The UJB issues a report affirming the principles of the judicial system and stating its rationale for adjudicating the cases against the AAS students.

March 4: The cited students are ordered to appear at a hearing on March 13 or face suspension proceedings.

March 10: White students disrupt recruiters for the Chase Manhattan Bank at Mallott Hall to protest the bank's dealings with South Africa. A special committee established by the administration declines to charge the students involved. The AAS interprets this decision as racial favoritism toward whites.

March 12: At an emergency faculty meeting, Corson calls for faculty support in the face of a breakdown of order. The faculty vote 306–229 to support the judicial board's citations of the five AAS members.

March 13: One hundred–fifty students appear before the conduct board in place of the cited students to protest the legitimacy of the judicial system. The board holds

suspensions "in abeyance" and asks the FCSA for assistance in reaching a decision.
March 14–15: Three white students are assaulted without provocation on campus at night. Two identified their attackers as black. A third, Joel Klotz, remembered nothing about the attack; he was beaten unconscious, remained in a coma for several days, and suffered brain damage.
March 26: After intense and laborious discussions, the FCSA publishes a lengthy report in the *Cornell Daily Sun* supporting the legitimacy of the judicial system and affirming the students' need to appear before the conduct board. The conduct board asks the defendants to appear on April 17, after spring break.
April 10–12: The Cornell Board of Trustees votes to establish an Afro-American studies center in which students would enjoy considerable decision-making power and pledges $215,000 to its first year of operation (1969–70) at Cornell and an additional $25,000 for an urban extension.
April 16: The AAS publishes a statement in the *Sun* presenting its case against the judicial system. The FCSA decides that student defendants may be tried in absentia.
April 17–18: The student conduct board holds its hearing with the defendants in absentia. At 2:00 a.m. it issues reprimands to three students for the December 13 disruptions by a vote of 4–1. False alarms break out in dormitories. Within an hour a cross is burned in front of Wari House, the black women's residence. The stage is set for the taking of Willard Straight Hall.

The Takeover and Crisis Week

Saturday, April 19: The AAS takes over Willard Straight Hall at 6:00 a.m. A day of tense negotiations, rumors, and ominous events ensues. Brothers from the Delta Upsilon fraternity invade the Straight in an attempt to liberate it from the AAS. After repelling the invaders, AAS allies begin bringing weapons into the building. Administrators find out late that evening that guns have been brought into the Straight, making it "a whole new ballgame."
Sunday, April 20: A deal is struck between administrators Keith Kennedy and Steven Muller and the AAS to end the takeover. The key provisions entail amnesty for the takeover and nullification of the judicial board's reprimands by the faculty as whole. At 4:00 p.m. the AAS walks out of Straight in a military procession, guns held high.
Monday, April 21: Perkins issues an emergency proclamation in the morning prohibiting arms and disruptive demonstrations on campus. Nonetheless, the AAS and other groups on campus remain armed. Perkins holds a convocation at Barton Hall at 3:00 p.m. before thousands of Cornellians in which he avoids addressing the issue at hand. After the convocation, the largest gathering of faculty in Cornell's history votes by an overwhelming majority to accept Perkins's seven-point proposal in place of the Kennedy-Muller deal and to delay nullifying the reprimands, citing the presence of arms and AAS coercion. The crisis intensifies.
Tuesday, April 22: Numerous meetings of colleges, faculty, and students are held, including a chaotic afternoon meeting at the Arts College. Fear begins to cause sen-

timent to change. In a radio broadcast, AAS member Tom Jones says that Cornell is on the edge of destruction if the faculty do not reverse their position on the sanctions. A faculty group vows to join students in a building takeover if the faculty as a whole prove recalcitrant. Several hundred armed sheriff's deputies assemble downtown, ready to move if another building is taken. An evening SDS meeting turns into a massive student takeover of Barton Hall. The decision to take over Day Hall (the administration building) is averted at the last second by astute speeches delivered by SDS member David Burak and Government Professor Eldron Kenworthy. The so-called Barton Hall Community pledges to take over Day Hall or another building if the faculty do not cave in at their meeting the next day. Students remain in Barton all night.

Wednesday, April 23: The faculty vote at noon to nullify the reprimands and to restructure governance of the university to include student power. Perkins addresses the victorious students at Barton Hall before the national and international media. In protest of this administration "capitulation,"Allan Sindler announces his resignation from Cornell.

Thursday, April 24: The Barton Hall Community continues discussion and debate about racism, power, and governance of the university. Government Department students hold a meeting in the afternoon at which Government Professor Walter Berns announces his resignation from Cornell. Walter LaFeber renounces his chairmanship of the History Department and threatens to resign from Cornell if threats to academic freedom persist. A counterrevolt of faculty begins as sixteen professors in History and Government refuse to teach unless order is restored.

Friday, April 25: Homer Bigart's coverage of the faculty revolt begins in the *New York Times*. The Government and History Departments hold a teach-in on academic freedom at Barton Hall.

Aftermath of the Crisis

April 27: The Group of Forty-One senior professors expresses concerns about academic freedom and standards at Cornell.

April 28: Professors Walter LaFeber, George Kahin, and Frederick Marcham meet with the former and current chairmen of the Board of Trustees (Arthur Dean and Robert Purcell) in New York City to discuss the situation at Cornell and problems associated with Perkins's remaining as president.

May 1: The trustees hold a marathon meeting at Cornell Medical College in New York City and issue a ten-point statement denouncing the "tactics of terror" and expressing "confidence" in Perkins (but falling short of an endorsement). The trustees also establish a committee to investigate the causes and implications of the crisis, chaired by trustee William Robertson.

May 2: The faculty vote to establish a constituent assembly to restructure the university.

May 14: Perkins addresses the Tower Club in New York City, defending the administration's handling of the crisis. Students led by Paul Rahe hold a demonstration outside the room to counter Perkins's claims. Perkins's speech is successful, representing the highwater mark of the administration's defense of its actions and policies.

May 23: Prominent professors in the Law School (led by Ian MacNeil) compose a letter to Perkins expressing loss of faith in his ability to protect academic freedom and to maintain law and order. Perkins receives the letter several days later.

May 28: The *New York Times* publishes Bigart's "blockbuster" article on Cornell, reporting the widespread senior faculty revolt, including moves by the new Group of Ten, led by Economics Professor George Hildebrand.

The June edition of the *Cornell Alumni News* is published. Editor John Marcham devotes the entire issue to a critical assessment of the crisis. Together with Bigart's "blockbuster," the *Alumni News* coverage undermines Perkins's position.

May 31: The Constituent Assembly meets, with much publicity. Perkins directs trustees to seek a successor. Dale Corson is soon named interim president.

June 2: Black Economics Professor Thomas Sowell resigns from Cornell, accusing Cornell of not holding black students to same standards as white students. James Turner accepts the directorship of the Africana Studies Center.

June 9: Perkins performs his last official act at Cornell, delivering an address at the 1969 commencement ceremonies.

June 29: Tom Jones delivers a speech at Willard Straight Hall threatening further disruption if black activists' demands concerning appointments in the Africana Studies Center and other matters are not met.

PARTICIPANTS

Listed here are individuals who played major roles in the events leading up to the crisis or the crisis itself, as well as others who were involved and went on to achieve national prominence.

Members of the Afro-American Society

Zachary Carter. Carter was the vice chairman of the Afro-American Society (AAS). Today he is the U.S. attorney for the eastern district of New York, appointed to the position by President Clinton. He was called on as district attorney in Brooklyn a few years ago to respond to a student takeover of Medgar Evers College in Brooklyn. He declined to be interviewed for this book.

Paul Du Bois. Today Du Bois is a nationally known community activist and media entrepreneur (and husband of Frances Moore Lappé, author of *Diet for a Small Planet*). He was a graduate student in government at Cornell, an activist for integration, and the creator of the initial black studies program that AAS militants displaced in 1969. During the year of the Straight crisis he experienced considerable pressure from more militant students. Today he is still active in interracial movements.

Harry Edwards. Edwards is now a professor of sociology at the University of California, Berkeley and was the founder of the discipline of sport sociology. He is currently the National Football League's top consultant on race relations. He was the organizer of the 1968 boycott by black athletes of the 1968 Olympic Games in Mexico City. Edwards was working on his Ph.D. at Cornell during the 1968–69 academic year. At Cornell he played an advisory role to the AAS during the conflict. He did not respond to my request for an interview.

John Garner. Garner was the leader of the revolutionary faction of the AAS in 1968 and 1969 and was probably the main force in the militarization of the AAS in the year leading up to the Straight crisis. A superb engineering student from Dayton, Garner left Cornell just before the Straight takeover to do political work in the ghetto. Eventually he went to medical school. He died of a kidney ailment during his residency.

Stephen Goodwin. Goodwin is now a Wall Street investment broker and winner of several awards for his ideas and contributions to minority advancement. Goodwin came from Harlem and was the AAS treasurer. He belonged to a white fraternity and had connections with numerous individuals and organizations at Cornell. Goodwin wrote the checks that paid for the guns the AAS ultimately brought into the Straight.

Robert Jackson. Jackson was president of the AAS in 1967–68 and a key player in the group's political and ideological development. Key administrators considered him a mature person with whom they could reason. Today he is a professor in nutritional science at the University of Maryland. He declined to be interviewed.

Thomas Jones. Jones emerged as the leading AAS militant during the Straight takeover. He came from a middle-class background—his father was a corporate physicist and his mother a teacher—and he moved deftly in both black and white domains at Cornell. He had been elected freshman class president in fall 1965, was named to the student judicial board, and joined a white fraternity before becoming active in the AAS. During the crisis he made the most inflammatory speeches against the university. Jones is now chief executive officer of the Smith Barney Asset Management division of Traveler's Group. He was also a member of the Cornell Board of Trustees and President Clinton's Social Security Council of 1996. In 1995 he donated $100,000 to Cornell to establish an annual "James Perkins Prize for Interracial Understanding and Harmony" for a student whose work has made a significant contribution to race relations. He and Perkins shook hands at the ceremony that inaugurated the prize. In 1997 black activists confronted Jones when he presented the award, calling him a "traitor to his people." Jones declined to be interviewed for this book.

Alan Keyes. Keyes was a candidate for the presidential nomination of the Republican Party in 1996. A graduate student in government and a disciple of Allan Bloom, Keyes dissented from the AAS's militancy. Before the Straight takeover an unidentified person threatened his life and that of his white girlfriend at an AAS meeting, according to a Security Division document. Like his mentors in the Government Department, Keyes left Cornell in the wake of the crisis. He completed his graduate work at Harvard. Keyes did not respond to my requests for an interview.

Andre McLaughlin. Today McLaughlin is a professor of African-American and women's studies at Medgar Evers College in Brooklyn, an institution she helped to develop. At Cornell she was involved with the social and intellectual aspects of the AAS. (She is the person who asked Zachary Carter to intervene in the takeover at Evers.)

Irving McPhail. Today president of a community college in inner-city St. Louis, McPhail has dedicated himself to minority education. He came to Cornell from Harlem and was a member of the Garner faction of the AAS.

Irene Smalls. Smalls is a nationally known writer of African-American children's stories. Hailing from Harlem, she helped to establish the AAS and the co-op for black women, Wari House.

Edward Whitfield. Whitfield served as AAS president during the crisis. He came to Cornell from Little Rock, Arkansas, and was a student in the six-year Ph.D. program. After the crisis he left Cornell to attend Malcolm X Liberation University. Today he is a community organizer and activist in North Carolina.

Administrators

Mark Barlow. As vice president for student affairs, Barlow was very involved with student issues. He was a member of the executive staff who helped make policy decisions during the crisis. Like many others, he was torn between his concern for students and his understanding of the principles of the university.

Stuart Brown. As dean of the College of Arts and Sciences during the crisis period, Brown wrote the most important document endorsing the AAS's interpretation of the McPhelin affair.

Dale Corson. Provost during the crisis, Corson became the president of Cornell after Perkins resigned. Corson's commitment to Cornell dated to 1946; he had risen through its ranks as a professor and an administrator. He was often delegated the authority to deal with crises during the 1960s, though some claimed his authority was limited during the 1969 crisis. He was the most level-headed of the executive staff in dealing with it. He was committed to the cause of racial integration.

Ruth Darling. As assistant dean of students during the crisis, Darling (along with Dean of Students Elmer Meyer) worked closely with the administration and students and was an important participant in the decisions of the judicial boards that precipitated the crisis. Darling also was in charge of the "rumor clinic" that played an important role in the crisis. Concerned about the principles of the university, she was also very sympathetic to the claims of student activists.

Gloria Joseph. The administrative head of the COSEP program, Joseph went on to write several novels with a feminist perspective. Joseph had to deal with many competing interests, including the administration, AAS activists, and nonmilitant black students. Many AAS students considered Joseph instrumental to their success at Cornell.

Keith Kennedy. Vice provost at Cornell during the crisis, Kennedy was the head of the committee that dealt with the development of the Afro-American studies program in 1969 and, along with Steven Muller, a negotiator with the AAS over the Straight takeover. Previously a director of research and associate dean of the College of Agriculture, Kennedy was a good administrator with practical wisdom.

Robert Miller. Miller was the dean of the faculty from 1967 to 1971. He played a key role in the negotiations with the AAS during their occupation of the Straight, pledging to resign if the faculty did not vote to nullify the sanctions against five AAS members that had precipitated the takeover. A professor of soil physics who had served with distinction as a first lieutenant in the air force during World War II, Miller was admired by many members of the administration for his sincerity and goodwill.

Steven Muller. A government professor and the vice president for public affairs who dealt with the press and public relations during the controversy, Muller was, with Keith Kennedy, one of the two negotiators inside the Straight. Muller was assigned the task of presenting the administration's interpretation of the events of 1969 to a skeptical world. He went on to become president of Johns Hopkins University.

James Perkins. Perkins was president of Cornell from 1963 to 1969, resigning under heat several weeks after the Straight crisis. He came to Cornell from the Carnegie Foundation and soon became a pioneer in increasing the admissions of students from the inner city at the predominantly white university. During his tenure as president he served on numerous prestigious national and international boards concerning education and racial justice. He was an educational consultant to the Educational Testing Service for many years until his death in August 1998. He steadfastly refused to discuss the crisis of 1969 publicly and declined my request for an interview in 1997. But I have examined much material on him from other sources, including his presidential papers and a lengthy interview he gave Keith Johnson, a journalist.

Professors

Walter Berns. Berns is a well-known scholar of the Constitution and of American politics at the American Enterprise Institute. He resigned from Cornell because of the threat to academic freedom and the failure of the administration to respond to threats against him made by Tom Jones and the AAS. Before the crisis he had been Jones's mentor. In 1994 Jones sent him a letter asking for forgiveness. Unlike Perkins, who had received a similar letter from Jones several years earlier, Berns refused to respond. Berns received the Clark Award for outstanding undergraduate teaching in the College of Arts and Sciences just before he resigned.

Allan Bloom. Bloom was a government professor who later wrote the controversial book *The Closing of the American Mind*, which was motivated in part by his experiences at Cornell in 1969. Deeply committed to the principles of liberal education and academic freedom, Bloom resigned in the aftermath of the crisis. He died several years ago.

David Brion Davis. Davis's book, *The Problem of Slavery in Western Culture*, won the Pulitzer Prize in History in 1967. Davis was respected by black and white students alike because of his intellectual stature and his scholarly contributions on race; he strove to develop a black studies program that had intellectual sophistication and diversity. The militant posture of the AAS and the crisis of 1969 ultimately took the program in a separatist direction.

Tom Davis. Tom Davis was chair of the Economics Department when the AAS took it over in reaction to the McPhelin incident. In the aftermath of the Straight crisis a year later, Davis pushed for controversial reforms in the governance of the department.

Douglas Dowd. Dowd was a professor of economics at Cornell. He was the leading faculty adviser to Students for a Democratic Society and a leading activist against the war, capitalism, and injustices in America. Dowd contributed to making many student radicals at Cornell intellectually serious and, according to some commentators, less inclined toward violence.

Andrew Hacker. A government professor who is perhaps the leading white writer on race relations in America today, Hacker taught a course on racial politics with Sindler, but he and Sindler stood on opposite sides of the fence on most issues, and he never joined the "counterrevolt" led by Sindler. At Cornell he was renowned as a maverick.

Donald Kagan. Kagan was a well-known professor of history who went on to become the dean of the Yale College of Arts and Sciences, where he found himself embroiled in the culture wars between multiculturalists and traditionalists (he was featured on the cover of the *New York Times Magazine* during this time). Kagan played a role in educational policy at Cornell and was a leading member of the "counterrevolt" mounted by the Government and History Departments.

Eldron Kenworthy. An assistant professor in the Government Department, Kenworthy sought a balance between the social justice and academic freedom missions of the university. Though he was a member of the Concerned Faculty during the Straight crisis, he was less angry and less confrontational than the leaders of that group. His speech at Barton Hall on Tuesday evening of the crisis week did more than any other factor to turn to tide away from potentially violent confrontation.

Walter LaFeber. A famous "revisionist" historian of American foreign policy, LaFeber served as an adviser to Perkins during the crisis of December 1968. He epitomized progressive liberals who were committed to the principles of liberal education and academic freedom. His credible threat to resign if Perkins remained at Cornell was a pivotal factor in Perkins's loss of support from trustees and many faculty in the wake of the Straight crisis. LaFeber was the first recipient of the Clark Award for outstanding undergraduate teaching in the College of Arts and Sciences.

David Lyons. Lyons was an associate professor of philosophy and a leader of the Concerned Faculty. Lyons represented the younger faculty, who were inclined to emphasize the social justice mission of the university. In 1976 he won the Clark Award for outstanding undergraduate teaching in the College of Arts and Sciences.

Father Michael McPhelin. McPhelin, visiting from the Philippines, taught a course on economic development in spring 1968 that precipitated the first major racial confrontation at Cornell. AAS leaders accused him of institutional racism and took over the Economics Department in response. The McPhelin affair heightened race consciousness at Cornell and posed the first serious challenge to academic freedom in the name of racial and social justice.

Chandler Morse. Morse was a professor of economics who chaired the first committee established by Perkins to develop a black studies program in the fall of 1968. The committee suffered from a lack of clear goals and inadequate communication with students, leading to AAS disaffection and the displacement of the Morse Committee by a committee of student activists led by John Garner.

Benjamin Nichols. Nichols was an engineering professor at Cornell who was deeply involved in the development of the black studies program and other areas of student activism. He served as the president of the Cornell chapter of the American Association of University Professors during the crisis period and also championed the social justice vision of the university. Years later he became mayor of Ithaca.

Clinton Rossiter. Rossiter was a government and history professor who wrote famous books about American politics and the founding of the nation. In 1953 he won the Bancroft and Wilson Prizes, the most prestigious book awards of the American Historical Association and the American Political Science Association, respectively, for *Seedtime of the Republic.* Rossiter initially spoke out against accepting the Straight agreement but switched his position at the next vote. He was threatened in Tom Jones's speech at Barton Hall. He fell into depression and was ostracized by colleagues who had refused to budge. A year later he committed suicide.

Allan Sindler. Sindler, chairman of the Government Department, was the first to resign in the wake of the Straight crisis. He went on to head the School of Public Policy at Berkeley. Though not as well known nationally as some of the other professors mentioned, he was the most important figure at Cornell for several reasons: he had been active in the civil rights movement in the South before he came to Cornell; he served on the key educational policy committee; he was the chair of the Government Department and a leader of the Government/History resistance; and he was the most important figure in the judicial system, having masterminded the liberal reforms that had just been adopted and having served on the key Faculty Committee on Student Affairs in 1969. He was the main force behind a lengthy defense of the system that the FCSA published in the face of AAS pressure, a defense that led to the decisive decision to issue the reprimands. Sindler epitomized the liberal defender of academic freedom and the rule of law.

Thomas Sowell. Sowell is a famous black conservative and a prolific author of books on race, economics, education, and civil rights who now resides at the Hoover Institution. Sowell was involved with COSEP students but became alienated from the racial pedagogy at Cornell, which he considered too race-conscious and insufficiently intellectually rigorous. He resigned from Cornell in June 1969.

Other Students

David Burak. Burak was a leader in SDS's Action Faction who was involved in a myriad of activities at Cornell, including political activism, teaching, and setting up the Sindler Commission. Burak joined Kenworthy in turning the Barton Hall takeover away from violent confrontation. Today he writes poetry and plays and also teaches at Santa Monica College. He taught at Ho Chi Minh University in Vietnam during the 1996–97 school year.

Stanley Chess. Editor of the *Sun* during the crucial year leading up to the Straight crisis, Chess strove to be fair to the competing groups and interests without losing sight of the broader interests of the university. Today he is in charge of running West Publishing Company's courses for bar examinations and has been writing a treatise on law.

Bruce Dancis. Dancis was a nationally prominent antiwar activist and founder of the movement at Cornell known as the Resistance. He was the first SDS member in the country to destroy his draft card, an act for which he served time in a federal prison right after the Straight crisis of 1969. Students depicted him as the moral leader of student movements at Cornell. Today he is the music and culture editor for the *Sacramento Bee*.

Art Kaminsky. Kaminsky was a leader in conventional student politics and the chair of the Scheduling, Coordination, and Activities Review Board (SCARB) in 1967 during the disputes over SDS and Resistance attempts to solicit pledges to destroy draft cards at the Straight. Kaminsky's senior thesis (1968) on the rise and fall of student government at Cornell is the definitive source on this topic. Today he is one of the leading sports agent attorneys in the country, working with National Hockey League athletes and others. He is based in New York City.

Chip Marshall. Marshall was a leader in the SDS Action Faction who pushed for a more confrontational stance during the Straight crisis. Marshall is now an international businessman living in Seattle.

Paul Rahe. A columnist for the *Sun* in 1969, Rahe was the most outspoken student critic of Perkins. He led a behind-the-scenes effort to undermine Perkins in the aftermath of the crisis. Today he is a history professor at the University of Tulsa.

Art Spitzer. Spitzer was an antiwar activist who became a leading member of the Faculty Committee for Student Affairs (FCSA) and a proponent of the Sindler position during the crisis. Today he is the chief attorney in the national office of the American Civil Liberties Union in Washington, D.C.

Stephen Wallenstein. Wallenstein was the other student member of the Faculty Committee on Student Affairs (FCSA), interviewer for the Oral History project on the crisis, and coauthor with George Fisher of the unpublished manuscript *Open Breeches: Guns at Cornell* (1970). Today Wallenstein is the executive director of the Global Capital Markets Center at Duke University, where he is also a professor of law and business.

The Radical Priests

Daniel and Phillip Berrigan. Daniel Berrigan was employed by Cornell University Religious Workers (CURW), and Phillip was often on campus. They did not play prominent roles in the Straight crisis (their main concern was Vietnam), but they are part of the story. Daniel Berrigan and Walter Berns engaged in some prominent debates on campus about the war and the validity of civil disobedience. During this time the Berrigans conducted highly publicized acts of civil disobedience, leading to major court cases. They set an example of activism for many students.

The Reporter

Homer Bigart. Bigart, a *New York Times* reporter who had won two Pulitzer Prizes for his war correspondence, played a major role in the aftermath of the Cornell crisis by reporting the side of the emerging faculty resistance. Perkins tried to get the *Times* to take him off the story but failed.

Trustees

Arthur Dean. Dean was the chairman of the Cornell Board of Trustees until just before the Straight crisis. He was a leading New York lawyer, a partner in the venerable firm Sullivan and Cromwell, and had been born in Ithaca and educated at Cornell, where he received a bachelor's degree (1921) and a law degree (1923). Described by LaFeber as "the toughest man I have ever known," Dean had numerous honorary law degrees and had served on national and international boards and been involved in as many negotiations over such issues as the law of the seas and nuclear arms. Dean was the first trustee to lose faith in Perkins.

Robert Purcell. Chairman of the Cornell Board of Trustees during the Straight crisis, Purcell had been educated at Cornell (B.A. 1932, LL.B. 1935). Purcell headed or served on the board of numerous companies; he was chairman of the board of International Basic Economy Corporation from 1958 to 1968. Purcell gave a million-dollar grant to launch the Africana Studies Center at Cornell in 1969 and was a Perkins supporter until the tide turned against Perkins in May 1969.

William Robertson. Robertson was a longtime member of the Cornell Board of Trustees. He headed the trustee committee that conducted interviews on the causes and effects of the Straight crisis and wrote the report that emerged from these hearings. He is now retired and living in New England.

NOTES

Chapter 1. Overview of the Crisis

1. In October 1967 police used guns on students at South Carolina State University. See Cleveland Sellers, with Robert Terrel, *The River of No Return: The Autobiography of a Black Militant and the Life and Death of SNCC* (Morrow, 1973).

2. Self-defense was part of the Black Power and Black Panther movements. It originated in the stand taken by Robert Williams in South Carolina in the early '60s against police violence. See Williams, *Negroes with Guns* (Marzani & Munsel, 1962); On Black Power, see George M. Frederickson, *Black Liberation: A Comparative History of Black Ideologies in the United States and South Africa* (Oxford University Press, 1995), ch. 7.

3. Thomas W. Jones, speech at Willard Straight Hall, June 29, 1969.

4. In general, see George Fisher and Stephen Wallenstein, *Open Breeches: Guns at Cornell* (unpublished manuscript).

5. See, e.g., Bayard Rustin, et al., *Black Studies: Myths and Realities* (A. Philip Randolph Educational Fund, 1969); John W. Blassingame, et al., *New Perspectives on Black Studies* (University of Illinois Press, 1971).

6. "It was only with the demonstrations in Birmingham, Alabama, in the summer of 1963 that race had become a central issue in the nation's public life. Suddenly Americans of all kinds took note; the moral power of black demands hit home." Tamar Jacoby, *Someone Else's House: America's Unfinished Struggle for Integration* (Free Press, 1998), p. 21.

7. John Leo, "Cornell Is Seeking Nation's Best Negro Scholars," *New York Times*, October 29, 1968, p. 44.

8. Ernest Dunbar, "The Black Studies Thing," *New York Times Magazine*, April 6, 1969. Reprinted in Meier, Rudwick, and Bracy (see note 9).

9. Jacoby, *Someone Else's House*, p. 58. The article Jacoby cited is from the *New York Times*, April 23, 1963. For articles on this rising split and related black politics in the 1960s, see August Meier, Elliot Rudwick, and John Bracy Jr., eds., *Black Protest in the Sixties: Articles from the New York Times* (Markus Wiener, 1991).

10. Stokely Carmichael and Charles V. Hamilton, *Black Power: The Politics of Liberation in America* (Vintage/Random House, 1967), p. 44. Emphasis in the original.

11. Interview with Denise Raynor, 1998. (All notes in this form refer to interviews I conducted personally over the course of the past few years.)

12. See Malcolm X, *By Any Means Necessary* (Pathfinder Press, 1970). The theme of black men protecting black women was a constant refrain in graduate student Cleveland Donald's perceptive portrayal of the AAS at Cornell in "Cornell: Confrontation in Black and White," in Cushing Strout and David I. Grossvogel, eds., *Divided We Stand: Reflections on the Crisis at Cornell* (Doubleday, 1970), pp. 152–204.

13. Fisher and Wallenstein, *Open Breeches*, p. 338.

14. Thomas J. Turner, *Cornell Daily Sun*, "Straight Takeover Twentieth Anniversary Supplement," April 19, 1989, p. 21.

15. Interview with Gloria Joseph, 1997.

16. Thomas L. Tobin, Oral History interview, p. 66. (All notes in this form refer to interviews conducted during and after the 1969 crisis as part of the Oral History Project.) I discuss the nature of these interviews at the end of this chapter.

17. Perkins's statement in executive staff transcript prepared after the crisis, which I call the "Executive Staff transcript," p. 6 (Perkins Papers, Cornell's Kroch Archive [hereafter referred to as "Perkins Papers"], #3/10/1022, Box 37).

18. Interview with Walter LaFeber, 1995.

19. Ibid.

20. Interview with Joyce Cima, 1997.

21. Edward Arlington Robinson, "Richard Cory," (1897) in Gerald Dewitt Sanders, John Herbert Nelson, and M. L. Rosenthal, eds., *Chief Modern Poets of England and America*, 4th edition (Macmillan, 1962).

22. Jean Jacques Rousseau, *Émile, or On Education* (1762).

23. E. D. Hirsch, *Cultural Literacy: What Every American Needs to Know* (Vintage, 1988), p. 119. On the progressive and pragmatic turn in education, see L. A. Cremin, *The Transformation of the American School: Progressivism in American Education, 1876–1952* (Knopf, 1964). On progressivism's emphasis on technical expertise (as applied by administrative and corporate elites) as the most appropriate form of knowledge, see Christopher Lasch, *Haven in a Heartless World: The Family Besieged* (Basic Books, 1975).

24. See the definitive work on Cornell's history until the 1960s, Morris Bishop, *A History of Cornell* (Cornell University Press, 1962).

25. James A. Perkins, interview with Keith Johnson, 1994, p. 20. Johnson conducted a lengthy interview of Perkins for his own research on Cornell during the post–World War II era. He provided me with a copy of it. Perkins declined my request for an interview.

26. James A. Perkins, "The Restless Decade," speech delivered in March 1968.

27. Perkins interview with Johnson, pp. 115–119.

28. Interview with James E. Turner, 1996.

29. James A. Perkins, *The University in Transition* (Princeton University Press, 1966), pp. 19, 80.

30. David I. Grossvogel, "The University in Transition," in Strout and Grossvogel, *Divided We Stand*, p. 132, quoting from ibid., p. 32.

31. Perkins interview with Johnson, pp. 15–18.

32. Allan Bloom, *The Closing of the American Mind: How Higher Education Has Failed Democracy and Impoverished the Souls of Today's Students* (Simon & Schuster, 1987), p. 339–340.

33. Clark Kerr, *The Uses of the University* (Harvard University Press, 1963).

34. Theodore Lowi, *The End of Liberalism: The Second Republic of the United States*, 2nd ed. (Norton, 1979). Originally published in 1969.

35. Perkins, *The University in Transition*, p. 33.

36. *Cornell Daily Sun*, February 28, 1968, p. 1.

37. Robert Hutchins, *The Higher Learning in America* (Transaction Books, 1995), p. 32. Originally published in 1936.

38. Bloom, *The Closing of the American Mind*, p. 343.

39. Hutchins, *The Higher Learning in America*, pp. 20, 44, 58.

40. Perkins interview with Johnson. pp. 26–27.

41. For example, see Alan Charles Kors and Harvey A. Silverglate, *The Shadow University: The Betrayal of Liberty on America's Campuses* (Free Press, 1998); Nat Hentoff, *Free Speech for Me, Not for Thee: How the American Left and Right Relentlessly Censor Each Other* (HarperCollins, 1994);

Roger Kimball, *Tenured Radicals: How Politics Has Corrupted Our Higher Education* (Harper-Collins, 1990). For a critique, see John K. Wilson, *The Myth of Political Correctness: The Conservative Attack on Higher Education* (Duke University Press, 1995).

42. For example, see the essays in Edith Kurzweil and William Philips, eds., *Our Country, Our Culture: The Politics of Political Correctness* (Partisan Review Press, 1994).

43. For example, see Nathan Glazer, *Remembering First Things* (Basic Books, 1970).

44. Barbara Johnson, quoted in Kimbal, *Tenured Radicals*, p. 68.

45. Jaroslav Pelikan, *The Idea of the University: A Reexamination* (Yale University Press, 1992), p. 48, quoting John Henry Newman, *The Idea of a University*. Newman's classic book is *The Idea of a University Defined and Illustrated* (Clarendon Press, 1976), edited with introduction and notes by I. T. Ker.

46. Ibid., p. 65.

47. American Association of University Professors, *Policy Documents and Reports 3–10*, 7th ed. (1990). A good source on the historical, normative, and legal aspects of academic freedom is William W. Van Alstyne, ed., *Freedom and Tenure in the Academy* (Duke University Press, 1993).

48. Alexis de Tocqueville, *Democracy in America*, vols. 1 and 2 (1835–1840).

49. Thomas Hobbes, *Leviathan* (1651); John Locke, *The Second Treatise of Civil Government* (1690). The original treatment of moral fury without the rule of law is Aeschylus, *The Oresteia*.

50. See the broad discussion in Todd Gitlin, *The Twilight of Common Dreams: Why America Is Wracked by the Culture Wars* (Metropolitan Books, 1995). See also Kenneth Hoover, with James Marcia and Kristin Parris, *The Power of Identity: Politics in a New Key* (Chatham House, 1997).

51. Lawrence Fuchs has shown how citizenship in America has consisted of a dialectical relationship between assertions of ethnic culture and identity and the acceptance of shared norms in the civic, constitutional culture. The relationship between ethnicity and universal citizenship is not a question of either-or, but rather one of dialectical balance. For the polity to work, however, the civic culture has to carry a trump card. Fuchs, *The American Kaleidoscope: Race, Ethnicity, and the Civic Culture* (Wesleyan University Press, 1990).

52. See Malcolm X, *By Any Means Necessary;* Georg Wilhelm Friedrich Hegel, *The Phenomenology of Mind* (Harper, 1967; originally published in 1807), pp. 229–233 . An excellent work that applies Hegel's theory of recognition to psychoanalysis and gender conflict is Jessica Benjamin, *The Bonds of Love: Psychoanalysis, Feminism, and the Problem of Domination* (Pantheon Books, 1988). I owe my understanding of this issue to Benjamin's work.

53. For an insightful treatment of the Deweyan-progressive defense of free speech in the name of furthering the democratic experiment, see Mark A. Graber, *Transforming Free Speech: The Ambiguous Legacy of Civil Libertarianism* (University of California Press, 1991). Even Alexander Meiklejohn's classic defense of free speech is based in this school of thought, though it also draws on other sources, especially classical thought. See Meiklejohn's "Free Speech and Its Relation to Self-Government," in *Political Freedom* (Oxford University Press, 1960; originally published in 1948).

54. Interview with Andre McLaughlin, 1996.

55. Interview with Irving McPhail, 1997.

56. Interview with Walter LaFeber, 1995.

57. Walter Berns, *Freedom, Virtue, and the First Amendment* (Louisiana State University Press, 1957). See also Berns, *The First Amendment and the Problem of American Democracy* (Basic Books, 1976).

58. Bloom, *The Closing of the American Mind*, p. 249.

59. See David J. Garrow, *Bearing the Cross: Martin Luther King Jr. and the Southern Christian Leadership Conference* (Vintage/Random House, 1986).

60. See Harry Kalven Jr., *The Negro and the First Amendment* (University of Chicago Press, 1965).

61. See Vaclav Havel, "Politics, Morality, and Civility," in *Summer Meditations* (Vintage/Random House, 1993), pp. 1–20. See also Hannah Arendt's classic essay on the fundamental difference between truth and power, "Truth and Politics," in Peter Laslett and W. G. Runciman, eds., *Philosophy, Politics and Society* (Blackwell, 1967).

62. Stephen Carter, *Reflections of an Affirmative Action Baby* (Basic Books, 1991), pp. 118–119.

Carter's father, Lyle, one of the few black professors at Cornell in 1969, played a role in the crisis that we will examine. Stephen was a student at Ithaca High School at the time.

63. Fisher was among the first journalists to use a tape recorder with interviews. The tapes (which are not available) and other research were the basis of the manuscript. Fisher's subsequent personal history included both successful journalistic endeavors and run-ins with the law. Nevertheless, sources (including press articles about him) have vouched for his journalistic integrity and his passion for disclosing the truth.

Chapter 2. Student Militancy

1. On Cornell's history up to the 1950s, the preeminent source is Morris Bishop, *A History of Cornell* (Cornell University Press, 1962).

2. Michael W. Miles, *The Radical Probe: The Logic of Student Rebellion* (Atheneum, 1971), p. 96.

3. Bishop, *A History of Cornell,* p. 407.

4. Interview with John Marcham, 1996.

5. Art Kaminsky, "Executive Board of Student Government: Success or Failure?" (senior honors thesis, History Department), p. 19. Sale became a noted journalist who wrote the definitive book on Students for a Democratic Society, *SDS,* (Random House, 1973), and Farina became a famous writer and novelist who wrote, among other books, *Been Down So Long It Looks Like Up to Me,* the setting of which is Cornell (Random House, 1966). Kaminsky is one of the leading sports agent attorneys in America.

6. Donald H. Moyer, "Student Conduct: Who's in Charge?" *Cornell Alumni News,* November 1967, p. 22.

7. Irving Louis Horowitz and William H. Friedland, "Five Years of Confrontation at Cornell," in Irving Louis Horowitz and William G. Friedland, eds., *The Knowledge Factory* (Aldine, 1970), p. 222. I am indebted to Keith Johnson's portrayal of the Morrison and Singer cases in the manuscript he is preparing on Cornell in the post–World War II years. On McCarthyism and academic freedom, see Ellen W. Schrecker, *No Ivory Tower: McCarthyism and the Universities* (Princeton University Press, 1986); Neil L. Hamilton, *Zealotry and Academic Freedom: A Legal and Historical Perspective* (Transaction Books, 1995), esp. pt. 1. The Supreme Court case that was the basis of the reversal in Singer's case was *Watkins* v. *United States,* 354 U.S. 178 (1957).

8. Kaminsky, "Executive Board of Student Government," p. 46.

9. Clark Kerr, *The Uses of the University* (Harvard University Press, 1963), p. 135. Traditional colleges or universities were often dedicated to specific normative objectives, and this often meant a lack of intellectual freedom. See Richard Hofstadter and Walter Metzger, *The Development of Academic Freedom in the United States* (Columbia University Press, 1955); Hamilton, *Zealotry and Academic Freedom.*

10. Savio's speech to Berkeley's Free Speech Movement, attacking Kerr's concept of the "knowledge factory" in David Lance Goines, *The Free Speech Movement: Coming of Age in the 1960s* (Ten Speed Press, 1993) pp. 151–153.

11. Miles, *The Radical Probe,* p. 91.

12. Tom Hayden, quoted in James Miller, in *Democracy Is in the Streets: From Port Huron to the Siege of Chicago* (Simon & Schuster, 1987), pp. 78–79. The concept of the public was first postulated by John Dewey in *The Public and Its Problems: An Essay in Political Inquiry* (Gateway, 1946), a work that influenced the early SDS. On the free speech movement, see David Lance Goines, *The Free Speech Movement.*

13. Allan Bloom, *The Closing of the American Mind: How Higher Education Has Failed Democracy and Impoverished the Souls of Today's Students* (Simon & Schuster, 1987), p. 268.

14. Interview with Walter Berns, 1995. Berns was more politely critical in a review of Kerr's book in the *Cornell Daily Sun,* March 14, 1969.

15. Paul Berman, *A Tale of Two Generations: The Political Journey of Two Utopias* (Norton, 1996), p. 12.

16. Horowitz and Friedland, "Five Years of Conflict at Cornell," p. 226.

17. See Miles, *The Radical Probe*, pp. 88–90.

18. Nathan Tarcov, "The Last Four Years at Cornell," *Public Interest*, Fall 1968, p. 126.

19. Interview with Dale Corson, 1996.

20. "Report of the Ad Hoc Committee on the Quality of Undergraduate Education" (Bowers-Kahn Commission Report), submitted to faculty on October 11, 1965 (Perkins Papers, #3/10/1022, Box 31); Morrison Commission Report, presented June 1, 1969 (Perkins Papers, #3/10/1022, Box 43).

21. Interview with Walter Berns, 1995 (Perkins Papers, #3/10/1022, Box 43).

22. W. J. Rorabaugh, *Berkeley at War: The 1960s* (Oxford University Press, 1989).

23. See Todd Gitlin, *The Sixties: Years of Hope, Days of Rage* (Bantam Books, 1987), esp. intro.; Sale, *SDS;* Miller, *Democracy Is in the Streets.*

24. Horowitz and Friedland, "Five Years of Conflict at Cornell," p. 244.

25. Interview with Bruce Dancis, 1996. See also "Dancis Rips Up Draft Card to Protest Selective Service," *Cornell Daily Sun,* December 15, 1969, p. 1.

26. Interview with David Burak, 1996. For a good overview of the antiwar movement, see Tom Wells, *The War Within: America's Battle over Vietnam* (University of California Press, 1994), in which Dancis and Cornell are discussed often.

27. The so-called D.C. Nine, led by Daniel Berrigan and his brother, Philip, were tried in 1972 for destroying draft files at a Selective Service office (see *United States* v. *Dougherty,* 473 F.2d 1113). Daniel Berrigan was a prolific author and poet as well as activist; see *The Dark Side of Resistance* (Doubleday, 1971) and *The Writings of Daniel Berrigan* (University Press of America, 1989). Philip Berrigan also published; see his autobiography, *Fighting the Lamb's War: Skirmishes with the American Empire* (1996).

28. Peter Agree, Oral History interview, pp. 10–11.

29. See Jerry Avorn and the Staff of the *Columbia Daily Spectator, Up against the Ivy Wall: A History of the Columbia Crisis* (Atheneum, 1968); Miles, *The Radical Probe,* chs. 1 and 2.

30. Interview with Charles ("Chip") Marshall, 1996.

31. See Perkins's calendar on "JP Student Involvement 9/5 to 11/28." Perkins had two one-hour meetings with Burak during this period (several other students are also listed). See also Perkins's letter to Mrs. John Newsom, July 5, 1967, describing Burak's role in research on "The problems of higher education for the Negro." Both documents in Perkins Papers, #3/10/1022, Box 33.

32. Interview with David Burak, 1996. Indeed, two officers asked me twenty-eight years later to say hello to Burak.

33. Interview with Sheila Tobias, 1995. For insight into how similar experiences among women in the civil rights movement sparked the second wave of the women's movement, see Sara M. Evans, *Personal Politics: The Roots of Women's Liberation in the Civil Rights Movement and the New Left* (Vintage, 1980). After leaving Cornell, Tobias went on to become a noted education writer and feminist. Among her recent works is *Faces of Feminism: An Activist's Reflections on the Women's Movement* (Westview Press, 1997).

34. *Cornell Daily* Sun, 1967; see also Douglas Dowd, Oral History interview; Dowd's memoir/analysis of America during his lifetime, *Blues for America: A Critique, a Lament, and Some Memories* (Monthly Review Press, 1997). Wells refers to Dowd often in *The War Within.*

35. Interview with Robert Kilpatrick, 1997, and others. Kilpatrick was a colleague of Dowd's in the Economics Department.

36. Interview with Bruce Dancis, 1996.

37. We will encounter such language in speeches throughout this book. See also Perkins's book, *The University in Transition* (Princeton University Press, 1966), which is replete with this type of discourse and logic.

38. Theodore Lowi, *The End of Liberalism: The Second Republic of the United States,* 2nd ed. (Norton, 1979), p. 63.

39. John Schaar, *Legitimacy in the Modern State* (Transaction Books, 1981). See also Schaar's critique of Erich Fromm and liberal notions of authority in *Escape from Authority* (Basic Books, 1961).

40. Miles, *The Radical Probe*, pp. 71–88, 161–162.

41. David B. Truman, *The Governmental Process: Political Interests and Public Opinion* (Knopf, 1951).

42. See, for example, John Searle, *The Campus War: A Sympathetic Look at the University in Agony* (World, 1971).

43. Kaminsky, "Executive Board of Student Government," pp. 152–156.

44. See, for example, E. E. Schattschneider, *The Semi-Sovereign People* (Holt, Rinehart and Winston, 1960).

45. Miles, *The Radical Probe*, p. 22.

46. Ibid., ch. 1.

47. Horowitz and Friedland, "Five Years of Confrontation at Cornell," p. 233.

48. Interview with Dale Corson, 1996.

49. Horowitz and Friedland, "Five Years of Confrontation at Cornell."

50. Front-page reports, *Cornell Daily Sun*, December 5, 1967; December 15, 1967; January 29, 1968. See also ibid., p. 237.

51. Interview with John Marcham, 1996.

52. Supreme Court doctrine at the time was as liberal concerning obscenity as it would ever be. See Donald Alexander Downs, *The New Politics of Pornography* (University of Chicago Press, 1989), ch. 1. This book links the development of Supreme Court doctrine to social and political events of the time.

53. Tarcov, "The Last Four Years at Cornell," p. 132.

54. See *Brandenburg* v. *Ohio*, 395 U.S. 444 (1969). But in 1968 the Court ruled that destroying a draft card is not protected expression under the First Amendment (*United States* v. *O'Brien*, 391 U.S. 367).

55. Dancis, Burak, and Kaminsky (next paragraph) quoted in Horowitz and Friedland, "Five Years of Confrontation at Cornell," pp. 249–250. I draw on their account of this event, as well as Kaminsky's in "Executive Board of Student Government."

56. For a good set of debates on this and related issues at the national level, see George F. Kennan, *Democracy and the Student Left: Angry Students vs. the Establishment: The Dialogue That Turned to Violence* (Bantam Books, 1968). Dancis's views were similar to Thoreau's in *On Civil Disobedience*, although Dancis was much more political and confrontational: moral conscience must trump rule of law. Walter Berns and Daniel Berrigan often squared off over this question, and Berns attacked Thoreau and Berrigan in lectures.

57. Wells, *The War Within*, p. 82.

58. Interview with Bruce Dancis, 1996.

59. Statement of the Faculty Council, December 5, 1967 (Perkins Papers, #3/10/1022, Box 25).

60. Ibid.

61. Interview with Isadore Blumen, professor of Industrial and Labor Relations, 1997. Economist Alfred Kahn led the university response, so he took the other side of the matter.

62. Interview with Walter Berns, 1995.

63. *Cornell Daily Sun*, February 13, 1968; February 27–March 1, 1968.

64. Ibid., November 20, 1967.

65. Interview with Sindler colleague Peter Sharfman, 1998.

66. Interviews with Andrew Hacker and John Marcham, both in 1996.

67. Sindler Commission Report, as reported in the *Cornell Daily Sun*, October 10, 1967.

68. Ibid.

69. Ibid., October 4, 1967, p. 10.

70. Ibid.

71. Ibid., p. 13.

72. Seth S. Goldschlager, "The Sindler Report: What Rules to Enforce," *Cornell Alumni News*, November 1967, p. 25.

73. Faculty Senate notes, November 8, 1967, p. 3433.

74. Interview with David Burak, 1996.

75. Interview with Neal Stamp, 1997. In a separate interview, Trustee William Robertson (1997) concurred with this concern.

76. *Cornell Alumni News*, November 1967, p. 25; *Ithaca Journal*, October 10, 1967, p. 1.

77. Interview with Isadore Blumen, 1997.

78. *Cornell University Policy Notebook for Students*, Trustees Declaration of May 1, 1968.

79. Notes provided to me by Allan Sindler, 1996.

80. Interview with William R. Robertson, 1997.

Chapter 3. The Rise of Racial Politics

1. Tamar Jacoby, *Someone Else's House: America's Unfinished Struggle for Integration* (Free Press, 1998), p. 34.

2. "Report of the Special Trustee Committee on Campus Unrest at Cornell" (Robertson Committee Report), presented September 5, 1969, p. 42.

3. Daryl Michael Scott, *Contempt and Pity: Social Policy and the Image of the Damaged Black Psyche, 1880–1996* (University of North Carolina Press, 1997), pp. 162–163.

4. James A. Perkins, interview with Keith Johnson, 1994, pp. 156–159.

5. Interview with Gloria Joseph, 1997.

6. Walter Slatoff, Oral History interview, p. 3.

7. Ibid., p. 4.

8. For example, in October 1966 U.S. President Lyndon Johnson appointed Perkins to plan an international conference on education, which Perkins then headed.

9. Walter Slatoff, Oral History interview, pp. 8–9.

10. Interview with William R. Robertson, 1997. See also Robertson Committee Report, p. 42.

11. George Hildebrand, Oral History interview, p. 51.

12. Robertson Committee Report, p. 42.

13. F. Dana Payne (assistant dean, Arts and Sciences) and Barbara Hirshfeld, Oral History interview, pp. 4–7.

14. Earlier version of George Fisher and Stephen Wallenstein, *Open Breeches: Guns at Cornell* (unpublished manuscript), p. BS1, made available to me by Professor Joel Silbey from his papers in the Kroch Archive. "BS" apparently stands for "Black Studies," which is a separate chapter.

15. Interview with Irving McPhail, 1997.

16. Interview with Andre McLaughlin, 1996.

17. Interview with Gloria Joseph, 1997.

18. Report on "Arts College Admissions" by Michael Shinagel, acting assistant dean for Arts College admissions, May 22, 1967, pp.13–14.

19. "Answers to Some Questions about COSEP," Committee on Special Education Projects, 1969 (Perkins Papers, #3/10/1022, Box 25).

20. Robertson Committee Report, p. 49.

21. Interview with Stephen Goodwin, 1996.

22. Interview with James E. Turner, 1996.

23. *Cornell Chronicle*, April 20, 1989, p. 6.

24. A few years ago, when Carter was in the Brooklyn district attorney's office, McLaughlin called him to deal with a student building takeover at Medgar Evers College, where she teaches.

25. Interview with Berns, 1995.

26. Interview with Irene Smalls, 1997.

27. Interview with Andre McLaughlin, 1996.

28. Interview with Stephen Goodwin, 1996.

29. Ibid.

30. Interview with Andre McLaughlin. 1996.

31. Interview with Stephen Goodwin, 1996. Goodwin marveled at the wealth around him. For example, one of his fraternity brothers was the son of the future owner of CBS, Lawrence Tisch, one of the wealthiest men in the world. Goodwin recalled fraternity brothers discussing renting a 747 to fly people to Florida for spring break.

32. Interview with Harris Raynor, 1998.

33. *Cornell Daily Sun*, November 8, 1966, pp. 1, 12.

34. Cleveland Donald, "Cornell: Confrontation in Black and White," in Cushing Strout and David I. Grossvogel, eds., *Divided We Stand: Reflections on the Crisis at Cornell* (Doubleday, 1970),

pp. 165–166. Black Power, derived from black nationalism, is a complex phenomenon, drawing on both radical and conservative forms of black thought. See, for example, George M. Frederickson, *Black Liberation: A Comparative History of Black Ideologies in the United States and South Africa* (Oxford University Press, 1995), ch. 7; Manning Marable, *Race, Reform, and Rebellion: The Second Reconstruction in Black America, 1945–1990* (University Press of Mississippi, 1991), ch. 5.

35. Gloria Joseph, "Black Power: Its Implications," *Cornell Daily Sun,* Supplement, October 21, 1966.

36. Walter Slatoff, Oral History interview, pp. 15–16.

37. Interview with Irene Smalls, 1997.

38. *Cornell Daily Sun,* February 16, 1968, p. 1.

39. Quoted in Fisher and Wallenstein, *Open Breeches,* pp. BS24–BS25.

40. Donald, "Cornell," p. 166.

41. This incident and the next were reported to me by a white student who was present in both cases and who said he was embarrassed by them.

42. Interview with Gloria Joseph, 1997.

43. This case was reported to me by the roommate of the black student.

44. Elmer Meyer Jr. Letter to associate deans and directors, May 14, 1969 (Kroch Archives; no date indicated on copy provided).

45. Security memo, March 13, 1964 (Corson Papers, Kroch Archives, #3/11/1665). Keyes was a contender for the presidential nomination of the Republican Party in 1996. Paul Rahe (1995) and Nathan Tarcov (1997) also discussed this matter with me.

46. Paul DuBois, Oral History interview, pp. 28, 93–94.

47. Interview with Denise Raynor, 1998.

48. Interview with Paul DuBois, 1996.

49. Pearl Lucas, Oral History interview, p. 4.

50. F. Dana Payne and Barbara Hirshfeld, Oral History interview, pp. 9–11.

51. F. Dana Payne, Oral History interview, p. 26.

52. Ernest Dunbar, "The Black Studies Thing," in August Meier, Elliot Rudwick, and John Bracy Jr., eds., *Black Protest in the Sixties: Articles from the New York Times* (Markus Wiener, 1991), p. 247. Originally published in the *New York Times Magazine,* April 6, 1969, Dunbar's article was ironic. Overall, it praised Perkins and the racial experiment at Cornell. Two weeks later the Straight takeover erupted.

53. Ibid., pp. 247–248.

54. Miles, *The Radical Probe,* p. 238.

55. Donald, "Cornell," pp. 156–157.

56. Interview with Irving McPhail, 1997.

57. Interview with Andre McLaughlin, 1996.

58. Interview with James E. Turner, 1996.

59. W.E.B. Du Bois, *Souls of Black Folk* (Chicago, 1903).

60. I draw throughout here on Miles, *The Radical Probe,* ch. 4, "The Black Resistance."

61. James Weldon Johnson, *Negro Americans, What Now?* (1938). Quoted in Miles, *The Radical Probe,* p. 196.

62. Miles, *The Radical Probe,* p. 217.

63. Ibid. p. 238.

64. See John Bunzel, "Black Studies at San Francisco State," *The Public Interest,* Fall 1968, pp. 22–39.

65. See Jacob N. Gordon and James M. Rosen, *The Black Studies Debate* (University of Kansas, 1974).

66. Donald, "Cornell," pp. 167–168. See Stanley Elkins, *Slavery* 2d. ed. (Grosset and Dunlap, 1963) and discussion in Scott, *Contempt and Pity,* pp. 114–118, 154, 193.

67. Ibid., p. 163.

68. Ibid., pp. 158–159.

Chapter 4. Racial Justice versus Academic Freedom

1. Cleveland Donald, "Cornell: Confrontation in Black and White," in Cushing Strout and David I. Grossvogel, eds., *Divided We Stand: Reflections on the Crisis at Cornell* (Doubleday, 1970), pp. 178–179.

2. Like many other Western intellectuals, McPhelin may have been inclined to impose his own intellectual values or models on other cultures. To understand how such thinking characterized American (liberal, conservative, radical, and African-American) intellectuals' understandings of African nationalism at the time, see Martin Staniland, *American Intellectuals and African Nationalists, 1955–1970* (Yale University Press, 1991).

3. "Initial Statement of Economics 103 Students," submitted to the Williams Commission (Kroch Archives, #47/5/1309).

4. Williams Commission transcript, April 10, 1968, p. 10.

5. Stokely Carmichael and Charles V. Hamilton, *Black Power: The Politics of Liberation in America* (Vintage/Random House, 1967), pp. 4–5. See also Michael Omi and Howard Winant, *Racial Formations in the United States from the 1960s to the 1990s,* 2nd ed. (Routledge, 1994).

6. See Lee Rainwater and William L. Yancey, *The Moynihan Report and the Politics of Controversy* (MIT Press, 1967).

7. Report of the Special Cornell University Commission of April 1968 (Williams Commission Report), p. 23. April 26, 1968 (Kroch Archives, #46/5/1309).

8. Williams Commission transcript, April 10, 1968, p. 12.

9. Ibid., pp. 12–16.

10. Ibid., pp. 27–28.

11. "Initial Statement of Economics 103 Students."

12. See Daryl Michael Scott, *Contempt and Pity: Social Policy and the Image of the Damaged Black Psyche, 1880–1996* (University of North Carolina Press, 1997).

13. Interview with Nathan Tarcov, 1997.

14. Williams Commission transcript, April 11, 1968, p. 9.

15. Ibid., April 13, 1968, p. 4.

16. Williams Commission Report, p. 9.

17. Interview with Andre McLaughlin, 1996.

18. Interview with Irving McPhail, 1997.

19. Williams Commission transcript, April 15, p. 25.

20. Ibid., April 12, pp. 20–21.

21. Ibid., April 10, p. 43.

22. Ibid., p. 44.

23. Ibid., April 15, p. 10.

24. Ibid.

25. Ibid., April 12, p. 29. According to Davis, DuBois "seemed to me under the circumstances at some risk of losing what standing he had in that particular group to leave the room and to go to the Provost's office." Davis was right. After this affair, DuBois began to lose status in the AAS as it moved away from his integrationist position.

26. This view is based on many accounts.

27. Williams Commission transcript, April 14, pp. 29–30.

28. Interview with Dale Corson, 1996.

29. George Fisher and Stephen Wallenstein, *Open Breeches: Guns at Cornell* (unpublished manuscript), p. 60.

30. Interview with Dale Corson, 1996.

31. Williams Commission transcript, April 13, p. 53.

32. Ibid., April 14, pp. 2–3.

33. Ibid., April 13, p. 47.

34. On the reaction to King's murder, see Manning Marable, *Race, Reform, and Rebellion: The Second Reconstruction in Black America, 1945–1990* (University Press of Mississippi, 1991), pp. 105–106.

35. *Cornell Daily Sun,* April 5, 1968, p. 16.

36. Interview with Denise Raynor, 1998.

37. See Donald, "Cornell," p. 177.

38. *Cornell Daily Sun,* April 8, 1968, p. 3.

39. Ibid., p. 3.

40. Fisher and Wallenstein, *Open Breeches,* p. 67.

41. The events discussed here were reported in the *Ithaca Journal* and the *Cornell Daily Sun* on April 5, 8, 10, 11, and 12, 1968.

42. This account of the memorial service draws heavily on Fisher and Wallenstein, *Open Breeches,* pp. 62–65; their account is more detailed than those in the *Cornell Daily Sun* and the *Ithaca Journal.*

43. *Cornell Daily Sun,* April 8, 1968, p. 3.

44. Ibid., April 10, 1968, pp. 1, 7; Fisher and Wallenstein, *Open Breeches,* pp. 67–68. Hacker would go on to write *Two Nations: Black and White, Separate, Hostile, and Unequal* (Ballantine Books, 1992) and other famous works on racism.

45. Edward Whitfield, "Whitfield," in Joan Morrison and Robert K. Morrison, eds., *From Camelot to Kent State: The Sixties Experience in the Words of Those Who Lived It* (Times Books, 1987), p. 257.

46. Donald, "Cornell," p. 171.

47. David Brion Davis, *The Problem of Slavery in Western Culture* (Cornell University Press, 1966).

48. Benjamin Nichols, Oral History interview, pp. 6–7.

49. Sowell would become one of the leading conservative black scholars in the country at the Hoover Institute. He is the author of numerous books on race, civil rights, economics, culture, and history.

50. Interview with Irving McPhail, 1997; similar thinking was reflected in Tom Jones's speech at Willard Straight Hall, June 29, 1969.

51. Federal policy had not yet begun the shift from a steadfast color-blind posture toward the race-conscious affirmative action positions that would soon characterize federal administrative policy. See Andrew Kull, *The Color-Blind Constitution* (Harvard University Press, 1992), ch. 11.

52. Benjamin Nichols, Oral History interview, pp. 31–32.

53. Letter in Perkins Papers, Kroch Archives.

54. Williams Commission transcript, April 15, p. 63.

55. Allan P. Sindler, "How Crisis Came to Cornell," paper presented to 1971 national meeting of the American Political Science Association (copy provided to me by Sindler).

56. Williams Commission transcript, April 15, p. 19.

57. Williams Commission Report, p. 23.

58. Ibid., p. 25.

59. Frederick Marcham, letter to James A. Perkins, April 8, 1968 (Perkins Papers, #3/10/1022, Box 25). See also Walter Slatoff letter to Stuart Brown, May 4, 1968, in same materials.

60. Robert Miller, Oral History interview, p. 31.

61. Ibid., p. 35.

62. That same year the Kerner Commission came to a similar conclusion about race relations. See *Report of the National Advisory Commission on Civil Disorders* (Times Books, 1968). I thank my colleague James Baughman for alerting me to the connection with the Kerner Commission.

63. Stuart Brown, letter to Perkins and faculty, May 22, 1968 (Perkins Papers, #3/10/1022, Box 43).

64. George Hildebrand, Oral History interview, pp. 29, 31.

65. Isadore Blumen, letter to Robert Miller, April 24, 1968.

66. Robert Miller reply to Isadore Blumen (provided to me by Blumen). Miller used the famous expression "all deliberate speed" from *Brown v. Board of Education of Topeka* (349 U.S. 294, 1955).

67. Fisher and Wallenstein, *Open Breeches,* pp. BS12–BS13.

68. For example, see American Association of University Professors, "1940 Statement of Principles on Academic Freedom and Tenure," in *Policy Documents and Reports 3,* 7th ed. (1990).

69. Executive Committee, Cornell Chapter, Association of American University Professors, letter to James A. Perkins, April 22, 1968 (Perkins Papers, #3/10/1022, Box 25).

70. Perkins reply to Cornell AAUP, May 1, 1968 (Perkins Papers, #3/10/1022, Box 25).

71. Interview with Benjamin Nichols, 1996.

72. This portrayal was simplistic, as academic freedom was a vital concept in the medieval university, which valued the dialectical method of learning. Interview with Professor James John, Department of History, Cornell University, 1996.

73. Notes in Perkins Papers, May 17, 1968, #3/10/1022, Box 43.

74. Sindler, "How Crisis Came to Cornell," pp. 14–15.

75. In *Mission of the University* (Norton, 1966), Jose Ortega y Gasset argues that the university must involve itself in the vital issues of the day. Yet in doing so it must not forsake its ultimate mission, which is to deal with science (broadly understood) and universal matters.

76. For example, see Kull, *The Color-Blind Constitution;* Lani Guinier, *The Tyranny of the Majority: Fundamental Fairness in Representative Democracy* (Free Press, 1994); Richard D. Kahlenberg, *The Remedy: Class, Race, and Affirmative Action* (New Republic/Basic Books, 1996).

77. Hofstadter Columbia University commencement address, *New York Times,* June 5, 1968, pp. 1, 34.

78. On racism as the denial of individuality, see Albert Memmi, *The Colonizer and the Colonized* (Beacon Press, 1965); Hadley Arkes, "Civility and the Restriction of Speech: Rediscovering the Defamation of Groups," in Philip Kurland, ed., *Free Speech and Association: The Supreme Court and the First Amendment* (University of Chicago Press, 1975).

79. Interview with Sheila Tobias, 1995. Tobias went on to gain national recognition as a writer on feminist and educational issues.

80. George M. Kahin, "Address in Barton Hall, April 25, 1969." In Strout and Grossvogel, *Divided We Stand,* pp. 34–41.

81. Sindler, "How Crisis Came to Cornell," pp. 15–17.

82. Interview with Peter Sharfman, 1998.

83. Kull, *The Color-Blind Constitution,* pp. 185–186. Trailblazing sociologists such as William Julius Wilson have also dealt with the implications of this phenomenon later in the 1980s. See Wilson, *The Truly Disadvantaged: The Inner City, the Underclass, and Public Policy* (University of Chicago Press, 1987).

84. For an insightful treatment of this reaction, see Peter Novick, *That Noble Dream: The "Objectivity Question" and the American Historical Profession* (Cambridge University Press, 1988), esp. pp. 481–488.

85. Jonathan Rauch, *Kindly Inquisitors,* pp. 68–69. See also Scott, *Contempt and Pity.*

86. For example, see Sara McLanahan and Gary Sandefur, *Growing Up with a Single Parent: What Hurts, What Helps* (Harvard University Press, 1994). As Richard Kahlenberg states, "For a long time, discussion of the subject was taboo, but today everyone from former Vice President Dan Quayle to Secretary of HHS Donna Shalala agrees that children who live with two parents have a better chance of making it in our society." See also Kahlenberg, *The Remedy,* p. 135.

87. Kull, *The Color-Blind Constitution,* pp. 187–188.

88. On the Republican strategy, see Kevin Phillips, *The Emerging Republican Majority* (Anchor Books, 1970). On the Democratic Party reforms, see Austin Ranney, *Curing the Mischief of Faction: Party Reform in America* (University of California Press, 1975). On the disintegration of the liberal consensus, see Walter Dean Burnham, *The Current Crisis in American Politics* (Oxford University Press, 1982).

Chapter 5. Separation or Integration?

1. See Tamar Jacoby, *Someone Else's House: America's Unfinished Struggle for Integration* (Free Press, 1998), chs. 6 and 7; Diane Ravitch, *The Great School Wars: A History of the New York City Public Schools* (Basic Books, 1974).

2. Jacoby, *Someone Else's House,* p. 216.

3. Interview with Irving McPhail, 1997.

4. Malcolm X, *By Any Means Necessary* (Pathfinder Press, 1970), pp. 24–25. Like most Westerners, Malcolm interpreted African nationalism through the prism of his own political agenda. On this phenomenon, see Martin Staniland, *American Intellectuals and African Nationalists, 1955–1970* (Yale University Press, 1991), esp. ch. 6.

5. Thomas W. Jones, speech at Willard Straight Hall, June 29, 1969.

6. See Georg Wilhelm Friedrich Hegel, *The Phenomenology of Mind* (Harper, 1967; originally published in 1807), esp. pp. 229–233. On Hegel's theory of citizenship, see Steven B. Smith, *Hegel's Critique of Liberalism: Rights in Context* (University of Chicago Press, 1989).

7. See David Brion Davis, *The Problem of Slavery in Western Culture* (Cornell University Press, 1966).

8. Frantz Omar Fanon, *The Wretched of the Earth* (Grove Press, 1968), pp. 293–294. Originally published in 1961.

9. For example, see Charles Taylor, "The Politics of Recognition," in Amy Gutmann, ed., *Multiculturalism: Examining the Politics of Recognition* (Princeton University Press, 1994).

10. Hegel, *The Phenomenology of Mind*, p. 229.

11. Tom Hayden, quoted in James Miller, in *Democracy Is in the Streets: From Port Huron to the Siege of Chicago* (Simon & Schuster, 1987), p. 59.

12. Interview with Paul DuBois, 1996.

13. Indeed, Hegel also taught that universal reason is the ultimate product of the dialectical struggle among consciousnesses and between master and slave. Reason results from the conflict of opposites.

14. In the 1990s this conflict has taken the form of the debate over critical race studies. Compare Mari J. Matsuda, Charles R. Lawrence III, Richard Delgado, and Kimberlè Williams Crenshaw, *Words That Wound: Critical Race Theory, Assaultive Speech, and the First Amendment* (Westview Press, 1993), with Daniel A. Farber and Suzanna Sherry, *Beyond All Reason: The Radical Assault on Truth in American Law* (Oxford University Press, 1997).

15. Cleveland Sellers, with Robert Terrell, *The River of No Return: The Autobiography of a Black Militant and the Life and Death of SNCC* (Morrow, 1973).

16. Ibid., p. 136. At one point, Sellers declares, "To us, *everything* was political."

17. This problem besets universities. See Lawrence C. Soley, *Leasing the Ivory Tower: The Corporate Takeover of Academia* (South End Press, 1995).

18. Notes of University Committee on Undergraduate Education, May 20, 1968 (Perkins Papers, #3/10/1022, Box 43).

19. David Brion Davis, Oral History interview, p. 3.

20. Paul DuBois, Oral History interview, p. 63.

21. Ibid., p. 14.

22. Benjamin Nichols, Oral History interview, p. 67.

23. Chandler Morse, Oral History interview, p. 9.

24. Benjamin Nichols, Oral History interview, pp. 78–79.

25. David Brion Davis, Oral History interview, p. 4.

26. Benjamin Nichols, Oral History interview, p. 4.

27. Cleveland Donald, "Cornell: Confrontation in Black and White," in Cushing Strout and David I. Grossvogel, eds., *Divided We Stand: Reflections on the Crisis at Cornell* (Doubleday, 1970), p. 168.

28. Paul DuBois, Oral History interview. The following accounts are based on this interview.

29. Interview with Dale Corson, 1996.

30. Donald, "Cornell," pp. 173–174.

31. Robert Browne, "Financing the Black University" (Perkins Papers, #3/10/1022, Box 37).

32. Chandler Morse, Oral History interview, p. 26.

33. Harold Cruse, *The Crisis of the Negro Intellectual* (Morrow, 1967).

34. Interview with Irving McPhail, 1997.

35. Interview with James E. Turner, 1996.

36. Chandler Morse, Oral History interview, p. 68.

37. Donald, "Cornell," p. 158.

38. "Communication to All Cornell Black Students," report of December 3, 1968 meeting of AAS on Afro-American Studies Program (Perkins Papers, #3/10/1022, Box 37).

39. Chandler Morse, Oral History interview, p. 40.

40. *Cornell Daily Sun,* December 9, 1968, p. 1.

41. Interview with Isadore Blumen 1997. The disposition of the case was reported in the *Ithaca Journal,* April 24, 1969. On Reppert's beating, see *Cornell Daily Sun,* December 9, p. 1.

42. See Chandler Morse, Oral History interview, p. 51.

43. Donald, "Cornell," p. 159

44. Anonymous source.

45. Donald, "Cornell," pp. 198–199. Emphasis in the original.

46. Allan P. Sindler, Oral History interview, p. 59.

47. Interview with Dale Corson, 1996.

48. James A. Perkins, memo to Gloria Joseph, December 10, 1968 (Perkins Papers, #3/10/1022, Box 37.).

49. Perkins interview with Keith Johnson, 1994, pp. 166–167.

50. Interview with Paul Rahe, 1995.

51. AAS document (Perkins Papers, #3/10/1022, Box 37).

52. Anonymous source.

53. Perkins's memo to AAS, "An Agreement with Respect to the Future of the Afro- American Studies Program," December 11, 1968 (Perkins Papers, #3/10/1022, Box 37).

54. Donald, "Cornell," p. 177. This purchase of bongo drums became a symbol of liberal patronization to many on the campus. The AAS had purchased the drums in late February for Malcolm X Day with university funds provided by Vice Provost Keith Kennedy. The students obtained the drums by embarking on an odd excursion to New York that involved a chartered university plane ride, a limousine ride, and one student getting lost in a rented car.

55. Ibid., pp. 177–178.

56. *Cornell Daily Sun,* December 16, 1968, p. 1.

57. Paul DuBois, Oral History interview, pp. 28–29.

58. The names were never made public, but I learned of them in a judicial board document, Memo to Student Faculty Board on Student Conduct, March 10, 1969, from Elizabeth S. McLellan, executive secretary of the board (Perkins Papers, #3/10/1022, Box 25). This memo includes the names of the students, but I refrain from publishing them in honor of the Privacy Act of 1974.

59. George Fisher and Stephen Wallenstein, *Open Breeches: Guns at Cornell* (unpublished manuscript, p. 113).

60. *Cornell Daily Sun,* December 16, 1968, p. 1.

61. Robert Miller, letter to James A. Perkins, December 15, 1968 (Perkins Papers, #3/10/1022, Box 37).

62. John Marcham, Oral History interview, p. 245.

63. David Brion Davis, Oral History interview, p. 21.

64. Anonymous source.

65. James A. Perkins, memorandum to the AAS, December 15, 1968 (Perkins Papers, #3/10/1022, Box 37). See also *Cornell Daily Sun* reports of the AAS constitution proposal and administration's reactions and memos during the week of December 15.

66. Anonymous source.

67. This person is my anonymous source.

68. Anonymous source.

69. Anonymous source.

70. Anonymous source.

71. Anonymous source.

72. Robert Miller, Oral History interview, p. 55.

73. Anonymous source.

74. Anonymous source.

Chapter 6. Progress or Impasse?

1. Cleveland Donald, "Cornell: Confrontation in Black and White," in Cushing Strout and David I. Grossvogel, eds., *Divided We Stand: Reflections on the Crisis at Cornell* (Doubleday, 1970, p. 189).

2. Donald, "Cornell," pp. 189–190. Donald named Berns as the professor Whitfield studied with, but sources told me it was Bloom; this makes sense because Bloom was the political theorist who taught Plato.

3. Interview with Andre McLaughlin, 1996.

4. Keith Kennedy, Oral History interview, p. 25.

5. Ibid., p. 26.

6. Robert Miller, Oral History interview, p. 64.

7. Paul Olum, quoted in George Fisher and Stephen Wallenstein, *Open Breeches: Guns at Cornell* (unpublished manuscript), pp. 132–133.

8. Interview with Irving McPhail, 1997.

9. James A. Perkins, letter to Earl Armstrong, January 7, 1969 (Perkins Papers #3/10/1022, Box 32).

10. Allan P. Sindler, Oral History interview, pp. 29–30.

11. Keith Kennedy, Oral History interview, p. 27.

12. Ibid., p. 31.

13. Ibid., pp. 42–43.

14. Donald, "Cornell," p. 200.

15. See Michael W. Miles, *The Radical Probe: The Logic of Student Rebellion* (Atheneum, 1971), ch. 1.

16. Allan P. Sindler, Oral History interview, pp. 63–64.

17. Ibid., p. 42.

18. Ibid.

19. Allan P. Sindler, "How Crisis Came to Cornell," p. 27. On the variety of approaches to black studies that emerged during this time frame, see Nathan Huggins, *Afro-American Studies: A Report to the Ford Foundation* (Ford Foundation, 1985), esp. pp. 26–27.

20. Allan P. Sindler, Oral History interview, pp. 32–33.

21. See Keith Kennedy, Oral History interview, p. 55–57; Allan P. Sindler Oral History interview, pp. 39–41.

22. *Cornell Daily Sun*, February 17, 1969, p. 6.

23. Keith Kennedy, Oral History interview, pp. 69–70.

24. On such symbols, see Murray Edelman, *The Symbolic Uses of Politics* (University of Illinois Press, 1964).

25. Interview with Bruce Dancis; *Cornell Daily Sun*, February 27, 1969.

26. Fisher and Wallenstein, *Open Breeches*, p. 141.

27. *Cornell Daily Sun*, March 3, 1969, pp. 1, 6.

28. Reported in Keith Kennedy, confidential report to Lowell George, March 18, 1969. This report is included in materials accompanying Kennedy's Oral History interview.

29. Ibid. This account also draws on the coverage in the *Cornell Daily Sun*, March 3, 1969, pp. 1, 6.

30. Interview with David Burak, 1996.

31. Harris Raynor interview, 1998.

32. *Cornell Daily Sun*, March 3, 1969.

33. Donald, "Cornell," p. 193.

34. *Cornell Daily Sun*, March 3, 1969, p, 5.

35. Fisher and Wallenstein, *Open Breeches*, p. 147.

36. See story in *Cornell Daily Sun*, March 10, 1969, p. 1.

37. Interview with Dale Corson, 1996. Corson made a similar statement during his extraordinary speech at the faculty meeting of March 12, 1969.

38. Faculty meeting minutes, March 12, 1969, p. 3610.

39. Interview with David Wall, 1996.

40. Interview with David Burak, 1996.

41. Interview with Robert Kilpatrick, 1997. Kilpatrick was an economics professor at Cornell who now works in the Office of Management and Budget in Washington, D.C.

42. Joel Silbey, Oral History interview, pp. 6–11. Emphasis in the original.

43. Edward Fox, letter, *Cornell Daily Sun,* March 14, 1969, p. 5.

44. All Corson quotations in this discussion are from the minutes of the faculty meeting of March 12, 1968, pp. 3605–3613.

45. Minutes of faculty meeting of March 12, 1968, p. 3614.

46. All quotations in this account are from Frederick G. Marcham, *Cornell Notes, 1967–1979* (unpublished manuscript, Marcham Papers, Kroch Archives).

47. Friedland's statement and the debate over the judicial system are in the minutes of the faculty meeting of March 12, 1969, pp. 3617–3629.

48. Peter Sharfman, Oral History interview, pp. 88–90.

49. Keith Kennedy, Oral History interview, p. 81.

50. Interview with Dale Corson, 1996. Corson read much of this statement from notes he wrote after the meeting.

51. See Jones's statements in the *Cornell Daily Sun,* "The Straight Takeover 20th Anniversary Supplement," April 19, 1969, p. 28, and in *From Camelot to Kent State: The Sixties Experience in the Words of Those Who Lived It,* Joan Morrison and Robert K. Morrison, eds. (Times Books, 1987), p. 250.

52. Keith Kennedy, Oral History interview, p. 82.

53. Interview with James E. Turner, 1996.

54. Keith Kennedy, Oral History interview, p. 87.

55. *Cornell Daily Sun,* April 10, 1969, p. 1; April 15, 1969, p. 1.

56. Sindler, "How Crisis Came to Cornell," p. 26.

57. *Cornell Daily Sun,* various issues; Sindler, "How Crisis Came to Cornell"; Allan P. Sindler, Oral History interview; Isadore Blumen Papers (material provided to me).

58. See Roger Rosenblatt, *Coming Apart: A Memoir of the Harvard Wars of 1969* (Little, Brown, 1997).

59. Interview with Irving McPhail, 1997.

60. Memo in Corson Papers (Kroch Archives, #3/11/1665).

Chapter 7. Liberal Justice or Racism?

1. Interview with Henry Ricciuti, 1997.

2. Ibid.

3. Interview with Neal Stamp, 1997.

4. Interview with John Marcham, 1996.

5. Interview with David Lyons, 1996. On the split between blacks and Jews in the New York education wars and on other fronts, see Jim Sleeper, *The Closest of Strangers: Liberalism and the Politics of Race in New York* (Norton, 1990).

6. Interview with Peter Sharfman, 1998.

7. Interview with Irving McPhail, 1997.

8. Interview with Andre McLaughlin, 1996.

9. Interview with Stephen Goodwin, 1996. A similar perceptual gap characterizes race relations today, especially in the reaction to the verdict in the O. J. Simpson criminal trial. See Andrew Hacker, *Two Nations: Black and White, Separate, Hostile, and Unequal* (Ballantine Books, 1992). On the Simpson trial and race relations, see Jeffrey Toobin, *The Run of His Life: The People v. O. J. Simpson* (Random House, 1996). See also Jewelle Taylor Gibbs, *Race and Justice: Rodney King and O. J. Simpson in a House Divided* (Jossey-Bass, 1997).

10. On Jones's resignation from the UJB, see Appendix "A" of Art Spitzer's Oral History interview, pp. IV B–3 and IV B–4. These materials and Appendix "B" are excerpts from documents on the history of the judicial system composed by a committee Spitzer headed in the Constituent

Assembly in the summer of 1969. In this chapter I draw on Appendix "B" and notes of FCSA meetings that are collected in the Spitzer Papers, provided to me by Spitzer (they will be submitted to the Kroch Archives); Art Spitzer, Oral History interview.

11. Interview with Paul Rahe, 1995.

12. Ruth Darling, Oral History interview, p. 19.

13. Interview with David Pimentel, 1997.

14. Ruth Darling, Oral History interview, p. 23.

15. Ibid., p. 25.

16. Ibid.

17. See memo to SFBSC members from Elizabeth S. McClallan, March 10, 1969 (Perkins Papers, #3/10/1022, Box 25).

18. *Cornell Daily Sun*, March 7, 1969.

19. *Cornell Daily Sun*, March 7, 1969; interview with Wayne Biddle, 1998. Biddle was a dissenter on the conduct board who went on to win two Pulitzer Prizes as a science reporter for the *New York Times*.

20. Ibid., March 12, 1969.

21. Art Spitzer, Oral History interview, p. 52.

22. *Cornell Daily Sun*, April 16, 1969, p. 16.

23. Ibid., March 14, 1969, p. 1.

24. Ruth Darling, Oral History interview, p. 31.

25. Ibid., p. 32.

26. On the attacks and Klotz's initial condition, see *Cornell Daily Sun*, March 17, 1969, p. 1, and March 18, 1969, p. 1. Peter Agree ('69) was an eyewitness to one of the attacks and confirmed this portrayal.

27. Ibid., March 17, 1969; March 18, 1969.

28. Ibid., March 18, 1969, op-ed page.

29. Art Spitzer, Oral History interview, p. 69.

30. Ibid., p. 73.

31. Ibid., p. 80.

32. Ibid., pp. 78, 81–82. Spitzer called Morse "the wettest noodle."

33. Ruth Darling, Oral History interview, p. 34.

34. Art Spitzer, Oral History interview, p. 90.

35. Allan P. Sindler, "How Crisis Came to Cornell," p. 41.

36. This irony lies at the heart of constitutional law and the famous case establishing judicial review, *Marbury* v. *Madison* (1 Cranch 137, 1803). According to scholars, Chief Justice John Marshall's great decision in the name of the rule of law was Machiavellian in its political astuteness in a politically dangerous time. See, for example, Robert G. McCloskey, *The American Supreme Court*, rev. ed. (University of Chicago Press, 1994).

37. Art Spitzer, Oral History interview, p. 96.

38. Interview with Spitzer, 1997.

39. FCSA Report; *Cornell Daily Sun*, March 26, 1969; Sindler, "How Crisis Came to Cornell," pp. 40–50.

40. Interview with Henry Ricciuti, 1997.

41. Sindler, "How Crisis Came to Cornell," p. 50.

42. Ruth Darling, Oral History interview, p. 32.

43. *Cornell Daily Sun*.

44. A week earlier, the *New York Times* had published a major article by Ernest Dunbar on the struggle for a black studies program at Cornell. The gist of the article was that the program could help solve America's racial dilemma. Dunbar, "The Black Studies Thing," *New York Times Magazine*, April 6, 1969. Reprinted in August Meier, Elliot Rudwick, and John Bracy Jr., eds., *Black Protest in the Sixties: Articles from the New York Times* (Markus Wiener, 1991).

45. George Fisher and Stephen Wallenstein, *Open Breeches: Guns at Cornell* (unpublished manuscript), p. 186.

46. Interview with George Taber, campus police sergeant, 1996; Fisher and Wallenstein, *Open Breeches*.

47. Fisher and Wallenstein, *Open Breeches,* p. 204.

48. Interview with Harris Raynor, 1998.

49. See Jerry L. Avorn and members of the staff of the *Columbia Daily Spectator, Up Against the Ivy Wall: A History of the Columbia Crisis* (Atheneum, 1969), pp. 38, 60ff; Michael W. Miles, *The Radical Probe: The Logic of Student Rebellion* (Atheneum, 1971), ch. 4.

50. The dissenter was Wayne Biddle, who told me in his interview that he considered the vote a form of racial insensitivity.

Chapter 8. Day 1: The Takeover and the Arming of the Campus

1. Pearl Lucas, Oral History interview, p. 2; F. Dana Payne and Barbara Hirshfeld, Oral History interview.

2. Interview with Dale Corson, 1996.

3. Thomas W. Jones, "Tom Jones," in Joan Morrison and Robert K. Morrison, eds., *From Camelot to Kent State: The Sixties Experience in the Words of Those Who Lived It* (Times Books, 1987), p. 250.

4. Cleveland Donald, "Cornell: Confrontation in Black and White," in Cushing Strout and David I. Grossvogel, eds., *Divided We Stand: Reflections on the Crisis at Cornell* (Doubleday, 1970), p. 20

5. Interview with Irving McPhail, 1997.

6. Caleb S. Rossiter, *The Chimes of Freedom Flashing: A Personal History of the Vietnam Anti-War Movement and the 1960s* (CTA Press, 1996), pp. 73–74. See also Cleveland Donald's analysis of black men protecting black women at Cornell, "Cornell: Confrontation in Black and White," in Cushing Strout and David I. Grossvogel, eds., *Divided We Stand: Reflections on the Crisis at Cornell* (Doubleday, 1970).

7. Interview with David Burak, 1996.

8. Interview with Charles ("Chip") Marshall, 1996.

9. All quotations in this account are from an interview with Sarah Diamant Elbert by Keith Johnson, a portion of which was provided to me by that source.

10. See Jerry Avorn and the Staff of the *Columbia Daily Spectator, Up against the Ivy Wall: A History of the Columbia Crisis* (Atheneum, 1968).

11. George Fisher and Stephen Wallenstein, *Open Breeches: Guns at Cornell* (unpublished manuscript), p. 216.

12. Jack Kiely, Oral History interview, p. 11.

13. Ibid., p. 6.

14. Fisher and Wallenstein, *Open Breeches,* p. 221.

15. Interview with Stephen Goodwin, 1996.

16. I am especially indebted to Fisher and Wallenstein, *Open Breeches,* for the details just provided and for many of the details surrounding the initial takeover, pp. 221–223.

17. Fisher and Wallenstein, *Open Breeches,* p. 228.

18. Interview with George Taber, 1996.

19. Fisher and Wallenstein, *Open Breeches,* p. 228.

20. Interview with Dale Corson, 1996.

21. Ruth Darling, Oral History interview, pp. 39–40.

22. *Cornell Daily Sun,* "Straight Takeover Twentieth Anniversary Supplement," April 19, 1989.

23. Carter Committee Report, p. 11. Report to president of special committee to investigate the Wari cross-burning and the attack on Willard Straight; Lisle Carter, chair, May 23, 1969 (Perkins Papers, #3/10/1022, Box 32).

24. Ibid., p. 1.

25. Fisher and Wallenstein, *Open Breeches,* p. 232.

26. Ibid., p. 234.

27. *Cornell Daily Sun,* April 20, 1969; ibid., p. 237.

28. Ibid.

29. Ibid., April 20, 1969, pp. 1, 3.

30. Letter to James A. Perkins, May 14, 1969 (Perkins Papers, #3/10/1022, Box 36). Another letter, from a mother to Keith Kennedy, enclosed for refund a ticket "to events I was unable to attend in my nightgown. . . . Also, I placed a deposit of eight dollars for the room from which I was so unwillingly and frighteningly evicted."

31. Fisher and Wallenstein, *Open Breeches*, p. 246–247.

32. Thomas L. Tobin, Oral History interview, p. 47.

33. Avorn and Staff, *Up against the Ivy Wall*.

34. Interview with Irving McPhail, 1997.

35. Interview with Andre McLaughlin, 1996.

36. Ibid.

37. Interview with Stephen Goodwin, 1996.

38. Interview with Irene Smalls, 1997. See also "Irene Smalls," in Morrison and Morrison, *From Camelot to Kent State*, pp. 262–267.

39. Fisher and Wallenstein, *Open Breeches*, p. 254.

40. Ibid., p. 253.

41. Interview with Dale Corson, 1996.

42. Interview with Neal Stamp, 1997.

43. Thomas L. Tobin, Oral History interview, pp. 42–43.

44. Keith Kennedy, Oral History interview, p. 102.

45. Fisher and Wallenstein, *Open Breeches*, pp. 260–261.

46. Ibid., p. 263. My account here is based in large part on this manuscript.

47. Ibid., p. 269.

48. Charles ("Chip") Marshall, Oral History interview, p. 7.

49. Fisher and Wallenstein, *Open Breeches*, p. 270.

50. Thomas W. Jones, speech at Willard Straight Hall, June 29, 1969.

51. Interview with Andre McLaughlin, 1996.

52. Interview with George Taber, 1996.

53. Interview with David Wall, 1996.

54. Charles ("Chip") Marshall, Oral History interview, p. 6.

55. Ibid., p. 9.

56. Interview with Keith Kennedy, 1996.

57. *Ithaca Journal*, April 21, 1969, p.16.

58. Interview with Andrew Hacker, 1996.

59. Mark Barlow, Oral History interview, p. 55.

60. Ibid., esp. p. 107.

61. Fisher and Wallenstein, *Open Breeches*, p. 288.

62. Interview with Keith Kennedy, 1996.

63. Thomas L. Tobin, Oral History interview, p. 50.

64. See folder entitled "Rumor Clinic Calls" (Kroch Archives, K-116-H-2-A, Box 2). See also *Ithaca Journal*, April 23, 1969, "Rumor Clinic Sifts Fact from Fiction."

65. Fisher and Wallenstein, *Open Breeches*, p. 313.

66. Ruth Darling, Oral History interview, p. 45.

67. Interview with Irving McPhail, 1997.

68. Fisher and Wallenstein, *Open Breeches*, p. 287.

69. Art Spitzer, Oral History interview, pp. 108–114. Emphasis added.

70. Fisher and Wallenstein, *Open Breeches*, pp. 308–309.

71. Robert Miller, Oral History interview, p. 120.

72. Jack Kiely, Oral History interview, p. 27.

73. Interview with Dale Corson, 1996.

74. Thomas L. Tobin, Oral History interview, pp. 55–56.

75. Ibid., pp. 48–49.

76. Harris Raynor interview, 1998.

77. Fisher and Wallenstein, *Open Breeches*, p. 322.

78. Keith Kennedy, Oral History interview, p. 108.

79. Robert Miller, Oral History interview, p. 121.

80. Robert Franklin Williams, *Negroes with Guns* (Marzani & Munsel, 1962); Cleveland Sellers, with Robert Terrel, *The River of No Return: The Autobiography of a Black Militant and the Life and Death of SNCC* (Morrow, 1973).

81. Interview with Stephen Goodwin, 1996.

82. Interview with SDS member who requested anonymity.

83. Interview with Dale Corson, 1996.

84. Interview with Andre McLaughlin, 1996.

85. Martin Luther King Jr., Atlanta speech, April 3, 1968. In this address King also spoke of the importance of freedom of speech and the responsibilities of public citizenship. See also David J. Garrow, *Bearing the Cross: Martin Luther King Jr. and the Southern Christian Leadership Conference* (Vintage/Random House, 1986), ch. 11.

86. Thomas W. Jones, speech at Willard Straight Hall, June 29, 1969, pp. 12–13.

87. Interview with Irving McPhail, 1997.

88. Interview with Donald Kagan, 1997.

89. Fisher and Wallenstein, *Open Breeches*, p. 312.

90. Mark Barlow, Oral History interview, p. 61.

91. Stuart Brown, Oral History interview, pp. 4–6.

92. See generally, Fisher and Wallenstein, *Open Breeches*.

Chapter 9. Day 2: The Deal

1. Stuart Brown, Oral History interview, pp. 7–8. Emphasis added.

2. Thomas L. Tobin, Oral History interview.

3. Robert Miller, Oral History interview, pp. 125–126.

4. Ibid., p. 127.

5. Ibid., p. 128.

6. Ibid., pp. 128–129.

7. Interview with Steven Muller, 1996.

8. "Chronology of Events: Willard Straight Seizure" (draft), April 19 and 20, 1969, p. 6 (Perkins Papers, #3/10/1022, Box 37 [henceforth referred to as "Chronology"]).

9. Interview with Neal Stamp, 1997.

10. George Fisher and Stephen Wallenstein, *Open Breeches: Guns at Cornell* (unpublished manuscript), p. 328.

11. Interview with Steven Muller, 1996.

12. Interview with Rudolph ("Barry") Loncke, 1996. Loncke is now a juvenile judge in Sacramento, California, who acknowledges that the Straight crisis influenced his career choice.

13. Ibid.

14. Interview with Steven Muller, 1996; Jack Kiely, Oral History interview; Fisher and Wallenstein, *Open Breeches*.

15. Interview with Steven Muller, 1996. See also details in "Chronology," p. 7.

16. While they spoke, Muller observed some interesting things in the background: students moved his car in the courtyard; people like Gloria Joseph and Stephanie Jones and baby entered the Straight, as did a large group with blankets and a "trombone" case. He wondered how people could get in and out of the Straight so easily. Fisher and Wallenstein, *Open Breeches*.

17. Interview with Neal Stamp, 1997.

18. Interview with Steven Muller, 1996.

19. Fisher and Wallenstein, *Open Breeches*.

20. Mark Barlow, Oral History interview, p. 70.

21. Interview with Dale Corson, 1996.

22. Robert Miller, Oral History interview, p. 141.

23. Ibid., pp. 141–147.

24. Interview with Keith Kennedy, 1996.

25. *Cornell Daily Sun*, April 21, 1969.

26. Robert Miller, Oral History interview, p. 138.

27. Thomas L. Tobin, Oral History interview, p. 61.

28. Matt McHugh, Oral History interview, p. 3.

29. Jack Kiely, Oral History interview, p. 13.

30. Keith Kennedy, Oral History interview, p. 116.

31. Interview with Steven Muller, 1996.

32. Ibid.

33. Fisher and Wallenstein, *Open Breeches,* p. 341.

34. Interview with Steven Muller, 1996.

35. Keith Kennedy, Oral History interview, p. 140.

36. Ibid., p. 117.

37. Interview with Keith Kennedy, 1996.

38. Ibid.

39. Interview with Steven Muller, 1996.

40. Fisher and Wallenstein, *Open Breeches,* p. 330.

41. Interview with Dale Corson, 1996.

42. Mark Barlow, Oral History interview, p. 66.

43. Fisher and Wallenstein, *Open Breeches,* p. 336.

44. Ibid., p. 337–338.

45. Ibid., p.338.

46. Interview with Steven Muller, 1996. See "Agreement Between the AAS and Cornell Relating to Black Student Departure from Willard Straight Hall" (Perkins Papers, #3/10/1022, Box 37).

47. Fisher and Wallenstein, *Open Breeches.*

48. Keith Kennedy, Oral History interview, pp. 163–165.

49. *Cornell Daily Sun,* April 21, 1969, p. 9.

50. Fisher and Wallenstein, *Open Breeches,* p. 348; Thomas L. Tobin, Oral History interview.

51. Interview with Neal Stamp, 1997.

52. Interview with Keith Kennedy, 1996.

53. Robert Miller, Oral History interview, p. 141.

54. Executive Staff Transcript (my name for this untitled document), p. 9.

55. Ruth Darling, Oral History interview, p. 51.

56. Matt McHugh, Oral History interview, p. 14.

57. Stuart Brown, Oral History interview, p. 9.

58. *Cornell Daily Sun,* April 21, 1969, p. 5.

59. Allan P. Sindler, letter to author , June 15, 1997.

60. John Searle, *The Campus War: A Sympathetic Look at the University in Agony* (World, 1971), p. 85.

61. Interview with Dale Corson, 1996.

62. Thomas L. Tobin, Oral History interview, p. 41.

63. *Cornell University News,* press release, 5:45 p.m., April 20, 1969 (Perkins Papers, Kroch Archives); Fisher and Wallenstein, *Open Breeches,* p. 352. See also Thomas L. Tobin, Oral History interview, which deals with the press's view of the deal as a capitulation, p. 61.

64. *New York Times,* April 23, 1969, p. 30.

65. Cox Commission, *Crisis at Columbia: Report of the Fact-Finding Commission Appointed to Investigate the Disturbances at Columbia University in April and May 1968* (Vintage/Random House, 1968); Jerry Avorn and the Staff of the *Columbia Daily Spectator, Up against the Ivy Wall: A History of the Columbia Crisis* (Atheneum, 1968).

66. "Assessment of Damages to Willard Straight Hall as a Result of Takeover" (Perkins Papers, #3/10/1022, Box 37). Whiting quoted in *Sun,* May 6, 1969, p. 1: "Straight Damages Exceed $15,000"; Fisher and Wallenstein, *Open Breeches.*

67. Interview with David Burak, 1996. The SDS national organization was at this time undergoing major factional strife, and the faction that became the Weathermen was becoming increasingly militant and violent. See Todd Gitlin, *The Sixties: Years of Hope, Days of Rage* (Bantam Books, 1987). Cornell's Action Faction was not as militant or violent as the Weathermen.

68. Fisher and Wallenstein, *Open Breeches;* Peter Sharfman, Oral History interview.

69. Interview with Harris Raynor, 1998.

70. Executive Staff Transcript, p. 6.

71. Jack Kiely, Oral History interview, p. 33.

72. Robert Miller, Oral History interview, p. 147.

73. FCSA chair Henry Ricciuti stressed this reneging in his interview with me in 1997. He said that this issue was ignored in the aftermath of the crisis.

74. Executive Staff Transcript, p. 7.

75. *Ithaca Journal,* April 22, 1969, [no page number].

76. Fisher and Wallenstein, *Open Breeches,* p. 364.

Chapter 10. Day 3: A "Revolutionary Situation"

1. *New York Times,* April 21, 1969, pp. 1, 35.

2. Max Black, Oral History interview, p. 5.

3. Robert Miller, Oral History interview, p. 148.

4. Interview with Steven Muller, 1996.

5. See document, "For Immediate Release," at 9:15 a.m., April 21, 1969. Cornell University News Office (Perkins Papers, #3/10/1022, Box 36).

6. Mark Barlow, Oral History interview, p. 74.

7. See Locke, *Second Treatise of Government,* in *Two Treatises of Government,* ed. Peter Lashett (Cambridge University Press, 1967).

8. Matt McHugh, Oral History interview, p. 15.

9. Mark Barlow, Oral History interview, p. 32.

10. Executive Staff Transcript, p. 12.

11. Ibid, pp. 13–14.

12. Ibid., pp. 14–15.

13. There had been accounts of SDS and AAS student informers hiding in hallways to avoid being seen with high-level administrators like Perkins and Corson. Corson reported that one AAS student begged him not to reveal the student as an informant. In his interview with me twenty-seven years later, Corson was still unwilling to identify the student. See also Mark Barlow, Oral History interview, p. 28.

14. Charles ("Chip") Marshall, Oral History interview, pp. 18–19.

15. These questions were right out of Hobbes, whose *Leviathan* is dedicated to the problem of creating a common and authoritative rule of law out of the competing and conflicting interpretations that characterize the state of nature.

16. Ruth Darling, Oral History interview, p. 65.

17. Peter Sharfman, Oral History interview, p. 4.

18. "Cornell Notes," 1967–1979, Frederick G. Marcham Papers (Kroch Archives), p. 557.

19. Interview with Steve Muller, 1996.

20. Interview with Walter LaFeber, 1995. LaFeber did not say who the hold-out was, but a reasonable guess would be Henry Guerlac.

21. George Fisher and Stephen Wallenstein, *Open Breeches: Guns at Cornell* (unpublished manuscript), p. 381.

22. Eldron Kenworthy, Oral History interview, pp. 4–7.

23. Strauss wrote many works, the most influential of which was probably *Natural Right and History* (University of Chicago Press, 1952).

24. Berns, for example, established his national reputation by publishing a book in 1957 that foresaw and criticized the liberal trends of the Warren Court in First Amendment jurisprudence. Berns argued in *Freedom, Virtue, and the First Amendment* (Louisiana State University Press, 1957) that free speech doctrine (concerning when it is permissible to engage in censorship) should be governed by the concept of virtue rather than a concept of freedom divorced from considerations of virtue. The book constituted a Straussian interpretation of constitutional freedom.

25. This point is a theme that recurs in Bloom's book *The Closing of the American Mind: How Higher Education Has Failed Democracy and Impoverished the Souls of Today's Students* (Simon & Schuster, 1987), and it was a theme in Berns's course on American government.

26. The basic point of Plato in *The Republic* is to lead individuals from narrow self-interest to more universal conceptions of justice. To Straussians this path is the product of liberal education. On the relationship between constitutional principles and the aristocratic aspects of liberal education, see Paul Eidelberg, *The Philosophy of the American Constitution: A Reinterpretation of the Intentions of the Founding Fathers* (Free Press, 1968). Berns taught this book in his introductory course to American government, Government 101. See also George F. Kennan, *Democracy and the Student Left: Angry Students vs. the Establishment: The Dialogue That Turned to Violence* (Bantam Books, 1968). In the aftermath of the Cornell crisis, students in many courses wrote papers on the implications of what happened. One paper I ran across dealt with the crisis in terms of Tocqueville's notion of the "tyranny of the majority." It was written for an anthropology course; as we will see, the Anthropology Department was among the most sympathetic to the student revolt. The paper received a B.

27. This theme runs throughout Strauss's work and Bloom's book.

28. Steven Muller, confidential memo to James A. Perkins, Dale Corson, Robert C. Sproul, Frank and A. Long, June 12, 1968 (Perkins Papers, #3/10/1022, Box 33).

29. Bloom, *The Closing of the American Mind*, pp. 363, 365.

30. Confidential memo from Dean Stuart Brown to Provost Corson on "The Ashford- Sindler Problem," May 27, 1968 (Perkins Papers, #3/10/1022, Box 25).

31. Allan Sindler, "Report on the Department of Government, Cornell University" (Perkins Papers, #3/10/1022, Box 25).

32. Walter Berns, *For Capital Punishment: Crime and the Morality of the Death Penalty* (Basic Books, 1979). Hobbes emerges as a villain in Berns's book because he would build a state on self-interest and survival rather than virtue and a commitment to justice.

33. After a stint at the University of Toronto, Berns eventually became a fixture at the American Enterprise Institute in Washington, D.C., and Sindler became the chair of Berkeley's School of Public Policy. Both became prolific authors of scholarly works. After his own tenure at Toronto, Bloom became the chair of the Committee on Social Thought at the University of Chicago and the author of *The Closing of the American Mind*.

34. Interviews with Walter LaFeber, Richard Polenberg, and Joel Silbey (all 1995).

35. See Concerned Faculty statements during the crisis (Kroch Archives, #47/5/1309).

36. David Lyons, Oral History interview, p. 27.

37. Lyons, *Forms and Limits of Utilitarianism*, (Clarendon Press, 1965).

38. Sheila Tobias, Oral History interview, p. 16. Tobias went on to become a noted feminist and education writer.

39. Interview with Richard Polenberg, 1995.

40. Interview with Eldron Kenworthy, 1995.

41. Quoted in Howard Feinstein, "April 1969: A Celebration of the Mass," in Cushing Strout and David I. Grossvogel, eds., *Divided We Stand: Reflections on the Crisis at Cornell* (Doubleday, 1970), p. 97.

42. Executive Staff Transcript, p. 11.

43. Ibid.

44. Fisher and Wallenstein, *Open Breeches*, p. 370.

45. *New York Times,* April 22, 1969, p. 34.

46. Joel Silbey, Oral History interview, p. 38–39.

47. Interview with Corson, 1996.

48. Fisher and Wallenstein, *Open Breeches*, p. 373. Emphasis added.

49. Ibid., p. 375.

50. Mark Barlow, Oral History interview, p. 78.

51. Cushing Strout, Oral History interview, p. 17.

52. Faculty Meeting Notes, pp. 3658–3659.

53. Fisher and Wallenstein, *Open Breeches*, p. 384.

54. This meeting was not mentioned in Chapter Nine.

55. Faculty Meeting Notes, p. 3662.

56. Ibid., p. 3663.

57. Peter Sharfman, Oral History interview, p. 12.

58. Faculty Meeting Notes, p. 3669.

59. Max Black, Oral History interview, p. 12.

60. Interview with Walter LaFeber, 1995.

61. Faculty Meeting Notes, p. 3665.

62. Ibid.

63. Interview with Walter LaFeber, 1995.

64. Faculty Meeting Notes, p. 3666.

65. Ibid., p. 3667.

66. Interview with Steven Muller, 1996.

67. Peter Sharfman, Oral History interview, p. 15.

68. Cushing Strout, Oral History interview, p. 17.

69. Joel Silbey, Oral History interview, p. 40.

70. Fisher and Wallenstein, *Open Breeches,* p. 389.

71. Ibid., p. 390.

72. Ibid, p. 392.

73. Thomas L. Tobin, Oral History interview, pp. 76–78.

74. Fisher and Wallenstein, *Open Breeches,* pp. 395–396.

75. Peter Sharfman, Oral History interview, pp. 15–16.

76. Fisher and Wallenstein, *Open Breeches,* pp. 396–397.

77. "5 Days" (anonymous manuscript in the Kroch Archives, #47/15/1309, Box 12).

78. *Ithaca Journal,* April 22, 1969, p. 11.

79. See Jerry Avorn and the Staff of the *Columbia Daily Spectator, Up against the Ivy Wall: A History of the Columbia Crisis* (Atheneum, 1968).

80. Michael Miles, *The Radical Probe: The Logic of Student Rebellion* (Atheneum, 1971), esp. ch. 1.

81. Thomas W. Jones, "Tom Jones," in Joan Morrison and Robert K. Morrison, eds., *From Camelot to Kent State: The Sixties Experience in the Words of Those Who Lived It* (Times Books, 1987), p. 251.

82. Executive Staff Transcript, pp. 26–27.

83. Fisher and Wallenstein, *Open Breeches,* pp. 397–398.

84. Interview with Donald Kagan, 1996.

85. Eldron Kenworthy, Oral History interview, pp. 15–16.

86. Executive Staff Transcript, pp. 19–20.

87. Fisher and Wallenstein, *Open Breeches,* p. 402.

Chapter 11. Day 4: Student Power

1. Norman Penny, Oral History interview, pp. 11, 12.

2. Clinton Rossiter, Oral History interview, p. 9.

3. Clinton Rossiter, quoted in *Cornell Daily Sun,* April 22, 1969, p. 9; *New York Times,* April 24, 1969, p. 1.

4. Norman Penny, Oral History interview, pp. 4–5.

5. George Hildebrand, Oral History interview, p. 43.

6. Norman Penny, Oral History interview, p. 7.

7. David Lyons, Oral History interview, p. 3.

8. See, for example, Jerry Avorn and the Staff of the *Columbia Daily Spectator, Up against the Ivy Wall: A History of the Columbia Crisis* (Atheneum, 1968); Roger Rosenblatt, *Coming Apart: A Memoir of the Harvard Wars of 1969* (Little, Brown, 1997).

9. Edwards became a professor of sociology at the University of California, Berkeley, and the

pioneer in the field of "sport sociology." He is also the consultant to the National Football League on race relations.

10. Henry Alker, quoted in George Fisher and Stephen Wallenstein, *Open Breeches: Guns at Cornell* (unpublished manuscript), p. 406.

11. Max Black, Oral History interview, p. 15.

12. Concerned Faculty Statement (Kroch Archives, #47/5/1309 [no box number]).

13. Eldron Kenworthy, Oral History interview, pp. 17, 18.

14. Max Black, Oral History interview, pp. 16–17.

15. Cushing Strout, Oral History interview, p. 21.

16. Executive Staff Transcript, pp. 24–25.

17. Fisher and Wallenstein, *Open Breeches*, p. 405.

18. Executive Staff Transcript, p. 25.

19. Tobin provided a humorous account of this incident; see Thomas L. Tobin, Oral History interview, pp. 85–87.

20. Ruth Darling, Oral History interview, p. 65–67.

21. Thomas L. Tobin, Oral History interview, p. 129; *Cornell Daily* Sun, April 23, 1969, p. 1.

22. Charles ("Chip") Marshall, Oral History interview, pp. 16–20. It is not clear exactly when the AAS changed its name to the Black Liberation Front, and Marshall may have used the new designation before the official change took place. I will not use the new name until after the faculty reversal on Wednesday.

23. Joel Silbey, quoted in Fisher and Wallenstein, *Open Breeches*, pp. 412–413.

24. Joel Silbey, Oral History interview, pp. 21, 29.

25. Interview with Walter Berns, 1995.

26. Stuart Brown, Oral History, p. 20.

27. "Cornell Notes, 1967–79," in Frederick G. Marcham Papers (Kroch Archives, p. 559.)

28. Joel Silbey, Oral History interview, pp. 25–26.

29. Executive Staff Transcript, p. 28.

30. Interview with John Marcham, 1996.

31. Executive Staff Transcript, pp. 28–29.

32. Fisher and Wallenstein, *Open Breeches*, p. 422. Most of the information on this session at the studio is based on Fisher and Wallenstein's account.

33. Ibid.

34. Jones's and Martin's words are from Fisher and Wallenstein's account.

35. *Wall Street Journal*, November 21, 1997, pp. 1, 8.

36. See for example, interview with David Burak, 1996.

37. Stuart Brown, Oral History interview, p. 82.

38. Executive Staff Transcript, pp. 29–30.

39. Thomas L. Tobin, Oral History interview, pp. 88–90.

40. Jack Kiely, Oral History interview, pp. 21–22. See also Thomas L. Tobin, Oral History interview, pp. 91–92.

41. Fisher and Wallenstein, *Open Breeches*, pp. 423–424.

42. Douglas Dowd told this to Robert Kilpatrick, among others; Kilpatrick repeated it to me.

43. Thomas L. Tobin, Oral History interview, pp. 90–112.

44. Fisher and Wallenstein, *Open Breeches*, p. 428.

45. Interview and correspondence with Allan Sindler.

46. Charles ("Chip") Marshall, Oral History interview, pp. 21–22.

47. "5 Days" (anonymous manuscript), p. 12.

48. For insightful analysis of the window of moral opportunity during the Holocaust, see Kristin R. Monroe, *The Heart of Altruism: Perceptions of a Common Humanity* (Princeton University Press, 1996).

49. Howard Feinstein, "April 1969: A Celebration of the Mass," in Cushing Strout and David I. Grossvogel, eds., *Divided We Stand: Reflections on the Crisis at Cornell* (Doubleday, 1970), p. 99.

50. Ibid.

51. Charles ("Chip") Marshall, Oral History interview, p. 22.

52. Fisher and Wallenstein, *Open Breeches,* p. 432.

53. Thomas W. Jones, quoted in *Cornell Alumni News,* June 1969, p. 20.

54. Eyewitness account.

55. Paul Marantz, quoted in Fisher and Wallenstein, *Open Breeches,* p. 432.

56. Feinstein, "April 1969," p. 100.

57. Interview with Charles ("Chip") Marshall, 1996.

58. Fisher and Wallenstein, *Open Breeches,* p. 437. Student paper, "Confrontation" (Kroch Archives, K-116-H-2-A, Box 13); at the top of the first page the grader wrote, "Paper not judged on the same criteria as those dealing with tribal governments." See also the packet of materials, "Outline of the Events at Cornell University, April 1969," compiled by Michael J. Malbin (class of '64 and Government graduate student); provided to me by Professor Jeremy Rabkin.

59. Eldron Kenworthy, Oral History interview, p. 18.

60. Charles ("Chip") Marshall, Oral History interview, pp. 19–20.

61. Fisher and Wallenstein, *Open Breeches,* pp. 436–437.

62. Eldron Kenworthy, Oral History interview, pp. 23.

63. Fisher and Wallenstein, *Open Breeches,* p. 439.

64. Ibid.; Eldron Kenworthy, Oral History interview, 22–23; interview with Eldron Kenworthy.

65. Charles ("Chip") Marshal, Oral History interview, p. 23.

66. Jack Kiely, Oral History interview, p. 19.

67. Interview with David Burak, 1996.

68. Interview with Randall Hausner, 1996.

69. Interview with David Burak, 1996.

70. Fisher and Wallenstein, *Open Breeches.*

71. Interview with David Burak, 1996.

72. "5 Days," pp. 20, 22.

73. *Ithaca Journal,* April 23, 1969, p. 15.

74. Fisher and Wallenstein, *Open Breeches,* p. 442.

75. Thomas L. Tobin, Oral History interview, p. 95.

76. Milton Konvitz, "Why One Professor Changed His Vote," *New York Times Magazine,* May 18, 1969, p. 61.

77. Ruth Darling, Oral History interview, p. 68.

78. Thomas W. Jones, speech at Willard Straight Hall, June 29, 1969.

79. Fisher and Wallenstein, *Open Breeches,* p. 454. See also generally, Allan P. Sindler, "How Crisis Came to Cornell."

Chapter 12. Day 5: A New Order

1. "5 Days" (anonymous manuscript); George Fisher and Stephen Wallenstein, *Open Breeches: Guns at Cornell* (unpublished manuscript).

2. "5 Days," p. 23.

3. Ibid.

4. Milton Konvitz, quoted in Fisher and Wallenstein, *Open Breeches,* pp. 456–457.

5. Executive Staff Transcript, p. 38.

6. See, for example, Frederick G. Marcham Papers, Cornell Notes, 1957–1969 (Kroch Archives).

7. Max Black, Oral History interview, pp. 22–23.

8. Ibid., pp. 26–27. The student interviewer was in fact Stephen Wallenstein.

9. Executive Staff Transcript, pp. 40–41.

10. *Albany Times-Union,* April 24, 1969.

11. Thomas W. Tobin, Oral History interview, p. 100.

12. Faculty Meeting Notes, pp. 3668–3675 (all quotations in the ensuing account of this meeting are from this source unless otherwise indicated); ibid., p. 102.

13. James John, *Alumni News,* June 1969. John also provided me with a copy of the speech.

14. Fisher and Wallenstein, *Open Breeches,* p. 461.

15. Max Black, Oral History interview, pp. 27–28.

16. Interview with Dale Corson, 1996. On Alcibiades, see Plutarch, *The Lives of the Noble Grecians and Romans* (Random House Library, no date).

17. Frederick G. Marcham Papers, Cornell Notes 1957–1969 (Kroch Archives), pp. 566–567.

18. Peter Sharfman, Oral History interview, pp. 40–41.

19. Fisher and Wallenstein, *Open Breeches,* p. 461.

20. David Lyons, Oral History interview, p. 27.

21. Joel Silbey, Oral History interview, pp. 26–27.

22. Interview with Donald Kagan, 1996.

23. Joel Silbey, Oral History interview, p. 29.

24. Clinton Rossiter, *Cornell Daily Sun,* April 24, 1969, p. 16.

25. Executive Staff Transcript, p. 41.

26. Interview with David Burak, 1996.

27. *Cornell Daily Sun,* April 24, 1969, p. 1.

28. Executive Staff Transcript, p. 42–43.

29. "It Can't Happen Here—Can It?" *Newsweek,* May 5, 1969, p. 29.

30. Executive Staff Transcript, p. 44.

31. James A. Perkins, *Cornell Alumni News,* June 1969, p. 24.

32. Fisher and Wallenstein, *Open Breeches,* p. 465.

33. Peter Sharfman, Oral History interview, p. 31.

34. Ari Zolberg, "Moments of Madness," *Politics and Society,* 1972, pp. 183–207.

35. Interview with Gould Coleman, 1995.

36. Quoted in Howard Feinstein, "April 1969: A Celebration of the Mass," in Cushing Strout and David I. Grossvogel, eds., *Divided We Stand: Reflections on the Crisis at Cornell* (Doubleday, 1970), pp. 103–104.

37. Fisher and Wallenstein, *Open Breeches,* pp. 474–475. See also, student letter (Kroch Archives, #47/5/1309, Box 13).

38. Fisher and Wallenstein, *Open Breeches,* p. 477.

39. Jonathan Rauch has shown how campaigns to eradicate evil, as opposed to its effects, leads to witch hunts. See also *Kindly Inquisitors: The New Attacks on Free Thought* (University of Chicago Press, 1993).

40. Interviews with Art Spitzer and Peter Harvey, 1997.

41. See, for example, Perry Miller, *Jonathan Edwards* (Meridian Books, 1959).

42. Cushing Strout, Oral History interview, p. 26.

43. Norman Penny, Oral History interview, pp. 12–13.

44. On how the "liberal model of science" supports empirical rationality over "revelation" or intellectual authority based on the status of the speaker, see Rauch, *Kindly Inquisitor: The New Attacks on Free Thought* (University of Chicago Press, 1993).

45. Alan Wolfe, "The New Class Comes Home," in Edith Kuzweil and William Phillips, eds., *Our Country, Our Culture: The Politics of Political Correctness* (Partisan Review Press, 1994), p. 288. For a case study of this type of political correctness in action in the '90s, see David O. Sacks and Peter A. Thiel's portrayal of the drive to eliminate the Western civilization requirement at Stanford in *The Diversity Myth: "Multiculturalism" and the Politics of Intolerance at Stanford* (Independent Institute, 1995).

46. See "The Plague in Literature and Myth," in René Girard, *To Double Business Bound: Essays on Literature, Mimesis, and Anthropology* (Johns Hopkins Press, 1978); Girard, *Violence and the Sacred* (Johns Hopkins Press, 1977).

47. Gunnar Mengers, quoted in Fisher and Wallenstein, *Open Breeches,* pp. 475–476.

48. Interview with Benjamin Nichols, 1996.

49. Walter Berns and Allan P. Sindler, "Academic Freedom Abridged," *Cornell Daily Sun,* May 2, 1969, op-ed page.

50. Interview with Andrew Hacker, 1996.

51. Feinstein, "April 1969," pp. 112–113.

52. Ibid., pp. 117–118.

53. Richard Polenberg provided me with several samples of such reactions; Feinstein's article provides many examples of psychological reactions.

Chapter 13. Reform, Reaction, Resignation

1. See, for example, Thomas L. Tobin, Oral History interview, pp. 111–113.

2. Norman Penny, Oral History interview, pp. 24–27.

3. George Hildebrand, Oral History interview, pp. 56–69; interview with Robert Kilpatrick, 1997. Kilpatrick also provided me with materials concerning this and other matters.

4. Thomas L. Tobin, Oral History interview, p. 108.

5. Though the university's legal counsel granted me access to the transcripts of the Robertson Committee's testimony, the conditions it set rendered it impossible to take advantage of the offer.

6. *Cornell Daily Sun,* April 25, 1969, p. 1.

7. Ibid.

8. Ibid.; *Sun,* April 25, 1969, p. 1.

9. Interview with Donald Kagan, 1996.

10. *Cornell Daily Sun,* April 25, 1969, p. 1.

11. Ibid., p. 16.

12. Peter Sharfman, Oral History interview, p. 50.

13. Ibid., pp. 54–59.

14. George Fisher and Stephen Wallenstein, *Open Breeches: Guns at Cornell* (unpublished manuscript), pp. 488–490.

15. *Cornell Daily Sun,* April 25, 1969, p. 1; ibid., p. 485; interview with Walter Berns, 1995.

16. See the introduction to Walter Berns, *For Capital Punishment: Crime and the Morality of the Death Penalty* (Basic Books, 1979); see also Berns, "The Assault on the Universities: Then and Now," in Stephen Macedo, ed., *Reassessing the Sixties: Debating the Political and Cultural Legacy* (Norton, 1997).

17. Interview with Walter Berns, 1995. Major studies on academic freedom crises (McCarthyism, the era of political correctness, and so on) have shown that cowardice of colleagues is one of the most salient factors in such incidents. See, for example, Neil L. Hamilton, *Zealotry and Academic Freedom: A Legal and Historical Perspective* (Transaction Books, 1995).

18. Interviews with Allan Sindler (1995), Donald Kagan (1996), and Walter LaFeber (1995).

19. *Cornell Daily Sun,* April 25, 1969, p. 16.

20. See George McTurnan Kahin and John Wilson Lewis, *The United States in Vietnam* (Dial Books, 1967). According to Jacob Heilbrunn, Kahin and LaFeber have had a major influence on the foreign policy views of a generation of individuals schooled in the "revisionist" school of American foreign policy (a school founded by LaFeber's mentor at Wisconsin, William Appleman Williams). See Heilbrunn, "Mr. Nice Guy: Sandy Berger's Sunny Foreign Policy," *New Republic,* April 13, 1998, pp. 19–23.

21. Peter Sharfman, Oral History interview, pp. 44–45.

22. George M. Kahin, "Address in Barton Hall, April 25, 1969," in Cushing Strout and David I. Grossvogel, eds., *Divided We Stand: Reflections on the Crisis at Cornell* (Doubleday, 1970), pp. 34–41.

23. Peter Sharfman, Oral History interview, p. 64.

24. Peter Sharfman, Oral History interview; Clinton Rossiter, Oral History interview.

25. Fisher and Wallenstein, *Open Breeches,* p. 488.

26. Kahn letter to Evelyn and David Major, April 27, 1969, and Kahn note (in material provided to me by Kahn).

27. James A. Perkins, letter to Robert Miller, April 30, 1968.

28. Norman Penny, Oral History interview, pp. 30–32.

29. Caleb S. Rossiter, *The Chimes of Freedom Flashing: A Personal History of the Vietnam Anti-War Movement and the 1960s* (TCA Press, 1996), p. 144. Caleb was a radical prodigal son and an-

tiwar activist who had come to question the legitimacy of the America his father had championed. Today he is an international rights and foreign rights activist in Washington, D.C.

30. Interview with Walter Berns, 1995.

31. Rossiter, *The Chimes of Freedom Flashing*, p. 12.

32. Interview with John Marcham, 1996.

33. Rossiter, *The Chimes of Freedom Flashing*, p. 13.

34. Clinton Rossiter, Oral History interview, p. 8.

35. Ibid., p. 5.

36. Conversation with Allan Sindler, 1997.

37. Clinton Rossiter, Oral History interview, pp. 32–34.

38. Interview with Alfred Kahn, 1996.

39. Interview with Joel Silbey, 1995.

40. Rossiter, *The Chimes of Freedom Flashing*, pp. 139–140.

41. Eldron Kenworthy, Oral History interview, p. 28.

42. Interview with Joel Silbey, 1995.

43. Interview with Dale Corson, 1996.

44. Fisher and Wallenstein, *Open Breeches*, p. 495.

45. Peter Sharfman, Oral History interview, p. 74.

46. Thomas L. Tobin, Oral History interview, p. 110, 113.

47. Peter Sharfman, Oral History interview, pp. 71–73.

48. Fisher and Wallenstein, *Open Breeches*, pp. 501–502.

49. *Cornell Daily Sun*, April 28, 1969, pp. 1, 10.

50. Fisher and Wallenstein, *Open Breeches*, pp. 505–506.

51. Interviews with Donald Kagan (1996) and Walter Berns (1995).

52. See Thomas L. Tobin, Oral History interview, pp. 114–115; Fisher and Wallenstein, *Open Breeches*, pp. 510–511.

53. Interview with Steven Muller, 1996.

54. An alumnus's letter to James A. Perkins, April 27, 1969 (Perkins Papers, #3/10/1022, Box 36). Other letters cited are from the same files.

55. Interview with Walter Berns, 1995. Allan Bloom discusses this split at Cornell and in higher education in general in *The Closing of the American Mind: How Higher Education Has Failed Democracy and Impoverished the Souls of Today's Students* (Simon & Schuster, 1987).

56. Alumnus letter to the president of the Cornell Alumni Association, May 10, 1969 (Perkins Papers, #3/10/1022, Box 36).

57. Thomas L. Tobin, Oral History interview.

58. Interview with Paul Rahe, 1995.

59. Interview with Stanley Chess, 1996.

60. These pieces appeared between April 22 and early May.

61. Interview with William Robertson, 1997.

62. Interview with Walter Berns, 1995.

63. John Marcham, Oral History interview, p. 242.

64. Salisbury, "Foreword," in *Forward Positions: The War Correspondence of Homer Bigart*, Betsy Wade, ed. (University of Arkansas Press, 1992), pp. xi–xii.

65. Thomas L. Tobin, Oral History interview, pp. 105–106.

66. Interview with Richard Polenberg, 1995.

67. Fisher and Wallenstein, *Open Breeches*, p. 512.

68. *New York Times*, April 24, 1969, p. 1.

69. Ibid., April 25, 1969, p. 1.

70. Ibid.

71. *New York Times*, April 26, 1969, p. 14.

72. John Marcham, Oral History interview, p. 239.

73. Interview with William Robertson, 1997.

74. George Hildebrand, Oral History interview, p. 69.

75. Ibid, pp. 43, 46.

76. Ibid., pp. 70, 73. I also had access to the Robertson Committee testimony of Isadore Blumen and James Whitlock.

77. Interview with Walter Berns, 1995.

78. Most of this and the following discussion is from "Cornell Notes, 1967–1979," in the Frederick G. Marcham Papers (Kroch Archives, pp. 572–582) and my interview with Walter LaFeber.

79. Interview with Neal Stamp, 1997.

80. Interview with Walter LaFeber, 1995.

81. *New York Times,* May 2, 1969, p. 1; Fisher and Wallenstein, *Open Breeches.*

82. Thomas L. Tobin, Oral History interview, pp. 120–122; interview with John Marcham; John Marcham, Oral History interview; Fisher and Wallenstein, *Open Breeches,* pp. 516–517.

83. Thomas L. Tobin, Oral History interview, p. 123.

84. Ibid., pp. 121–123.

85. Allan P. Sindler, "How Crisis Came to Cornell," April 27, 1969, pp. 69–70.

86. Thomas L. Tobin, Oral History interview, pp. 114–116. See "Transcript of Talk Given by Steven Muller: Annual Meeting, Cornell Club of Buffalo," April 30, 1969 (Perkins Papers, #3/10/1022, Box 37).

87. Fisher and Wallenstein, *Open Breeches,* p. 564.

88. Jack Kiely, Oral History interview, pp. 16–17.

89. *Cornell Daily Sun,* May 15, 1969, p. 7. See Tower Club Speech (Perkins Papers, #3/10/1022, Box 37).

90. Interview with Paul Rahe, 1995; Fisher and Wallenstein, *Open Breeches,* pp. 568–569.

91. Interview with Patricia and Charles Stewart, 1997.

92. *Cornell Daily Sun,* May 16, 1969, p. 1.

93. Interview with Allan Sindler, 1995; Fisher and Wallenstein, *Open Breeches,* p. 573; *Ithaca Journal,* May 24, 1969.

94. Fisher and Wallenstein, *Open Breeches,* p. 576.

95. Cushing Strout, Oral History interview, pp. 34–35.

96. *Ithaca Journal,* May 24, 1969; Fisher and Wallenstein, *Open Breeches,* p. 574.

97. Cushing Strout, Oral History interview, p. 33. These comments suggest that Perkins actually agreed — despite his disclaimers to the faculty — with comments Muller had made in the *Wall Street Journal* (August 23, 1968) about the progressive university's need for student-administrative alliances against the faculty. This article sparked a heated controversy at the first faculty meeting of that year in which Perkins dissociated himself from Muller's points. Muller also said he was quoted out of context.

98. Interviews with William Robertson, Neal Stamp, and Joyce Cima (secretary of the Board of Trustees); all interviews 1997.

99. Interview with William Robertson, 1997.

100. "Report of the Special Trustee Committee on Campus Unrest at Cornell" (Robertson Committee Report), presented September 5, 1969, pp. 28, 37.

101. Sindler, "How Crisis Came to Cornell," pp. 79–80.

102. Robertson Committee Report, p. 60.

103. Ibid., p. 59. See Association of American University Professors, "1940 Statement of Principles on Academic Freedom and Tenure," in *Policy Documents and Reports 3,* 7th ed. (1990). One of the best sources on academic freedom is William W. Van Alstyne, ed., *Freedom and Tenure in the Academy* (Duke University Press, 1993).

104. James A. Gross, letter to Perkins, April 28, 1969 (Perkins Papers, #3/10/1022 [no box provided]).

105. Richard Hofferbert letter to the Faculty Committee on Academic Freedom and Tenure, May 14, 1969; emphasis in original (Kroch Archives, #47/5/1309 [no box provided]).

106. Arthur W. Rovine, letter to the Faculty Committee on Academic Freedom and Tenure, May 16, 1969 (Kroch Archives, #47/5/1309 [no box provided]).

107. Fisher and Wallenstein, *Open Breeches*, p. 587.

108. Homer Bigart, "Cornell Bears Scars of Conflict: Faculty Is Divided over Perkins," *New York Times,* May 28, 1969, p. 1.

109. Steven Muller, *Cornell Alumni News,* June 1969, p. 35.

110. John Marcham, ibid., pp. 30, 32.

111. John Marcham, Oral History interview, pp. 206–207.

112. Ibid., p. 205; Fisher and Wallenstein, *Open Breeches,* pp. 584–585.

113. John Marcham, Oral History interview, pp. 205–206.

114. Interview with Ian MacNeil, 1997.

115. Ibid.

116. Law School letter, May 23, 1969 (Perkins Papers, Kroch Archives).

117. Fisher and Wallenstein, *Open Breeches,* pp. 590–592.

118. Interview with William Robertson, 1997.

119. *New York Times,* June 1, 1969, p. 1.

120. Fisher and Wallenstein, *Open Breeches,* pp. 596–599.

121. James A. Perkins, Commencement Address, quoted in Peter Kihss, *New York Times,* June 10, 1969, p. 1; ibid., pp. 601–604.

122. Peter Kihss, *New York Times,* June 11, 1969, p. 32.

123. Sindler, "How Crisis Came to Cornell," p. 78.

Chapter 14. Cornell and the Failure of Liberalism

1. Much of the information regarding this matter is drawn from Keith Kennedy, Oral History interview, esp. pp. 122–129.

2. See James E. Turner, "Turner Accepts Director of Afro-American Center, " *Cornell Daily Sun,* June 2, 1969, p. 7.

3. Thomas W. Jones, speech at Willard Straight Hall, June 29, 1969.

4. Thomas W. Jones, letter to James A. Perkins, July 18, 1980; provided by Keith Johnson.

5. James A. Perkins, letter to Thomas W. Jones, August 15, 1980; provided by Keith Johnson.

6. *Wall Street Journal,* August 15, 1997, p. C1.

7. Jonathan Kaufman and Anita Raghavan, "The Jones Brother's Frame a 'Great Debate' over Success and Race," *Wall Street Journal,* November 21, 1997, p. 1.

8. Interview with Walter Berns, 1995.

9. Clarence Page, "Second Thoughts and Hope"; (article provided to me by Berns; neither publication nor date was legible.)

10. Walter Berns, letter to Clarence Page, May 20, 1995. Berns told me that Jones denies that Berns convinced him to stay.

11. Resolution July 1969, from the papers of Robert Kilpatrick; provided by Kilpatrick.

12. Peter Sharfman, Oral History interview, p. 94.

13. Barbara Hirshfeld, in F. Dana Payne and Barbara Hirshfeld, Oral History interview, p. 19.

14. Interview with Irving McPhail, 1997. Andre McLaughlin's experience was similar, though less transformative.

15. Interview with James E. Turner, 1996.

16. Interview with a Cornell professor who asked to remain anonymous in connection with this issue.

17. Interview with James Turner, 1996.

18. Provost Robert Plane, memorandum to President Dale Corson, October 27, 1969 (Corson Papers, Kroch Archives, #3/11/1665, Box 33).

19. Interview with Isadore Blumen, 1997. A similar issue broke out in 1976 in relation to a Regents' case against the university. John M. Freyer (Cornell's attorney), letter to Robert D. Stone, State Education Department, December 13, 1976 (Corson Papers, Kroch Archives #3/11/1665 [no box provided]).

20. Ujamaa Statement of Purpose, July 7, 1972 (Corson Papers, #3/11/1665).

21. For example, Keith Kennedy, letter to Robert Plane, May 12, 1970 (Corson Papers, #3/11/1665, Box 33).

22. Dale Corson, "Confidential Memorandum Concerning Regents Hearing on Ujamaa," submitted to the Executive Committee of the Board of Trustees, August 6, 1976 (Corson Papers, #3/11/1665, Box 123).

23. A leading insider in the Corson administration informed me of this issue, which alerted me to look for Ujamaa materials in the Corson Papers. This individual had played a pivotal role in the Ujamaa matter and in later issues of a similar nature. He was critical of the university's policies in this area.

24. Thomas Sobol, letter to the editor, *Wall Street Journal*, June 11, 1996, p. A15. Sobol, a professor at Teachers College, Columbia University, assisted New York State's investigation of the Cornell programs.

25. "Cornell Battles Anew over Ethnic Dormitories," *New York Times*, May 6, 1996, p. B5; "No Violation of Rights Is Found in Cornell Dorms for Minorities," *New York Times*, September 24, 1996, p. B2.

26. "Cornell Battles Anew," p. B5.

27. The *Wall Street Journal* has had some thought-provoking pieces on the Cornell situation. See the editorial on Meyers's suits against Cornell, "Racial Balkanization at Cornell," July 25, 1995, p. A12. See also Michael Meyers, "Cornell's Insult to Brown Decision," *Wall Street Journal*, May 17, 1996, p. A14; Tamar Jacoby, "The Content of Our Character: Have We Abandoned Dr. King's Vision?" *Wall Street Journal*, January 19, 1998, p. A14.

28. Paul A. Batista, letter to the editor, *Wall Street Journal*, May 30, 1996, p. A15.

29. Nat Hentoff, "Burning Newspapers at Cornell," *Liberal Opinion Weekly*, August 25, 1997. I obtained the details of this confrontation from Hentoff's article and from the *Cornell Daily Sun*, April 29, 1997, p. 1.

30. Caleb S. Rossiter, *The Chimes of Freedom Flashing: A Personal History of the Vietnam Anti-War Movement and the 1960s* (TCA Press, 1996), p. 73.

31. Interview with Andre McLaughlin, 1996.

32. Sindler, "How Crisis Came to Cornell," pp. 84–85. See also Walter Berns, "The Assault on the Universities: Then and Now," in Stephen Macedo, ed., *Reassessing the Sixties: Debating the Political and Cultural Legacy* (Norton, 1997). ("Cornell," Berns wrote, was the "prototype of the university as we know it today," having "jettisoned every vestige of academic integrity"; p. 157.)

33. Ellis Cose, *Color-Blind: Seeing Beyond Race in a Race-Obsessed World* (HarperCollins, 1997), p. 215.

34. Aristotle, in *The Politics*, depicts politics as the struggle of reaching agreement out of the conflict of viewpoints, of making one out of the many. See also Hannah Arendt, *The Human Condition* (University of Chicago Press, 1958).

35. Tamar Jacoby, "The Next Reconstruction," *New Republic*, June 22, 1998, pp. 19–20.

36. Hannah Arendt, *The Origins of Totalitarianism* (Harcourt Brace, 1952).

37. Philosophers have written about the concept of "moral luck": that the commitment to moral action is partly a function of circumstance. See, for example, Thomas Nagel, "Moral Luck," in Thomas Nagel, *Mortal Questions* (Oxford University Press, 1979). John Searle applies a logic along these lines in his evaluation of administrations beset by the campus wars of the 1960s in *The Campus War: A Sympathetic Look at the University in Agony* (World, 1971).

38. Jonathan Rauch, *Kindly Inquisitors: The New Attacks on Free Thought* (University of Chicago Press, 1993), p. 86.

39. David I. Grossvogel, "The University in Transition," in *Divided We Stand: Reflections on the Crisis at Cornell*, Cushing Strout and David I. Grossvogel, eds. (Doubleday, 1970), p. 139.

INDEX

CPSIA information can be obtained
at www.ICGtesting.com
Printed in the USA
LVHW112000250719
625352LV00003B/285/P